Communication
and Human
Behavior

UNITED STATES OF AMERICA
B 13595376 J
TALKING
MICHELANGELO
I ♥ NY
ULYSSES
CAN FOOL

Communication and Human Behavior

Brent D. Ruben
Rutgers University

Macmillan Publishing Company
New York

Collier Macmillan Publishers
London

For Jann, Robbi and Marc
in friendship, love, and appreciation

Copyright © 1984, Brent D. Ruben

Printed in the United States of America

Macmillan Publishing Company
866 Third Avenue, New York, New York 10022

Collier Macmillan Canada, Inc.

Library of Congress Cataloging in Publication Data

Ruben, Brent D.
  Communication and human behavior.

  Includes index.
  1. Communication   2. Human behavior.   I. Title.
P90.R78 1983   302'.2   82–4692
ISBN 0–02–404270–6

Printing: 12345678   Year: 456789012

ISBN   0-02-404270-6

Foreword

Cave drawings and other relics and reconstructions of prehistoric times tell a story of the first attempts to grapple with fundamental questions about existence, life, death, meaning, and purpose. In a very real sense, it was with these questions and humankind's first efforts to address them that the study of human behavior began.

Historians generally trace the beginnings of the systematic study of behavior to the early Greeks. Interest in the study of human activity grew primarily out of philosophy, at a time when that field was the single discipline concerned with the pursuit of knowledge. Eventually, given the influence of scientific methods and a growing trend toward specialization in the pursuit of knowledge, separate disciplines evolved for the study of behavior, as they had earlier in the study of physical and biological phenomena.

In the 1860s, August Comte gave the name *sociology* to the study of society and social existence, and a decade later the psychological laboratories of Wilhelm Wundt and William James were established. The origins of anthropology also date to the middle of the nineteenth century and to the work of the British scholars Maine, Tylor, and Frazer. The fields of political science and communication, with roots that extend to the early Greeks, took on identities as disciplines in their own right in the 1900s.

Today, the study of human behavior is of interest not only to those in sociology, anthropology, psychology, political science, and communication but also to scholars dispersed in perhaps a dozen other disciplines, including literature, history, biology, religion, art, law, medicine, and philosophy. For the individuals working in each of these fields, the challenges and opportunities today are very much what they were thousands of years ago. As did our earliest ancestors, contemporary humans confront situations that are difficult to comprehend and to which it is not easy to adjust: the

v

miracle of birth, the trauma of illness, the tragedy of death, and the search for purpose and meaning in life.

As in each generation, a number of tributaries that bear the distinctive mark of a given culture and time flow from these larger issues. Today's society must deal with problems and prospects of fast-paced technological change, evolving concepts of marriage and family, old age and obsolescence, increasing crime rates, energy and economic pressures, and so on. Individuals also face a host of smaller, but no less significant, problems on a daily basis: a relationship that doesn't work out, a promotion that doesn't come through, a friend who no longer seems to care, a job that doesn't materialize, the prejudice or discrimination that inflicts pain, a parent who doesn't understand, a marital conflict that is difficult to reconcile, or a child who disappoints loved ones.

Whether approached from the perspective of psychology or communication, political science or art, a knowledge of human behavior can be of great value in trying to comprehend and deal with the cirucumstances of existence, as well as in helping to understand one's self, one's actions, motives, feelings, and aspirations.

One can choose to explore behavior from any number of disciplinary perspectives. In this book the selected point of view is communication. The goal will be to provide a comprehensive, yet basic, introduction to this field and its approach to explaining human activity. The contributions of general system theory, symbolic interaction, general semantics, sociology of knowledge, and cognitive science have been particularly useful in developing the framework of this book. The general systems approach directs attention to the various diverse disciplines in which communication has been studied and provides both the motivation and the means for consolidating these often divergent points of view. Systems theory encourages exploration of the role of communication not only in human life but also in the essential activities of all living things. Further, the systems approach indicates the importance of examining communication at various levels—biological and psychological, along with the social, cultural, and technological. And, finally, systems theory provides a way of characterizing the interrelationships between these levels of human activity.

The perspectives of symbolic interaction, sociology of knowledge, general semantics, and cognitive science focus attention on the roles of symbols, information, and interpretative processes in human life. The concepts of symbolic interaction and sociology of knowledge also provide a basis for comprehending the complex web of relationships that link individuals to the many social units in which they function.

Communication and Human Behavior is composed of chapters organized into sections. Each chapter presents visual as well as verbal materials. The photographs, drawings, and tables are intended to add to the book in a substantive, as well as aesthetic, manner. Their purpose is to clarify, elaborate upon, and extend the ideas discussed in the text.

Section I provides the frame of reference for the entire volume. In Chapter 1, the reader is reminded of the multiplicity of meanings of the word *communication* and introduced to some factors that have contributed to this diversity. Chapter 2 provides a view of communication as a basic life process, drawing together the perspectives of various definitions and disciplines. Chapter 3 reviews highlights in the evolution of communication study from its early days to the present, providing a context for understanding the various traditions that influence contemporary thinking in the discipline.

The nature of human communication is explored in depth in Section II, beginning in Chapter 4 with an explanation of the nature and role of symbols. Chapters 5 and 6 discuss the sources of the verbal and nonverbal information of significance to human life, and Chapter 7 considers the way in which people select, interpret, and retain information. Chapter 8 examines the nature of communication technology and its function in extending our human information processing capabilities.

The third section of the book looks at various uses and consequences of human communication. Chapter 9 focuses on the individual. Chapters 10, 11, and 12 consider the role of communication in relationships, groups and organizations, and societies and cultures, respectively.

Brent D. Ruben
Belle Mead, New Jersey

Acknowledgments

It has rightfully become tradition to acknowledge the contributions of some of the many significant persons who have helped to stimulate an author's creative efforts, thanking them for their valued assistance and publically relieving them from any culpability for inadequacies in the final product.

There are a number of persons I would like to acknowledge in this way, many of whom I know personally, others only through their work. Among those individuals who have contributed in major ways to the substance of this volume are Peter Berger, Ludwig von Bertalanffy, Gregory Bateson, Herbert Blumer, Kenneth Boulding, Dick Budd, Jim Campbell, Michael Cheney, George Dickscheid, Hugh Duncan, Ken Frandsen, Erving Goffman, Nancy Harper, Dick Hixson, Todd Hunt, Dan Kealey, Mark Knapp, Linda Lederman, Jim McCroskey, Thomas Kuhn, Desmond Morris, Jack Prince, Fred Smith, and Lee Thayer.

A number of other persons provided much appreciated assistance in the preparation of this manuscript at various stages. My sincere thanks to Jan Sirois, Marsha Bergman, Jean Ericson, Jacqueline McGuiness, Helen Weitz, Linda Vignec, Barbara Robb, and Sue Sebastian. I am grateful, also, to Jim Anderson, Mike Kaminsky, Bill Fort, and Leny Struminger for their guidance in the use of computerized word processing technology. For his creative energy, I am most thankful to Patrick Carter of Camden, Delaware, whose original painting, "Images We Hold in Common," painted especially for this volume, appears on the cover, title page, and at the beginning of each section. Another painting by the artist, "Ad Infinitum," is reproduced on the title page of Chapter 9.

I am grateful, also to Chris Kilyk, Nat Clymer, Jon Jacobson, Bill Gilhooly, Robert Conoy, Rick Budd, and Bill Gudykunst who provided a number of the photos used in the volume, and to Chris, Bill, and Rick for their assistance in processing those photographs taken by me.

A well-deserved word of thanks to George Carr, Production Supervisor; Eileen Burke, Book Designer; and most especially to Executive Editor, Lloyd Chilton, for his encouragement through all phases of this project. And lastly, a special note of appreciation to my parents, Nate and Ruth Ruben, for much of the impetus to do a book such as this.

Contents

Communication and Human Behavior

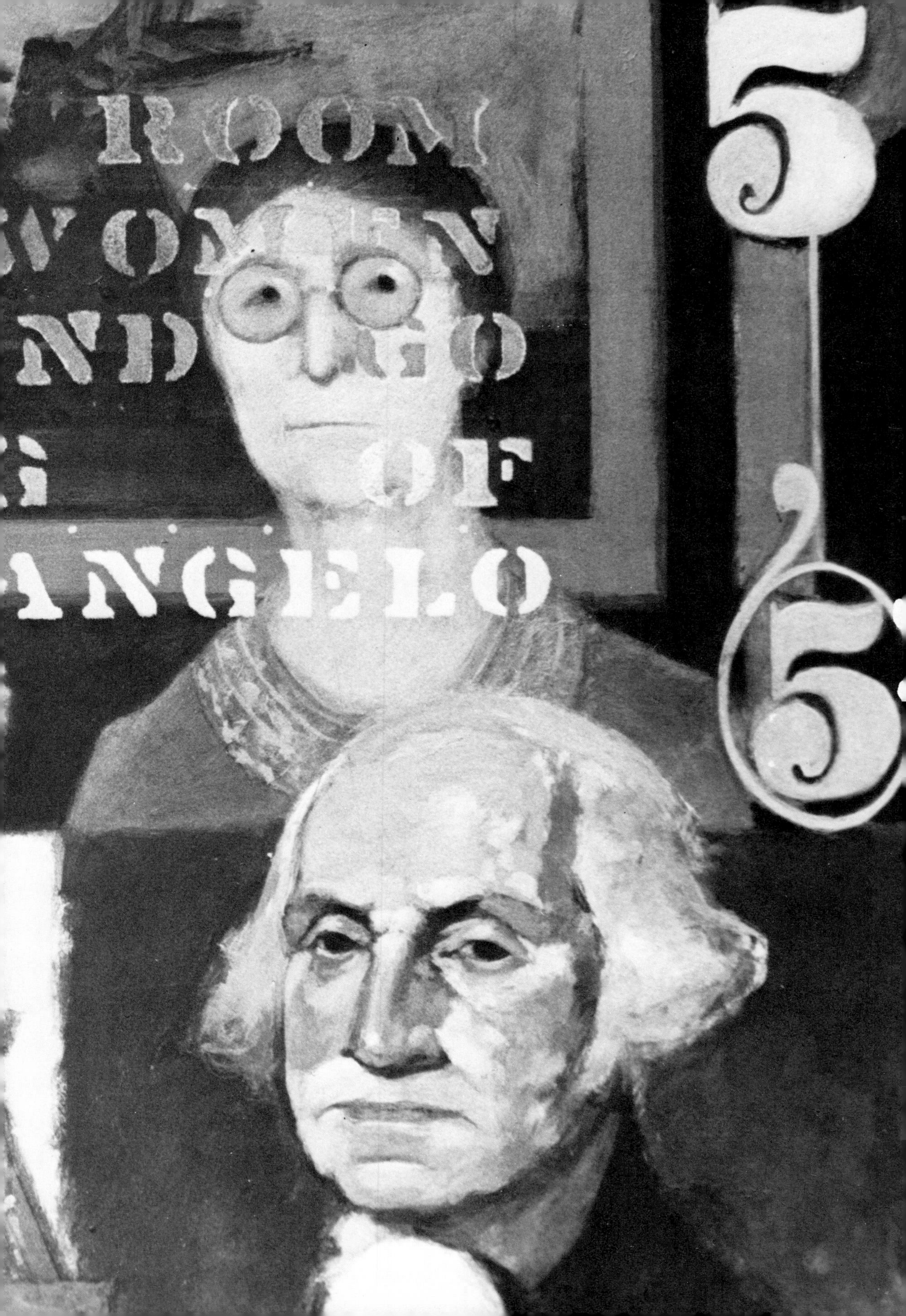
ROOM
OF
ANGELO
5
5

An Integrating Framework

Introduction

What Is Communication?

I know you believe you understand what you think I said but, I am not sure you realize that what you heard is not what I meant

Few words are used in as many different ways by as many different people as *communication*. To some, *communication* brings to mind an image of a speaker addressing an audience from behind a lectern, the lively discussion of colleagues at a meeting, or an exchange of glances between lovers. Others associate the term primarily with mass media—newspapers, television, books, magazines, radio, or the recording industry. For still others, communication has to do with computers, cathode-ray tubes, terminals, telephone lines, and satellites.

Communication is a debate, videodisc, cable television, a sermon, a memorable night at the theater, the efforts of a child striving to conquer stuttering, and a field of study. Or it may be used to refer to Morse code, a roadside sign, signal flags, a uniform, CB radio, or a long-distance phone call. *Communication* can be a thoughtful walk on the beach at sunset, a tear, an outstretched arm, a knowing smile, the sign language of a deaf mute, a kiss, a four-letter word scrawled on a restroom wall, even silence.

Characteristics of Communication

The reasons for the many differing uses of communication may seem puzzling at first. As we shall see in Chapter 3, however, the various meanings of the term are a natural outgrowth of the lengthy and, in many respects, intriguing history of communication study. For now it is important only to be

aware of the incredibly broad range of actions and activities that are referred to as *communication* and to be familiar with some of the factors that have contributed to its diversity of meanings.

Field and Activity

One of the most significant factors in this regard is the use of *communication* to refer both to a field of study and a set of activities. People study communication and people communicate (or, more accurately, engage in communication). This kind of confusion does not occur in most other disciplines. For example, people study psychology and English, but they do not "psychologize" or "Englishicate." They study English and engage in writing, or they study psychology and engage in therapy or counseling. In these fields, as in most others, different terms are used to distinguish the discipline from the activity practiced within it, whereas with communication a single term refers to both the field and the activity.

Science and Art

A second factor that has contributed to the diversity of meanings of the term is the variety of approaches for studying the communication process. During Greek times, *communication* was studied in the tradition of the humanities and arts, much like philosophy or literature. In the years that followed, the

methods of the physical and life sciences came to have a great impact on the study of communication, as they did in other fields concerned with the study of human behavior.

In the more recent past the popularity of the scientific approach in communication study has grown steadily. Throughout these years, however, a number of scholars have continued to study communication in the tradition of the humanities and arts. Thus, even within the discipline, some see communication as a precise phenomenon to be understood by using mathematics and complex research methods, whereas others regard it as a creative, personal, artistic, and subjective activity.

Interdisciplinary Tradition

Not only has communication been studied in various ways but also in various disciplines. Beyond being of interest to scholars within the field, the process of communication has also been of concern to psychologists, sociologists, political scientists, linguists, zoologists, anthropologists, and philosophers, who regard the topic as important to their own areas of study.

In psychology the focus has been on communication and the individual; in sociology, communication and social processes; in political science, communication and political behavior; in zoology, communication among animals; and so on. As these perspectives have contributed greatly to the breadth and richness of our understanding of the communication process, so, too, have they added to the multiplicity of meanings for the term.

Natural and Purposeful

When one thinks of communication as an activity, rather than a field of study, even greater diversity of meaning exists. From one point of view, for instance, communication can be thought of as the natural and unconscious talking and listening that is a routine part of daily affairs. From another perspective, it can be viewed as an intentional, purposeful, and highly conscious activity in which people engage when they deliver a speech or write a report.

Amateur and Professional

In one usage of the term, *communication* refers to such activities as talking, reading, or writing, which most people carry out without special training or expertise. The same term is also used to refer to activities engaged in by professionals in sales, advertising, marketing, counseling, public relations, management, and journalism.

In most other areas, more precise terminology is available to help avoid such ambiguity. For example, there are many persons who doodle, draw, or paint as a hobby or pastime, but the term *artist* is reserved for those who have special expertise and who exercise these talents as professionals. The same is true in athletics, in which such phrases as *professional baseball player* or *professional golfer* differentiate the expert from the amateur. With *communica-*

EAST
FLORIDA'S TURNPIKE

INTERSTATE
FLORIDA
4

BUS STOP

HELLO PETE

EPT HOLIDAY

A.M.	P.M.	A.M.	P.M.	A.M.	P.M.
11:01	12:46	11:16			12:4
	3:16				
	5:0				

SUNDAY

HOLIDAY
A.M. | P.M.
12:46

OX LOCATION FOR LATER COLLECTION 172 St ¢ Ft. WASH

A FINE OF $1,000 OR THREE YEARS IMPRISONMENT
FOR TAMPERING WITH THIS BOX, LOCK OR CONTENTS

LOCATION OF THIS BOX 171 St. 2 B'WAY

tion, a single term is used to describe the activities of both professionals and novices.

Communications and Communication

Another factor contributing to the multiplicity of meaning is confusion between *communication* and *communications.* Many of those persons who have focused attention on communication have been predominantly interested in technology and media. The term *communications* has traditionally been used to refer to these technologies or to specific messages that are transmitted through these media. *Communication,* as we have seen, has generally been used to refer to the activity of sending and receiving messages, and to the discipline as a whole.

With the growing availability and interest in communication technology in recent years, increasingly the term *communications* is used interchangeably with *communication.* The effect of this usage has been to further contribute to the already substantial lack of clarity of terminology.

Popularity

A final factor that has contributed to the diversity of meaning is the widespread interest and popularity of communication in recent years. Within the last twenty years, the number of communication books, journals, media, teachers, students, departments, and courses has grown more rapidly than in any previous stage in the history of the discipline. With this growth has come an expansion in the scope of the field, bringing changes to both the discipline and the concept that have not always been systematic or orderly.

The popularity of *communication* in the academic domain has been paralleled or even surpassed in the popular arena. In 1975, the *Harper Dictionary of Contemporary Usage* listed *communication* as a "vogue word—a word...that suddenly or inexplicably crops up...in speeches of bureaucrats, comments of columnists...and in radio and television broadcasts." Today, there are books on communication with oneself, in marriage, in families, in groups, in therapy, with one's boss, colleagues at work, potential mates, and one's children. And there are more books and magazines on television, movies, comic strips, video games, personal computers, shyness, trust, assertiveness, and so on.

Because of this popularity, most people are comfortable using the term and confident in their understanding of it, though, again, there is certainly no clear concensus as to its meaning. As a consequence, they are generally quite willing to render "expert" judgments regarding the quality of their own, a friend's, a relative's, or a colleague's communication skills and effectiveness. In this respect, at least, the increased popularity of *communication* in everyday discourse has been a mixed blessing. On the one hand, it has ensured the growth and relevance of the field. On the other hand, it has contributed to the misleading view that communication is easily understood, thereby lending further confusion to the subject.

Information and Behavior

For all the reasons noted, to be explored more fully in Chapter 3, the question "What is communication?" is a difficult one to answer. The issue, however, must be addressed by anyone seriously interested in understanding the process, field, or technology of communication. Ideally, the answer should provide a view of communication that gives some sense of unity amidst the diversity.

If one looks broadly at the topic, drawing upon the wide range of viewpoints that have been developed about communication, it is possible to

create this kind of integrating perspective. Regardless of whether one is using *communication* to refer to the field or the activity, an intentional or natural process, a science or an art, mass media or human relations, personal computers or counseling, public speaking or journalism, one finds a fundamental concern with *information* and *behavior*.

Using these two concepts, one can formulate a useful working definition of the communication process: *Communication is information-related behavior*. By extension, the study of communication is *the study of information-related behavior*. The concepts of *information* and *behavior* draw together diverse notions of communication and provide the foundation for a broad view of the role of communication in human affairs.

What exactly does it mean to say, "Communication is information-related behavior"? What types of information? What types of behavior? How is communication technology involved? These are the questions with which this book is concerned. Chapter 2 will explore the basic question with which the study of behavior is concerned: What is the nature of life? In answering this question, we will examine the central role of information in virtually every facet of life as we know it.

Summary

Communication means many things to many people. Some think of it as a discipline; others as an activity. For some it is a science; for others, an art. It may be an unconscious activity or a premeditated and deliberate technique.

The diversity of meanings associated with the term are an outgrowth of the history of the field. Some factors that have contributed to the multiplicity of usages are (1) the use of the same term to refer both to the name of the discipline and the activity within it; (2) the methods of study drawing on traditions of the sciences, on the one hand, and of the arts and humanities on the other; (3) the interdisciplinary heritage of communication study; (4) the use of a single term to refer both to natural and purposeful activities; (5) the association of the word with everyday activities that require no special training, as well as with techniques that demand professional expertise; (6) the blurring distinction between *communication* (discipline or process) and *communications* (technology or messages); and (7) the popularity of the field.

Central to the many uses of the term is a common concern with *information* and *behavior*. Accordingly, one can formulate a useful working definition of the communication process using these two notions: *Communication is information-related behavior*, and *the study of communication is the study of information-related behavior*. This book is devoted to exploring the many implications of this definition.

Chapter 2

Communication

A Basic Life Process

FEEDING • LEARNING • IDENTITY IMPRINTING • DEVELOPMENT OF COMMUNICATION CAPABILITIES • ADAPTATION • LOCOMOTION • SELF-DEFENSE • TERRITORIALITY • COOPERATION • COMPETITION • DIVISION OF LABOR • MOBILIZING FOR GROUP ACT-TION • DOMINANCE-SUBMISSION • STATUS CONFERRAL • SOCIAL ORGANIZATION • SPECIES CONTINUITY • MATING • REPRODUCTION • PARENT-OFF SPRING RELATIONS • FEEDING • LEARNING • IDENTITY IMPRINTING • DEVELOPMENT OF COMMUNICATION CAPABILITIES • ADAPTATION • LOCOMOTION • SELF-DEFENSE • TERRITORIALITY • COOPERATION • COMPETITION • DIVISION OF LABOR • MOBILIZING FOR GROUP ACT-TION • DOMINANCE-SUBMISSION • STATUS CONFERRAL • SOCIAL ORGANIZATION • SPECIES CONTINUITY • MATING • REPRODUCTION • PARENT-OFF SPRING RELATIONS • FEEDING • LEARNING • IDENTITY IMPRINTING • DEVELOPMENT OF COMMUNICATION CAPABILITIES • ADAPTATION • LOCOMOTION • SELF-DEFENSE • TERRITORIALITY • COOPERATION • COMPETITION • DIVISION OF LABOR • MOBILIZING FOR GROUP ACT-TION • DOMINANCE-SUBMISSION • STATUS CONFERRAL • SOCIAL ORGANIZATION • SPECIES CONTINUITY • MATING • REPRODUCTION • PARENT-OFF SPRING RELATIONS • FEEDING • LEARNING • IDENTITY IMPRINTING • DEVELOPMENT OF COMMUNICATION CAPABILITIES • ADAPTATION • LOCOMOTION • SELF-DEFENSE • TERRITORIALITY • COOPERATION • COMPETITION • DIVISION OF LABOR • MOBILIZING FOR GROUP ACT-TION • DOMINANCE-SUBMISSION • STATUS CONFERRAL • SOCIAL ORGANIZATION • SPECIES CONTINUITY • MATING • REPRODUCTION • PARENT-OFF SPRING RELATIONS • FEEDING • LEARNING • IDENTITY IMPRINTING • DEVELOPMENT OF COMMUNICATION CAPABILITIES • ADAPTATION • LOCOMOTION • SELF-DEFENSE • TERRITORIALITY • COOPERATION • COMPETITION • DIVISION OF LABOR • MOBILIZING FOR GROUP ACT-TION • DOMINANCE-SUBMISSION • STATUS CONFERRAL • SOCIAL ORGANIZATION • SPECIES CONTINUITY • MATING • REPRODUCTION • PARENT-OFF SPRING RELATIONS • FEEDING • LEARNING • IDENTITY IMPRINTING • DEVELOPMENT OF COMMUNICATION CAPABILITIES • ADAPTATION • LOCOMOTION • SELF-DEFENSE • TERRITORIALITY • COOPERATION • COMPETITION • DIVISION OF LABOR • MOBILIZING FOR GROUP ACT-TION • DOMINANCE-SUBMISSION • STATUS CONFERRAL • SOCIAL ORGANIZATION • SPECIES CONTINUITY • MATING • REPRODUCTION • PARENT-OFF SPRING RELATIONS • FEEDING • LEARNING • IDENTITY IMPRINTING • DEVELOPMENT OF COMMUNICATION CAPABILITIES • ADAPTATION • LOCOMOTION • SELF-DEFENSE • TERRITORIALITY • COOPERATION • COMPETITION • DIVISION OF LABOR • MOBILIZING FOR GROUP ACT-TION • DOMINANCE-SUBMISSION • STATUS CONFERRAL • SOCIAL ORGANIZATION • SPECIES CONTINUITY • MATING • REPRODUCTION • PARENT-OFF SPRING RELATIONS • FEEDING • LEARNING • IDENTITY IMPRINTING • DEVELOPMENT OF COMMUNICATION CAPABILITIES • ADAPTATION • LOCOMOTION • SELF-DEFENSE • TERRITORIALITY • COOPERATION • COMPETITION • DIVISION OF LABOR • MOBILIZING FOR GROUP ACT-TION • DOMINANCE-SUBMISSION • STATUS CONFERRAL • SOCIAL ORGANIZATION • SPECIES CONTINUITY • MATING • REPRODUCTION • PARENT-OFF SPRING RELATIONS • FEEDING • LEARNING • IDENTITY IMPRINTING • DEVELOPMENT OF COMMUNICATION CAPABILITIES • ADAPTATION • LOCOMOTION • SELF-DEFENSE • TERRITORIALITY • COOPERATION • COMPETITION • DIVISION OF LABOR • MOBILIZING FOR GROUP ACT-TION • DOMINANCE-SUBMISSION • STATUS CONFERRAL • SOCIAL ORGANIZATION • SPECIES CONTINUITY • MATING • REPRODUCTION • PARENT-OFF SPRING RELATIONS • FEEDING • LEARNING • IDENTITY IMPRINTING • DEVELOPMENT OF COMMUNICATION CAPABILITIES • ADAPTATION • LOCOMOTION • SELF-DEFENSE • TERRITORIALITY • COOPERATION • COMPETITION • DIVISION OF LABOR • MOBILIZING FOR GROUP ACT-

One can use a number of approaches to explore the relationship between communication and behavior. The perspective we will use begins by considering the nature of life itself and the characteristics that distinguish *living* things from nonliving entities.

Some Basic Concepts

Systems

A *system* is any entity or whole that is composed of interdependent parts. Systems have characteristics and capabilities which are distinct from those of the separate parts. A simple example of a system is a cake. The ingredients of a typical cake are sugar, flour, salt, eggs, butter, vanilla, and baking powder and/or soda. When these are combined and baked, the result is an entity that is much different than any of the individual ingredients.

The organs of the body are also systems in that the cells, blood, and tissues all operate together to make the organ a unique, functioning unit that is capable of performing operations none of its parts could accomplish independently. An automobile—composed of tires, radiator, alternator, engine, drive train, and a variety of other parts—is yet another example of a system. Societies, organizations, groups, relationships, and individuals are also systems. Each has interconnected component parts, and as a whole has attributes and performs functions that would be impossible for any one part alone.

Most systems have physical properties, as, for example, the solar system, a society, a transportation system, a neurological system, a skeletal system, a stereo system, an exhaust system, an animal, or a cell. The nature of these properties varies greatly, and, depending on the particular system, may consist of such ingredients as atoms, stars, individuals, bones, machines, neurons, genes, muscles, or gases.

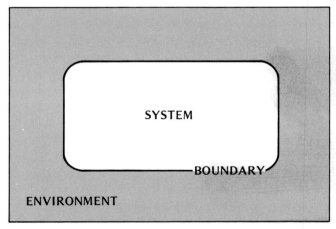

FIGURE 2.1

Boundaries

Boundaries define the edges of a system and hold the parts together. They protect the system from environmental stresses and exclude or admit substances to ensure the system's continued functioning. For a cake, the pan in which the ingredients are baked serves as a boundary. It holds together the components and allows for the exchange of heat and air. The boundaries of cells are walls. Organs have membranes. Animals have skin, shells, fur, or external skeletons that hold the parts together and protect the system.

Environment

Beyond the boundaries of a system is the *environment* in which it exists and upon which it may well depend. The immediate environment of a cake being baked is the inside of the oven and the heated air contained within. In a broader sense, the environment is everything beyond the edges of the pan. Generally, one can think of the environment as the physical area and influences separated from a system by its boundary.

Closed and Open Systems

Some systems interact with their environments; others do not. *Closed systems* are so named because they operate in isolation of their environment. An example of a closed system is the reaction of several chemicals mixed together in a sealed container. The action of the ingredients that defines the system is totally a consequence of the dynamics that occur among the chemicals with no influence from the environment outside the test bottle.

Open systems are engaged in a continual give-and-take exchange with their environment. Such systems influence and are influenced by their environment. Because they interact with their environment, the dynamics of open systems are usually less predictable than in closed systems, in which the outcome depends only on the isolated exchange among parts of the system.

Living Systems

Of all those systems that influence and are influenced by their environment, our particular concern is with *living systems*—open systems that go through a life cycle. For all living things, that cycle begins with birth or initial emergence, moves through various stages of growth and development, and eventually leads to deterioration, decay, and death.

As with other open systems, the dynamics of living systems involve an ongoing interaction between the entity and its environment. The basic process is one in which a living system takes in certain materials that are necessary to its life functioning through openings in its boundary and gives off into the environment other materials as wastes.

With plants, the critical environmental exchange involves a give-and-take of chemicals and other substances necessary to growth. The process through which this development occurs is called *photosynthesis*. Necessary to this process are the presence of a number of environmental inputs, including sunlight, heat, water, and carbon dioxide. As a by-product of photosynthesis, plants give off oxygen into the environment.

Animals, on the other hand, require the intake of oxygen, and they give off carbon dioxide. Animal metabolism also requires the intake of food substances. The food is transformed into living tissue and energy by the animal, and organic wastes are returned to the environment.

Animal and Human Systems

As one moves up the scale of life from plants to animals, the nature of the system-environment interaction becomes increasingly complex. Animals not only depend for their survival upon chemical and physical exchanges but also upon *communication—the exchange of information.* This latter process—communication—enables animals to create, gather, and use information about the events, objects, and living things in their environment as a basis for their behavior.

Just as animals take in oxygen and foodstuffs and transform them into materials necessary to their functioning, they also take in *data* and transform them into *information* that is equally necessary to their life processes.[1] In this most basic sense, *communication is the essential life process through which animal*

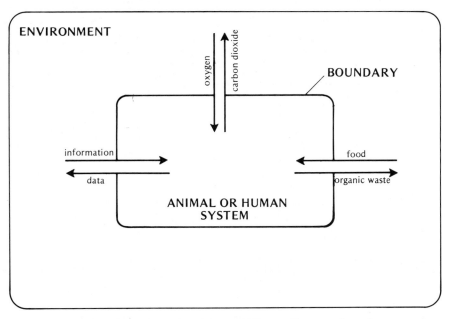

FIGURE 2.2 Basic Processes of Animal and Human Systems. In order to survive, higher-order living systems must be open to exchanges with the environment. These exchanges take place through the boundary of the system. In this manner, living systems exchange oxygen for carbon dioxide, and food inputs for organic wastes. In a similar way they process data and information through permeable areas in the system boundaries—eyes, ears, nose, mouth, and skin.

and human systems create, acquire, transform, and use information to carry out the activities of their lives.

Communication Modes

The information used as the basis for behavior is derived by producing and responding to environmental *data* or *cues*. The world in which living systems exist is filled with a vast array of such data or cues. Some of these data, such as the mating call of a bird or the words exchanged between friends, are purposefully created by another living system. Other cues, such as the sound of a rainstorm, light reflecting off an object, the heat given off by a fire, or the odor of decaying organisms, are not. Both types of data are vital as potential sources of the information necessary to behavior.

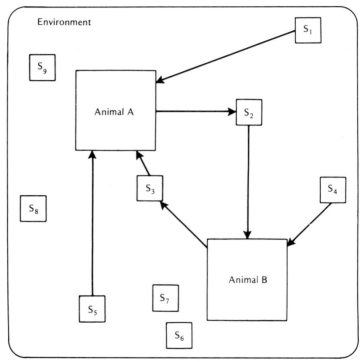

FIGURE 2.3 Communication Sources and Modes. Within an environment, there are numerous potential data and data sources to which a living system may attend and react, represented by S_1 through S_9 in the illustration above. Some of these data may be produced by inanimate sources, such as the sounds of thunder, the visible flash of lightning, or the touch of a leaf blowing past in the wind—S_1, S_4, and S_5. Other data, taking the form of a smell, taste, sound or sight are produced by other living systems—S_2 and S_3. Such data may be unintended byproducts of the systems' life activities, like the sound of flapping wings as a bird rushes to flee to avoid a predator. Or, they may be more purposeful, such as the mating call of male birds. At any instant, many potential data sources are not taken account of at all—S_6, S_7, S_8, and S_9.

Visual Information

For humans, visual data are particularly important; a wave and a smile from a friend, a blush of embarrassment, a tear, a new dress or a new car, and the headlines of a newspaper are all potential sources of information that can hold great significance for us. Some other animals also make substantial use of visual data. The color and acrobatics of male birds, the luring colored wings of the male butterfly, the rhythmic light of the firefly, and the movement of head, ears, or tail by primates all serve as valuable information sources.

As significant as sight is for humans and some animals, it is generally not as crucial as other communication modes among most species. Many animals lack the visual capacities necessary for processing light and depend instead on touch, sound, smell, or taste to relate to their environment or to one another.

FIGURE 2.4 Many mammals respond to environmental conditions with particular positioning of the body, tail, and head. These postures provide visual cues as to the disposition of the animal in the situation, and serve to attract, repel, or simply inform other animals who take account of them.

TABLE 2.1 Communication Modes

Modality	Form of Data
Visual ...	*Sight* —facial displays —movement of body parts —distance and spacing —position —dress —other symbols, adornment, and emblems
Tactile ...	*Touch* —vibration —stroking —rubbing —pressure —pain —temperature
Olfactory and Gustatory ...	*Smell and Taste* (Pheromones) —body odors —special chemicals —food sources, fragrances, and tastes
Auditory ...	*Sound* —incidental sounds —vibrations —whistling —drumming —rubbing —vocalization

Tactile Information

For many animals, touch, bumping, vibration, and other types of tactile data are important. From before birth through the first months and years of life, physical contact plays a critical role in the biological and social development of human infants, as well as in the young of other species. Tactile data remain crucial through the lives of many animals, in parent-young relations, courtship and intimate relations, social greetings, play, and aggression and combat. Tactile cues also play a vital role in self-defense and self-preservation. Receptors in the skin and other locations throughout the body detect heat, cold, pressure, and pain and serve as signals that the safety of the system is threatened. For humans, tactile data are the major source of symptoms, such as fatigue, nausea, dizziness, muscular strain, or apprehension that are used to determine if one is ill and to identify the problem and its location.

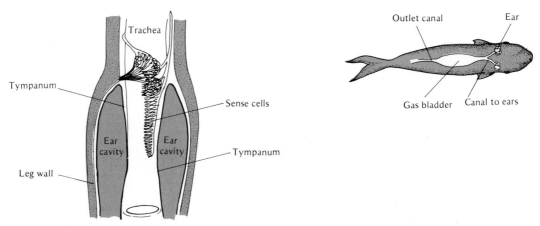

FIGURE 2.5 Insect and Fish Hearing. The drawings to the left illustrate how insects receive auditory messages through small openings in their legs. Many fish receive auditory data by means of a gas bladder that serves a function similar to the eardrum, as shown in the illustration at the right. Sound is conveyed from the gas bladder through tubes to an inner ear.

Olfactory and Gustatory Information

Many animals also use olfactory and gustatory information to relate to their environment and to one another. Some of the chemically based data, or *pheromones,* are produced by other animals; others, such as the scent of a flower or the smell of rain, have inanimate sources. Pheromones are carried through water or air to the specialized receptor at the boundary of the living system. Vertebrates acquire these data through a nose, fish through a nose or odor-sensitive cells on the body, and insects by means of sensors located in their antennae.

As Jack Prince explains:

> ...(the odor sensitive cells) are situated so air or water passes over them and allows them to absorb the odor particles it carries. In air these cells pick up more particles with each sniff or breath, so the odor builds up in the receptor cells and becomes stronger. Each cell is connected by a nerve fiber with the brain...which is more developed in animals that use smell as the dominant sense than in animals that rely on vision or hearing.[2]

As with other modes, the brain filters out irrelevant data, responding only to those cues to which the system is attuned or to which it has learned to attend. Although humans have the set of organs thought necessary for chemical data production and reception, olfactory information plays a much less substantial role in the activities of humans than in the lives of many other animals.

Auditory Information

For many animal and human systems, auditory data provide critical links to the environment and to one another. Some sounds—thunder, an earthquake,

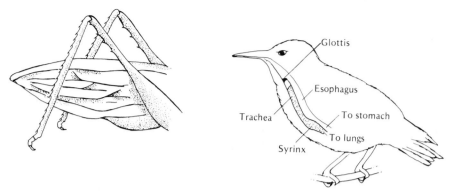

FIGURE 2.6 Insect and Bird Sound Production. Many insects produce a sound called *stridulation* by rubbing their hind legs against their bodies. The inner thigh of the hind legs contains a saw-like ridge of teeth (a *file*) that produces a range of sounds when pulled across a wing vein (or *scraper*). Birds, which lack the larynx associated with sounds of most mammals, produce sounds by means of a *syrinx*.

SOURCE: *Languages of the Animal World*, J. H. Prince (Nashville: Nelson), 1975.

or the surf splashing against the shore—have nonliving sources. Other auditory data are produced by living things through speaking, whistling, drumming, or striking a part of the body against an object, the ground, or another part of the body. Additional data are created as an extension of human activity, such as results from the firing of a rifle or operating an engine. Actions of this kind produce vibrations that are transported through air or water.

In order for auditory data to be useful to a living system, the vibrations must be detected, received, and processed by means of a special organ which converts the data into electrical impulses that can be utilized by the brain. Lower-order animals generally respond to sound either by approaching or moving away from the data source; most higher-order systems are able to act upon auditory cues in any number of ways as a product of prior learning. Auditory data are important in the lives of a wide range of species, including birds, insects, primates, and humans, who depend upon these cues in caring for the young, learning, courtship and mating, and language acquisition and use.

Basic Functions of Communication

The significance of communication and the various information-processing modes of animal and human systems is perhaps clearest when one considers some of the basic biological functions they serve: (1) *survival of the species;* and (2) *adaptation.* Each of these has a number of facets.

Survival of the Species

The perpetuation of a particular species of living thing from one generation to the next involves three activities in which communication is vital: (1) mating; (2) reproduction; and (3) parent-offspring relations and socialization.

Mating Although many differences exist in the specific mating practices of various species, many share certain things in common. An animal must be able to identify other individuals of its species and be able to determine gender relative to its own. Also, individuals must attract and sometimes persuade one another. And the animals must synchronize their actions in time and physically orient with one another. Each of these endeavors centrally involves communication.

Members of one species identify, locate, and attract one another by emitting and responding to cues of one kind or another. The songs of grasshoppers and crickets serve this purpose, as does the odor of moths and the light-flashing of fireflies. With birds, mating involves the creating and reception of auditory data ranging from a simple repetitive and not necessarily musical call to a complex song-and-dance presentation, acrobatics, and rituals. In some species the male birds build and decorate nests, which they use to advertise their availability to prospective mates.

For many animals, mating involves not only identifying and attracting an individual but also synchronizing the time of sexual activities in order for fertilization to occur. The oyster and certain other marine animals apparently acquire the information needed for the proper timing of fertilization from the ocean tides. Reproduction begins in the spring, following a migration toward a breeding ground. The increased daylight in this season cues the change in hormonal functions through which reproductive cycles are coordinated.[3]

For some insects, recognition, attraction, synchronization, and coordination occur as a result of data provided by chemicals. With moths, for example, the female sex pheromone triggers a sequence of activities in the male, starting with the activation of the animal, followed by its movement toward the chemical source, and culminating in courtship and copulation. The pheromone is so vital an information source in the mating process that the female's body need not even be present. If a small quantity of the chemical is placed on some nonliving object, nearby male moths exhibit toward the object the entire sequence of mating and copulation actions that are normally associated with the presence of the female moth.[4]

As with other species, human courtship involves the identification and attraction of mates. These processes occur primarily through visual, auditory, and tactile modes, although some studies suggest that chemical data may also play a role. To a far greater extent than with other animals human courtship and mating involves persuasion and negotiation. Humans arrange the terms, timing, and implications of their intimate relations, and in these interactions communication plays an indispensible role.

Reproduction It is almost too obvious to note that offspring of any species as they reach adulthood bear strong physical resemblance to their parents. A bear cub grows up to look and act like a bear, not a cat or a dog. Physiologically, structurally, in general appearance, and in a number of behavioral patterns, the young of any species replicate or reproduce their parents. This replication or reproduction comes about through a communication process in which the sperm cell of the male parent and female egg cell merge to provide a blueprint for the growth and development of the offspring.[5]

The cell is the basic system involved in this process. All living systems, their subsystems, and their subsubsystems are composed of cells. The general pattern of growth of living things is through division of cells. A single cell divides to produce two, each of which divides to produce two more, and so on. In some organisms, this continues until thousands, millions, or billions of cells are produced. Division, growth, and development proceed according to the blueprint as the cells form into layers and masses that fold together and intermesh to form systems—tissues, bones, and organs.

Cells contain *chromatin*, which forms into chromosomes during cell division. Just before a cell divides, pairs of chromosomes pull apart, and one of each pair goes into each of the cells. Within these chromosomes is nucleic acid, which has been given the name *DNA*. DNA apparently contains the information that determines the characteristics of a particular cell. The DNA also carries the data, often termed the *genetic code*, which provide the instructions that guide the growth and development of the entire organism.

Reproduction of offspring by their parents begins at the moment of conception as the male sperm and the female egg join. The egg cell, most of which is filled with food, is about one-two hundredth of an inch across. In this space are all the instructions that represent the mother's contribution to the inherited characteristics of the child. The sperm cell, which is only about $\frac{1}{80,000}$ the size of the egg, carries only the information necessary to the father's contribution to the developmental blueprint.[6] Through the union of these two cells, all the information needed for the continuity of the species is transmitted in what is undoubtedly life's most fundamental communication process.

Parent-Offspring Relations and Socialization In lower-order animals, the survival of a species and the communication capabilities necessary to this end are largely assured through inheritance. For this reason, among amphibians, reptiles, and fish, little or no contact between adults and their offspring is necessary. However, with social insects, birds, and mammals, early parent-offspring relations are essential to survival. Even before baby ducklings are born, for example, sounds in the egg may help the parents prepare for the task ahead. Visual, auditory, tactile, gustatory, and olfactory signals are also necessary to the feeding process—often in ways that one might not predict. Adult birds, for instance, seem to react to auditory cues from their babies,

---

FIGURE 2.7 Visual Signal Patterns of Firefly Messages. Male lightning bugs begin their flight during early evening hours of the spring or summer, flashing the luminescent light on the abdomen to attract a mate. In many species, the female does not fly, but rather signals the male from the grass, guiding him to her location. Because there are often a number of different varieties of fireflies in any one area, different codes are necessary in order for individuals to identify and attract members of their own species. These codes consist of distinctive flash and flight patterns—dots, swoops, curves, lines, zigzags and the timing of flashes.

SOURCE: Margaret Cosgrove, *Messages and Voices.* Copyright © 1974 by Margaret Cosgrove. Reprinted with permission.

FIGURE 2.8 Communication plays a basic, and in many ways similar, role in the courtship and mating practices of many animals, humans included.

Crowned Cranes

rather than to visual data, in determining how many offspring are present and, therefore, how much food to bring.[7]

With many social animals, extended contact between parent and young is required. When this contact does not occur, the important role of communication in the survival of a species is underscored. Some birds that are raised without interaction with others of their kind become totally confused about their identity. Konrad Lorenz was the first to study the processes by which birds and other animals learn or *imprint* their identity in early social interaction. He observed:

One of the most striking as well as pathetically comical instances...con-

cerned an albino peacock in an Australian zoo, the lone survivor of a brood that had succumbed to a spell of bad weather. The peafowl chick was placed in the only warm room available during the meagerly funded postwar years. The room just happened to be the one in which the giant tortoises were housed. Although the young peacock flourished in these surroundings, the peculiar effect of its reptilian roomates on the bird became apparent not long after it had attained sexual maturity and grown its first train: Beginning then and forever after, the peacock displayed his magnificent plumes in the famous "wheel" position *only* to giant tortoises, eagerly if vainly courting these reptiles while ignoring even the most handsome peahens with which the zoo supplied him.... In the case of the albino peacock, (imprinting) condemned the unfortunate bird to a life in involuntary celibacy.[8]

Humans are among those animals whose survival depends directly upon relations with adults. The human infant, in fact, is dependent on others of his or her species longer than are other creatures.

Adaptation

Beyond the role communication plays in the survival of a species from one generation to the next is its important function in the day-to-day adaptation of animal and human systems. Among the most fundamental facets of this adaptation, in which information processing plays a role, are (1) locomotion and food identification; (2) self-defense; and (3) establishment and maintenance of territories.

Locomotion The term *locomotion* refers to the purposeful movement of a living system through space, from one location to another. Goal-directed movement of this kind is necessary for nearly all of life's activities, including mating, food location, and self-defense.

Anyone who, as a child, experimented with ants or other insects by placing sticks or rocks in their path probably remembers well how skilled they were at determining the presence of an obstacle and adjusting their course accordingly. Even in a simple example of this sort the role of communication is apparent. In order to move systematically from one position to another, a substantial amount of data must be processed. At a minimum, a living system must use data—sound, sight, odor, temperature, or other cues—to determine its present location. It must also process information relative to the direction it wants to proceed and its progress toward a desired endpoint. Adjusting for impediments, cracks in a sidewalk, or rocks and sticks requires the acquisition and processing of still more data.

Many animals have highly developed locomotion capabilities and can travel great distances with precision. The skills of cats, horses, and homing pigeons are well known in this regard, as are those of ducks and geese, who maintain two seasonal homes several hundred miles apart. Apparently, some

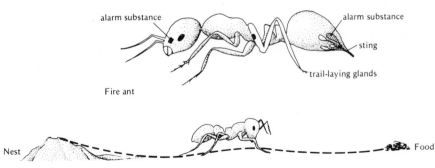

FIGURE 2.9 The Ant's Olfactory Message-Making. The extended sting at the rear of the ant's body lays an odor trail between the nest and the food source that lasts about 100 seconds, and that other ants can easily follow.

SOURCE: The Insect Societies, Edward O. Wilson (Cambridge, MA: Belknap Press-Harvard University Press), 1971.

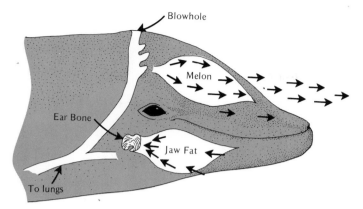

FIGURE 2.10 Dolphin Sound Production and Reception. Dolphins send out click-like echolocation signals through the forehead and receive returning data through the jaw and throat. Whistles are apparently created by forcing air back and forth between the lungs and air sacks connecting to the channel leading to the blowhole.

animals who travel great distances orient themselves by processing data about landmarks, the sun, or stars. Other animals use a sonarlike system of sounds and echoes to find their way about. The echo location skills of bats are so well developed that in total darkness they can pass between two black silk threads placed less than a foot apart without touching. And, the dolphin's echo system has such sensitivity that the animal can distinguish two different fish at a distance of fifteen to eighteen feet.[9]

One of the most elaborate locomotion processes is that used by social bees in locating and securing food. Karl von Frish found that when a worker bee locates a desirable source of food, it announces the find to other bees in the hive by either a "round dance" or a "tail-wagging dance."[10] If the food is located closer than fifty or sixty meters, the bee dances in circles in the hive,

FIGURE 2.11 Echolocation Techniques of Dolphins. The clicks created by dolphins are transmitted through the water, striking any object in the area. The time it takes the echo to return to the dolphin indicates the distance of the object.

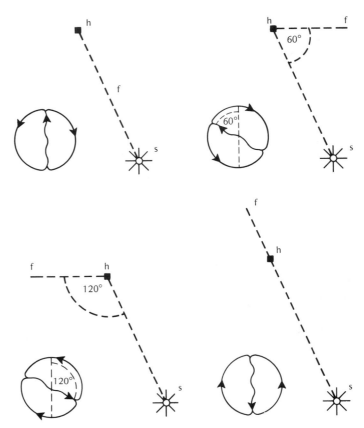

FIGURE 2.12 Bee Locomotion and Food Finding. The scout bee conveys the *distance* of the food by rhythmic tail wagging. The closer the food, the more the tail wags back and forth. The *direction* of the food is indicated by the path traveled by the bee. The direction of movement of the bee while it dances indicates the relationship of the hive (h), the food source (f), and the sun (s). If the tail-wagging dance points straight upward, the food lies in the direction of the sun. If the dance runs 60° left of straight up, the food is 60° to the left of the sun; if the dance is straight down, the food is in the opposite direction (180° away from the sun), and so on.

SOURCE: Reprinted from Karl von Frisch, *Bees: Their Vision, Chemical Senses, and Language, Revised Edition.* Copyright © 1950, 1971, by Cornell University. Used by permission of the publisher, Cornell University Press.

indicating to others that the food is located nearby. If the food is further away, the scout bee performs a tail-wagging dance. The closer the food, the more the tail wags back and forth. The direction of the bee's flight while carrying out the dance indicates the direction in which the food is located.

Locomotion processes are also essential for humans, although the form and communication modes involved differ. Walking across a room to turn on a stereo set, for instance, requires the processing of data relative to one's present location, the destination, and one's progress toward it. When the task is completed, the return trip across the room requires another series of information-processing steps. In a basic sense, the man or woman scurrying

TABLE 2.2

Function		Activities Involved
Survival	. . .	*Mating* (species and gender identification, attraction, persuasion, synchronizing actions)
		Reproduction
		Parent-offspring Relations and Socialization (feeding, learning, identity imprinting, development of communication capability)
Adaptation	. . .	*Locomotion*
		Self-defense
		Territoriality
		Cooperation-competition
		Division of Labor
		Mobilizing for Group Action
		Dominance-submission
		Status Conferral
		Social Organization

along a busy sidewalk at rush hour or driving on a crowded multilane highway has a great deal in common with the locomotion activities of the ant, bat, dolphin, or songbird. Each must analyze an immense quantity of data in order to arrive safely at the intended destination.

Self-Defense Communication also plays an important role in the processes through which living systems identify and respond to potential sources of threat to their safety and well-being. If an animal notes the presence of a danger—a predator, a falling tree, the headlights of an auto, and so on—the animal prepares instinctively to defend itself or to flee. As a part of what has been termed the *stress response*, hormonal and muscular systems are activated, readying the animal for maximum physical output.[11]

The outlet for this stress energy—the act of fighting or retreating—is often the basis for information used by other animals. To the predator, for example, such data are useful in anticipating, countering, and overpowering the actions of its prey. Other animals may use data generated by fight or flight as a signal that their safety is also threatened. This is so, for instance, when the alarm response of one bird evokes a reaction in others who in turn produce their own distress calls. Similarly, as a part of the fight and flight response, injured or disturbed fish give off chemical signals that serve to alert other fish of impending danger.

Thus, for living systems, communication is necessary for identifying and reacting to environmental stressors and for signaling others of the need to

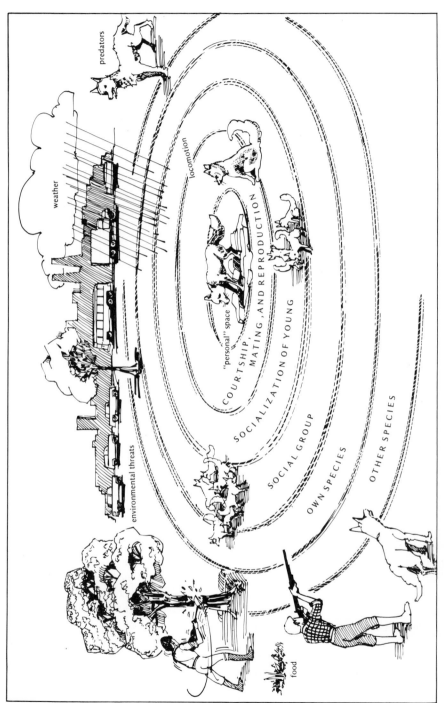

FIGURE 2.13 Communication serves living systems in a variety of respects. In addition to providing a fundamental means for survival of a species from one generation to the next, communication is the means by which animals inform themselves of the conditions, threats, opportunities, and challenges of their environment. Through communication animals define a territory and personal space, conduct activities of courtship and mating, rear their young, carry out social activities with members of their own species, and relate to members of other species and the physical environment.

SOURCE: Adapted from Margaret Cosgrove, *Messages and Voices*, Dodd, Mead & Company, 1974.

mobilize for action or dispersal. Among humans, the natural fight-or-flight response is often constrained or channeled into other culturally sanctioned actions. When this occurs, communication also plays a central role in ways that will become clear in later discussion.

Territoriality The establishment and maintenance of a home or territory is another basic activity in which communication plays a vital role. Almost all animals become attached to particular places, often to those locations where they were born, spent their youth, or mated, and many mark and even defend these territories.

Perhaps the best examples of territoriality are provided by birds. In the spring, male birds take possession of an area, hedge, or portion of a meadow. Thereafter, they make an effort to keep out other males by singing. Some birds create songs with two distinct forms, one by which they maintain contact with their partners, and another by which they define and display their territory. Because each male bird has a unique song pattern, it is not difficult for other birds to determine when a song belongs to a "neighbor" and a "familiar face," and when it is that of a stranger.[12] Whereas the neighbor whose home is already established represents no threat to the territory, the foreigner may, and his presence therefore evokes a much different reaction. Territories also play an important role in the lives of social insects. Many species go to great lengths to construct their dwellings and to compete for prime housing sites; often such insects can determine the presence of a foreigner and will often attack if an individual violates their territory.[13] Some animals also establish and maintain what might be thought

FIGURE 2.14 Some birds, such as wrens, construct a number of nests and conduct the female on a guided tour of the construction sites. She selects the one she likes best for their home. Typically, of the various nests the male builds, one is more carefully constructed and frequently the female selects this nest. Occasionally the male bird takes other females on a tour of the remaining nests; if one is reasonably well-made, he may end up with a second companion in a "downtown apartment."

FIGURE 2.15 Through various forms of communication, individuals of various species define and maintain personal space.

of as *mobile* or *transitory territories*, and these, too, involve communication. Some fish and birds, for example, travel or rest in groups, and a stranger that violates the boundary may well meet with considerable resistance from the group.

In a number of respects, territoriality seems to be as important to human life as it is to the lives of many other animals, although often less obviously so. In many situations, humans maintain *personal space*—portable or transitory territories—in a manner similar to other animals, In face-to-face discussions, for example, a certain amount of space usually is maintained between individuals. When this space is violated, substantial discomfort often occurs. A coat or briefcase on an empty seat in a bus, or a towel or

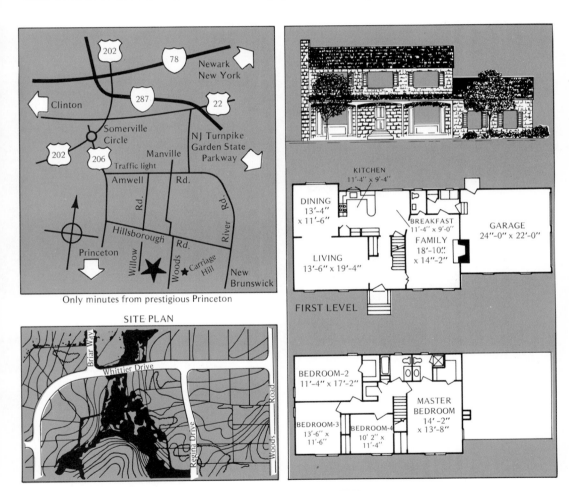

FIGURE 2.16 Human Territories. The human tendency to create and construct elaborate dwellings would seem to be unsurpassed in the animal world. Whether a garden apartment, brownstone, acreage, or home in the suburbs, the acquisition, maintenance and decoration of home territories becomes an important life activity of most humans. In addition to providing shelter from the elements, such territories serve other communicative functions, including the establishment and display of personal, social, economic, and occupational identity and status.

FIGURE 2.17 The use of communication in marking geographic territories is not unique to the nonhuman world. Borders of various sorts play a role in human life, as well.

umbrella on the beach may also serve to mark transitory territories, in much the same way as the bird's song claims a section of a grove.

Over the years a great deal of human effort has also been directed toward acquiring, dividing, and maintaining nontransitory territories of one kind or another—countries, states, counties, municipalities, and personal properties. And people spend a considerable amount of time selecting, allocating, and decorating homes, offices, and apartments, as well, As with other animals, our territories are extensions of ourselves, defined and maintained through communication.

Summary

Communication is the necessary life process through which animal and human systems acquire information about their environment that is necessary to carry out their life activities. The process involves taking in data from the environment and transforming those data into information that can be used to guide behavior.

Animal and human systems use visual, tactile, olfactory, gustatory, and auditory data or cues as sources of information and the bases for behavior. The processing of these data provides information that serves two primary functions: survival of the species and adaptation. Survival of the species involves mating, reproduction, and parent-offspring relations and socialization. Adaptation necessitates locomotion, self-defense, and territoriality. Each of these activities centrally involves communication.

Communication, then, is viewed as an essential, ongoing life process through which animal and human systems maintain themselves—emerge, develop, grow, and eventually deteriorate—in their environments. A recognition of the common role communication plays in the lives of all such systems provides a useful background for exploring the nature of human communication in the chapters ahead.

Notes

1. Cf. James G. Miller, "Living Systems," *Behavioral Science*, **10**:193–237 (1965), and Lee Thayer, *Communication and Communication Systems* (Homewood, IL: Irwin, 1968), p. 17.
2. Jack H. Prince, *Languages of the Animal World* (Nashville, TN: Nelson, 1975), p. 33.
3. Niko Tinbergen, *Social Behaviour in Animals with Special Reference to Vertebrates* (London: Methuen, 1965), p. 25.
4. H.H. Shorey, *Animal Communication by Pheromones* (New York: Academic Press, 1976), p. 99.
5. A fascinating discussion of this complex topic is provided by Isaac Asimov in *The Genetic Code* (New York: New American Library, 1962), and Chester Lawson in "Language, Communication, and Biological Organization," in *General Systems Theory and Human Communication*, edited by Brent D. Ruben and John Y. Kim (Rochelle Park, NJ: Hayden, 1975), p. 88. A related discussion is presented in *The Selfish Gene* by Richard Dawkins (New York: Oxford University Press, 1976).
6. Isaac Asimov, op. cit., p. 19.
7. Gerhard A. Theilcke, *Bird Sounds* (Ann Arbor, MI: University of Michigan Press, 1970), pp. 65–66.
8. Hilda Simon, *The Courtship of Birds* (New York: Dodd, Mead, 1977), p. 23. Parentheses added
9. Fernand Méry, op. cit., p. 3; for further discussion of echo location, see Jack R. Prince, *Languages of the Animal World* (Nashville, TN: Nelson,

1975), p. 23; Jacques-Yves Cousteau and Philippe Diolé, op. cit., pp. 138–139; and Forrest G. Wood, *Marine Mammals and Man: The Navy's Porpoises and Sea Lions* (Washington, D.C.: Robert Luce, 1973), pp. 70–83.

10. Martin Lindauer, *Communication Among Social Bees* (Cambridge, MA: Harvard University Press, 1961), p. 33. A more detailed discussion of dance and communication among social bees, of which this is a summary, is provided in Martin Lindauer, op. cit., pp. 32–58. See also *The Insect Societies,* by Edward O. Wilson (Cambridge, MA: Belknap Press, 1971).

11. Cf. Hans Seyle, *The Stress of Life* (New York: McGraw-Hill, 1956), The notion of stress and its relationship to communication will be discussed in more detail in subsequent chapters.

12. Cf. Gerhard Thielcke, op. cit., pp. 43–47.

13. H.H. Shorey, op. cit., pp. 81–82.

References and Suggested Reading

Amon, Aline. *Reading, Writing, Chattering Chimps.* New York: Atheneum, 1975.

Ashby, W. Ross. "General Systems Theory as a New Discipline." *General Systems,* **3** (1958).

Asimov, Issac. *The Genetic Code.* New York: New American Library, 1962.

Barash, David P. *Sociobiology and Behavior.* New York: American Elsevier, 1977.

Boulding, Kenneth E. "General Systems Theory—Skeleton of Science." *Management Science,* **2** (1956), 11–17.

Buckley, Walter. *Modern Systems Research for the Behavioral Scientist.* Chicago: Aldine, 1967.

Cannon, Walter B. *The Wisdom of the Body.* New York: Norton, 1932.

Churchman, C. West. *The Systems Approach.* New York: Delacorte, 1968.

Cosgrove, Margaret. *Messages and Voices.* New York: Dodd, Mead, 1974.

Cousteau, Jacques-Yves, and Philippe Diolé. *Dolphins.* Translated by J.F. Bernard. Garden City, NY: Doubleday, 1975.

Dawkins, Richard. *The Selfish Gene.* New York: Oxford University Press, 1976.

Dimond, Stuart J. *The Social Behavior of Animals.* London: Batsford, 1970.

Farb, Peter. *Ecology.* New York: Time–Life, 1963.

Frings, Hubert. "Zoology" in *Interdisciplinary Approaches to Human Communication.* Ed. by Richard W. Budd and Brent D. Ruben. Rochelle Park, NJ: Hayden, 1979, 33–35.

——and Mable Frings. *Animal Communication.* 2nd ed. Norman, OK: University of Oklahoma, 1975.

Fuller, J.L., and M.W. Fox. "The Behavior of Dogs." In *The Behavior of Domestic Animals.* Ed. by E.S.E. Hafez. Baltimore: Williams & Wilkins, 1969, 439–481.

Geldart, Frank A. *The Human Senses.* New York: Wiley, 1972.

Gerard, R.W. "A Biologist's View of Society." *General Systems,* 1 (1956), 155–160.

Grinker, R.R., Sr., Ed. *Toward a Unified Theory of Human Behavior.* New York: Basic Books, 1967.

Guhl, A.M. "The Social Environment and Behavior." In *The Behaviour of Domestic Animals.* Ed. by E.S.E. Hafez. Baltimore: Williams & Wilkins, 1969, 85–94.

Hafez, E.S.E., Ed. *The Behaviour of Domestic Animals.* Baltimore: Williams & Wilkins, 1969.

Hall, A.D., and R.W. Fagen. "Definition of System." *General Systems,* 1 (1956), 18–28. Reprinted in *General Systems Theory and Human Communication.* Ed. by Brent D. Ruben and John Y. Kim. Rochelle Park, NJ: Hayden, 1975, 52–65.

Hancocks, David. *Master Builders of the Animal World.* New York: Harper, 1973.

Haney, Alan. *Plants and Life.* New York: Macmillan, 1978.

Hartshorne, Charles. *Born to Sing: An Interpretation and World Survey of Bird Song.* Bloomington, IN: Indiana University Press, 1973.

Hinde, Robert A. *Biological Bases of Human Social Behavior.* New York: McGraw-Hill, 1974

Laszlo, Ervin, Ed. *The Systems View of the World.* New York: Braziller, 1972.

Lawson, Chester A. "Language, Communication and Biological Organization." *General Systems,* 8 (1963). Reprinted in *General Systems Theory and Human Communication.* Ed. by Brent D. Ruben and John Y. Kim. Rochelle Park, NJ: Hayden, 1975, 80–95.

Lindauer, Martin. *Communication Among Social Bees.* Cambridge, MA: Harvard University Press, 1961.

Méry, Fernand. *Animal Language.* Translated by Michael Ross. Westmead, England: Saxon House, 1975.

Miller, James G. "Living Systems." *Behavioral Science,* 10, (1965), 193–237.

Miller, Jonathan. *The Body in Question.* New York: Random House, 1978.

Novitski, Edward. *Human Genetics.* New York: Macmillan, 1977.

Prince, Jack H. *Languages of the Animal World.* Nashville, TN: Nelson, 1975.

Ruben, Brent D. "Communication and Conflict: A System-Theoretic Perspective." *Quarterly Journal of Speech* 64:2 (1978), 202–210.

———"General Systems Theory." In *Interdisciplinary Approaches to Human Communication.* Ed. by Richard W. Budd and Brent D. Ruben. Rochelle Park, NJ: Hayden, 1979, 95–118.

———and John Y. Kim, Eds. *General Systems Theory and Human Communication.* Rochelle Park, NJ: Hayden, 1975.

Ruesch, Jurgen, and Gregory Bateson. *Communication: the Social Matrix of Psychiatry.* 2nd ed. New York: Norton, 1968.

Scott, J.P. "Introduction to Animal Behaviour." In *The Behaviour of Domestic Animals*. Ed. by E.S.E. Hafez. Baltimore, MD: Williams & Wilkins, 1969, 3–21.

Sebeok, Thomas A. *Animal Communication: Techniques of Study and Results of Research*. Bloomington, IN: Indiana University Press, 1968.

Sebeok, Thomas A. *How Animals Communicate*. Ed. by Thomas A. Sebeok. Bloomington, IN: Indiana University Press, 1977.

Selye, Hans. *The Stress of Life*. Rev. ed. New York: McGraw-Hill, 1976.

Shorey, H.H. *Animal Communication by Pheromones*. New York: Academic Press, 1976.

Simon, Hilda. *The Courtship of Birds*. New York: Dodd, Mead, 1977.

Thayer, Lee. *Communication and Communication Systems*. Homewood, IL: Irwin, 1968.

Thielcke, Gerhard A. *Bird Sounds*. Ann Arbor, MI: University of Michigan Press, 1970.

Tinbergen, Niko. *Social Behaviour in Animals with Special Reference to Vertebrates*. London: Methuen, 1953.

von Bertalanffy, Ludwig. *General Systems Theory*. New York: Braziller, 1968.

———."General System Theory." *General Systems*, **1** (1956), 1–10.

von Frisch, Karl. *Bees: Their Vision, Chemical Senses and Language*. Ithaca, NY: Cornell University Press, 1950.

———.*The Dance Language and Orientation of Bees*. Cambridge, MA: Belknap Press-Harvard University Press, 1967.

Wilson, Edward O. *The Insect Societies*. Cambridge, MA: Belknap Press-Harvard University Press, 1971.

Wood, Forrest G. *Marine Mammals and Man: The Navy's Porpoises and Sea Lions*. Washington, D.C.: Robert Luce, 1973.

Chapter 3

History

The Traditions of Communication Study

To fully appreciate the significance and unifying value of the approach to information and behavior discussed in Chapters 1 and 2, it is important to have a sense of the process by which communication study has developed over the years. This chapter will briefly review some of the highlights of this evolution.

Early Communication Study

It is difficult to determine precisely when and how communication first came to be regarded as a significant factor in human life. According to historians, considerable concern about communication and its role in human affairs was expressed prior to the fifth century B.C., in classical Babylonian and Egyptian writings and in Homer's *Iliad*.[1]

Perhaps the most familiar historic statement suggesting the importance of communication was provided in the Bible. In the opening section of the Old Testament the spoken word is described as the incredibly powerful force through which God created the world—God said, "Let there be light; and there was light."

As with other disciplines that have sought to explain human behavior, the beginning of systematic theory development in communication can be traced to the Greeks. Their initial interest sprang from the practical concerns of day-to-day life. Greece had a democratic form of government, and virtually all facets of business, government, law, and education were carried on orally. Greek citizens also had to be their own lawyers. Accused and accuser alike presented their cases before a jury of several hundred persons who would have to be convinced of the rightness of a position. Lawsuits were common in Athens, and, as a result, legal public speaking became a preoccupation.

Rhetoric and Speech

What might be considerd as the first theory of communication was developed in Greece by Corax and later refined by his student Tisias. The theory dealt with courtroom speaking, which was considered the craft of persuasion. Tisias became convinced that persuasion could be taught as an art and provided encouragement for instructors of what was called *rhetoric*.

Aristotle (385–322 B.C.) and his teacher Plato (427–347 B.C.) were central figures in early communication study. Both regarded communication as an *art* or *craft* to be practiced on one hand, and as an *area of study* on the other. As Aristotle noted in the opening paragraph of his classic work, *Rhetoric:*

> To a certain extent all men attempt to discuss statements and to maintain them, at random or through practice and from acquired habit. Both ways being possible, the subject can plainly be handled systematically, for it is possible to inquire the reason why some speakers succeed through practice and others spontaneously; and everyone will at once agree that such inquiry is the function of science.[2]

Aristotle described communication in terms of an *orator* or *speaker*

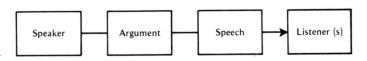

FIGURE 3.1 Aristotelian View.

constructing an *argument* to be presented in a *speech* to *hearers*—an *audience*. The speaker's goal was to inspire a positive image of himself or herself and to encourage the members of the audience to be receptive to the message:

> rhetoric exists to affect the giving of decisions...the *orator* must not only try to make the argument of his *speech* demonstrative and worthy of belief; he must also make his own character look right and put his *hearers*, who are to decide, into the right frame of mind.[3] (Italics added)

For Aristotle, then, communication was a verbal activity in which a speaker tried to persuade—to achieve his or her own purposes with a listener through skillful construction of an argument and delivery of a speech.

During this same period, Plato outlined what he thought would be necessary for the study of rhetoric to contribute to a broader explanation of human behavior. The field would need to include the study of the nature of words, the study of the nature of human beings and their ways of approaching life, the study of the nature of order, and the study of the instruments by which human beings are affected.[4] Thus, although the earliest interest in communication focused on political speaking, it was recognized that in order to fully understand how persuasion operated it would be necessary to develop a broader and more comprehensive theory.

The writings of two other scholars—Cicero (106–43 B.C.) and Quintilian (35–95 A.D.)—began to contribute to that broadening theory of communication. Like Plato and Aristotle, Cicero saw communication as both an academic and practical matter. His view of communication was so comprehensive as to include all of what is now considered the domain of the social sciences. Quintilian is remembered primarily as an educator and synthesizer, bringing together in his writing the previous five hundred years' thinking about communication.[5]

The notion that communication was critical to virtually all aspects of human life was widely held during the Classical period. Unfortunately, the unity and direction that had characterized communication during this era was largely reversed in the Medieval and Renaissance periods. With the decline of the oral tradition and democracy, much of the interest in communication also waned. The study of rhetoric was dispersed among several different fields, and by the end of the fourteenth century, most of the communication theory that had originally been developed in rhetoric was now being studied in religion.

Eventually, the work of Augustine led to a rediscovery of classical Greek theory. His writings applied communication to the interpretation of the *Bible* and other religious writings, and to the art of preaching. In so doing, Augustine once again united the *practical* and *theoretical* aspects of communication study.

During the eighteenth and nineteenth centuries, emphasis in communication study was placed on written argument and literature. There was also great interest in speaking style, articulation, and gesture, leading to the formation of the National Association of Elocutionists in 1892.

By the end of the nineteenth century, most colleges and universities were organized into departments, and rhetoric and speech were often within departments of English rather than being separate units. In 1909, the Eastern States Speech Association—now the Eastern Communication Association—was formed, and in 1910, held its first annual conference. The National Association of Teachers of Public Speaking, which became the Speech Association of America and more recently the Speech Communication Association, was formed in 1914. In 1915, the *Quarterly Journal of Public Speaking* was first published, followed soon after by the *Quarterly Journal of Speech*. By 1920, speech had become a discipline in its own right.[6]

Journalism

The other field that has long contributed to the heritage of communication study is *journalism*. Like rhetoric and speech, journalism also dates back several thousand years. Writers indicate that perhaps the earliest practice of journalism occurred some 3,700 years ago in Egypt, when a record of the events of the time was transcribed on the tomb of an Egyptian king. Years later, Julius Caesar had an official record of the news of the day posted in a public place, and copies of it were made and sold.[7]

Predecessors of today's newspaper were a mixture of newsletters, ballads, proclamations, political tracts, and pamphlets describing various events. The mid-1600s saw the emergence of the newspaper in its modern form, and the first paper published in the United States, *Publick Occurrences Both Forreign and Domestick*, appeared in 1690 in Boston.

Although the practice of journalism dates back many years, formalized study in the area did not progress rapidly until the early 1900s. In 1905, the University of Wisconsin offered what were perhaps the first courses in journalism, at a time when there were few, if any, books on the topic. By 1910, there were half a dozen volumes available, and between 1910 and 1920, some twenty-five works on journalism and newspaper work were compiled, signaling a pattern of continued growth.[8]

Recent History: Early Twentieth Century

In the first half of the twentieth century, interest in communication continued in rhetoric and speech. In journalism, the advent of radio in the 1920s and television in the early 1940s, resulted in the wider application of journalistic concepts. At the same time, these new media gave impetus to the development of a broadened view of the nature of journalism and paved the way for the emergence of new areas of study—*mass media* and *mass communication*.

Concern with communication was not limited to rhetoric, speech, and journalism, however. In philosophy, for example, a number of scholars wrote about the nature of communication and its role in human life. A number of anthropologists, psychologists, and sociologists were also interested in communication and its role in individual and social process, and writers in the area of language also contributed to the advancement of communication study.

The Late 1940s and 1950s: Interdisciplinary Growth

In the late 1940s and early 1950s, the scope of the field of communication broadened substantially. During these years, a number of scholars from the various behavioral and social science disciplines began to develop theories of communication which extended beyond the boundaries of their own fields. In anthropology, for example, research concerned with body positioning and gestures in particular cultures laid the groundwork for more general studies of nonverbal communication. In psychology, interest focused on persuasion. social influence, and, specifically, attitudes—how they form, how they change, their impact on behavior, and the role of communication in these dynamics.

Sociologists and political scientists studied the nature of mass media in various political and social activities, voting behavior, and other facets of life. In zoology, communication among animals began to receive considerable attention among researchers. During these same years, scholars in linguistics, general semantics, and semiotics, fields that focused on the nature of language and its role in human activity, also contributed to the advancement of communication study.

Studies in rhetoric and speech in the late 1940s and 1950s broadened to include oral interpretation, voice and diction, debate, theater, physiology of speech, and speech pathology. In journalism and mass media studies, growth and development were even more dramatic, spurred on in no small way by the popularity of television and efforts to understand its impact. In a number of classic works in the 1950s, the focus on specific media—newspapers, magazines, radio, and television—began to be replaced by a more general concern with the nature and effects of *mass media* and *mass communication*.

By the end of the 1950s a number of writings had appeared that paved the way for the development of more integrated views of communication. It was during these years that the National Society for the Study of Communication (now the International Communication Association) was established with the stated goal of bringing greater unity to the study of communication by exploring the relationships among speech, language, and media.[9] These developments set the stage for the rapid growth of communication as an independent discipline.

Lasswell's View of Communication

Along with other developments during this period were a number of writings that sought to provide descriptions of the nature of the communication process. One of the most often cited characterizations of communication was

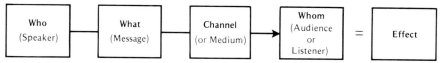

FIGURE 3.2 Lasswell Model.

advanced by political scientist Harold Lasswell in 1948 as an outgrowth of his work in the area of propaganda. Lasswell provided a general view of communication that extended well beyond the boundaries of political science. He said that the communication process could best be explained by the simple statement: "Who says what to whom in what channel with what effect."[10]

Lasswell's view of communication, as had Aristotle's some two thousand years earlier, focused primarily on verbal messages. It also emphasized the elements of *speaker*, *message*, and *audience*, but used different terms. Both men viewed communication as a one-way process in which one individual influenced others through messages.

Lasswell offered a broadened definition of *channel* to include mass media along with verbal speech as part of the communication process. His approach also provided a more generalized view of the *goal* or *effect* of communication than did the Aristotelian perspective. Lasswell's work suggested that there could be a variety of outcomes or effects of communication, such as to inform, to entertain, to aggravate, and to persuade.

Shannon and Weaver's Model

About one year after the introduction of the Lasswell approach, Claude Shannon published the results of research he had undertaken for Bell Telephone to study the engineering problems of signal transmission. The results of this work provided the basis for the often cited Shannon and Weaver model of communication.

In their book *The Mathematical Theory of Communication*, the authors describe the nature of the communication process:

> communication will be used here in a very broad sense to include all the procedures by which one mind may affect another. This, of course, involves not only written and oral speech, but also music, the pictorial arts, the theatre, the ballet, and in fact all human behavior.[11]

As shown in Figure 3.3, Shannon and Weaver described communication in terms of six elements:

> The *information source* selects a desired message out of a set of possible messages.... The selected message may consist of written or spoken words, or of pictures, music, etc.

> The *transmitter* changes this *message* into the *signal* which is actually sent over the *communication channel* from the transmitter to the *receiver*. In the case of telephony, the channel is a wire, the signal a varying electrical current on the

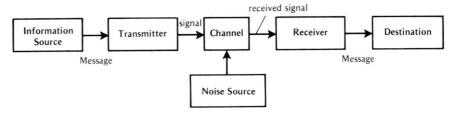

FIGURE 3.3 Shannon and Weaver Model.

SOURCE: The Mathematical Theory of Communication, Claude E. Shannon and Warren Weaver. Copyright © 1949 by the University of Illinois. Renewed 1977. By permission.

> wire; the transmitter is the set of devices (telephone transmitter, etc.) which change the sound pressure of the voice into the varying electrical current.... In oral speech, the information source is the brain, the transmitter is the voice mechanism producing the varying sound pressure (the signal) which is transmitted through the air (the channel)....
>
> The *receiver* is a sort of inverse transmitter, changing the transmitted signal back into a message, and handing this message on to the destination. When I talk to you, my brain is the information source, yours is the destination; my vocal system is the transmitter, and your ear and associated eighth nerve is the receiver.[12]

This view represented an important expansion of the idea of communication to include such activities as music, art, ballet and the theater—in fact, all human behavior, although these more far-reaching implications were not to be elaborated upon for some time. The Shannon and Weaver perspective, like that of Lasswell, included not only verbal and mediated channels but also gestures, body position, and other forms of nonverbal behavior.

In discussing their view of communication, Shannon and Weaver also introduced the term *noise,* which was a label for any distortion that interfered with the transmission of a signal from the source to the destination, such as static on a radio, a blinding fog, or blurred, rain-soaked pages of a newspaper. They also advanced the notion of *correction channel,* which they regarded as a means of overcoming problems created by noise. The correction channel was operated by an observer who compared the initial signal that was sent with that received; when the two didn't match, additional signals would be transmitted to correct the error.[13]

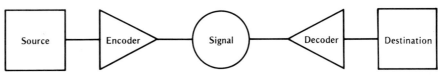

FIGURE 3.4

SOURCE: The Process and Effects of Mass Communication. Ed. by Wilbur Schramm. Copyright © 1965 by the University of Illinois Press. By permission.

Schramm's Models

In a noteworthy article published in 1954 and entitled, "How Communication Works," Wilbur Schramm provided several additional models of the dynamics of the communication process. The first, shown in Figure 3.4, was essentially an elaboration of that advanced by Shannon and Weaver. Describing this model, Schramm said:

> A *source* may be an individual (speaking, writing, drawing, gesturing) or a communication organization (like a newspaper, publishing house, television station or motion picture studio). The *message* may be in the form of ink on paper, sound waves in the air, impulses in electric current, a wave of the hand, a flag in the air, or any other signal capable of being interpreted meaningfully. The *destination* may be an *individual* listening, watching, or reading; a member of a *group*, such as a discussion group, a lecture audience, a football crowd, or a mob; or an individual member of a particular group we call the mass audience, such as the reader of a newspaper or a viewer of television.[14]

Schramm saw communication as a purposeful effort to establish a *commonness* between a source and receiver, noting that the word *communication* comes from the Latin *communis,* which meant *common:*

> what happens when the source tries to build up this commonness with his intended receiver? First, the source encodes his message. That is, he takes the information or feeling he wants to share and puts it into a form that can be transmitted. The pictures in our heads can't be transmitted until they are coded.... Once coded and sent, a message is quite free of its sender.... And there is good reason...for the sender to wonder whether his receiver will really be in tune with him, whether the message will be interpreted without distortion, whether the picture in the head of the receiver will bear any resemblance to that in the head of the sender.[15]

In this model, Schramm introduced the concept of *field of experience,* which he thought to be essential to determining whether or not a message would be received at the destination in the manner intended by the source.

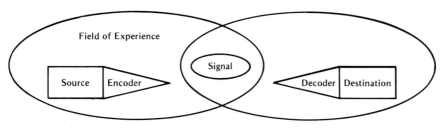

FIGURE 3.5

SOURCE: *The Process and Effects of Mass Communication.* Ed. by Wilbur Schramm. Copyright © 1965 by the University of Illinois Press. By permission.

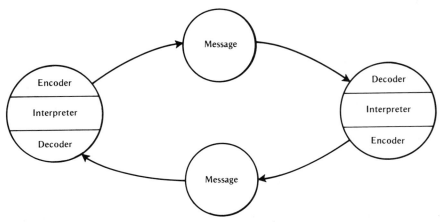

FIGURE 3.6

SOURCE: *The Process and Effects of Mass Communication*. Ed. by Wilbur Schramm. Copyright © 1965 by the University of Illinois Press. By permission.

He contended that without common fields of experience—a common language, common backgrounds, a common culture, and so forth—there was little chance for a message to be interpreted correctly (Figure 3.5).

Following a similar line of reasoning as Shannon and Weaver, Schramm suggested the importance of *feedback* as a means of overcoming the problem of noise. He said that feedback "tells us how our messages are being interpreted.... An experienced communicator is attentive to feedback and constantly modifying his messages in light of what he observes in or hears from his audience."[16] As shown in Figure 3.6, Schramm believed that when a receiver provided feedback he or she became a sender, thus eliminating the need for a distinction between the two in describing the communication process. Each individual was viewed as both source and recipient of messages, and communication was viewed as circular, rather than one-way, as with earlier models.

The Schramm view of communication was more elaborate than many others developed during this period and added new elements in describing the process. In addition to reemphasizing the elements of *source, message,* and *destination,* it suggested the importance of the *encoding* and *decoding* process and the role of *field of experience.* Further, whereas other models had acknowledged that the *receiver* might be either a single person or a large audience, this model suggested that a *source* could also be one individual or many, and in actual operation, *source* and *receiver* were often indistinguishable.

Katz and Lazarsfeld's Model

In 1955, political scientists Elihu Katz and Paul Lazarsfeld presented their *two-step flow* concept of communication in their book *Personal Influence.* The model was based on earlier research in which they found that information presented on the mass media did not reach and have an impact upon receivers

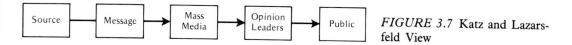

| Source | Message | Mass Media | Opinion Leaders | Public |

FIGURE 3.7 Katz and Lazars-feld View

as previous views of communication seemed to suggest it would. Specifically, their research indicated that political radio and print messages seemed to have a negligible effect on individuals' voting decisions.

In searching for an explanation for this lack of effect, they developed a view that linked interpersonal dynamics to mass communication. Their follow-up studies indicated that undecided voters were influenced more by people around them than by information provided by the mass media; husbands and wives were influenced by their spouses, club members by other club members, workers by their colleagues, children by their parents, and so on. Their research also indicated that some people were consistently more influential than others, leading them to conclude that "ideas often seem to *flow* from radio and print *to* opinion leaders and *from them* to the less active sections of the population"—in a two-step flow.[17] (See Figure 3.7.)

In some respects, the two-step flow concept was quite similar to earlier views of communication. Although subsequent research has suggested that the two-step concept is applicable in only a restricted range of situations, the formulation served to link face-to-face and mass communication and to introduce the idea of opinion leaders.

Westley and MacLean's Model

During this same period, Bruce Westley and Malcolm S. MacLean, Jr. also developed an important characterization of the communication process. Their model departed from previous popular approaches by suggesting that communication does not begin with a *source* but, rather, with a series of *signals* or potential messages. In Westley and MacLean's view, there are a large number of signals—potential messages—in a communicator's environment, which they referred to as "X's" in their model. Signals may involve single (X), or multiple modalities, such as hearing, touch, and sight (X_{3m}).

The model suggested that in a given situation some of the many signals (X's) in one's environment at any point in time were selected by an individual—A—and combined to form a new message (X^1)—a news story, advertisement, or speech, for example. Person A was seen as passing along the new message (X^1) to a second person, C. If Person C happened to be present in the circumstances to which A was referring, C would also have some firsthand information about the situation (X_3 and X_4). And, if he or she desired, C might question A on his or her account of the event. This questioning would be classified as feedback, designated in the model as (fb_{ca}). (See Figure 3.8.)

For purposes of illustration, suppose that A is a reporter who has witnessed a serious fire, then written and passed along a story about it to his or her editor, C. Person C might rewrite, shorten, or otherwise alter the message; eventually, a revised version would be published and distributed to a receiver (B), a newspaper or magazine subscriber, in our example. Person B

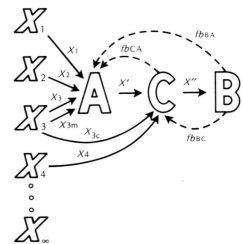

FIGURE 3.8 Westley-MacLean Model.

SOURCE: Bruce Westley and Malcolm S. MacLean, Jr., "A Conceptual Model for Communication Research," *Audio-Visual Communication Review*, Winter, 1955. By permission.

might decide to provide feedback to C (*fb bc*), sending a letter to the editor, for instance. Or Person B might elect to provide feedback to A (*fb ba*), perhaps writing a note to the reporter offering congratulations on the story.

The Westley-MacLean model was considerably more complicated than previous models, and the additional components, lines, and arrows led to a view of communication that was expanded in several significant ways: The model accounted for both mass communication and interpersonal communication, as well as the relationship between the two. Also, it broadened and elaborated the feedback concept. The approach also suggested that communication began with a communicator receiving messages rather than sending them. Additionally, the model provided a different concept of messages or signals than had other models. This represented a fourth important contribution. Previous models were predominately concerned with verbal and nonverbal messages that were purposeful, intentionally created, and transmitted by a sender to achieve specific effects upon a receiver. The Wesley-MacLean model, by implication, suggested that not all messages that were important to the communication process were intentionally sent or necessarily the result of human activity. In their concept, a fire, a sneeze, a traffic accident, a tear, one's clothing, even silence were messages to the extent that they were of significance to the people involved. Finally, the model suggested that messages are transformed as they are transmitted from individual to individual. What began as X_1, X_2, X_3, or X_{3m} for A were transmitted to C in a form once removed from the original event—(X^I). And the message C sent to B was twice removed from the original event—(X^II).

Recent History: Late Twentieth Century

The 1960s: Integration

In the 1960s, a good deal was done to synthesize thinking from rhetoric and speech, journalism and mass media, as well as the other social science disciplines. Among the noteworthy contributions to this integration were a number of landmark books published in the early 1960s, including *The Process of Communication* (1960), *The Effects of Mass Communication* (1960), *On Human Communication* (1961), *Diffusion of Innovations* (1962), *The Science of Human Communication* (1963), *Understanding Media* (1964), and *Theories of Mass Communication* (1966).

The generalized views of communication reflected in these volumes were applied to other areas beginning in the middle of the decade. The term *communication* was linked to *speech* and *rhetoric* in basic books of the field during these years. In 1966, *Speech Communication: A Behavioral Approach* appeared, and two years later, *An Introduction to Rhetorical Communication* was published. In the middle 1960s , major volumes also appeared, linking *communication* with *culture* and *persuasion*. The first books with *interpersonal communication* in their titles were also published during this decade.

Communication continued to be of interest in many other disciplines during the 1960s, as well. Sociologists focused on group dynamics, social relations, and the social origins of knowledge. Political scientists wrote about the role of communication in governments, governance, public opinion, propaganda, and political image building, providing the foundation for the development of the area of political communication that was to blossom a decade later.

In administrative studies, writings on organization, management, leadership, and information networks provided the basis for the growth of *organizational communication*, an area of study that also emerged in the 1970s. In a similar manner, writings in anthropology and linguistics, together with those in communication, set the stage for the emergence of intercultural communication as an area of study. Advances by zoologists during the 1960s encouraged the study of animal communication.

The 1970s and 1980s: Growth and Specialization

The late 1960s and early 1970s were years of unprecedented growth in communication, as more and more persons were drawn to the field. The expansion and specialization which began in the late 1960s reached new heights in the early 1970s. *Interpersonal communication* became an increasingly popular area, as did the study of nonverbal interaction. Information science, information theory, and information and communication systems were other topics of increasing interest. During these same years, *group, organizational, political, international,* and *intercultural communication* emerged as distinct areas of study.

Rhetoric, public speaking, debate, theater, speech pathology, journalism, mass media, photography, advertising, and public relations continued to grow and prosper alongside communication, speech communication, and mass communication. Such new areas as instructional, therapeutic, and developmental communication also became attractive to researchers and practitioners.

Perhaps the most dramatic indication of the growth and diversification in communication study was the remarkable increase in the publication of books and periodicals.[18] Beyond the many books appearing in interpersonal, group, organizational, cross-cultural, political, speech, and mass communication, other volumes dealt with animal communication, audio-visual techniques, communication in education, and communication in business and personnel. Other more specialized books focused on communication and children, intimate communication, dyadic communication, satellite communication, communication and ethics, classroom communication, cable communication, and communication and sex differences. Some books sought to provide summaries and overviews of the expanding field.

Increased interest in communication study during the 1970s was also evident in periodicals and scholarly journals. The first publications with the term *communication* in their titles were published in the mid-1930s, and during the 1950s four more appeared. Eight new periodicals appeared during the 1960s, and the 1970s brought the arrival of seventeen new publications bearing *communication* in their titles. A number of new academic journals were introduced, and several other journals of speech and journalism added the word *communication* to their titles to reflect a broadened focus. By the end

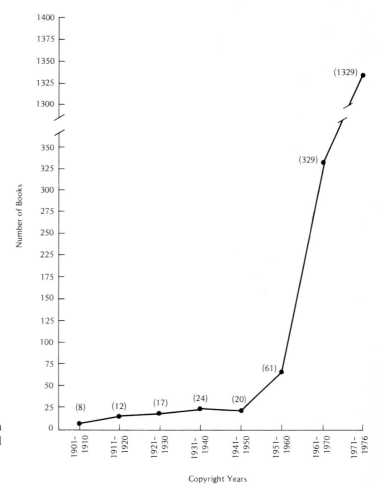

FIGURE 3.9 Communication and Communication Related Books Currently in Print.

SOURCE: *Books in Print*, 1979.

of the decade, *Ulrich's International Periodical Dictionary* listed one hundred thirty-seven publications on communication.

The expansion and diversification of communication study was reflected in college and university curricula. A number of new departments of communication were formed throughout the 1970s, and some programs in *speech* were changed to programs in *speech-communication* or *communication*. The same was true in some journalism departments, where the shift was from *journalism* to *mass communication* or *communication*.

Growth in the field during the late 1970s and early 1980s has been steady, although less dramatic than in the preceding years. In addition to continued interest in the various specialization areas within the field, a major concern with communication technology and policy relative to its use has also been evident. The impact of video games, personal computers, video discs, video cassette recorders, word processors, cable television, and on-line data bases of various types may be even more far-reaching than was the advent of television nearly a half-century earlier. As will be discussed in some detail in Chapter 8, the scope of these changes are such that they are likely to provide a major focus for communication study in the latter half of the decade and beyond.

Berlo's Model

In the last twenty-five years a number of models of the communication process have been advanced, expanding on the work of earlier scholars. One of the most frequently mentioned of these was set forth by David Berlo in 1960 in his book *The Process of Communication*. In some respects the model looked much like the original Aristotelian view of communication, including the traditional elements of *source, message, channel,* and *receiver*.

For each of these elements, controlling factors were listed. The *skills,*

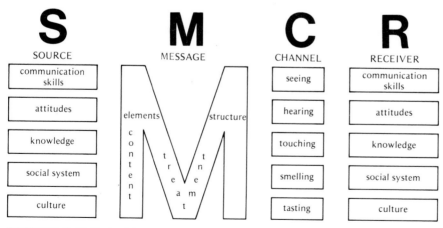

FIGURE 3.10 Berlo Model.

SOURCE: *The Process of Communication: An Introduction to Theory and Practice,* by David Berlo. Copyright © 1960 by Holt, Rinehart and Winston. Reprinted by permission of Holt, Rinehart and Winston, CBS College Publishing.

attitudes, knowledge, culture, and *social system* of the *source* were all seen as important to understanding the way communication operates, as were the *content, treatment,* and *code* of the *message*. The model acknowledged all five senses as potential information channels and indicated that the same factors influenced receivers as sources (Figure 3.10).

In his discussions of the model, Berlo more than others before emphasized the idea that communication was a *process*.[19] He also stressed the idea that "meanings are in people, not in words"—another way of saying that the interpretation of a message depended mainly on the meaning of the words or gestures to the sender and receiver, rather than on the elements of the message in and of themselves.[20] In emphasizing the importance of the meaning attached to a message by a source and receiver, the Berlo framework reinforced a shift away from views of communication that emphasized the *transmission* of information to perspectives that focused on the *interpretation* of information.

Newcomb's Model

In 1961, a *coorientation* model of communication was advanced by psychologist Theodore Newcomb in his book *The Acquaintance Process*. The model was initially developed to describe what happens when two individuals who are attracted to one another engage in interaction. The resulting view of communication has not only been significant in its own right but has also had a major impact on the development of subsequent theory and research.

Newcomb's view was based on *consistency* or *balance theory*, which suggested that human beings had a need to maintain a harmony among their attitudes, beliefs, and behavior. For purposes of illustration, let's assume that Person *A* had a positive regard for Person *B*, a positive attitude toward a given object or message—a political candidate, for instance—and, further, that Person *A* assumed that Person *B* shared his or her opinion of the candidate. If, as the two individuals began to discuss the candidate, Person *A* were to learn that *B* did not share his or her view, a state of imbalance would occur, according to Newcomb. In such a situation, one or more of the following five changes were thought necessary to restore harmony and balance:

> (1) a change in A's attitude toward X, such as to reduce the perceived discrepancy with B; (2) a discrepancy-reducing change in his perception of B's attitude; (3) a reduction in the importance assigned by A to his attitude toward X; (4) a reduction in the strength in degree of A's positive attraction to B; or (5) a reduction in the degree of perceived common relevance that A attributes to X for himself and B.[21]

Thus, the Newcomb framework would indicate that Person *A* in our example would be likely to change his or her opinions toward the political candidate, change his or her perceptions of *B*'s attitude toward the candidate, reduce the importance attached to the matter, reduce the strength of his or her attraction to *B*, and/or reduce his or her present assessment of the extent to which he or she and *B* have a common perspective on these kinds of issues.

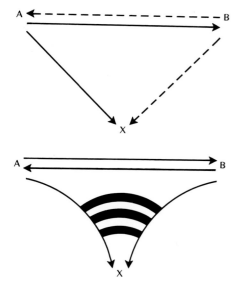

FIGURE 3.11

SOURCE: *The Acquaintance Process* by Theodore M. Newcomb. Copyright © 1961, by Holt, Rinehart and Winston, Inc. Reprinted with permission of Holt, Rinehart and Winston, CBS College Publishing.

FIGURE 3.12

SOURCE: *The Acquaintance Process* by Theodore M. Newcomb. Copyright © 1961, by Holt, Rinehart and Winston, Inc. Reprinted by permission of Holt, Rinehart and Winston, CBS College Publishing.

Figure 3.11 portrays the Newcomb perspective on the communication process from the point of view of Person *A*. The same circumstance could also be analyzed from the perspective of Person *B*, who is presumably going through the same stages, more or less simultaneously, as depicted in Figure 3.12.

Like earlier models, the Newcomb formulation included references to *people* and *messages; source* and *receiver* were not specifically differentiated. Unlike many of these perspectives, however, the Newcomb approach described the communication processes in terms of the interpretive processes that occur *inside* individuals, rather than on the transmission of information *between* them, further contributing to the movement away from transmission-oriented theories.

Dance's Model

In 1967, Frank Dance's interesting helical-spiral model of communication was published. The Dance model is substantially different in appearance from others it post-dates. The choice of this form was intended to reflect a sense of communication as a complex and evolutionary process:

> If communication is viewed as a process, we are forced to adapt our examination and our examining instruments to the challenge of something in motion, something that is changing while we are in the very act of examining it.[22]

As shown in Figure 3.13, the helix was seen as a way of combining the desirable features of the straight-line models with those of the circle, while avoiding the weaknesses of each.[23] To the circular feedback models, the Dance perspective added a concern with the dimension of *time*, suggesting that each communicative act builds upon the previous communication experiences of all parties involved.

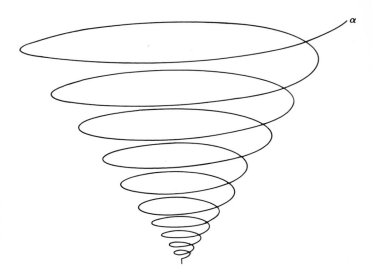

FIGURE 3.13 Dance Model.

SOURCE: "Toward A Theory of Human Communication," in *Human Communication Theory: Original Essays.* Ed. by Frank E.X. Dance. Copyright © 1967. By Permission.

Watzlawick, Beavin, and Jackson's Model

In that same year, 1967, Paul Watzlawick, Janet Beavin, and Don Jackson wrote *Pragmatics of Human Communication*, which provided a general view of communication on the basis of psychiatric study and therapy. Their approach and many of the concepts and propositions they provided have been influential in communication thinking since that time.

The Watzlawick-Beavin-Jackson view of communication, presented in a general form in Figure 3.14, portrayed communication as a *process* involving a give-and-take of messages between individuals.[24] The perspective stressed the view that communication is not something that occurs only when a source chooses intentionally to send messages. Rather, they asserted, in the tradition of Shannon and Weaver, that because we are always behaving, "one cannot not communicate."[25]

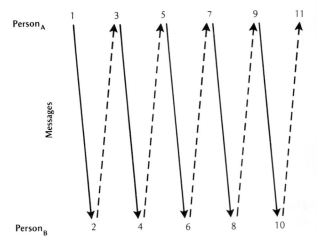

FIGURE 3.14 Watzlawick-Beavin-Jackson Model.

SOURCE: Adapted from *Pragmatics of Human Communication*, Paul Watzlawick, Janet H. Beavin and Don D. Jackson. Copyright © 1967 by W.W. Norton. By Permission.

Communication was seen as an ongoing, cumulative activity between individuals who function alternatively as source and receiver. As with other works of this period, their writings suggested that in order to understand how communication worked, one needed to look beyond the messages and channels to the meanings the individuals involved attach to the words and actions they created. (See Figure 3.14.)

Rogers and Kincaid's Model

One of the more recent models of the communication process is provided by Everett Rogers and D. Lawrence Kincaid in *Communication Networks: Toward a New Paradigm for Research*, published in 1981. The authors described what they termed a convergence model of communication that stressed the importance of information and the manner in which information links individuals together in social networks. They described communication as a process in which individuals

> create and share information with one another in order to reach mutual understanding. This cyclical process involves giving meaning to information that is exchanged between two or more individuals as they move toward convergence... (which is) the tendency for two or more individuals to move toward one another, and to unite in a common interest or focus.[26]

In explaining the manner in which the convergence process was thought to operate, they indicated that communication

always begins with "and then..." to remind us that something has occurred

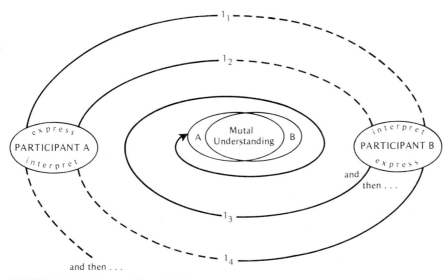

FIGURE 3.15 Rogers-Kincaid Model.

SOURCE: *Communication Networks* by Everett M. Rogers and D. Lawrence Kincaid. Copyright © 1981 by the Free Press, a Division of Macmillan Co., Inc.

before we begin to observe the process. Participant A may or may not consider the past before he shares information (I_1) with Participant B. This individual must perceive and then interpret the information which A creates to express his/her thoughts, and then B may respond by creating information (I_2) to share with A. Individual A interprets this new information and then may express himself again with more information (I_3) about the same topic. Individual B interprets this information, and they continue the process ($I_4 \ldots I_n$) until one or both become satisfied that they have reached a sufficient mutual understanding of one another about the topic for the purpose at hand.[27]

As in a number of early views, the convergence model explained communication in terms of a progressive sending and receiving of messages between two individuals in which the goal and predicted outcome are mutual understanding of a topic. Although acknowledging the role of interpretive processes that occur *within* individuals, the Rogers-Kincaid view emphasized the information exchanges and networks *between* them. Their perspective also carried forth the view of communication as a *process* rather than a *single event*, a point of view emphasized in nearly all models in recent years.

The Evolution of Communication Study

It is clear that a number of changes have occurred in the nearly 2,500-year history of communication study—changes both in our understanding of the communication *process* and in the *discipline* in which it has been studied. The following sections will briefly summarize these changes.

The Development of Communication Theory

In the most general sense, a theory of communication, like theories about other facets of human behavior, is an idea about the nature of human action developed to describe, explain, or predict what one observes. This chapter has explored the evolution of the idea of communication by reviewing some of the more frequently cited models of the process. Models are often a useful way to examine the workings of a phenomenon such as communication, because they miniaturize, simplify, and highlight major facets of a theory.

Paradigms and Anomalies A number of models of the communication process have been advanced over the nearly 2,500-year history of the field. Through an analysis of these models, a number of changes are apparent. The earliest perspectives on communication were concerned with public speaking to a listener or listeners with persuasion as the goal. Gradually, concern broadened to private as well as public speaking, nonverbal and mediated as well as verbal channels, multiple speakers and listeners as well as single individuals, outcomes such as entertainment along with persuasion.

Amidst all the noticeable change, one also notes certain patterns that have changed very little. Throughout much of the history of communication study, the process has been described in terms of a *source* constructing

FIGURE 3.16

messages to be transmitted to a *receiver* to bring about a desired effect. In this way of thinking, communication has essentially been regarded as a one-way transfer of information from source to receiver, as portrayed in Figure 3.16. This S→M→R perspective has been so pervasive in theories and models of communication that it represents what Thomas Kuhn and others refer to as a *paradigm*—a broad framework that guides the thinking of scholars as they advance specific theories over a substantial period of time.[28]

In communication, as in other fields, paradigms do not endure forever. Often they change in response to *anomalies*—research findings, observations, or events that cannot be explained by, or are inconsistent with, existing paradigms.[29] When one reviews the recent history of the field, it is evident that this kind of change has been occurring in communication. Further examination reveals that the anomaly that has given impetus to this transition is relatively simple: *Message sent is not equal to message received—MS ≠ MR.* Or, to put it in a somewhat different way, using the terms presented in Chapters 1 and 2: *Data sent does not equal information received (D ≠ I).*

Even as Aristotle advanced his orator-to-listener view of communication, he and his contemporaries acknowledged that the persuasive efforts of the speaker were not always successful. It was presumed, however, that the match between the message sent and that received could be made more predictable if a source knew more about how to effectively construct and deliver messages.

In the models and writings of Shannon and Weaver, and most especially Schramm, is evidence of an initial recognition of the *MS ≠ MR* anomaly and the beginnings of changing views of communication. Shannon and Weaver's concept of *noise* represented the first formal acknowledgement in a basic communication model that the message as sent by a source, and the message as received by the destination were often not the same. At the same time the concept of *noise*, as they explained it, offered an explanation as to why the two often did not coincide. The notion of a *correction channel* or *feedback*, suggested by Shannon and Weaver and elaborated upon by Schramm and others, went one step beyond acknowledging that data sent and information received often didn't match, by providing a mechanism for remedying the "problem."

The work of Westley and MacLean dealt head on with the *MS ≠ MR* anomaly by creating a model that did not begin with the purposeful sending of messages, but rather with an individual surrounded by "*X*'s—data—some of which were intentionally provided by others and some not. This way of thinking provided a logical and broadened explanation as to why the message as interpreted by a receiver often had little in common with the message as intended by the source.

The *field of experience* concept, introduced by Schramm, represented yet another means of explaining why the "picture in the head" of the source was not duplicated in the head of the receiver, following the transmission of a message. Similarly, the idea of *opinion leaders*, first suggested in the work of Katz and Lazarsfeld, again reflected an awareness of the fundamental anomaly. Like *feedback*, it also provided a means for explaining the lack of predictive value of the classical paradigm.

Other changes in the ways scholars described the communication process occurred as a consequence of the recognition that the message as received often did not correspond well to the message that was sent. The Katz and Larzarfeld model, for instance, presented the view that sender-to-receiver effects are more often *mediated* than *direct*. Schramm's perspective indicated that communication was *circular* rather than *unidirectional*. The Newcomb view placed great emphasis on message reception and message interpretation, and Berlo's writings stressed the role of *meaning* rather than *messages*. Berlo also characterized communication as *a process*, not *a single event*, a point-of-view that was carried forward by Dance, and more recently by Rogers and Kincaid.

Communication Theory Today This review of communication models suggests that whereas the S→M→R predominated during much of the history of the field, the past quarter-century has brought the beginnings of some fundamental change to this perspective. The evolution has been from a sender and message-centered concept to a receiver and meaning-centered view, from a one-way perspective to a circular or spiraling framework, from a static view to a process-oriented way of thinking, from a view centered on public speaking to a perspective that potentially includes all behavior.

Taken collectively, the theories and models advanced in the past twenty-five years have substantially broadened our understanding of the nature of communication and have pointed out some of the shortcomings of earlier approaches. They have provided the foundation for the development of a more comprehensive explanation of the role of communication in human affairs of the sort outlined in Chapter 2.

As we leave the S→M→R paradigm behind, we leave with it the view of communication as the intact transmission of messages or information from a source to a receiver. In its place is a view of communication as the process

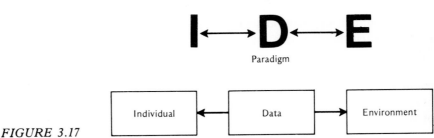

I ←→ D ←→ E

Paradigm

| Individual | ← | Data | → | Environment |

FIGURE 3.17

TABLE 3.1

Model	How Communication Works	Major Factors Stressed in Explaining Communication Outcomes	Directional Flow
Aristotle	Speaker constructs messages that brings about persuasive effects among listeners	source and message	one-way
Lasswell	Speaker constructs messages, selects a channel, and thereby brings about a range of effects among listeners	source, message and channel	one-way
Shannon-Weaver	Source encodes message and transmits through channel to receiver	source, message, noise	one-way with feedback
Schramm[1]	Source encodes message and transmits through channel to receiver	source and message	one-way
Schramm[2]	Source encodes message and transmits information through channel to receiver if they have shared field of experience	source, message, receiver	one-way
Schramm[3]	An individual encodes message and transmit information through channel to another person who in turn transmits message to source, etc., providing feedback to enable both persons to improve communication fidelity	source, message, receiver, feedback	circular (through feedback)
Katz-Lazarsfeld	Source encodes messages and transmits information through mass media to opinion leaders who relay it to public	channel, message, receiver, opinion leader	one-way (mediated)
Westley-MacLean	Source selectively encodes messages and transmits information in modified form to receiver who decodes, encodes, and transmits information in modified form to other individual(s) with feedback at every step	receiver, meaning, feedback	circular (through feedback)

Model	How Communication Works	Major Factors Stressed in Explaining Communi-cation Outcomes	Directional Flow
Berlo	Source encodes messages based on his/her skills and experience and transmits through one of the five senses to receiver whose interpretation of the message depends on his/her meanings for the words which compose the message	source, receiver meaning, process	one-way
Newcomb	Individuals react to one another's messages based on their attitudes toward the topic and one another, with a goal of maintaining consistency and harmony	meaning, receiver	triangular
Dance	Individuals encode and de-code messages based on previous communication experiences	process, time	helical-spiral
Watlawick-Beavin-Jackson	Individuals exchange mes-sages through behavior, the meaning of which varies with each person depending largely upon the communicative rela-tionship between them	receiver, meaning, process, metacommunication	two-way
Rogers-Kincaid	Individuals linked to one another through networks create and share information in order to reach mutual understanding	social networks, information, time	spiral

through which individuals (I)—all animal and human systems—create and use data(D) to establish what the Latins termed *communis*—commoness—with the environment and its inhabitants (E)—what could be termed an $I \leftarrow D \rightarrow E$ paradigm. (See Figure 3.17.)

The Development of the Field of Communication

In addition to looking at the evolution of communication theory, this chapter also traced the development of the discipline from its early beginnings, through periods marked by interdisciplinary development, to its emergence and growth as a discipline in its own right. From this overview, one can draw a number of conclusions that are helpful in understanding communication study today.

Ancient and Newly Emergent The core of modern communication study has its origins in the work of the early Greek philosophers. The 1900s, however, brought a number of changes to the discipline, including a new name. Within the last twenty-five years, the scope of the field has broadened, its structure has changed, and every facet of it has grown substantially. In this respect, communication can be viewed as a newly emergent field, the newest of the disciplines concerned with the study of human behavior.

Interdisciplinary Heritage Throughout its history, communication has been greatly influenced by a wide range of diverse intellectual disciplines and points of view. Although communication is a distinctive field in its own right, the communication process continues to be of interest to scholars in a number of other fields. This is not unique to communication but is characteristic of nearly all disciplines concerned with the study of human behavior. Social processes are of interest in psychology, political science, and anthropology, as well as in sociology. The individual is a topic of concern in sociology, history, and literature, as well as in psychology. Similarly, information processes play a significant role in psychology, sociology, and political science, as well as in the field of communication.

Field of Study, Profession, and Activity From its early beginnings, communication has been the subject of scholarly thought, as well as the label for a range of activities such as speaking and writing. This duality has led to a good deal of confusion about both the term and the discipline; yet the dual meaning has not been without benefit. Perhaps in part because of a broad range of meanings of the term, theorists, researchers, and professionals have been drawn to this single field of study. The consequences has been a generally productive stress among those with different orientations and the formulation of more comprehensive ways of thinking than would be likely to be formulated by any group in isolation.

This duality has had yet another consequence. Because the word *communication* has throughout its history been used to refer to activities such as speaking and listening, as well as to a scholarly field, the word has popular, as well as academic and technical, meanings. This has further contributed to both the richness and relevance of the field on the one hand, and the diversity of meaning associated with the term *communication* on the other.

Traditions of Science, Arts, and Humanities Communication has been approached in a variety of ways over the years. Early on, the field developed primarily in the tradition of the humanities. The influence of the scientific tradition was great, however, and in the past twenty-five years, there has been increased commitment to more systematic observation, quantitative measurement, and ultimately to the development of more valid and reliable generalizations about the role of communication in human affairs.

During these same years, many scholars have continued to study and write about communication from the humanistic and artistic perspective. Such scholars regard the methods of the humanities and arts as most appropriate for determining the relevance of communication to human life. It seems likely, given the subject matter of the field, that the perspective of the sciences and that of the arts and humanities will continue to coexist in the future as they have in the past.

Technology Owing primarily to its journalistic heritage, a concern for media and technology has long been a part of the traditions of communication study. Initially, interest was focused on specific forms, such as newspapers, radio, or television. More recently the perspective has broadened to include the nature and function of communication technology in general along with particular media.

Summary

Communication has a rich and lengthy history, which can be traced back to Babylonian and Egyptian writings prior to the fifth century B.C. The initial contributions to communication study came from scholars in what was termed *rhetoric*. They viewed communication as the practical art of persuasion. Aristotle and Plato, who were particularly significant to early communication study, saw rhetoric and the practice of public speaking not only as an art but also as a legitimate area of study. From its early beginnings, communication was seen as a process in which a speaker constructed messages to bring about desired responses in his or her receiver—the classical S→M→R perspective.

Along with rhetoric and speech, journalism also contributed to the heritage of communication study. As with rhetoric, initially, journalism was concerned primarily with practical rather than theoretical matters. By the beginning of the twentieth century, rhetoric and speech were clearly established as disciplines in their own right, and journalism began to take shape as a field, as well.

During the early twentieth century, interest in communication continued in rhetoric and speech, and in journalism the advent of radio and later television led to the wider application of journalistic concepts and the development of more theories of the overall process. The late 1940s and 1950s were years of interdisciplinary growth, as scholars from various disciplines advanced theories of communication that extended beyond the boundaries of their own fields. Among those to provide such descriptions of communication were Lasswell, Shannon and Weaver, Schramm, Katz and Lazarsfeld, and Westley and MacLean.

The 1960s was a period of integration. A good deal was done to synthesize the writings of rhetoric and speech, journalism and mass media, as well as other disciplines. A number of landmark books appeared in this period within the field. The decade of the 1970s was a time of unprecedented growth within the field. It was also a period in which much specialization occurred, giving rise to research and writing in interpersonal, group, organizational, political, international, and intercultural communication. The late 1970s and early 1980s were also characterized by a renewed concern for communication technology and the development of policy relative to its use.

During this most recent period of history, a number of additional models of the communication process were advanced, extending the work of earlier scholars. Among these were the writings of Berlo; Newcomb; Dance; Watzlawick, Beavin, and Jackson; and Rogers and Kincaid.

The overview of the history of communication reveals a number of changes during the nearly 2,500-year heritage of the field—changes both in the theory of the communication process and in the discipline in which it is studied. The earliest perspectives on communication were concerned with public speaking to a listener with persuasion as the goal. With increasing evidence that the message as sent and that received seldom equalled one another, movement away from the S→M→R paradigm has taken place, providing impetus for a broadened view such as that presented in Chapter 2.

Communication is both ancient and newly emergent, interdisciplinary in heritage, the home of scholars and proessionals, a science and an art, or humanity, and is also concerned with technology.

Notes

1. For a detailed summary of the early history of speech and rhetorical communication study overviewed here, see *Human Communication Theory: History of a Paradigm* by Nancy L. Harper (Rochelle Park, NJ: Hayden, 1979), pp. 16–68.
2. Aristotle, *Rhetoric and Poetics*, translated by W. Rhys Roberts (New York: Random House, Modern Library, 1954) in Harper, op. cit., p. 20.
3. W. Rhys Roberts, *Works of Artistotle.* (Oxford: Clarendon Press, 1924), p. 1377b.
4. Nancy L. Harper, op. cit., p. 22.
5. Nancy L. Harper, op. cit. pp. 27–30.
6. E.G. Bormann, *Theory and Research in the Communicative Arts* (New York: Holt, 1965), pp. 16–17.
7. J.F. Frank, *The Beginnings of the English Newspaper 1620–1660* (Cambridge, MA: Harvard University Press, 1961), p. 2.
8. Grant M. Hyde, "Forward," in *Survey of Journalism,* ed. by G.F. Mott (New York: Barnes & Noble, 1937), p. viii.
9. Carl H. Weaver, "A History of the International Communication Association," in *Communication Yearbook 1.* Ed. by Brent D. Ruben (New Brunswick, NJ: Transaction-International Communication Association, 1977), pp. 607–609.
10. Harold D. Lasswell, "The Structure and Function of Communication in Society," in *Mass Communications,* edited by Wilbur Schramm (Urbana, IL: University of Illinois Press, 1960), p. 117.

11. Claude E. Shannon and Warren Weaver, *The Mathematical Theory of Communication* (Urbana, IL: University of Illinois Press, 1949) p. 3.
12. Ibid., p. 7.
13. Ibid., p. 68.
14. Wilbur Schramm, "How Communication Works," in *The Process and Effects of Mass Communication*, ed. by Wilbur Schramm (Urbana, IL: University of Illinois Press, 1954), pp. 3–4.
15. Ibid., p. 4.
16. Ibid., p. 9; Cf., also, Norbert Wiener, *The Human Use of Human Beings: Cybernetics and Society* (New York: Avon Books, 1967), pp. 47, 81, who advanced a similar view of feedback.
17. Elihu Katz and Paul F. Lazarsfeld, *Personal Influence: The Part Played by People in the Flow of Mass Communications* (New York: Free Press, 1956), p. 32.
18. Figures shown are for those books copyrighted during the years indicated and still in print as of 1978.
19. David K. Berlo, *The Process of Communication* (New York: Holt, 1960) pp. 23–28.
20. Ibid., p. 175.
21. Theodore M. Newcomb, *The Acquaintance Process* (New York: Holt, 1961) p. 17.
22. Frank E.X. Dance, "Toward a Theory of Human Communication," in *Human Communication Theory: Original Essays*, ed. by Frank E.X. Dance (New York: Holt, 1967), pp. 293–294.
23. Ibid., pp. 294–295.
24. Paul Watzlawick, Janet H. Beavin, and Don D. Jackson, *Pragmatics of Human Communication: A Study of Interactional Patterns, Pathologies, and Paradoxes* (New York: Norton, 1967), pp. 48–51.
25. Ibid., pp. 51–54.
26. Everett M. Rogers and D. Lawrence Kincaid, *Communication Networks* (New York: Free Press, 1981), p. 65.
27. Ibid.
28. Cf. Thomas S. Kuhn, *The Structure of Scientific Revolutions*, 2nd ed. (Chicago: University of Chicago Press, 1970), pp. 1–42.
29. Ibid., pp. 52–65.

References and Suggested Reading

Aristotle. *Rhetoric*. Translated by W.R. Roberts. New York: Modern Library, 1954.

Barnlund, Dean. *Interpersonal Communication*. Boston: Houghton Mifflin, 1968.

Berlo, David K. *The Process of Communication*. New York: Holt, 1960.

Bettinghaus, Erwin P. *Persuasive Communication*. New York: Holt, 1968.

Bormann, E.G. *Theory and Research in the Communicative Arts*. New York: Holt, 1965.

Bochner, Arthur P., and Dorothy Lenk Krueger, "Interpersonal Communication Theory and Research: An Overview," in *Communication Yearbook III*. Ed. by Dan Nimmo, (New Brunswick, NJ: Transaction-International Communication Association, 1979), 197–212.

Brown, W.R., and M.J. Schaefermeyer, "Progress in Communication as a Social Science," in *Communication Yearbook IV*. Ed. by Dan Nimmo. New Brunswick, NJ: Transaction-International Communication Association, 1980, 37–48.

Budd, Richard W. "Perspectives on a Discipline: Review and Commentary." In *Communication Yearbook 1*. Ed. by Brent D. Ruben. New Brunswick, NJ: Transaction-International Communication Association, 1977, 29–36.

———— and Brent D. Ruben, Eds. *Approaches to Human Communication*. Rochelle Park, NJ: Spartan-Hayden, 1972.

Burke, Kenneth. *Language as Symbolic Action*. Berkeley, CA: University of California Press, 1968.

Campbell, James H., and Hal W. Hepler. *Dimensions in Communication*. Belmont, CA: Wadsworth, 1965.

Carroll, John B. *The Study of Language*. Cambridge, England: Cambridge University Press, 1953.

Cherry, Colin. *On Human Communication*. New York: Science Editions, 1961.

Chomsky, Noam. *Aspects of the Theory of Syntax*. Cambridge, MA: M.I.T. Press, 1965.

————. *Syntactic Structures*. The Hague, Netherlands: Mouton, 1957.

Cochran, Barbara D. "The Evolution of Journalism." In *Survey of Journalism*. Ed. by G.F. Mott. New York: Barnes & Noble, 1937, 16–31.

Dance, Frank E.X., Ed. *Human Communication Theory: Original Essays*. New York: Holt, 1967.

————. "Toward a Theory of Human Communication." In *Human Communication Theory: Original Essays*. Ed. by Frank E.X. Dance. New York: Holt, 1967, 228–309.

DeFleur, Melvin. *Theories of Mass Communication*. New York: McKay, 1966.

Dixon, P.D. *Rhetoric*. London: Methuen, 1971.

Erikson, K.V., Ed. *Aristotle: The Classical Heritage of Rhetoric*. Metuchen, NJ: Scarecrow, 1974.

Fabbro, Janet. "A History of the Idea of Communication." Unpublished paper. New Brunswick, NJ: Rutgers University, Department of Human Communication, 1979.

Foley, Joseph M. "Mass Communication Theory and Research." In *Communication Yearbook III*. Ed. by Dan Nimmo, New Brunswick, NJ: Transaction-International Communication Association, 1979, 263–270.

Frank, J.F. *The Beginnings of the English Newspaper 1620–1660*. Cambridge, MA: Harvard University Press, 1961.

Frings, Hubert, and Mable Frings. *Animal Communication*. New York: Wiley, 1964.

Gavin, Joan. "A History and Analysis of the Field of Communication." Unpublished paper. New Brunswick, NJ: Rutgers University, Department of Human Communication, 1979.

Hall, R.N., Ed. *Direction of Graduate Programs in the Speech Communication Arts and Sciences*. Ephrata, PA: Speech Communication Association.

Hardt, Hanno. "Philosophy: An Approach to Human Communication." In *Approaches to Human Communication*. Ed. by Richard W. Budd and Brent D. Ruben. New York: Spartan-Hayden, 1972, 290–312.

Harper, Nancy L. *Human Communication Theory: History of a Paradigm*. Rochelle Park, NJ: Hayden, 1979.

Hovland, Carl I., Irving, Janis, and Harold Kelly. *Communication and Persuasion*. New Haven: Yale University Press, 1953.

Hyde, Grant M. "Foreward." In *Survey of Journalism*. Ed. by G.F. Mott. New York: Barnes and Noble, 1937, vii–viii.

Katz, Elihu. "The Two-Step Flow of Communication." In *Mass Communications*. Ed. by Wilbur Schramm. Urbana, IL: University of Illinois Press, 1960, 346–365.

———, and Paul F. Lazarsfeld. *Personal Influence*. New York: Free Press, 1955.

———. *Personal Influence: The Part Played by People in the Flow of Mass Communications*. New York: Free Press, 1955.

Kim, John Y. "Feedback and Human Communication: Toward a Reconceptualization." Unpublished Doctoral dissertation. University of Iowa, 1971.

Klapper, Joseph. *The Effects of Mass Communication*. New York: Free Press, 1960.

Kuhn, Thomas S. *The Structure of Scientific Revolutions*. Chicago: University of Chicago Press, 1970.

Lasswell, Harold D. "The Structure and Function of Communication in Society." In *The Communication of Ideas*. Ed. by Bryson Lyman. Institute for Religion and Social Studies, 1948. Reprinted in *Mass Communications*. Ed. by Wilbur Schramm. Urbana IL: University of Illinois Press, 1960, 117–130.

Larson, Charles U., and Thomas C. Wiegele. "Political Communication Theory and Research: An Overview." In *Communication Yearbook III*. Ed. by Dan Nimmo, New Brunswick, NJ: Transaction-International Communication Association, 1979, 457–474.

Lazarsfeld, Paul F., Bernard Berelson, and Hazel Gaudet. *The People's Choice*. New York: Columbia University Press, 1944.

Lippman, Walter. *Public Opinion*. New York: Free Press, 1922.

Littlejohn, Stephen W. *Theories of Human Communication*. Columbus, OH: Merrill, 1978.

Manca, Luigi D. "Seven Notes on MacLean." *The Journal of Communication Inquiry*. (Spring 1976), 36–60.

McCroskey, James. *An Introduction to Rhetorical Communication*. Englewood Cliffs, NJ: Prentice-Hall, 1968.

McLuhan, Marshall. *The Mechanical Bride*. New York: Vanguard, 1951.

———. *Understanding Media*. New York: McGraw-Hill, 1964.

Miller, Gerald R. *Speech-Communication: A Behavioral Approach.* New York: Bobbs-Merrill, 1966.

———— and Michael Burgoon. "Persuasion Research: Review and Commentary." In *Communication Yearbook 2.* Ed. by Brent D. Ruben. New Brunswick, NJ: Transaction-International Communication Association, 1978, 29-47.

Morris, W., and M. Morris. *Dictionary of Contemporary Usage.* New York: Harper, 1975.

Mott, Frank Luther. *American Journalism—A History 1690–1960.* New York: Macmillan, 1962.

Muskat, Lori. "Communication: Attempt Toward a History." Unpublished paper. New Brunswick, NJ: Rutgers University, Department of Human Communication, 1979.

Newcomb, Theodore M. *The Acquaintance Process.* New York: Holt, 1961.

Nimmo, Dan. "Political Communication Theory and Research: An Overview." In *Communication Yearbook 1.* Ed. by Brent D. Ruben. New Brunswick, NJ: Transaction-International Communication Association, 1977, 441–452.

Nordenstreng, Kaarle. "European Communication Theory: Review and Commentary." In *Communication Yearbook 1.* Ed. by Brent D. Ruben. New Brunswick, NJ: Transaction-International Communication Association, 1977, 73–78.

Ogden, C.K., and I.A. Richards. *The Meaning of Meaning.* London: Kegan Paul, 1923.

Redding, W. Charles. "Organization Communication Theory and Ideology: An Overview." In *Communication Yearbook III.* Ed. by Dan Nimmo. New Brunswick, NJ: Transaction-International Communication Association, 1979, 309–342.

Richetto, Gary M. "Organizational Communication Theory and Research: An Overview." In *Communication Yearbook 1.* Ed. by Brent D. Ruben. New Brunswick, NJ: Transaction-International Communication Association, 1977, 331–346.

Rogers, Everett M., and D. Lawrence Kincaid. *Communication Networks.* New York: Free Press, 1981.

Ruben, Brent D. "Intrapersonal, Interpersonal, and Mass Communication Processes in Individual and Multi-Person Systems." In *General System Theory and Human Communication.* Ed. by Brent D. Ruben and John Y. Kim. Rochelle Park, NJ: Hayden, 1975, 164–190.

Ruesch, Jurgen, and Gregory Bateson. *Communication—The Social Matrix of Psychiatry.* New York: Norton, 1951.

Saral, Tulsi B. "Intercultural Communication Theory and Research: An Overview of Challenges and Opportunities." In *Communication Yearbook III.* Ed. by Dan Nimmo. New Brunswick, NJ: Transaction-International Communication Association, 1979, 395–406.

Schramm, Wilbur. "The Beginnings of Communication Study in the United States." In *Communication Yearbook IV.* Ed. by Dan Nimmo. New Brunswick, NJ: Transaction-International Communication Association, 1980, 73–82.

———. "How Communication Works." In *The Process and Effects of Mass Communication.* Ed. by Wilbur Schramm. Urbana IL: University of Illinois Press, 1954, 3–26.

———. *The Science of Human Communication.* New York: Basic, 1963.

———. Ed. *The Process and Effects of Mass Communication.* Urbana, IL: University of Illinois Press, 1954.

Shannon, Claude E., and Warren Weaver. *The Mathematical Theory of Communication.* Urbana, IL: University of Illinois Press, 1949.

Skinner, B.F. *Verbal Behavior.* New York: Appleton-Century-Crofts, 1957.

Smith, Alfred G. "Taxonomy of Communication: Review and Commentary." In *Communication Yearbook 1.* Ed. by Brent D. Ruben. New Brunswick, NJ: Transaction-International Communication Association, 1977, 79–88.

———. "The Discipline of Communication: 1966–1978–1990." Unpublished paper presented at the National Seminar, Universidad Iberoamericana, Mexico, 1978.

———, Ed. *Communication and Culture.* New York: Holt, 1966.

Smith, David H. "Communication Research and the Idea of Process." *Speech Monographs,* **39** (1972), 175–182.

Smith, Ronald L. "General Models of Communication." Paper presented at the Summer Conference of the National Society for the Study of Communication, 1962.

Stewart, Charles J. "Historical Survey: Rhetorical Criticism in Twentieth Century America." In *Explorations in Rhetorical Criticism.* Ed. by Charles J. Stewart, Donovan J. Oches and Gerald P. Mohrmann. University Park, PA: Pennsylvania State University Press, 1973, 1–31.

———, Donovan J. Ochs, and Gerald P. Mohrmann, Eds. *Explorations in Rhetorical Criticism.* University Park, PA: Pennsylvania State University Press, 1973.

Subject Guide to Books in Print, 1978–1979. New York: Bowker, 1978.

Thayer, Lee. "Communication—*Sine Qua Non* of the Behavioral Sciences." In *Vistas in Science.* Ed. by D.L. Arm. Albuquerque, NM: University of New Mexico Press, 1968. Reprinted in *Interdisciplinary Approaches to Human Communication.* Ed. by Richard W. Budd and Brent D. Ruben. Rochelle Park, NJ: Hayden, 1979, 7–32.

Thayer, Lee. *Communication: Theory and Research.* Springfield, IL: Thomas, 1967.

——— Ed. *Communication: Concepts and Perspectives.* New York: Spartan, 1967.

——— Ed. *Communication: Ethical and Moral Issues.* New York: Gordon and Breach, 1973.

———. *Communication and Communication Systems.* Homewood, IL: Irwin, 1968.

———. "On Theory-Building in Communication: Some Conceptual Problems." *Journal of Communication,* **13** (1963) 217–235.

Watzlawick, Paul, Janet H. Beavin and Don D. Jackson. *Pragmatics of Human Communication: A Study of Interactional Patterns, Pathologies, and Paradoxes.* New York: Norton, 1967.

Weaver, Carl H. "A History of the International Communication Association." In *Communication Yearbook I*. Ed. by Brent D. Ruben. New Brunswick, NJ: Transaction-International Communication Association, 1977, 607–609.

Westley, Bruce H., and Malcolm S. MacLean, Jr. "A Conceptual Model for Communication Research." *Audio-Visual Communication*, **3** (Winter, 1955), 4. Reprinted in *Journalism Quarterly*, **34** (1957), 31–38.

Wheeless, Lawrence R., and H. Thomas Hurt. "Instructional Communication Theory and Research: An Overview of Instructional Strategies and Instructional Communication Systems." In *Communication Yearbook III*. Dan Nimmo, Ed. New Brunswick, NJ: Transaction-International Communication Association, 1979, pp 525–542.

Wiener, Norbert. *The Human Use of Human Beings: Cybernetics and Society*. Boston: Houghton Mifflin, 1950. Reprinted in 1967 by Avon Books, New York.

———. *Cybernetics or Control and Communication in the Animal and the Machine*. Cambridge, MA: M.I.T. Press, 1948.

Wright, Charles R. *Mass Communication*. New York: Random House, 1959.

The Process of Human Communication

Human Communication

The Symbol-Using Animal

We have seen that for human and animal systems, alike, communication involves the creation, reception, and processing of data in order to adapt to the environment. Yet for all that humans have in common with other living systems in these respects, it is important that we not overlook the sense in which humans are very special kinds of animals.

There have been many attempts to identify, precisely, what it is that makes us unique among animals.[1] A number of writers have pointed to our social nature and its pervasive role in human life. However, many animals depend for their survival on other members of their species. Still other scholars have suggested that our capacity for communication might be the distinguishing characteristic. As we know, however, the production, trans-

Letter	Morse Code	Manual (Deaf)	Braille	ASCII	Letter	Morse Code	Manual (Deaf)	Braille	ASCII
A	·—			01000001	L	·—··			01001100
B	—···			01000010	M	——			01001101
C	—·—·			01000011	N	—·			01001110
D	—··			01000100	O	———			01001111
E	·			01000101	P	·——·			01010000
F	··—·			01000110	Q	——·—			01010001
G	——·			01000111	R	·—·			01010010
H	····			01001000	S	···			01010011
I	··			01001001	T	—			01010100
J	·———			01001010	U	··—			01010101
K	—·—			01001011	V	···—			01010110

mission, and reception of data is essential to the social lives of many species, and communication in one form or another is necessary to the adaptation and survival of all animals. With regard to our communication capability, however, as humans we do have a unique capability: We can create and use symbols and symbolic language, and it is this skill and the many consequences of it which perhaps best highlights the special nature of the human animal.

But what exactly, does it mean to say that *humans create and use symbolic language*. A *language*, in the most general sense, is *a set of characters, or elements, and rules for their use in relation to one another*. There are all sorts of languages. Most familiar are spoken and written languages such as English,

	Morse Code	Manual (Deaf)	Braille	ASCII
W	· – –			01010111
X	– · · –			01011000
Y	– · – –			01011001
Z	– – · ·			01010110
1	· – – – –			00110001
2	· · – – –			00110010
3	· · · – –			00110011
4	· · · · –			00110100
5	· · · · ·			00110101
6	– · · · ·			00110110
7	– – · · ·			00110111

	Morse Code	Manual (Deaf)	Braille	ASCII
8	– – – · ·			00111000
9	– – – – ·			00111001
0	– – – – –			00110000

FIGURE 4.1 The English alphabet, Morse Code, sign language, braille, and the ASCII (American Standard Code for Information Interchange) computer code are among our most used languages. Each has evolved to meet a specialized set of human needs. The languages differ from one another in their structure, yet in terms of the more basic functions served, they have much in common. Each is composed of a number of symbols, the meanings of which are arbitrary and a matter of social convention. They are useful for message sending and receiving only when their significance is agreed upon by the persons who wish to use them.

French, Swahili, or German. The Morse code, Braille, genetic code, BASIC, COBOL, and computer machine-language, are other less obvious types of languages.

Using language, data can be coded and transmitted from one point to another with one or more communication modes. Oral, spoken, and other acoustically-coded languages make use of the auditory mode. Written or light-utilizing languages use the visual channel.

Symbols are data—characters, letters, words, objects or actions—which stand for or represent something besides themselves. As humans, we are able to invent symbols, their meanings, and the responses we make to them. Consider the word *dog* as an example. *Dog* has no inherent, intrinsic meaning or significance. It is simply a particular pattern of auditory vibrations that comes about by the manipulation of the vocal cords, lips, tongue, and mouth, or a configuration of ink on paper in the case of written language. The characteristics of the words and sounds of their spoken pronunciation comprise a symbolic code that is useful only to those who have learned to decipher it. The word is arbitrary in the sense that it has no relation to the animal to which it refers other than that which we have invented, agreed upon, learned, and accepted through use. Any word could have been chosen in its place.

While letters and words are the most obvious elements in our symbolic language, there are many others which are important to human life. For example, an illuminated red light located on a sign near the corner of an intersection is a symbol. It "means" stop. Actually, of course, the light means nothing itself. It is rather that through custom and habitual use—and, in this case, legislation—people have come to interpret the symbol as an indication to stop.

A rectangular piece of cloth with thirteen red and white stripes and fifty white stars on a blue field in the upper corner is another kind of symbol. In some circumstances, the presence of the symbol will lead people to stand, salute, or place their right hand over their hearts. In other situations, people may drive or walk past the symbol without even taking notice of it. In each case, it is the significance people have learned to attach to the symbol and the situation in which they encounter it which determines how they will react.

Another classic, yet subtle, example of symbolic language is our monetary system. We think little about the communication process which occurs when we go into a store, pick out an item priced at $15, go to the cashier, hand over a ten and a five dollar bill, and leave the store with a "thank you" and the item in a bag. This exchange is very much a communication event, one in which symbolic language plays a crucial role. When we give the clerk a ten and a five dollar bill, in effect, we are only handing over two pieces of paper. They have no inherent value, other than the cost of the paper and ink. They are symbols. They "work" because we believe in them, because the data has a shared informational value. The store owner who trades pieces of paper for goods or services does so because he or she believes other customers will also accept them in change. He or she also assumes that whatever is left at the end of the business day can be deposited

GOOD LUCK SYMBOLS

Symbol	Name	Meaning
	Thunderbird	*Bearer of Happiness*
	Sun Symbols	*Happiness*
	Crossed Arrows	*Friendship*
	Arrow	*Protection*
	Arrow	*Warding off Evil*
	Broken Arrow	*Peace*
	Thunderbird Track	*Bright Prospects*
	Bear Track	*Good Omen*
	Deer Track	*Plenty Game*
	Fence	*Guarding Good Luck*
	Rain Cloud	*Good Prospects*
	Rain Drop	*Good Luck*
	Rain	*Good Crops*
	Leaf	*Wealth*
	Mountain	*Abundance, Plenty*
	Mountain Range	*Abundance*

DESCRIPTIVE SYMBOLS

Symbol	Name	Meaning
	Teepee	*Temporary Home*
	Hogan	*Permanent Home*
	Lasso	*Captivity*
	Eagle Feathers	*Chief*
	Hopi Horse	*Journey*
	Saddle Bags	*Journey*
	Path Crossing	
	Headdress	*Ceremonial Dance*
	Enclosure	*Ceremonial Dance*
	Days and Nights	*Time*
	Cactus	*Sign of the Desert*
	Gila Monster	*Sign of the Desert*
	Butterfly	*Everlasting Life*
	Running Water	*Constant Life*
	Morning Stars	*Guidance*
	House of Water	*Cave Spring*

CHARACTERISTICS

Symbol	Name	Meaning
	Arrowhead	*Alertness*
	Buffalo Eye	*Alertness*
	Medicine Man's Eye	*Wisdom*
	Snake	*Wisdom*
	Sun Rays	*Constancy*
	Rattlesnake's Jaw	*Strength*
	Bird	*Lighthearted*
	Najahe	*Beauty, Love*
	Squash Blossom	*Fertility*
	Lightning Arrow	*Swiftness*

FIGURE 4.2 These symbols presumably have their origin in the picture writing of primitive Indians. Some are still used in their ceremonials; others are used mainly for their decorative value.

FIGURE 4.3 As humans we are literally enveloped in a sea of symbols, an understanding of which are essential to even simple activities like traveling from one place to another, shopping for consumer goods, or enjoying a favorite hobby.

in the bank, and that those symbols will retain their value so that they can be used later in the week, month, or year. The system works because people believe the monetary symbols have value, generally agree on the symbolic meaning of coins and currency, and have sufficient confidence in the stability of the government which "stands behind" the value of the symbol.

Animal and Human Communication

The origins and functioning of languages used by most other animals contrasts quite dramatically with human symbolic language. Birds are born knowing how to build the nest necessary for mating and survival; the instructions are inscribed on the chromosomes of the fertilized egg cell from which it developed.[2] Lightning bugs inherit the knowledge needed to emit and respond to luminescent messages of a potential mate, and bees are apparently born programmed with the information needed to create and interpret the waggle dance. As Rapoport suggests:

> Every species is adapted to a particular way of life in a more or less circumscribed environment. In non-humans, adaptation is almost entirely a matter of their own anatomy and physiology being shaped in the long process of evolution and natural selection. A beast of prey has teeth and

claws appropriate to its predatory life; the grass eaters can live on grass because they can digest cellulose, which does not yield to the digestive processes of the meat eaters. Fish are streamlined; birds have very light bones and very strong forelimb muscles, and so can fly.[3]

Humans are born less well equipped, lacking many of the faculties necessary to the survival of less complex animals.

Man can do a little of what most animals do, but nothing of it very well. He can run, but not as fast as a deer or a cheetah; he can climb, but not as well as a monkey or a squirrel; he can swim, but not as well as a seal. He eats meat, but his teeth are not as well adapted to meat-eating as a tiger's. His claws are practically worthless for the purposes for which most claws are used. His skin is almost bare; naked, he could survive only in the tropics.[4]

In purely biological terms, the human animal could certainly appear to be one of the least capable of creatures. Not only do we lack the outstanding physical capabilities of other animals, but we are less efficient communicationally, as well. Human communication, after all, involves symbol language. As such, symbols and their meanings have to be created and agreed upon by others if they are to be useful for the sending and receiving of coded data. To be agreed upon they have to be taught and learned. To achieve this end, considerable resources must be expended on socialization and education, and even then we seem to be only moderately successful at teaching each other even basic symbol systems like math and language.

Characteristics of Human Communication

For all our own inadequacies, our species has survived on the planet a remarkably long time compared with most other animals. In the case of birds, for example, the average length of time between the appearance of a species and its extinction is estimated at about 40,000 years, and the average for mammals is about 20,000 years. Humans, by way of comparison, have lived at least 500,000 years and perhaps as long as one million years.[5] In spite of our inadequacies, our human symbol-using capacity has given our species some very special advantages which help to explain our survival.

Permanence and Portability

Perhaps the most significant of these advantages is the potential for permanence of human symbolic language. For most animals, visual, tactile, olfactory, gustatory, and auditory signals are transitory in nature. A sound, a gesture, a touch, a sensation, or an odor may effectively link animals to one another and their environment, but each is short-lived, and once the data has served its original informational function, no traces of it remain. In most cases, such animals must be within sight or hearing range in order to respond to messages from another individual, and even olfactory cues used to make a territory or provide a trail are generally short-lived.

In this regard, humans have greater capability than other animals. Because human communication involves symbols, and symbols represent something besides themselves, they can have permanence and significance apart from the situation in which they were originally used. Data provided in a letter sent to a friend, a book, a poem, a scientific formula, the blueprint for a building, signs along a highway, or a recipe are not transitory in nature. They may have a virtually unending existence and use. In fact, their life is limited only by our human capacity for preserving the physical materials on which they were initially recorded. Through photocopying, computer storage, video and audio recordings, microfilm and microfiche, and video disc, the life of the symbols may be extended by transferring the coded data to more permanent materials, making their life virtually limitless. The contrast between the instantaneous flash of the firefly to a potential mate and the survival of human knowledge across many generations is almost overwhelming.

The permanent nature of symbols makes it possible for us to accumulate experience and transmit large quantities of data from one generation to the next. This enables humans to "bind" time—to draw upon learnings of the past as well as the present, and to create messages today which will be a part of the environment of future generations of humans.

Humans also have a well-developed capacity to "bind" space. The objects or persons to which particular symbols refer need not be present in order for that symbol to be useful as information. Using any one of a number of communication technologies, data coded and packaged at one geographic location can be transmitted to persons thousands of miles away. Thus, a

FIGURE 4.4

BUDDHISM	ISLAM	CHRISTIANITY	JUDAISM
Buddha	Star and Crescent	Latin Cross	Star of David
CONFUCIANISM	UNITARIANISM	HINDUISM	TAOISM
Conjugal Bliss	Chalice	Shiva	Yin-Yang

FIGURE 4.5 Among the symbols that have transcended many generations are those associated with religion.

phone call to a friend, a popular song recorded by British artists, a magazine article, or a network television program may have significance to their viewers, though the place where they were produced and the ultimate destination may be thousands of miles apart.

The Physical and Symbolic Environment

A second characteristic which distinguishes human communication from the communication of other animals is the relative complexity of our human surroundings. Like other animals, our survival depends upon our ability to successfully adapt to our environment. We share, in common with other animals, a world composed of physical entities and dynamics—land masses, trees, oceans, thunderstorms, living organisms, earthquakes, and so on. To a far greater extent than other living things, as humans we must also adapt to a *symbolic* environment. Because of the permanent and portable nature of symbols, the environment is literally filled with coded data to which we must adapt in order to function effectively in our lifetimes. This makes for a very special kind of existence, with special opportunities and special problems.

There are some one hundred languages in use today, and perhaps another five hundred languages and dialects that are of regional importance. Although most human languages have fewer than one hundred distinct sounds, these can be combined in almost a limitless number of ways which are meaningful to other persons who have learned the meanings of individual words and the grammatical rules for combining them to form sentences.[6] In addition to these languages, there are pictural symbols and numerals—over twenty thousand in all, according to one source.[7] In combination, these symbols can produce virtually an infinite set of coded messages about communication, automobiles, love, human behavior, trust, or whatever.

FIGURE 4.6 We make choices in a symbolic environment.

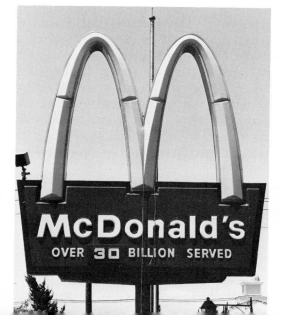

Beyond letters, words, sentences, paragraphs, illustrations, gestures, and numerals, there are myriads of other human creations that can be of symbolic significance for us—the food we eat, the buildings in which we live and work, the places where we play, the clothes we wear, and the cars we drive. Lee Thayer provides an excellent description of this symbolic world, which he refers to as our *communicational environment*.

> What is uniquely characteristic of human communication...is the fact that the (human)...sophistication...has made possible the emergence and evolution of a purely communicational environment or reality—i.e., an environment or reality comprised of anything that can be and is talked about. Whatever can be and is talked about comprises a reality in the sense that it must be adapted to and dealt with in much the same way as that reality which is subject to sensory validation (physical environment). In other words, man's position on the phylogenetic scale has made possible the emergence and evolution of a communicational environment which has as much or more significance for man than does the physical environment for the "lower" animals.[8]

Meaning

A third important characteristic of human communication which distinguishes us from other animals is our relative ability to invent and internalize meanings for the objects, places, and people that surround us in our symbolic environment.

Like other animals, we are born with certain message-responding tendencies, or reflexes, which play an important role in our lives from the time we are infants. The touch of a nipple to the mouth of a newborn infant, for example, is a tactile cue which triggers the sucking response necessary for eating, and, hence, survival. In a similar manner, when we accidentally place a finger on a hot stove, a signal is sent to the brain, and in an instant we pull our hand away in pain. Responses such as these are automatic and do not involve symbols. They are what we might term *first-order communication events*.

As humans, however, these sorts of automatic, nonsymbolic experiences account for only a small percentage of our communication activities. Most of our experiences involve *symbols* and *meaning*. This is often the case in many of the most fundamental data-responding situations. In the case of placing a finger on the stove, for example, as soon as we begin to think about the experience of being burned, try to comprehend the reasons for the pain, consider various medical remedies, relate the pain to other sensations in our previous experience, or talk about the event with other persons, we are involved in a *second-order communication event*. It is a *second*-order event because we are not dealing directly with the physical environment, but rather with our symbolic representations and interpretations of it—our thoughts, feelings, and memories.

We have little way to relate to our physical world apart from the symbols

FIGURE 4.8 Some symbols that we have learned to associate with particularly valued, meaningful, or painful aspects of our lives come to have a special significance for us.

we have learned to associate with our experiences, and as a result, most of human communication events are second-order, in nature. We may respond directly to impulses of various sorts, but as soon as we endeavor to describe those experiences to ourselves or others we have returned to the world of symbols.

Even in the simplest of activities, like a race, this uniqueness and complexity is apparent.[9] When an athlete hears a starting gun, his or her initial response to the auditory cue is identical to the response of a gazelle. The heartbeat speeds up, and at top running speed the heart pumps five times more blood than normally. Most of the blood is needed for the muscles. There is also a need for twenty gallons of air per minute to supply oxygen to the blood. For the runner and gazelle alike, most of the energy needed by the muscles is lost as heat. Since chemical burn-up by the muscles is too fast to be complete, waste products remain in the blood, leading to fatigue that can be eliminated only when fresh oxygen is introduced into the blood supply.

In all of these respects, the behavior of the runner and that of the gazelle are alike. Both creatures function in a way that is normal for an animal in flight. But the key point is that the man or woman in the example is *not* in flight. Where the gazelle's behavior is a first order communication event, directed solely by reflex, the runner's actions are not. The behavior of the gazelle could only occur in response to uncontrolled and uncontrollable fear; the runner's response, on the other hand, is a consequence of the symbolic *meaning* he or she has for the situation itself and the information he or she derives from the data which comprise it. The runner's behavior is self-initiated, deliberate, and directed by desire.

As humans, we are not only capable of creating events, but also the significance and meaning those events will have for us. We can invent and organize contests, plan and train to participate in them, voluntarily direct our actions during the activity, experience pride and satisfaction upon receiving a ribbon or trophy, and later reflect upon ourselves and our experience. We do all this because of our capacity for inventing and bestowing meaning and significance upon the data which surrounds us and upon our own activities.

For humans, unlike other animals, even matters as basic as determining what and how to eat, where to live, and how to mate are not solely matters of biology and genetic programming. While many North Americans, for example, look forward with enthusiasm to a juicy barbecued steak, an individual who is of the Hindu faith might well choose the prospect of death by starvation rather than eating the meat of the sacred cow, the holiest of animals. In a similar sense, decisions as to whether to eat with fingers, fork and knife, or chopsticks, whether to use one's left hand to eat, as would be acceptable in many countries, or only one's right hand, as is necessary in Arab cultures, and whether to regard ants and squid as delicacies or as repugnant, depend upon the symbolic meanings we as humans have developed for the objects, people, and situations around us.

The same contrast between humans and other animals is also evident in the area of mating and courtship. Determinations as to whether individuals who will "mate" will simply move in together or marry in a religious or legal ceremony, whether partners are selected by the individuals themselves or by their parents; as well as whether, where, how, and when mating takes place, all depend upon the meanings particular humans have learned to attach to the circumstances in which they find themselves, rather than upon innate or universal first-order responses.

The words, flags, courtship practices, laws, monetary symbols, eating customs, and the host of other standardized practices that are important in our relationships, groups, organizations, and societies have their origins in individuals creating and responding to data.

Through human communication our symbols and individual meanings for them become shared and standardized—*intersubjectified*. With continued use, our symbols and the meanings we come to attach to them take on an objective quality, and in fact, become a part of the environment to which we

FIGURE 4.9 What to eat, what utensils to use, what order to eat this and that, where to place one's hands when they are not in use, and how to signal one's satisfaction with a meal, exemplify the sorts of concern that distinguish human symbolic communication from that of other animals. Humans go to great lengths to invent and standardize symbolic practices even with regard to basic biological activities such as eating. Being familiar and fluent with these symbolic realities is often crucial to assuring one's acceptance by those who have themselves learned and accepted a particular symbolic pattern. Knowing not to ask for a straw with your drink at a $70-per-dinner restaurant, realizing that it's "improper" to rest one's elbows on the table, using your "salad fork" only for the salad, being able to manage to eat and appear composed with chop sticks when others at he table can, are often the sort of skills that others take as an indication of refinement, proper upbringing, worldliness, and being "cultured."

must adapt. The creation and use of these intersubjectified symbols is no doubt one of the most intriguing aspects of human communication.

Artist, Ben Shahn makes this point very eloquently:

> It is the images we hold in common, the characters of novels and plays, the great buildings, the complex pictorial images and their meanings, and the symbolized concepts, principles, and great ideas of philosophy and religion, that have created the human community. The incidental items of reality remain without value or common recognition until they have been symbolized, recreated, and imbued with value.[10]

Communication technology and the mass communication process play a major role in the symbol creation and intersubjectification process. The content of media programming is created by humans, and these programs are reflective of the symbolic meanings of their creators. Once the programs are created and transmitted, they take on a life of their own—an objective quality. They confront both creator and viewer or reader as something very

FIGURE 4.10 In addition to performing a number of mechanical functions, hands serve important symbolic functions, as well. For example, it is the *right* hand we place over our heart and raise to our head in a salute to the flag. It is also the right hand which makes new acquaintances and greets old ones, concludes contracts, presents religious offerings, transmits spiritual messages in benedictions, takes possession, and lends assistance. If the right hand symbolizes *strength, honor, dignity,* and *cleanliness,* the *left* hand often is symbolic of the opposite qualities. Arabs, for example reserve the right hand for eating, while delegating responsibilities having to do with affairs of the toilet exclusively to the left. And, among certain tribes in lower Niger, women are forbidden from using their left hands in preparing food, presumably because the left hand is an instrument of sorcery and the medium for evil spirits. Similarly, many inhabitants of the Guinea Coast cling to the belief that when having a drink at the

real, rather than simply as extension of the images of their producers. Through the mass media we are presented with images of various life styles, occupations, gender roles, marital standards, eating habits, religious practices, and so on. These images both *reflect reality* as envisioned by its creators and *create a reality* which must be in some way be adapted to by those who come in contact with these data.[11]

News programming, for instance, provides us with a shared agenda of the concerns of the day.[12] In so doing it contributes to the standardization of the symbols in our environment and our meanings *for* those symbols. This function, however, is by no means limited to the mass media. Sports, drama, schools, museums, libraries, films, theater, architecture, and even restaurants also play a vital role in the creation and intersubjectification of our symbols, images, and meanings in that they contribute to the commonness of experiences of the many persons who are exposed to or use them.

Self-Reflexiveness

A final distinguishing characteristic of human communication is self-reflexiveness or self-consciousness. Because of our symbol-using capacity, we are able to reflect upon ourselves and our actions, to set goals and priorities, and to have expectations. This human capacity which allows "man to view himself as a 'self,' as part of and apart from his environment, is the core of the communication process."[13]

It is our capacity for self-reflexiveness that allows us to theorize about ourselves, our encounters, our technologies, and our existence, about communication, and about human behavior. This capability is a mixed blessing. On the one hand it is self-reflexiveness that enables us to set goals and measure our progress toward them, to have expectations of ourselves and recognize when we have met them. On the other hand, it is also through self-reflexiveness that we recognize our own failures, the expectations we do not meet, the qualities we admire but do not possess.

---

dwelling of a local resident, it is necessary to watch their host closely, because even the slightest contact between his or her left hand and the drink to be served might result in poisoning the liquid. Members of many cultures go to great lengths to insure that their young develop a preference for using their right hands rather than their left. In the Netherlands Indies, for example, children have been observed with their left arms completely bound—no doubt a rather effective teaching technique. It is quite likely that the preference for right-handedness over left-handedness apparent in many cultures including our own, is reflective of the often subtle symbolic realities which have come to be associated with each hand over the years.

SOURCE: R. Hertz, "The Hands," in *Rules and Meanings*, Mary Douglas, ed., (New York: Penguin), 1973, pp. 118–124.

FIGURE 4.11 The fable of "The Emperor's New Clothes," provides an excellent, though exaggerated illustration of the manner in which our meanings for symbols, people, and circumstances come to be standardized and evolve through communication.

The Emperors New Clothes

In the great city in which he lived many strangers came every day. One day two rogues came. They said they were weavers, and declared they could weave the finest stuff anyone could imagine. Their colors and patterns were unusually beautiful, they said, and explained that the clothes made of the stuff possessed the wonderful quality that they became invisible to anyone who was unfit for the office he held or was not very bright or perceptive.

"Those would be most unusual clothes!" thought the Emperor. "If I wore those, I should be able to find out what men in my empire are not fit for the places they have; I could tell the clever ones from the idiots." He asked the men to begin weaving immediately.

They put up two looms, and pretended to be working. They at once demanded the finest silk and the costliest gold; this they put into their own pockets, and worked at the empty looms till late into the night.

After a few weeks passed, the Emperor said to himself, "I should like to know how far they have got on with the stuff." But he felt quite uncomfortable when he thought that those who were not fit for their offices could not see it. He believed, of course, that he had nothing to fear for himself, but he preferred first to send someone else to see how matters stood.

"I will send my honest old Minister to the weavers," thought the Emperor. "He can judge best how the stuff looks, for he has sense, and no one understands his office better than he." So the good old Minister went out into the hall where the two rogues sat working at the empty looms.

"Mercy!" thought the old Minister, and he opened his eyes wide. "I cannot see anything at all! Can I indeed be so stupid? Am I not fit for my office? It will never do for me to tell that I could not see the stuff."

"Haven't you anything to say about it?" asked one of the rogues, as he went on weaving. "It is charming—quite enchanting!" answered the old Minister, as he peered through his spectacles. "What a fine pattern, and what colors! Yes, I shall tell the Emperor that I am very much pleased with it."

The Emperor soon sent another honest officer of the court to see how the weaving was going on, and if the stuff would soon be ready. He fared just like the first: he looked and looked. "Isn't that a pretty piece of stuff?" asked the two rogues; and they displayed and explained the handsome pattern which was not there at all.

"I am not stupid!" thought the man. "Yet it must be that I am not fit for my office. If that is the case, I must not let it be noticed." And so he praised the stuff which he did not see, and expressed his pleasure at the beautiful colors and charming pattern. "Yes, it is enchanting," he told the Emperor.

All the people in the town were talking of the gorgeous stuff. The

FIGURE 4.11 (Continued)

Emperor wished to see it himself while it was still upon the loom. With a whole crowd of chosen men, among whom were also the two honest statesmen who had already been there, he went to the two cunning rogues.

"Isn't that splendid?" said the two statesmen, who had already been there once. "Doesn't your Majesty approve of the pattern and the colors?" And they pointed to the loom, assuming that the others could see the stuff.

"What's this?" thought the Emperor. "I can see nothing at all! That is terrible. Am I stupid? Am I not fit to be Emperor?" He said aloud, "oh, it is very beautiful! It is our highest approval." He nodded in a contented way, and gazed at the loom. . . .

Summary

In this chapter we have examined the nature of symbols and symbolic language and the manner in which our symbol-creating capacity distinguishes human communication from the communication processes of other animals. Symbolic language is a means for creating and transmitting coded data which are composed of abstract elements—letters, words, sentences, drawings, emblems, or gestures. The relationship between a symbol and the aspects of the environment to which it refers is arbitrary, learned, and a matter of consensus.

Unlike other animals whose messages are transitory, human symbols have permanence and portability, and with them we can span years and generations. Using these symbols, humans create, and in turn adapt, not only to a *physical* environment like other animals, but also to a *symbolic* environment. Because of our communication abilities we, of necessity, invent, internalize, and intersubjectify the meanings for our symbols. Symbols are the basis for the images we share in common. It is also through human communication that we are able to be conscious of and reflect upon ourselves, our actions, our achievements, our frustrations, as well as our failures.

The characteristics of human communication largely explain how it is that humans have survived on our planet as long as we have. Human communication affords us the opportunity for a unique and, so far as we know, unparalleled existence. Like other animals, we humans have not improved perceptibly in our breathing, our sight, our hearing, nor the circulation of our blood within the past several thousand years. Unlike other animals, however, we have evolved incredibly in our ability to use our faculties in ingenious ways our ancestors of no more than a generation ago could scarcely have imagined. In our biological processes, humans continue, like other animals, to follow biological habit. But in our communication processes, we are limited in our development only by our capacities for the creation and use of symbols.

DANGER

HARD HAT
AREA

Canadian Club

The Best In The House

Welcome
HELP KEEP REHOBOTH BEACH CLEAN

BEACH RULES

BATHERS MUST WEAR TOPS ON
SIDEWALKS AT ALL TIMES

STREET CLOTHES AFTER 7:30 P.M. ON BOARDWALK

NO ALCOHOLIC BEVERAGES ON BOARDWALK, BEACH, OR STREET

NO DOGS ON BEACH OR BOARDWALK AT ANYTIME

NO LITTERING · USE LITTER RECEPTACLES

NO SLEEPING ON BEACH OR BOARDWALK AFTER 7 P.M.

ORDINANCES STRICTLY ENFORCED
POLICE DEPT.

Notes

1. For many of the ideas concerning the unique nature of human symbolic language, and for the title of this chapter, I am indebted to Anatol Rapoport and his work, "Man, The Symbol User," in *Communication: Ethical and Moral Issues*, edited by Lee Thayer (New York: Gordon and Breach, 1973), especially pages 23–30.
2. Ibid., p. 27.
3. Ibid., p. 27.
4. Ibid., p. 27.
5. Ibid., p. 28.
6. Ibid., p. 27.
7. Henry Dreyfuss, *Symbol Sourcebook* (New York: McGraw-Hill, 1972), pp. 16–19.
8. Lee Thayer, "Communication—*Sine Qua Non* of the Behavioral Sciences," in *Interdisciplinary Approaches to Human Communication*, edited by Richard W. Budd and Brent D. Ruben (Rochelle Park, NJ: Hayden, 1979), p. 12.
9. The example and discussion of the runner and gazelle is based upon that provided by Jacob Bronowski, *The Ascent of Man* (Boston: Little, Brown, 1973), pp. 30–36.
10. Ben Shahn, *The Shape of Content* (Cambridge, MA: Harvard University Press, 1967), pp. 130–131.
11. Cf. Peter Berger, The Sacred Canopy (Garden City, N.Y.: Doubleday, 1969), Ch 1.
12. Cf. Maxwell E. McCombs, and Donald L. Shaw. "The Agenda-Setting Function of Mass Media." *Public Opinion Quarterly* (1972) 36: 176–187.
13. Richard W. Budd and Brent D. Ruben, *Beyond Media* (Rochelle Park, NJ: Hayden, 1979) p. 109.

References and Suggested Reading

Baker, Stephen. *Visual Persuasion*. New York: McGraw-Hill, 1961.

Berger, Peter L. and Thomas Luckmann. *The Social Construction of Reality*. Garden City, NY: Anchor, 1966.

Blumer, Herbert. *Symbolic Interactionism*. Englewood Cliffs, NJ: Prentice-Hall, 1969.

Boulding, Kenneth. *The Image*. Ann Arbor, MI: University of Michigan Press, 1950.

Bronowski, Jacob. *The Ascent of Man*. Boston: Little, Brown, 1973.

Budd, Richard W. "General Semantics: An Approach to Human Communication." In *Approaches to Human Communication*, edited by Richard W. Budd and Brent D. Ruben, 97–119. New York: Spartan–Hayden, 1972, and *Interdisciplinary Approaches to Human Communication*, edited by Richard W. Budd and Brent D. Ruben, 71–93. Rochelle Park, NJ: Hayden, 1979.

————and Brent D. Ruben. *Beyond Media: New Approaches to Mass Communication*. Rochelle Park, NJ: Hayden, 1979.

————eds. *Interdisciplinary Approaches to Human Communication*. Rochelle Park, NJ: Hayden, 1979.

Burke, Kenneth. *Language as Symbolic Action*. Berkeley, CA: University of California Press, 1968.

Dewey, John and Arthur F. Bentley. *Knowing and the Known*. Boston: Beacon, 1949.

Douglas, Mary, ed. *Rules and Meanings*. New York: Penguin, 1973.

Dreyfuss, Henry. *Symbol Sourcebook*. New York: McGraw-Hill, 1972.

Duncan, Hugh D. *Symbols and Social Theory*. New York: Oxford University Press, 1969.

————.*Symbols in Society*. New York: Oxford University Press, 1968.

Fabun, Donald. *Communications*. Beverly Hills, CA: Glencoe, 1968.

Goffman, Erving. *Frame Analysis*. Cambridge, MA: Harvard University Press, 1974.

Hertz, R. "The Hands." In *Rules and Meanings*, edited by Mary Douglas. New York: Penguin, 1973.

Holzner, Burkhart. *Reality Construction in Society*. Cambridge, MA: Schenkman, 1968.

Ittelson, William H., ed. *Environment and Cognition*. New York: Seminar, 1973.

Johnson, Wendell. *People in Quandaries*. New York: Harper, 1946.

Jung, Carl G. *Man and His Symbols*. New York: Doubleday, 1964.

Korzybski, Alfred. *Selections from Science and Sanity*. Lakeville, CN: International Non-Aristotelian Library, 1948.

McHugh, Peter. *Defining the Situation*. Indianapolis, IN: Bobbs-Merrill, 1968.

Mead, George H. *Mind, Self and Society*. Chicago: University of Chicago Press, 1934.

Morris, Desmond. *Manwatching*. New York: Abrams, 1977.

Morris, Charles. *Signification and Significance*. Cambridge, MA: MIT Press, 1964.

Pelletier, Kenneth R. *Mind as Healer, Mind as Slayer*. New York: Delacorte, 1977.

Prince, Jack H. *Languages of the Animal World*. Nashville, TN: Nelson, 1975.

Rapoport, Anatol. "Man, The Symbol User." In *Communication: Ethical and Moral Issues*, edited by Lee Thayer. New York: Gordon and Breach, 1973.

Ruben, Brent D. "General Systems Theory: An Approach to Human Communication." In *Approaches to Human Communication*, edited by Richard W. Budd and Brent D. Ruben, pp. 120–144, New York: Spartan–Hayden, 1972, and *Interdisciplinary Approaches to Human Communication*, edited by Richard W. Budd and Brent D. Ruben, pp. 95–118. Rochelle Park, NJ: Hayden, 1979.

————. "Human Communication, Semiotics, and General Systems: Personal and Social Communication." In *Information Utilities*, edited by Pranus Zunde, pp. 169–174. Washington, D.C.: American Society for Information Science, 1974.

————. "Intrapersonal, Interpersonal and Mass Communication Processes in Individual and Multi-Individual Systems." In *Human Communication and General Systems Theory*, edited by Brent D. Ruben and John Y. Kim, pp. 164–190. Rochelle Park, NJ: Hayden, 1975.

Selye, Hans. *The Stress of Life*. rev. ed. New York: McGraw-Hill, 1976.

Shands, Harley C. *Thinking and Psychotherapy*. Cambridge MA: Harvard University Press, 1960.

Shahn, Ben. The *Shape of Content*. Cambridge MA: Harvard University Press, 1967.

Thayer, Lee. *Communication and Communication Systems*. Homewood, IL: Irwin, 1968.

————. "Communication—*Sine Qua Non* of the Behavioral Sciences." In *Interdisciplinary Approaches to Human Communication*, edited by Richard W. Budd and Brent D. Ruben, pp. 7–32. Rochelle Park, NJ: Hayden, 1979.

————ed. *Communication: Concepts and Perspectives*. New York: Spartan–Hayden, 1967.

Watzlawick, Paul. *How Real is Real?* New York: Random House, 1969.

Whorf, Benjamin Lee. *Language, Thought and Reality*. Cambridge, MA: MIT Press, 1956.

Wood, Charles W. *Myth of the Individual*. New York: Day, 1927.

Verbal Codes

Language and Its Use

In order for elections to serve the people as

rolling political policy four conditions must b

ng candidates should offer clear policy alterna

rs; (2) Voters should be knowledgeable on the i

Assuming the issues are clear, the majority pre

be identified; and (4) After the election, the

:e should be bound by his election mandate.

However, in the American political system, th

ot fulfilled and the people do not

y. In actuality, partie

tives simply b

date

Introduction

Producing and responding to symbols are fundamental to our lives as humans. Compared to many other animals, whose means of communication are largely determined through inheritance, the human capacity for inventing and reacting to various kinds of data may be nearly limitless. As we go about the activities that fill our lives, virtually every aspect of our behavior—our words, appearance, or actions—are potential stimuli or *data* that provide the basis for *information* when attended to and interpreted by others.

Some of the data that become significant for others we create or encode intentionally, with a specific goal in mind, as when we prepare a speech, gesture to a friend, create a data base for computerized retrieval, dress for a job interview, or write copy for an advertisement. Even in situations such as these, no matter how well we plan or rehearse, we also are likely to create data that are unintended. A trembling hand, shaky voice, misspelled word, poorly pronounced phrase, lack of eye contact, or sweaty brow can easily have as much information value to others as the words and gestures created intentionally.

To illustrate the variety of sources for the data that play a role in human behavior, consider the following scenario:

> After months of being frustrated and unhappy in your current job, you decide that it is time to look seriously at the alternatives. A friend calls your attention to an advertisement in the newspaper for a position that sounds interesting at a well-known firm. You update your resumé and send it off with a cover letter to the company's personnel office.
>
> Several days hence, you receive a call indicating that they would like to schedule you for an interview. In preparation for the interview you have done a fair amount of planning. You've considered what to say about why you want the new position and why you want to leave the old one. You also have a list of questions you would like to ask, and have given some thought to the general approach you will take in presenting yourself, as well as to your attire.
>
> By the time the appointed hour arrives, you feel well prepared. You greet the interviewer with a purposely hearty, "Hello, there! How are you, today," shake his hand, and take a seat next to the desk. As you situate yourself comfortably in the chair, you give some conscious attention to your posture and try to relax. As the questions begin to come, you try to speak in a way that will lead him to see you as comfortable yet not overly informal, interested but not overly aggressive, composed yet spontaneous, self-assured but not arrogant.
>
> After what seems like an hour, the interviewer says he has no more questions, and asks if you do. You inquire about salary range, opportunities for advancement, and benefits—questions you selected because they would provide information you wanted, while creating the sort of impression of interest and alertness you hoped to project.
>
> After providing brief responses, the interviewer thanks you for coming and indicates that he will be in touch with you regarding the position as soon as

all the applicants for the position have been considered. You exchange closing pleasantries, and leave.

Considering the same circumstance from the point of view of the personnel department and the interviewer provides a somewhat different perspective. The task of finding a qualified person began long before the interview with the collection of data for the job description and advertisement. In a more general sense, from their point of view, communication began with the firm's advertising and public relations efforts over the years in that the company's image was a key factor in your decision to apply in the first place.

In constructing the advertisement for the new position, the personnel department sought to describe the job in a way that would attract highly qualified applications with reasonably accurate expectations about what the position would involve. After screening applications from many applicants, the list to be interviewed was finalized. The interviewer greeted each candidate as he or she arrived and devoted a few minutes to building rapport. As the interview proceeded, the overall goals were to create a positive, yet realistic, impression of the company and the job and to evaluate candidates' suitability for the position.

Questions that were asked were likely from a standardized interview guide, developed to ensure that all interviews followed a similar format. Some of the questions were designed to probe candidates' technical qualifications, as well as to provide the interviewer a sense of how composed and confident interviewees were, how they approached problems, dealt with people, felt about themselves, and so on.

Many of the questions were designed to generate information on several of these topics simultaneously. *Where did you go to school? What was your major area of study? What did you like best about that discipline? What were you looking for in this position? What previous experience had you had? Why were you thinking of leaving your present position? What were your greatest assets? What were your weaknesses? What were your career objectives? Did you prefer to work alone or with others?* In responding to your questions at the end of the interview, the interviewer tried to provide the requested information in a way that would further contribute to a positive regard for the company and the position.

Even in such a routine circumstance as a job interview, the richness and complexity of human communication is apparent. Consider, for example, the broad range of messages created before the interview—the chat with a friend, resumé, job description, advertisement, and the standardized interview guide. In the interview, messages included the exchange of verbal pleasantries, handshake, facial expressions, posture, arrangement of questions, elements in the responses, as well as the questions each person asked.

Behind the scenes, the interviewee thought about his or her feelings, what to say next, how long to talk, how he or she was reacting to the interviewer, how the interviewer seemed to be reacting to him or her, and so on. These self-reflective data helped both individuals transform internal feelings into observations and instructions for action. The immediate environment in which the interview took place, the type and arrangement of furniture in the room, time of day, temperature, and other situational factors were also sources of data that may have played a role in the dynamics of the interview.

Data and Information

In a situation such as the one described, each person is putting forth a good deal of effort to create particular sorts of impressions in the hope of achieving a predetermined outcome. We have some degree of control over the ways we express ourselves through our words and deeds, and to that degree, we have influence over the verbal and nonverbal data we create. However, for reasons we will explore in detail when we discuss information reception, we have only a limited control over whether and how the data we create become transformed into information that is of significance to others.

In the preceding scenario, for instance, the interviewee could have initiated the meeting by saying, "Hi, how are you doin'?" Or he or she could have opened the conversation with, "Hello. How are you this morning? Quite a nice day, isn't it?" Perhaps one of these openings was selected in an effort to create a particular impression—informal in the first case, more formal in the second. Alternatively, either of these greetings could have been "selected" through habit.

It is conceivable that the interviewer would have taken note of and reacted to the interviewee's remarks precisely as intended. It is also possible that any of a number of other things could have happened. The interviewer might not have paid any attention to the comment because he or she was concentrating on the appearance, dress, or demeanor of the individual. Or the greeting might go unnoticed because the interviewer was preoccupied with thoughts of the candidate who just left the office. Yet another possibility is that the greeting was unattended to because the interviewer was concentrating on what he or she was about to say.

Even if the interviewer were aware of and able to understand the words used in the greeting, a range of alternative interpretations might result. The individual's attempt to achieve informality might lead the interviewer to conclude that the candidate was unprepared, careless, presumptuous, or frivolous. A greeting designed to create a formal or self-confident image might be read as arrogance. Language and actions intended to convey assertiveness could be read as aggressiveness. The interviewee's attempts to be seen as a good listener and not overly pushy could be interpreted as suggesting that he or she is shy or withdrawn, perhaps even unintelligent and uninteresting.

As even the simple example of the interview illustrates, human communication is a complex, multifaceted, and often unpredictable endeavor. In any given situation, each of us generates a good deal of data—verbal and nonverbal, intended and unintended. The results of our activities in various situations contribute over time to a much larger database.

Anything we have said or written, done or not done, as well as the way we have looked, clothes we have worn, and documents and projects we have created may serve as the basis for information about us.

This chapter and Chapter 6 will focus on the information sources that play a central role in human behavior. Let us first consider verbal sources of information, specifically, *language* and *paralanguage*—what we say (orally and on paper), and how we say it.

Language

The creation and use of alpha-numeric language is one of humankind's most impressive accomplishments. About 10,000 distinct languages and dialects are in use today, and each of these language systems is unique in many respects.[1] There are, however, some surprising commonalities among them, as well. All languages, for instance, make use of a distinction between vowels and consonants, and in nearly all languages the subject precedes the object in declarative sentences.[2]

Beyond these specific kinds of similarities are more general commonalities in structure and use. Every language, for example, has an indentifiable pattern and set of rules of *phonology*, which indicate how sounds are combined to form words; *syntax*, which describes how words are combined into sentences; *semantics*, which concerns the meanings of words on the basis of their relationship to one another and to elements in the environment; and *pragmatics*, which pertains to the way in which language is used in practice.[3]

Physiological Factors

Some general similarities among various languages may be the result of a common ancestry. Major similarities, however, appear to be more the result of physical and mental capacities of the human species which creates and uses these languages.

Although a number of animal species can produce auditory data, even primates with their ability for vocalization lack the basic physiological capacity of humans. The human larynx located at the upper end of the trachea or windpipe is strengthened by cartilage that supports the vocal cords. When air from the lungs passes over the vocal cords with a greater force than occurs during normal breathing, the cords vibrate. The vibrations that result are called *voicing*. As the vocal cords are tightened, the pitch of the voice rises; as they are loosened, the pitch lowers. Additional variation in sound production is afforded humans because of the position of the tongue.

As the air is projected with voice-producing force, it is affected by the vocal cords and the tongue, as well as by the lips, mouth, teeth, and jaw. The position of the tongue, lips, and jaw are the primary factors involved in the creation of the vowel sounds. When the outflowing breath creates friction against the teeth, lower lip, or the upper parts of the mouth or tongue, sounds such as *f, v, s, z, th, sh,* and *zh* are produced in English pronunciation.

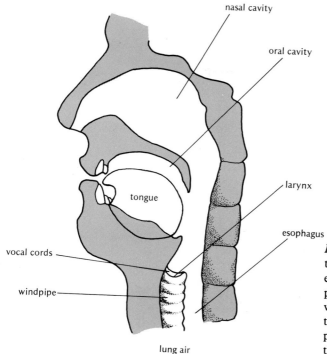

nasal cavity

oral cavity

larynx

esophagus

tongue

vocal cords

windpipe

lung air

FIGURE 5.1 Human sound production. The larynx is located at the upper end of the trachea or windpipe. Air passing through the vocal cords causes vibrations that produce human voice patterns. Tightening of the vocal cords produces high-pitched sounds; loosening the cords results in a lower pitch.

If the breath is stopped momentarily by movement of the lower lip or some part of the tongue, another sort of friction results, creating such sounds as the English pronunciation of *p. b, t, d, k,* and *g.* If the breath is rapidly and intermittently stopped, *trills* or *flips* result, which are associated with the pronunciation of *rr* in Spanish, and *butter* or *letter* in English. If the breath stream is stopped in the mouth such that it is forced through the nasal passages, the result is a nasal sound common to French, and to the English pronunciation of the letters *b, m, d* and *g.*[4] Sounds of letters are combined to form words, and words to form phrases and sentences. This wide range of sounds combined with variations in pitch, volume, and rate of speech produces the wide variety of vocal cues characteristic of spoken human language.

Cognitive Factors

As with other animals, human physiology only partially explains the workings of the communication process. Controlling these mechanisms are the brain and nervous system, which enable us to sense, make sense of, and act on environmental data. Here, the differences between humans and other animals are even more apparent.

One example will help to illustrate the point. Studies of chimps and gorillas who have been taught American sign language indicate clearly that primates can be taught to use language. However, the total vocabulary of the

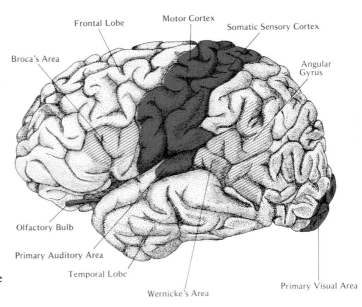

FIGURE 5.2 Left hemisphere of the human brain.

Labels on figure: Frontal Lobe, Motor Cortex, Somatic Sensory Cortex, Broca's Area, Angular Gyrus, Olfactory Bulb, Primary Auditory Area, Temporal Lobe, Wernicke's Area, Primary Visual Area

most successful of these students was four hundred words. In contrast, the average human has a vocabulary nearly two hundred times that large.[5]

Findings from neurophysiological research have pointed to the importance of particular areas of the brain for linguistic functioning. Especially important in this regard are what are termed Broca's Area and Wernicke's Area, both of which are located in the left half or *hemisphere* of the brain.[6]

Much remains to be learned about the manner in which the brain processes and uses information in speech. It is thought that information to be vocalized is associated with an appropriate auditory pattern in Wernicke's Area and is then transmitted to Broca's Area, which activates the electrical impulses needed to mobilize the voice-producing mechanisms and to create the intended vocalization.[7] This conclusion is supported by studies which have shown that damage to Broca's Area of the brain disturbs the production of speech but has much less impact on comprehension, whereas damage to Wernicke's area disrupts all aspects of language-use.[8]

Thus, through a process that we only partially understand, the individual is able to convert an idea, a joke, or a feeling into a coded data pattern, using a language he or she has learned. Once coded and vocalized, the words and sentences become a part of the environmental data pool to which others may attend and attach significance.

Language Acquisition

A good deal of attention has been devoted to determining precisely how and when we first develop competency in the use of language. Some linguists contend that the basic structure of language is innate in humans and that the child needs to learn only the surface details of the language spoken in his or her environment. Others see language acquisition as a part of the general development of the individual.[9] Both groups agree that interaction between the individual and environment is essential to linguistic competence. Studies have demonstrated that without the capacity and opportunity to talk with others no language capability develops.[10]

Studies of the first few months of life suggest that language acquisition begins with random "coos" and "giggles" in the presence of family members and other familiar persons. At age six to nine months, the "coos" and "giggles" are replaced by babbling sounds, and by eighteen months, most children can form a few simple words—dada, papa, mama, or nana.[11]

The speech patterns of others in the environment are important in this stage and throughout language acquisition. Generally, the speech of those who care for the child differs from standard language use in that the vocabulary is simplified, intonation patterns are exaggerated, sentences are simple, and frequent questions are asked (by mothers), and assertions are provided (by fathers).[12]

During the earliest stages of language development, single words are utilized to *label*, *assert*, or *question*.[13] In addition to describing an important person, for example, "mama" may be used as assertion. "Mama!" may mean, "I want you!" or "I need you, now!" Posed as a question, "Mama?" is a way of saying, "Where are you?" or "Will you come help me?" or "Is that you?"

As the child reaches the age of two and beyond, he or she begins to form two-word sentences:

> The two-word stage is a time for experimenting with many binary semantic-syntactic relations such as possessor-possessed ("Mommy sock"), actor-action ("Cat sleeping"), and action-object ("Drink soup").[14]

Although the child's vocabulary is growing, words are being used primarily to define specific, concrete actions and objects. A "car" may be understood as "a way to go to the store," and a "jack-in-the-box" is "what plays music and pops up." From this point on, the child's vocabulary and ability to form sentences progresses rapidly. Before youngsters are three, most are able to use their three-hundred to four-hundred-word vocabularies to create well-formed sentences of three, four, and more words.[15]

As the child grows older, his or her phonetic, syntactic, semantic, and pragmatic skills increase. Words are used in increasingly more abstract ways. Whereas "dog" to the toddler meant "my dog Spot," to the youngster it may refer to "my dog Spot and John's dog Rusty." And in later stages of development, "dog" becomes "a kind of pet," and later "a specific kind of four-legged animal."

What began as the use of words and sentences to refer to the *immediate* and the *tangible* gradually evolves to a capability for referring to the *abstract* and the *distant*. Thus, as a child develops increasing skill in the use of language, the linkage between his or her words and the particular events of the immediate surroundings becomes progressively more remote. For adults, meanings for particular words are abstractions based on a lifetime of experiences.

Accompanying the development of skill in using spoken language comes competency in the use of written forms. Combined with the use of various

CHILD'S AGE	COORDINATION	LANGUAGE
4 months	Johnny can hold his head up by himself.	Johnny coos and chuckles when people play with him.
6 to 9 months	Johnny can sit alone and can pull himself up into a standing position.	Johhny babbles continually, sounding like this: "gagagag yayayaya; dadadada."
12 to 18 months	Johnny first stands alone, then he walks along furniture, and, finally, he walks by himself.	Johnny uses a few words, follows simple commands, and knows what "no" means.
18 to 21 months	Johnny's walking looks stiff and jerky but he does well. He can sit in a chair (his aim is only "fair"), he can crawl down stairs, and he can throw a ball (clumsily).	Johnny understands simple questions and begins to put two or three words together in sentences.
24 to 27 months	Johnny runs well, but falls when making a quick turn. He can also walk up and down stairs.	Johnny uses short sentences composed of words from a 300–400 word vocabulary.
30 to 33 months	Johnny has good hand and finger coordination; he can manipulate objects well.	Johnny's vocabulary increases in size, and three- and four-word sentences are prevalent His language begins to sound adultlike.
36 to 39 months	Johnny runs smoothly and negotiates sharp turns; he walks stairs by alternating feet; he can ride a tricycle, stand on one foot (briefly), and jump twelve inches in the air.	Johnny talks in well-formed sentences, following rather complex grammatical rules; others can generally understand what he is talking about.

communication technologies, a host of expanded uses of language become possible. Adults use language in a variety of ways—to describe, assert, explain, argue, entertain, persuade, and express emotion and humor. Language is used not only in vocal but also in written form, not only in single messages but in lengthy documents and databases, not only face-to-face but also in mass communication.

Words, Things, and People

From the time an infant's first words are uttered, language begins to play a central and pervasive role in his or her life. Through formal and informal schooling, the child learns the accepted dictionary definitions—*denotative meanings*—for the terms he or she and others use. The child also learns the shades of meaning associated with particular words that are not necessarily a part of the explicit definition—their *connotative meaning*. He or she learns, for instance, that denotatively, *negro* and *Black* may have essentially the same meaning, but connotatively, they often evoke quite different reactions. A phrase such as "intimate sexual relations" is an acceptable way to refer to intercourse in everyday discussion, but "four-letter words" that may "mean" the same thing have quite a different connotation.

The impact of language acquisition is so subtle and thorough that the symbols—words, phrases, and sentences—are easily confused with the people, behaviors, actions, events, or ideas to which they refer. In many of the affairs of daily life, language seems to work "as if it were real." Most often, when we ask people how they are, for instance, they respond in a way which reassures us that our confidence in words is well justified.

But there are also a number of circumstances in life which remind the reflective person that an uncritical belief in the "reality of language" can lead to difficulties. Talking about quitting smoking, losing weight, changing one's lifestyle, or "turning over a new leaf" is often much different from carrying out the behavior.

Similarly, a woman saying that she is "in love" may not tell us much about the way she feels, how she will behave, or what she really thinks about the concepts and people to which her words refer. We use the words *I do*, for example, to seal the bonds of marriage. Although these two words have great symbolic value to the parties involved at that moment, the stability of the marriage will depend not upon the words but upon the behaviors and ideologies to which they refer.

Beyond the problems that arise from confusing words, phrases, and

---

FIGURE 5.3

SOURCE: Barbara S. Wood, *Children and Communication* (Englewood Cliffs, N.J.: Prentice-Hall, 1976), pp. 24–26; adapted from Eric Lenneberg, "The Natural History of Language," in *The Genesis of Language*, eds. Frank Smith and George A. Miller (Cambridge, MA: M.I.T. Press, 1968), p. 222. By permission of Prentice-Hall and the MIT Press, Cambridge, Massachusetts.

FIGURE 5.4 The nature of the relationship between language and the elements in environment to which they refer has long been an issue of importance in human life. In the Middle Ages, for example, the word *Abracadabra* was believed to be capable of curing fever. Apparently, the first prescription for its use came from a poem on medicine by Quintus Serenus Sammonicus, a doctor who accompanied the Roman Emperor Severus on an expedition to Britain in 208 A.D. The word was to be written in on a triangular piece of paper. The sheet of paper was to be worn on a piece of flax around the patient's neck for nine days and then thrown backwards over the shoulder into a stream that ran eastward. Presumably, when the word disappeared, so would the ills of the patient. The same belief in the relationship between symbols and physical reality is evidenced in an ancient Jewish spell against a demon named Shabriri. To get rid of the demon, one would say Shabriri Briri Riri Iri Ri, whittling him away to nothing.

SOURCE: *Man, Myth, and Magic,* Volume 1, New York: Marshall Cavendish, 1970.

sentences with the people, behaviors, actions, or ideas to which they refer, additional complexity in language results because in actual use words seldom mean the same thing to two different people. Even though there may be a general consensus on the denotative and connotative meanings of a particular word, the precise meanings each of us attaches to words and phrases depend upon our experiences. As a consequence, the meanings of words are subjective and, to some extent, unique to each individual. The following exchange illustrates the point:

Fred: "Ray, I need that breakdown on the Johnson deal that you've been working on for this afternoon's meeting."

Ray: "Okay, Fred, you'll have it."

Ray: "Sally, that memo for sales has got to go out this morning."

Sally: "I'll get it right out."

Fred: (4:30 that afternoon) "Ray, where's that information you promised to get me this afternoon?"

Ray: "You should have had it this morning. I asked Sally to get it right over to you."

Fred: "Well, it's not here and you know this isn't the first time something like this has happened..."

"I can't think of a better companion than a dog. They are faithful, kind, affectionate. . . Sunshine is like a member of the family."

"I'd never think of going out at night without my dog by my side"

DOG

"I've never cared much for dogs as pets."

"I agree, dogs make great pets."

FIGURE 5.5

As a result of the day's events Ray has accumulated more evidence that Sally is incompetent. Fred has decided once and for all that he simply can't count on Ray, and Sally is convinced that Ray is looking for a reason to try to get rid of her. Although all of these conclusions may be justified, it is also quite possible that at least a partial explanation of what occurred is to be found in the words and phrases each person used and how they were interpreted. Initially, Fred indicated to Ray that he needed the information for the afternoon meeting. Ray told Sally that it had "to go out this morning." But what did "go out this morning" mean? To Sally, who sent it out at 11:00 through the inter-office postal system—it meant "go *out* this morning." To Fred and Ray it meant *"be delivered* this morning."

The same sorts of difficulties arise in many other settings as well. Hour after hour is spent in labor negotiations, for instance, arguing over the precise terminology to be used in a contract. In such a situation, the interpretation of such seemingly innocent words as *shall, will,* or *may* can become complex. Often, whether mass media news reporting provokes a lawsuit or not often depends upon the use and individual interpretation of a few words.

A major difficulty in classifying information for use as an index or data base also has to do with the subjectivity of meaning. Whether information on the impact of a Middle Eastern oil price increase should be classified and stored under "oil," "Middle East," "inflation," "home fuel costs," "the economy," "OPEC," or one or more of several other possibilities is a

```
——— POOL RULES ———
HOURS 9AM - 10PM
-wwwwwwwwwwwwwww-

1. NO CUT-OFFS, PLEASE. SWIM SUITS ONLY
2. GLASS, FOOD & DRINK SHOULD BE KEPT AWAY FROM POOL
3. NO PETS IN POOL AREA
4. NO HORSEPLAY OR RUNNING IN THE POOL AREA  PLEASE

6. BATHING CAPS SHOULD BE WORN OVER LONG HAIR
7. CHILDREN UNDER 14 SHOULD BE WITH AN ADULT
8. PLEASE DO NOT REMOVE PATIO FURNITURE FROM DECK
9. THE POOL IS FOR GUESTS USE ONLY

SWIM AT YOUR OWN RISK
```

```
PRIVATE PROPERTY
ALL INCOMING & OUTGOING
PACKAGES. ATTACHE CASES.
BAGS. ETC. ARE
SUBJECT TO INSPECTION
BY THE SECURITY OFFICER
```

FIGURE 5.6 Minor differences in word choice—such as "should" versus "are" in the signs shown—may have a substantial impact on the significance a message will have.

language problem for the individual who complies an index or database and for those who want to use it.

Words as Labels

Another use of language that often plays a subtle but significant role in other's inferences about us are our labels—names and titles. In addition to identifying or classifying us in one way or another, names may also be the basis of first impressions. Many surnames, for instance, provide clues to ancestry. Inferences as to nationality or ethnic background can become the basis for a stereotype long before face-to-face interaction with the individual.

Even first names may not be the neutral, value-free labels they are generally assumed to be. There is evidence, for example, that first names can be important to first impressions. Studies suggest that certain first names are more often seen as being associated with qualities such as intelligence, attractiveness, strength, or femininity than others. "John" and "Robert" are regarded far more positively than "Frederick," and "Joan" more favorably than "Donna" or "Cynthia."

With only our first names as information, others can and sometimes do make assessments of the quality of our work, as well as how desirable and attractive we are. While it is generally argued that common names tend to be more positively regarded in initial impressions than more unusual names, it has also been noted that a number of the senior executives of the nation's largest companies have had uncommon names. In circumstances in which our names are the first or only data available, they may well have an impact on impressions others form before meeting us.

Titles such as *Dr., Ph.D., M.D., Prince, Professor, Ms., Mrs., Mr.* or *Senator* also serve as identifiers that may be used to infer qualities such as gender, occupation, education intelligence, financial security, prior experience, age, and marital status, long before one meets an individual. Depending upon the context in which a title is used, people may infer any number of other qualities as well. If an individual were to introduce himself to a next-door neighbor as *Dr. John Johnson,* that may well say something quite different than if he presents himself as *John Johnson.* Similarly, when a man walks up to an unaccompanied woman in a singles bar, the response to her introducing herself as *Mrs. Jim Johnson* would likely be quite different than if she referred to herself as *Ms. Jane Johnson.*

One's occupational title can also be an identifying message. Studies suggest, for instance, that occupations such as physician, university professor, trial lawyer, engineer, banker, airline pilot, high school teacher, pharmacist, armed forces officer, clergyman, artist, and primary grade teacher are generally regarded, in that order, as prestigious titles.[17] On the other hand, occupational labels such as miner, barber, shoemaker, waiter, farmhand, street vendor, janitor, servant, and street sweeper evoke the opposite response. One's occupational title alone can give rise to a number of inferences about an individual, such as status, gender, presumed levels of financial well-being, power and influence, and education.

	Men's Names	Men's Ranking	Women's Ranking
First Names			
	Daniel	10	13
	David	7	9
	Edward	18	10
	Frederick	25	25
	James	13	17
	John	11	1
	Joseph	9	2
	Robert	1	12
	Thomas	19	24
	Ronald	16	8
Short Names			
	Dan	24	15
	Dave	2	3
	Ed	13	16
	Fred	16	27
	Jim	3	5
	Jack	6	6
	Joe	4	19
	Bob	8	4
	Tom	5	11
	Ron	22	7
Nicknames			
	Danny	23	26
	Davey	28	28
	Eddy	27	30
	Freddy	29	23
	Jimmy	20	21
	Johnny	26	14
	Joey	30	29
	Bobby	11	18
	Tommy	14	20
	Ronnie	21	22

Women's Names	Men's Ranking	Women's Ranking
Anne	9	5
Barbara	10	12
Carol	6	15
Cheryl	7	14
Cynthia	20	18
Diane	11	19
Donna	16	17
Janet	8	4
Jean	12	3
Joan	4	2
Judith	15	11
Karen	1	7
Kathleen	5	16
Linda	19	10
Margaret	17	8
Mary	3	6
Nancy	2	13
Patricia	18	9
Sharon	14	20
Susan	13	1

FIGURE 5.7 What's in a name? Names are not necessarily the neutral, value-free labels that many people might assume or desire them to be. Often, for example, surnames serve as data from which nationality and/or religion can be inferred. And based upon these inferences, first impressions may be formed. There is also evidence to suggest that even first names by themselves provide the basis for the formation of impressions and stereotypes.

In several studies individuals were asked to indicate how much they associate qualities such as goodness, strength, and potency with various men's and women's names. The results indicate that people do associate certain qualities with particular names, and that, in general, people are more positively disposed toward some names than others. The list shows the ranking of preferences for men's and women's names that resulted.

SOURCE: (Left) Men's First Names, Nicknames, and Short Names: A Semantic Differential Analysis." *Names*, 21:1 (March, 1973), pp. 22–27. By permission. (Right) E. D. Lawson, "Women's First Names: A Semantic Differential Analysis", *Names* (June, 1974), pp. 52–58. By permission.

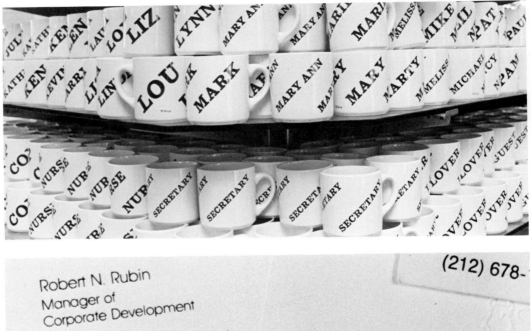

FIGURE 5.8 Our names and titles are personal and professional symbols by which we identify and refer to one another. By their very nature and depending upon the way they are used, they also often serve as the basis for inferences about our education, nationality, financial status, or personality.

Paralanguage[18]

Although *what we say*—the words, phrases, and sentences—is important verbal communication, the *way* we use language can be even more important than our words as sources of information. Long before children develop skill in language use, they acquire a familiarity with the tonal pattern of the language in their environment. Some recent studies suggest that it is possible to identify the language environment in which a child lives from babbling tonal contours during the second year of life.[19] These paralinguistic patterns children acquire not only reflect the larger language environment in which they are being raised but also the unique patterns of family and friends.

Unlike language, paralanguage provides *information about information—* what has been called *metacommunication*.[20] That is, a sigh, a monotone, a loud voice, or a raspy mutter may serve as important cues in helping the individual decide how to interpret the informational content of a message. With spoken language, loudness, rate of speaking, tone, pitch variation, and uses of pauses can have a major influence on whether and how one reacts to the words. On the basis of *pitch*, for example, we are able to determine whether a particular utterance is a statement or a question, a serious comment or a sarcastic barb. Whether *really* spoken orally is intended to be interpreted as *really?* or *really!* is determined through paralanguage rather than through the word itself. In the same way, we decide whether *that's beautiful* is to be taken literally or to mean quite the opposite.

Interjections, such as *a, huh, really*, and *you know*, stuttering, and stammering may also have an impact upon the way any utterance is interpreted. Although there is no difference in the words used in "come in," and "cooommme iiinnn," the meanings we would attach to these two messages would likely be very different.

In written language, the form of a word or statement is also important to interpretation. Punctuation, spelling, cross-outs, too much or too little space between words, sentence structure, handwriting, or color of ink are likely to influence the reader's reaction to the words.

In addition to shaping the interpretation of the spoken utterance, paralanguage and form may provide a basis for a number of inferences about the author or speaker. Rate of speed and accent, for example, can provide information from which inferences are drawn as to nationality or the region of the country in which the person was raised, and other characteristics associated with stereotypes about the geographic locale. "The *fast-talking* New Yorker" or "the *slow drawl* of the Southerner," for example, are often associated with behavioral, as well as geographic, characteristics.

Particularly in oral speech, paralanguage can also provide the basis for assumption as to the speaker's educational level, interest in the topic, level of comfort and self-concept, regard for the audience, personality, and mood. Tone, pitch, rate of speech, and volume provide clues as to an individual's emotional state.

Similarly in written language, punctuation marks, tone, correctness or incorrectness of spacing, spelling, sentence structure, and neatness or lack of

Bodoni Bold

Light, rich, beautiful,
expensive, meaningful,
graceful, tight, formal,
soft, perfect, good,
clean, harmonious, honest

Bodoni Book Italic

Perfect, soft, plain,
feminine, good, rich,
beautiful, rounded, ex-
pensive, graceful, clean,
harmonious

Bodoni Ultra

Active, ugly, hard,
strong, dark, masculine,
rugged

Cheltenham Bold

Imperfect, hard, con-
strained, old, ugly, old-
fashioned, cheap, active,
honest, plain, strong,
dark, simple, masculine,
usual, rugged

Garamond

Light, rich, beautiful,
rounded, expensive,
meaningful, formal, plain,
perfect, good, clean, harmonious, honest

Garamond Italic

Perfect, good, rich,
beautiful, rounded, mean-
ingful, harmonious,
honest, ornate, weak, soft,
light, expensive, feminine,
delicate, graceful, clean

Tempo Bold

New, modern, hard, plain,
good, strong, dark,
simple, masculine,
rugged, honest

Karnak intermediate

Hard, constrained, strong
masculine, rugged, awk-
ward, stiff, good, sim-
ple, clean, honest

Kaufman Script

New, active, modern,
informal, soft, femi-
nine, light, delicate

Type Script

Old-fashioned, weak,
beautiful, soft, ornate,
light, complex, rich,
rounded, expensive,
feminine, delicate,
graceful, clean, har-
monious, formal

Garamond Bold

Old, meaningful, hard,
plain, usual, rugged,
perfect, strong, dark,
masculine, clean, har-
monious, honest

Flash

Free, new, active, strong,
rounded, modern, cheap,
masculine, relaxed,
dark, rugged, informal

FIGURE 5.9 Beyond a linguistic symbol itself, factors such as the style, shape, size, manner of reproduction, and placement of that symbol may substantially influence its ultimate significance. Each of the type faces shown provoked quite different reactions in a research project aimed at determining which styles of type are most effective for particular types of advertising.

SOURCE: Stephen Baker, *Visual Persuasion* (New York: McGraw-Hill, 1961. By permission of Stephen Baker.)

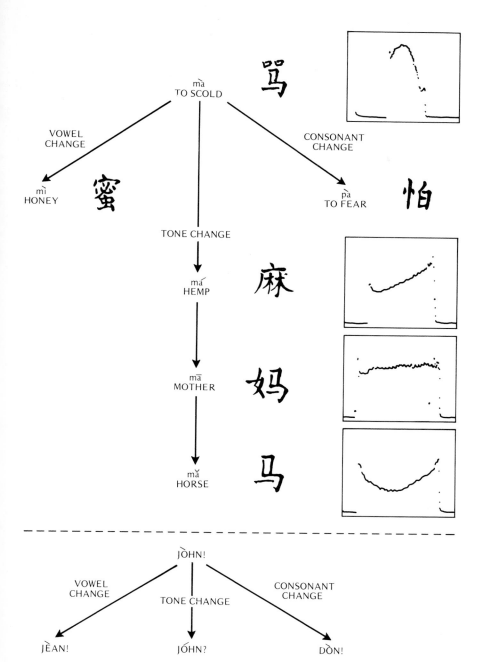

FIGURE 5.10 In some languages, paralanguage is even more essential to language usage than in English. In Chinese, for instance, tones alter the meaning of words. Standard Chinese has only four tones: falling (as in *mà*), rising (*má*), level (*mā*) and dipping, or falling and then rising (*mǎ*). The drawings on the right show the voice pattern as the words are spoken. In Chinese, changing tone has the same kind of effect on the meaning of a word as changing a vowel or a consonant would in English.

SOURCE: William S-Y Wang, "The Chinese Language," in *Human Communication: Language and its Psychobiological Bases* (San Francisco: Freeman, 1982), p. 58. By permission.

FIGURE 5.11

it, and whether something is handwritten and barely legible or neatly typed may well serve as a basis for generalized inferences as to how educated, careful, respectful, or serious a person is and provide clues as to his or her mood or emotions at the time of writing.

Types of Verbal Information

When an individual has a well-defined objective to achieve through verbal data, he or she is likely to anticipate difficulties that may result from the subjectivity of language and confusion of words and meanings. In writing a book, preparing for a speech, creating a film documentary, developing an information classification system, or planning an important discussion with an intimate friend or colleague, we may devote a great deal of attention to selecting the appropriate words, sentences, and sentence structures to achieve our goals. In such circumstances we use words as tools to achieve a predetermined objective.

In many situations we are far less conscious of the words we use and the way we use them. Especially in casual conversation with a friend, family member, lover, or colleague at work, we are likely to say "what comes to our minds," without a great deal of attention to setting objectives or word selection.

Whether we use our words in a planned, intentional way or in a less systematic, unintentional fashion, they are data of potential significance to others. In either kind of situation, verbal data provide potential information of three types: (1) information about *the topic under discussion;* (2) information about *the source;* and (3) information about *how the source regards the intended recipient(s).*

A written or spoken presentation designed to convince us to vote for a particular candidate, for instance, provides the basis for information about the candidate, his or her qualifications, campaign promises, and potentials. Also, the presentation provides data as to the level of preparation, interest, education, intelligence, attitudes, beliefs, mood, and motives of the speaker. Finally, the speech may provide clues as to how the speaker regards his or her intended audience. Does the speaker "look down" on the audience? Does he or she consider them to be powerful, authoritative, educated? Does he or she fear or resent them? Clues are often provided by one's use of language.

To clarify the distinction between these three kinds of information, consider the following statement:

Marge: "Carol is an incompetent and uncaring person!"

First, from a topical point of view, Marge is indicating that there are some things about Carol that bother her. Beyond that, Marge may also be providing some clues about herself. She seems to feel quite strongly about Carol. Perhaps she is a fairly outspoken individual. She may be quite an emotional person. Perhaps she is judgmental and intolerant of individual differences. Perhaps she is jealous or envious of Carol.

In addition to providing data that serves as the basis for information about Carol and herself, she may also be providing clues as to how she regards the person to whom she is speaking. It is likely that Marge sees herself as closer to the person she's talking to than she is to Carol. It is also probable that Marge assumes the listener is closer to her than to Carol. One could also infer that she trusts the listener, or alternatively, that she simply doesn't care who knows how she feels about Carol—which would be additional information about Marge. At the least, we can safely assume that Marge has some reason for wanting to share her reaction with the listener.

Let's consider two slightly more complex examples:

1. Daddy: (Following the sound of breaking glass): "Marc."
   Marc: "Daddy, I didn't do it."

2. Ed: "Mary, I want to talk to you."
   Mary: "Ed, I know what you're going to say. I'm sorry, I never intended for you to get hurt.... It just happened."

In all respects except the topic, these two exchanges are quite similar. In each instance the first speaker is really saying very little from a topical point of view. In fact, in both cases, the speakers provide no information that identifies a topic for discussion. The second speakers, however, provide the basis for a number of inferences. Both Marc and Mary seem to be saying that they *assume* they are being asked about a particular act, even though this is not necessarily accurate. They respond as though they have been verbally attacked. Their responses are *defensive*, perhaps motivated by guilt or fear, or both. In addition to providing data from which one could infer something about their feelings and attitudes, their responses also provide clues as to how they feel about the persons with whom they are interacting. Both Marc and Mary are concerned with their relationships, of necessity or choice. For whatever reasons, both seem to see themselves in a "one-down" or inferior position, in which they must justify, explain, and/or seek forgiveness or approval from Daddy and Ed.

Let's consider a slightly more complicated situation:

Bill: "Well, Todd, my wife and I are really excited. We've got a chance to go to Las Vegas this weekend on a special half-price package. It wasn't really the time we had picked to go, but we just can't pass it up.... Doubt we'll ever have a chance to go so cheaply again."

Todd: "I considered going, but with the economy the way it is, decided it's not smart to spend money on travel this year."

In the brief exchange, Bill is providing data about the prospect of an upcoming trip. He's also explaining that it will cost only one-half the normal amount. The fact that Bill is talking about the trip at all may suggest that he's the type of person who enjoys sharing his excitement. Or, perhaps he is boasting; perhaps he is seeking attention or recognition.

In explaining that he got a special price, he may provide a clue that he wishes to be seen as clever, shrewd, or economical. Or, alternatively, it may suggest that he is the sort of person who feels a need to justify or apologize for his good fortune. The decision to share his plans with Todd suggests that Bill cares about or values Todd. Perhaps he is seeking to impress Todd, or trying to solicit support or encouragement.

In responding as he did, Todd indicates that he does not think it is a smart time to spend money on a trip. Beyond this, his response may provide a clue that Todd is unwilling to share in Bill's excitement. Perhaps he is jealous. Or, perhaps he fails to detect Bill's excitement. Todd's response also may suggest that he wishes to be seen as more rational than Bill—at least in this instance. He seems to feel no obligation to acknowledge or contribute to Bill's excitement, and has no particular interest in providing an audience for further discussion of Bill's trip.

Our language and paralanguage serve a number of functions, some intentional, others not. They are a primary means for creating and transmitting data in our human endeavors. It is our means of recording information for ourselves and the mechanism by which we provide data for others on various topics. These data also provide the basis for other kinds of information that is used to infer our interest in a particular topic, our preparation, attitudes, education, mood, motives, age, personality, concepts of ourselves, and regard for and estimation of our listeners, readers, or viewers.

Summary

Through our behavior—words, sentences, tone, appearance, actions, and the like—we create data that are potentially significant sources of information for others. Some of the data we create intentionally, others more by accident.

Most of our purposeful data creation involves the use of language and paralanguage. Languages are similar to one another in several respects. All have rules relative to phonology, syntax, semantics, and pragmatics. Still more basic similarities result from the physiological and cognitive capacities of humans. The physiology of human speech is more advanced than that necessary for vocalizations in other species, and the differences between human mental abilities and those of other animals are even more pronounced. Particular areas of the brain—Broca's Area and Wernicke's Area—both of which are located in the left hemisphere, are thought to be critical to language use.

Our capacity for language develops from the time we are infants through a progressive series of stages. As adults, we use language not only to refer, as does the child, to the immediate environment but also to record, describe, assert, express emotion, question, identify ourselves, entertain, humor, defend, and for a host of other purposes.

Because of the pervasiveness of human language, it is easy to confuse words and phrases with the events, people, behaviors, and circumstances to which they refer. Even though words may have generally agreed upon denotative and connotative meanings, their ultimate significance depends on the personal past experiences of the persons involved.

Paralanguage—the way language is used—can be as important as words and sentences in written and spoken communication. Tone, pitch, punctuation, volume, spelling, and other facets of language use become significant sources of data, providing information about information—*metacommunication*. They provide clues as to mood, education, country and region of origin, as well as the attitude of the speaker or author.

Language and paralanguage provide the bases for three types of information: (1) information about the topic under discussion; (2) information about a source; (3) information about how the source regards the intended recipients. Overall, language and paralanguage serve a number of functions, some intentional and others by accident.

Notes

1. William S-Y Wang, "Language and Derivative Systems," in *Human Communication: Language and its Psychobiological Basis*, Ed. by William S-Y Wang (San Francisco: Freeman, 1982) p. 36.
2. Ibid.
3. Breyne Arlene Moskowitz, "The Acquisition of Language," in *Human Communication: Language and its Psychobiological Basis*, p. 122. For discussions of various facets of language study and their relation to one another, see *Communication and Culture*, Alfred G. Smith, Ed. (New York: Holt, 1966); George A. Miller and Frank Smith, Eds., *The Genesis of Language* (Cambridge, MA: M.I.T. Press, 1966); Leonard Bloomfield, *Language* (New York: Holt, 1933); Noam Chomsky, *Aspects of the Theory of Syntax* (Cambridge, MA: M.I.T. Press, 1965); Joseph DeVito, *The Psychology of Speech and Language* (New York:

Random House, 1970); J.A. Fodor and J.J. Katz, *The Structure of Language* (Englewood Cliffs, NJ: Prentice-Hall, 1964); Edward Sapir, *Language* (New York: Harcourt, 1921); and F. de Saussaure, *Course in General Linguistics*, translated by W. Baskin (New York: Philosophical Library, 1959).

4. Harold Whitehall, "The English Language," in *Webster's New World Dictionary of the American Language* (Cleveland: World, 1964), pp. xv–xxix.

5. Morton Hunt, *The Universe Within* (New York: Simon and Schuster, 1982), pp. 36–37.

6. What is named Broca's Area is based on the pioneering research by Paul Broca during the late 1800s. Wernicke's Area is named for German neurologist Karl Wernicke, who is acknowledged as the first to discover that damage to that section of the left hemisphere would lead to difficulties in speech comprehension. For a detailed discussion of the history and present significance of this work to neurophysiology and speech, see *Left Brain, Right Brain*, by Sally P. Springer and George Deutsch (San Francisco: Freeman, 1981); "Specializations of the Human Brain," by Norman Geschwind in *Scientific American* (September 1979); and an overview provided by Morton Hunt, op. cit.

7. Norman Geschwind, "Specializations of the Human Brain," in *Human Communication: Language and Its Psychobiological Basis*, William S-Y Wang, Ed., op. cit., 1982, pp. 113–115.

8. Ibid., p. 112. Cf., also, discussion in Morton Hunt, op. cit., pp. 33–36.

9. Breyne Arlene Moskowitz, op. cit., p. 122.

10. Ibid., p. 123.

11. The summary of stages in language acquisition is based upon an in-depth discussion provided in Barbara S. Wood, *Children and Communication* (Englewood Cliffs, NJ: Prentice-Hall, 1976), pp. 24–27, adapted from Eric Lenneberg, "The Natural History of Language," in *The Genesis of Language*, Frank Smith and George A. Miller, Eds. (Cambridge, MA: M.I.T. Press, 1968), p. 222. Cf. also, Breyne Arlene Moskowitz, op. cit.

12. Breyne Arlene Moskowitz, op. cit., p. 123.

13. Cf. Barbara Wood, pp. 112–113.

14. Breyne Arlene Moskowitz, op. cit., p. 125.

15. Barbara Wood, op. cit., pp. 25–26.

16. Cf. E.D. Lawson, "Men's First Names, Nicknames, and Short Names: A Semantic Differential Analysis," *Names*, **21,** 1 (March 1973), pp. 22–27. See also, E.D. Lawson, "Women's First Names: A Semantic Differential Analysis," *Names*, **22,** 2 (June 1974) pp. 52–58; E.D. Lawson, "Semantic Differential Analysis of Men's First Names," *The Journal of Psychology*, **78:** (1971) pp. 229–240; and John W. McDavid and Herbert Harari, "Stereotyping of Names and Popularity in Grade School Children," *Child Development* **37** (1966), pp. 453–459.

17. Based upon studies of the perceived prestige of fifty common occupations in the United States and fifty-five other countries, reported in Donald J. Treiman, *Occupational Prestige in Comparative Perspective* (New York: Academic Press, 1977), pp. 155–156.

18. Although paralanguage is often classed with nonverbal communication, it is discussed here with verbal because it is so directly related to language use; unlike other behaviors to be considered in Chapter 6, paralanguage cues cannot be created in the absence of vocalization.
19. Breyne Arlene Moskowitz, op. cit., pp. 130–131.
20. The term *metacommunication* was advanced by Paul Watzlawick, Janet Beavin, and Don D. Jackson in *Pragmatics of Human Communication* (New York: Norton, 1967).

References and Suggested Reading

Bloomfield, Leonard. *Language*. New York: Holt, 1933.

Brown, Roger. *Words and Things*. New York: Free Press, 1958.

Budd, Richard W. "General Semantics." In *Interdisciplinary Approaches to Human Communication*. Ed. by Richard W. Budd and Brent D. Ruben. Rochelle Park, NJ: Hayden, 1979, 71–94.

Burling, Robbins. *Man's Many Voices*. New York: Holt, 1970.

Chomsky, Noam. *Aspects of the Theory of Syntax*. Cambridge, MA: M.I.T. Press, 1965.

de Saussaure, F. *Course in General Linguistics*. Translated by W. Baskin. New York: Philosophical Library, 1959.

DeVito, Joseph. *The Psychology of Speech and Language*. New York: Random House, 1970.

Dunkling, Leslie Alan. *First Names First*. New York: Universe, 1977.

Fodor, A., and J.J. Katz. *The Structure of Language*. Englewood Cliffs, NJ: Prentice-Hall, 1964.

Geschwind, Norman. "Specializations of the Human Brain." *Scientific American* (September 1979), 180–182.

Hayakawa, S.I. *Language in Thought and Action*. New York: Fawcett, 1962.

Hubel, D.H. *Scientific American* (September 1979), 44–53.

Hunt, Morton. *The Universe Within*. New York: Simon and Schuster, 1982.

Johnson, Wendell. *People in Quandaries*. New York: Harper, 1946.

Korzybski, Alfred. *Science and Sanity*. Lakeville, CT: The International Non-Aristotelian Library, 1948.

Lawson, E.D. "Men's First Names, Nicknames, and Short Names: A Semantic Differential Analysis." *Names*, **21** (1973), 22–27.

————"Women's First Names: A Semantic Differential Analysis." *Names*, **22** (1974), 52–58.

Lee, Irving J. *Language Habits in Human Affairs*. New York: Harper, 1941.

McDavid, John W., and Herbert Harari. "Stereotyping of Names and Popularity in Grade School Children." *Child Development*, **37** (1966), 453–459.

Miller, George A., and F. Smith, Eds. *The Genesis of Language*. Cambridge, MA: M.I.T. Press, 1966.

Moskowitz, Breyne Arlene. "The Acquisition of Language." *Scientific American* (November 1978), 92–94.

Sapir, Edward. *Language*. New York: Harcourt, 1921.

Smith, Alfred G., Ed. *Communication and Culture*. New York: Holt, 1966.

Springer, Sally, and Georg Deutsch. *Left Brain, Right Brain*. San Francisco: Freeman, 1981.

Thieme, Paul. "The Indo-European Language." *Scientific American* (October 1958), 63–74.

Treiman, Donald J. *Occupational Prestige in Comparative Perspective*. New York: Academic Press, 1977.

Wang, William S-Y. "The Chinese Language." *Scientific American* (February 1973), 50–60.

————. "Languages and Derivative Systems." In *Human Communication: Language and Its Psychobiological Bases*. Ed. by William S-Y Wang. San Francisco: Freeman, 1982, 36–38.

Whorf, Benjamin L. *Language, Thought, and Reality*. Ed. by J.B. Carroll. New York: Wiley, 1956.

Williams, Frederick, Robert Hopper, and Diana S. Natalicio. *The Sounds of Children*. Englewood Cliffs, NJ: Prentice-Hall, 1977.

Wood, Barbara S. *Children and Communication*. Englewood Cliffs, NJ: Prentice-Hall, 1976.

Nonverbal Codes

Appearance, Action, Touch, Space, and Time

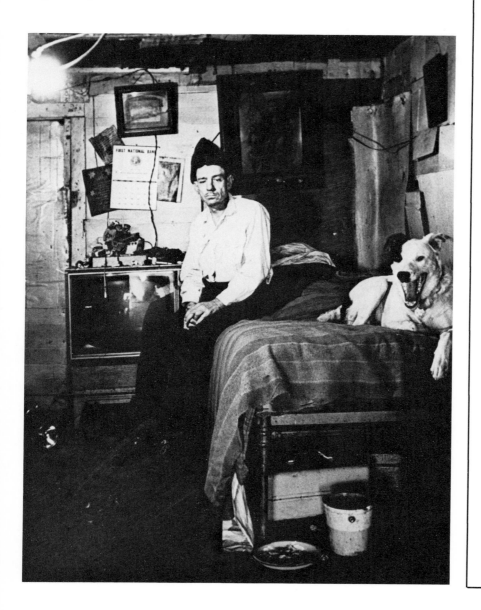

Kim walked over to a row of unoccupied chairs, placed the briefcase and purse she was carrying on the seat to her right, and situated a Saks Fifth Avenue bag near her on the floor. She began to leaf casually through the pages of a *Psychology Today* magazine, glancing periodically at the TV monitor listing incoming flights, and then down at her watch.

After about five minutes had passed, a middle-aged man in a three piece suit walked over and selected a seat directly across from her. As Kim glanced up out of the corner of her eye to see where he was looking, her eyes caught his. He smiled, and she looked away in embarrassment. Kim concentrated her attention on the magazine in front of her, but she sensed the man was still staring. Finally, she noticed him get up and walk away.

Several minutes later he reappeared, walked over to the seat next to her and sat down without saying a word. Kim picked up her brief case and shopping bag and walked rapidly down the concourse toward the gift shop.

As the brief scenario illustrates quite clearly, nonverbal cues play a significant and pervasive role in human communication. Though no words were spoken, the individuals' appearance, dress, actions, movement, positioning, and timing provided the basis for information that had an impact on behavior.

Differences Between Verbal and Nonverbal Codes

Awareness and Attention

In a number of respects, nonverbal codes have much in common with verbal language systems. Before turning to a discussion of these similarities, however, it is useful, first, to consider several noteworthy differences.

The first distinction has to do with the general lack of awareness of, and attention devoted to, nonverbal codes in comparison with language. This difference is perhaps most evident when one considers the contrast between the manner in which training in the two areas is handled in our schooling.

In the case of verbal language, great effort is expended to ensure that students are taught rules of pronunciation, syntax, semantics, and pragmatics as a part of their formal education. Frequent opportunities for guided experience in the written and oral use of language are provided at virtually all educational levels. Competence in the use of verbal codes is, in fact, considered to be so important that it is regarded as one of the most "basic" skills.

In comparison, nonverbal codes receive little attention in most schools. Music, art, and physical education *are* generally included as part of the curriculum. However, no skills training comparable to composition, literature, or public speaking, is provided for the nonverbal competencies that are critical to face-to-face interaction.

Definition Does the lack of attention to nonverbal codes imply that they are of less importance to human behavior than language? Certainly not. Rather the differing levels of emphasis suggest still other distinctions between verbal and nonverbal codes. The first, and perhaps most obvious explanation for the stress placed on language, is to be found in the relatively explicit rules and structure of language, compared to the less specifiable and specified nature of most nonverbal codes.

For any given language, documentation of these patterns is provided in various sources—dictionaries, style manuals, and the like. However, there are no comparable nonverbal dictionaries or style manuals beyond popular books on etiquette, dress, and body language, which lack the precision and reliability of guides to language use.

Intention Another difference between verbal and nonverbal codes lies in their use. While individuals may devote considerable attention to their appearance, dress, or gestures, in general, more overt attention is given to planning, executing, and monitoring the impact of verbal messages. Simply stated, language is more often used in purposeful message-sending attempts than nonverbal codes, a factor which helps to further explain why greater attention has been devoted to verbal than nonverbal competence.

Public vs. Private Status Language usage patterns—except speech problems such as stuttering or stammering—have long been regarded as a *public* or *social* matter, and an appropriate area for instruction. By way of contrast, matters pertaining to one's appearance, mannerisms, and body positions are generally considered *private* and *personal*, and have therefore been less likely topics of discussion and analysis in schools and other public settings.

Finally, perhaps for all these reasons and others, much more systematic attention has been devoted to the study of language and language patterns than to nonverbal behavior. Only in the last several decades has nonverbal communication emerged as an area of intensive study, and the topic of a growing collection of popular articles and books.

Hemispheric Specialization

Another major difference, the topic of increasing scholarly interest, pertains to the location in the brain where nonverbal activities are centered. As we noted, the left hemisphere of the brain is thought to play a predominant role in language processes. Other activities which require the sequential processing of information, such as mathematics, seem also to rely heavily on the left hemisphere.[1] By way of contrast, the right hemisphere is of special significance in the recognition of faces and body images, art, music and other endeavors where integration, creativity, or imaging are involved.[2]

Studies show, for instance, that some individuals with damage in the right hemisphere have difficulty with location and spatial relationships, recognition of familiar faces, or the recognition of scenes or objects. Other research, which argues convincingly in favor of right-hemisphere specialization, has shown that even where damage to the language centers in the left hemisphere is so severe that the patients may have difficulty speaking, the ability to sing is often unaffected.[3]

There is substantial evidence that the contributions of the two hemispheres of the brain are in some senses distinctive. What remains to be determined is the extent to which *differences in the locations* where verbal and nonverbal information is processed are indicative of even more fundamental *differences in the manner* in which these two sorts of information are handled by the brain.

Similarities Between Verbal and Nonverbal Codes

Multiple Uses

Language is used for purposeful message-sending more often than nonverbal codes, but both kinds of data can be produced and transmitted either intentionally or unintentionally. For example, one may smile to indicate friendliness, in much the same way that he or she might use language to convey cordiality. And, unintended cues like mismatched socks or a lack of eye engagement, can have as much information value as poor grammar or misspellings.

Rules and Patterns

While the structure and patterns of nonverbal codes are less specifiable and less specified than those of language, rules and patterns can nonetheless be identified in nonverbal communication. Some of these rules and patterns pertain to the *production* of nonverbal data, others to the ways in which emotions may be *displayed*, still others are necessary to comprehend the significance of cues produced by others.[4]

Rules associated with the *creation* of many nonverbal behaviors—a handshake, for instance—can be seen as similar to *phonetics*. Rules prescribing the appropriate sequence of nonverbal cues relative to one another—in meeting someone for the first time, for example—are a type of *syntax*. There are also generalizable *semantic* patterns for many nonverbal behaviors which can be identified, and conventions as to *when* and *how* particular cues are to be used—a kind of *pragmatics* of nonverbal codes.

As is the case with verbal codes, some of these rules and patterns are common to the behavior of all individuals, regardless of personal or cultural differences. In facial expressions, for instance, studies have suggested that there appears to be a predictable relationship between emotions such as happiness, sadness, anger, or fear, and distinctive movements of facial muscles.[5] And gestures, such as the head nodding which we associate with "yes" and "no," also seem to be universal, though their precise meanings may not be. To a large extent these shared patterns are the result of physiological and cognitive capacities common to all humans.

Beyond the universal characteristics of nonverbal and verbal code systems, are a great many more patterns that are unique to a particular region, occupational or cultural group, or individual.

Relationship to Other Data Sources

Any of the various types of verbal or nonverbal behaviors—language, paralanguage, appearance, action, gestures, facial expressions, or others— may bear any one of several relationships to one another. First, they may be duplicative of one another, as when a person says "Sit down," and points downward to a chair. They can also be *complementary* such as when an individual smiles and says, "Come in, I'm glad to see you." Verbal and nonverbal cues may also be sources of potentially *contradictory* data as would be the case if one were told how interested another person was in what was being said, while the "listener" stared across the room at a member of the opposite sex.[6]

Types of Nonverbal Cues

In this chapter we will focus our discussion on five general categories of nonverbal cues: *appearance, action, touch, the use of space,* and *the use of time.* The discussion of whether and how verbal and nonverbal data become information of significance to the others' behavior we will leave for the next chapter.

Appearance

It is often said that "beauty is only skin-deep." While this is not wholly accurate, there is little doubt that, particularly when other sources of information are lacking, "surface-level" data play an important role in human communication.

Particularly in the formation of initial impressions, appearance is probably the single most important information source. Perhaps the most dramatic evidence as to the importance of appearance comes from studies of dating preferences, from which it has been determined that attractiveness was more important than such factors as religion, race, self-esteem, academic achievement, aptitude, personality, or popularity, in determining how well partners would like one another.[7] Evidence from other studies suggests that physical attractiveness is not only important to dating preferences, but also is often a predictor of how successful, popular, sociable, sexually attractive, persuasive, and even how happy people are.[8] A number of factors contribute to appearance, among them one's *face, eyes, physique, dress,* and *adornment.*

Face and Eyes

When we think of a person's face, we generally think of it as a whole, rather than in terms of the distinctive features of which it is composed:

> The human face comes in many sizes and shapes. There are triangular, square, and round faces; foreheads may be high and wide, high and narrow, low and wide, low and narrow, protruding or sunken; the complexion of a

face may be light, dark, coarse, smooth, wrinkled, or blemished; eyes may be balanced, close, far apart, recessed or buldging; noses can be short, long, flat, crooked, "humpbacked," a "bag," or a "ski slope"; mouths may be large and small with thin or thick lips; ears, too, may be large or small, short or long; and can bulge or appear sunken."[9]

A *face* is a system. The forehead, eyes, nose, ears, lips, chin and mouth are interrelated components which collectively serve functions that no part alone could. Beyond their significance in contributing to one's overall appearance, facial expressions serve as data sources in their own right, providing probably the best source of information as to an individual's emotional state—happiness, fear, surprise, sadness, anger, disgust-contempt, and interest.[10] Our feelings are often, as the adage suggests,

TABLE 6.1 Nonverbal Message Sources

Appearance

- Face
- Eye Gaze
- Pupil Dilation
- Dress
- Adornment
- Badges
- Physique

Actions

- Gestures
  - Baton Signals
  - Guide Signs
  - Yes-no Signals
  - Greetings and Salutation Displays
  - Tie Signs
  - Isolation Gestures
  - Preening Gestures

Touch

Space

- Personal Space
- The Physical Environment

Time

- Timing
- Timeliness

TABLE 6.2 Specific Nonverbal Behaviors That Contribute to Attractiveness Beyond Dress and General Appearance

Warm Behaviors	Cold Behaviors
Looks into eyes	Gives a cold stare
Touches hand	Sneers
Moves toward individual	Gives a fake yawn
Smiles frequently	Frowns
Works eyes from head to toes	Moves away
Has a happy face	Looks at the ceiling
Smiles with mouth open	Picks teeth
Grins	Shakes head negatively
Sits directly facing individual	Cleans fingernails
Nods head affirmatively	Looks away
Puckers lips	Pouts
Licks lips	Chain-smokes
Raises eyebrows	Cracks fingers
Has eyes wide open	Looks around the room
Uses expressive hand gestures while speaking	Picks hands
Gives fast glances	Plays with hair
Stretches	Smells hair

SOURCE: G. L. Clore, N. H. Wiggins, and S. Itkin, "Judging Attraction from Nonverbal Behavior: The Gain Phenomenon," *Journal of Consulting and Clinical Psychology* **43** (1975), pp. 491–497. Copyright © 1975 by the American Psychological Association. Adapted by permission of the author.

"written all over our faces." Researchers believe that the role of the face in relation to emotion is common to all humans. Describing what has been termed a "neurocultural theory of facial expression," Paul Ekman explains: "What is universal in facial expressions of emotion is the particular set of facial muscular movements when a given emotion is elicited."[11] The specific events and circumstances that trigger various emotions, vary from one individual and culture to another.[12] The emotions evoked by ceremonies accompanying death, for instance, may vary greatly from one person to another depending upon the individual's personality and the way the event is viewed in the given culture.

The customs and rules guiding the display of particular emotions also may vary from person-to-person, and culture-to-culture. For any emotion, exaggeration, understatement, and masking (deception), may occur. An individual might exaggerate or mask an emotion, for example, when an employer announces that he or she will receive a "healthy raise"—but the amount turns out to be one-third that expected by the employee.[13]

FIGURE 6.1

Eye Gaze

Probably the most impactful elements of the face in terms of communication are the eyes.

As Ellsworth notes:

> ...Unlike many nonverbal behaviors having a potential cue-value which is rarely realized, such as foot movements,...subtle facial or postural changes, a direct gaze has a high probability of being noticed. For a behavior that involves no noise and little movement, it has a remarkable capacity to draw attention to itself even at a distance...."[14]

As children, we have heard many times that "it's not polite to stare." And as adults there are frequent reminders of the "rule." If one stops at a traffic light, and the person in the next car looks interesting, we may "steal a glance," but are careful not to appear to stare. Similarly, while waiting in line at a grocery store, or sitting in a restaurant or other public place, one may casually glance at the persons around, but generally must try at the same time to appear as though he or she is not actually noticing the other person or persons at all.

Actually, the rule that we apply as adults is, "It's not polite to stare at people whom you don't know very well, unless you can do so without having them notice you." When and if you are noticed, it is necessary to pretend not to have been looking, unless the intent is to violate the other's expectations.

The "rules" for eye contact with friends and acquaintances are quite different from those for strangers. Among close friends, for instance, staring is not only acceptable, but may even be expected. When conversing verbally with even a casual acquaintance, some degree of mutual eye contact is regarded as essential. In such circumstances, "looking" may help in grasping the ideas being discussed and is often taken as an indication of interest and attention. Among intimate friends and lovers, prolonged glances may be exchanged periodically even when no accompanying words are spoken.

There are a number of situations where eye glances are "optional." For instance, when a speaker asks a question of a large audience, each member of the group may choose to engage or avoid the glance of the speaker. The likelihood of being called on to answer the question is considerably greater if one looks at the speaker than if one looks away. In such a situation, *nonverbal* engagement is read as an expression of interest and as a desire and willingness for *verbal* engagement. Other situations where eye contact is "optional" include cocktail parties, bars, airplanes, trains, and many work situations, where one may choose to engage the looks of others or systematically avoid them.

As significant as eye behavior is to human communication, most of us are relatively unsophisticated in our awareness of eye behaviors and ability to characterize them with any precision. Among those who study this facet on nonverbal behavior, a number of terms have been advanced which assist in description. A distinction can be drawn, for instance, between *face contact* and *eye contact* (or *eye gaze*), the former referring to looking at another person's face, the latter at another's eyes. *Mutual gaze* refers to reciprocal gazing by two individuals at one another's face. *One-sided gaze* describes the circumstance where one person looks at another, but the behavior is not reciprocated. *Gaze avoidance* refers to actively avoiding another's eye gaze, while *gaze omission* describes the situation where one individual fails to look at another, but without the intention of doing so.[15]

At what and whom we look, for how long, under what circumstances, whether the gaze is one-sided or mutual, whether we are engaged in gaze omission or gaze avoidance provide the basis for inferences as to one's interests, focus of attention, intentions, and even attitudes. Looking may be a matter of observing, orienting, inspecting, concealing, avoiding, or searching for pacification.[16]

Researchers have demonstrated that a primary function of eye gaze or the lack thereof, is to regulate interaction. Eye contact serves as a signal of readiness to interact, and the absence of such contact, whether intended or accidental, tends to reduce the likelihood of such interaction.[17] Other studies suggest that eye gaze also plays an important role in the personal attraction. Generally speaking, positive feelings toward an individual and high degree of eye contact go together. Perhaps for this reason, we often assume that persons who look our way are attracted to us. Other studies indicate, further, that individuals who engage in high levels of eye gaze are typically seen as more influential and effective in their dealings than others.

FIGURE 6.2 In addition to contributing to over-all appearance, one's face and hair provide the basis for inferences as to one's emotional state, age, mood, interest level, personality, and reaction to events and people.

A number of factors have been shown in research to be related to the extent of eye gaze, including distance, physical characteristics, personality, topic, situation, and cultural background.[18] Based on this research, one can predict that, generally, more eye contact will occur when one is physically distant from others, when the topic being discussed is impersonal, and when there is a high degree of interest in the other person's reactions. Greater eye contact also occurs when one is trying to dominate or influence others, comes from a culture which emphasizes eye contact during conversation, is generally outgoing, striving to be included, listening rather than talking, or when one is dependent on the other person.[19]

One would expect less gazing between persons who are physically close, when intimate topics are being discussed, when there are other relevant objects of people nearby, or when one is not particularly interested in another's reactions or is embarrassed. Similarly if an individual is submissive, shy, sad, ashamed, attempting to hide something, or of higher status than the person with whom he or she is talking, less eye contact is likely.[20] Obviously, these are generalities which may not apply in a given circumstance.

Pupil Dilation

The pupils of the eye can also serve as sources of data as to one's interest or attraction. As one looks at people or objects that are seen as appealing, the pupils tend to enlarge. And, in at least some experimental settings, there is evidence that pupil size can be a factor in judgments of a person's attractiveness. In these studies, pictures of females with enlarged pupils were consistently rated as more attractive by males than were those of women with small pupils.[21] It is also interesting to note, in this regard, that the drug Belladonna (meaning literally, "beautiful woman") has a tradition of use by women as a cosmetic to increase the size of their pupils with the thought that in so doing they would enhance their attractiveness.

The extent to which pupil size is actually a useful source of information, is still a question. Particularly in a culture such as ours, in which we stand so far apart during most conversations, it is difficult to discern the size of another person's pupils, even when making an effort to do so. In Middle Eastern cultures, however, where the standard distance separating people during conversations is much smaller, information based on pupil size is more usable. Some authors have noted in this connection that sunglasses are often worn by persons in these cultures as a means of concealing pupil size.[22]

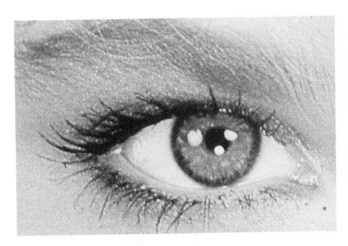

FIGURE 6.3 Research suggests that when one looks at an individual or object that is of interest or seen as attractive, the viewer's pupils dilate. Baby pictures shown to single women, married but childless women, and mothers resulted in pupil dilation. The same pictures shown to single men and married but childless men resulted in pupil constriction. Fathers viewing the picture experienced pupil dilation.

SOURCE: H. Hess, *The Tell-Tale Eye* (New York: Van Nostrand Reinhold, 1975) and Desmond Morris, *Manwatching* (New York: Abrams, 1977).

FIGURE 6.4 In addition to providing a source of basic information as to sex, age, occupation, and group affiliation, dress also often plays a critical role in the first impressions.

Dress and Adornment

Dress fulfills a number of functions for us as humans including decoration, physical and psychological protection, sexual attraction, self-assertion, self-denial, concealment, group identification, and display of status or role.[23] Cosmetics, jewelry, eyeglasses, tatoos, hair pieces, false eyelashes, and perms serve many of these same ends, as do objects one carries such as a purse, radio, newspaper, or briefcase.

Because of their many functions, dress and adornment are noteworthy and often utilized as the basis for judgments as to gender, age, personality, approachability, financial well-being, class, tastes, values, and cultural background

Dress may also provide the data from which inferences can be drawn relative to more basic facets of our personalities. It has been suggested by some researchers, for instance, that individuals who show particular interest in their dress are often conventional, compliant, persistent, suspicious, and insecure.[24] Persons who were particularly concerned with economy in dress were found to be responsible, efficient, precise, and intelligent. Others who dressed in close conformity with current styles were generally sociable, traditional, and submissive.

Badges of various kinds also provide the basis for information as to the identity, status, or affiliations of an individual. Often one's dress serves as an *occupational badge*, as is generally the case with police officers, nurses, prostitutes, doctors, priests, military personnel, and members of particular atheltic teams. In such instances, the "costume" each wears is designed, standardized, and used with the goal of making one's occupation easy to determine. The "*uniforms*" of college students, businessmen, factory

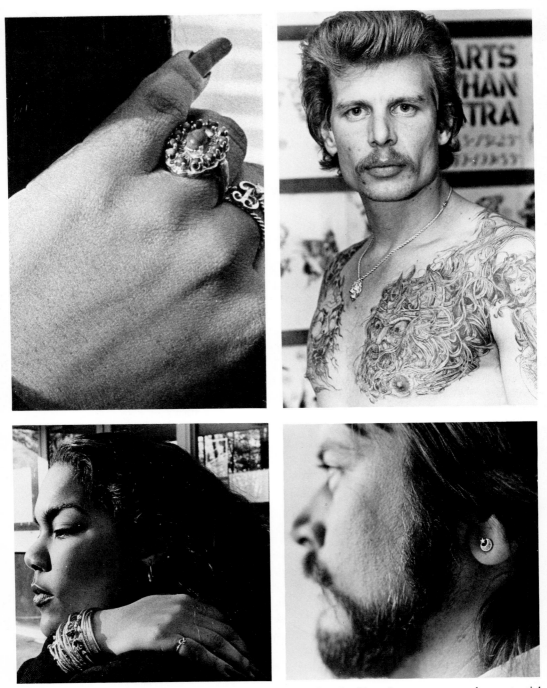

FIGURE 6.5 Jewelry, hair, beards, make-up, and other bodily adornments are also potential information sources.

workers, or housewives may serve much the same function, though they are not necessarily intended to do so.

Other badges are hats, shirts, sweatshirts, or jackets which bear the name of an individual, school, employer, manufacturer, favorite auto or musical performer. Specialized jewelry such as a wedding or engagement ring or a necklace with a letter, name, or religious symbol may also serve to provide information as to one's identity, status, group, or organizational affiliation.

One's car and home can provide additional data from which others draw inferences as to financial resources, aesthetic preferences, status, or occupational category. In much the same way, a club membership, a particular credit card, briefcase, fraternity or sorority pin, or a business card may also serve as cues to which people react as they form impressions based on one's appearance.

Physique

An additional factor that contributes to appearance is *physique*. Studies have suggested, for example, that inferences are often drawn about personality based on body shape and size. Persons who appear to be "soft," "round," and overweight may be assumed to be affable, affectionate, calm, cheerful, complacent, extroverted, forgiving, kind, soft-hearted, and warm. Persons who appear to be muscular, bony, and athletic-looking are often stereotyped as being active, argumentative, assertive, competitive, confident, dominant, hot-tempered, optimistic, reckless, and noncomforming. And persons who are tall and thin in appearance are often assumed to be aloof, anxious, awkward, cautious, cool, introspective, meticulous, sensitive, shy, and conforming.[25]

One's height alone may also provide the basis for stereotyping. For males in our culture, greater height is generally associated with positive qualities, while, beyond a certain point, the opposite is the case for females. Interestingly, the taller of the two candidates for president has been the consistent winner since 1900, with the exception of Jimmy Carter who is 5'9".[26]

Actions

It has often been said that "actions speak louder than words." What we do—and don't do—may have much more significance to others than what we say or how we appear. Based largely on an individual's collective actions in various situations, others decide what the person is like, how he or she is likely to react to future situations, whether he or she is trustworthy, courageous, compassionate, charitable, and so on. If one runs from a physical or symbolic confrontation, lets others down when entrusted with a responsibility, or gives willingly in a time of need, these actions may have more impact than anything one might say. And, in group contexts, actions such as strikes, demonstrations, job actions, picketing, marches, walkouts, protests, even wars, often dramatize a point far more forcefully than words.

TABLE 6.3 Stages in Emotional Development and Nonverbal Expression

Stage	Age	Characteristics	Sample Emotions
1	to 3 mos.	Wild, irregular, jerky movements of the entire body.	excitement, distress
2	3–5 mos.	Regular, rhythmic movements of the entire body.	anger, delight
3	5–14 mos.	Making faces, turning the head and poking: specific movements.	affection, fear, elation
4	14–24 mos.	Contact movements (pokes, hits, caresses) to others.	affection for child, affection for adult, jealousy, joy

SOURCE: Barbara S. Wood, *Children and Communication* (Englewood Cliffs, N.J.: Prentice-Hall, 1976), p. 197, adapted from "Emotional Development in Early Infancy," *Child Development*, 1932, 3. By permission of Prentice-Hall.

Gestures

Gestures—movement of body, head, arms legs, or feet—also play an important role in human communication. Studies suggest that we progress in our capacity for gesturing through four basic stages.[27] In the first stage, from birth to three months, irregular, jerky movements of the entire body indicate excitement and distress. In the next stage, three to five months, the infant is able to move the entire body more rhythmically, in patterns associated with anger and delight. In the third stage, five to fourteen months, children develop specialized gestures such as making faces, turning the head, and poking. Between the ages of fourteen and twenty-four months, the child is able to express affection for particular people, as well as joy and jealousy, through contact movements such as poking, hitting, and caressing.

Gestures, as well as other cues, may either be *purposeful*—messages which are intended to achieve a particular purpose—or *incidental* and *unintended*. Some gestures are used as substitutes and complements for language, such as when, upon being asked a question, we shake our head back and forth while saying "no." In other instances we use gestures in place of words. A shrug of the shoulders, for instance, is used to indicate confusion or uncertainty, a frown and slow horizontal back-and-forth motion of the head to indicate frustration or annoyance, or the circle sign made by the thumb and forefinger to mean "OK."

Inherited, Discovered, Imitated and Trained Actions

Desmond Morris, an anthropologist who has written a good deal in this area, suggests that gestures are acquired through *inheritance, discovery, imitation,* and *training.*[28] Examples of actions which are inborn include the sucking response of the baby, the use of body contact gestures as a part of courtship,

FIGURE 6.6 Folding one's arms can be considered a *discovered action*. There are no significant differences from one culture to another as to how individuals cross their arms, but there are differences between persons. These differences occur because we "discover" the action rather than learning it from others. Once one has arrived at a way of crossing his or her arms, it becomes very natural, and it is only with some difficulty and conscious attention that it can be done in another way.

SOURCE: Desmond Morris, *Manwatching* (New York: Abrams, 1977).

and the pattern of greeting between individuals when coming together or parting company.

Some gestures we discover as we identify the limitations and capabilities of our bodies. The way people cross their arms is an example. There is little variation from one culture to another, but there are differences between individuals within any one culture. And each individual tends to be fairly consistent over time. Some of us fold left hand over right, and others right over left. Regardless of which we have become accustomed to, it is difficult to reverse the pattern without considerable effort.[29]

A good many of our gestures we acquire unknowlingly from the people around us as we grow up. The typical handshake, for instance, is acquired through imitation, as are many other greeting forms and cultural and subcultural mannerisms.

Actions like winking, playing tennis, jumping on one foot, whistling, or walking on one's hands, require active training in order to master. The wink, for example, taken so much for granted by the adult, is a formidable challenge for a child. Like other trained actions, substantial observation and systematic effort is required for mastery.

Origins of Gestures

It is interesting to speculate as to the origins of human gestures. Some gestures displayed by adults seem to be carried over from our activities as children. Smoking, pencil chewing, nail-biting, candy and gum chewing, and "nervous eating" may well have their roots in our early feeding experiences, when oral satisfaction was associated with safety and security.

Other gestures may have even more ancient origins. Kissing and erotic gestures of the tongue associated with lovemaking may have their roots in the feeding habits of our ancestors. At early points in human history, mothers apparently fed their young by chewing food in their mouths first and then passing the food to their child's mouth in a gesture which very much resembles the tongue-kissing of adult lovers today.[30]

Another gesture, the horizontal head shaking which we use to say "no," may well have its origins in the infant's gesture indicating he or she wants no more milk from the mother's breast, bottle, or spoon.[31]

Types of Gestures

There are many ways of classifying gestures. Morris, who provides what is perhaps the most exhaustive listing, includes the following:[32]

Baton Signals and Guide Signs One sort of gesture, the baton signal, is used to underscore or emphasize a particular point being made verbally. Examples of baton signals include a downward clipping motion of the hand, a forward jabbing movement of the fingers and hand, and the raised forefinger. Another similar kind of gesture is the *guide sign,* by means of which we indicate directions to others, as when we point, direct, or beckon another person nonverbally.

Yes-No Signals *Yes-no Signals* are another category of gesture. Movements of the head are the primary means for creating these signals. While many gestures are unique to one or several cultures, the vertical, "yes" head nod appears to be universal. Even though we might assume that the meaning of the "yes" nod is fairly specific, further thought reminds us that there a number of variations:

> The Acknowledging Nod: "Yes, I am still listening."
> The Encouraging Nod: "Yes, how fascinating."
> The Understanding Nod: "Yes, I see what you mean."
> The Agreeing Nod: "Yes, I will."
> The Factual Nod: "Yes, that is correct."[33]

The "no" gesture, of course, consists of a horizontal movement of the

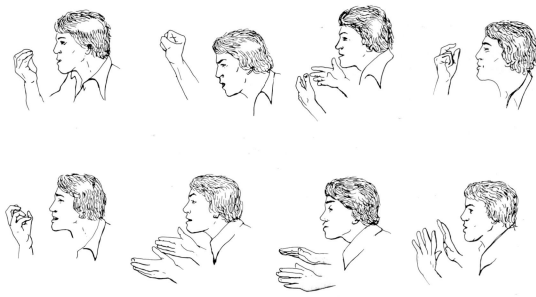

FIGURE 6.7 Baton gestures.

SOURCE: Desmond Morris, *Manwatching* (New York: Abrams, 1977).

FIGURE 6.8 A circle sign made with the thumb and forefinger illustrates how the significance of a single gesture can very substantially from one culture to another. In England and North America, the sign means, "okay." For the French, it signifies "okay" when the gesture is made while smiling. If it is accompanied by a frown, it is taken to mean "worthless" or "zero." In Japan, the same sign is often used as a sign for "money."

SOURCE: Desmond Morris, *Manwatching* (New York: Abrams, 1977).

head. In many parts of the world a side-to-side swaying of the head is also used to say "maybe yes, maybe no." In addition to the head, the hand and fingers can also be used to express yes-no signals. For instance, in our North American culture a shaking of the forefinger from side to side is a way of saying "no."

Greetings and Salutation Displays Greetings or salutations are another kind of gesture. The most familiar greeting forms are the handshake, embrace, and kiss by which we signal our pleasure at someone's arrival or the significance of their departure.

One can differentiate several stages in the greeting or salutation process. The first phase is the *inconvenience display:*

> To show the strength of our friendliness, we 'put ourselves out' to varying degrees. We demonstrate that we are taking the trouble. For both host and guest, this may mean 'dressing up.' For the guest it may mean a long journey. For the host it entails a bodily shift from the centre of his home territory. The stronger the greeting, the greater the inconvenience. The Head of State drives to the airport to meet the important arrival. The brother drives to the airport to greet his sister returning from abroad. This is the maximum form of bodily displacement that a host can offer. From this extreme there is a declining scale of inconvenience, as the distance travelled by the host decreases. He may only go as far as the local station or bus depot. Or he may move no farther than his front drive, emerging from his front door after watching through the window for the moment of arrival. Or, he may allow a child or servant to answer the door and remain in the room, the very centre of his territory, awaiting the guest who is then ushered into his presence. The minimal inconvenience display he can offer is to stand up when the guest enters the room, displacing himself vertically but not horizontally.[34]

The second stage is *the distant display*. From the moment the guest and host see each other, they indicate the other's presence by several other gestures including a smile, eyebrow flash, head tilt, wave, and sometimes an outstretching of arms indicating an upcoming embrace. As the two individuals approach one another, they will signify pleasure at the other's presence by hugging, squeezing, patting, kissing, or pressing their cheeks together, coupled often by extended eye contact, laughing, smiling, sometimes even crying. The particular greeting used depends upon a number of factors including the nature of the relationship, the situation in which they are meeting one another, the length of time that has past since they have seen one another, and the extent of change in either person's status since last they were together.

Tie Signs The *bonding, or tie sign* is yet another category of gesture. Through tie signs individuals indicate that they are in a relationship. In much the same way that indications such as wedding rings, fraternity pins, or matching clothing suggest the existence of a relationship between two or more persons, certain gestures serve the same purpose. Handholds, linked arms, a single drink shared by two people, close physical proximity when sitting or walking, and the simultaneous sharing of objects of all sorts provide cues about the individuals and the nature of their relationship.

Isolation Gestures Other sorts of common gestures are the body positionings such as crossing arms or legs, through which we conceal or block portions of the body from view. In some instances, *isolating gestures* may serve as intentional messages, though more often they are less purposeful. These and other gestures, including hugging oneself, supporting the chin or cheek with an arm, or touching one's mouth, may signal our discomfort or anxiety, even though we are unaware of these feelings.[35]

Other Gestures Gestures also play a major role in courtship, mating, and sexual affairs, with humans as with other animals. In addition to handholding, kissing, petting, and forms of sexual contact, other gestures, often termed *preening behavior* also come into play. For instance, stroking one's hair, adjusting makeup or clothing in the mirror, leaving buttons open, or stroking one's own arms or legs can also play a role in sexual attraction.[36]

In religion also gestures have significant functions. Kneeling, standing at appropriate times, bowing, and folding one's hands in prayer are symbolic means through which one participates in the central rituals of any faith.

Touch

When a gesture is extended to the point where physical contact is involved, tactile data are created. For humans the significance of tactile data begins well before birth, in the prenatal contact between mother and infant. From the first moments of life, touch is the primary means through which child and

FIGURE 6.9 Even when no words are spoken, nonverbal sources often provide clues as to who "goes with" whom in any given situation.

FIGURE 6.10

parents relate to one another. Through this tactile mode, feeding takes place and affection is expressed.

Through the early years, touch continues to be the central means for expressions of warmth, caring, and concern between family members and close friends. Beginning with the preschool and elementary years, physical contact also takes on a role in play, and especially sports and fighting among boys in our culture. We also learn the significance of tactile messages in greeting rituals such as the handshake, hug, and kiss during this period. In the teen-age and preadult years touching takes on increasing significance as a way of expressing warmth, love, and intimacy.

Tactile messages are also important among members of the same sex. Especially among males, athletic endeavors provide a primary medium for physical contact, both in the actual activity of the sport, and in the pats and slaps of assurance and encouragement among players and coaches. For some, the role of touch in aggression continues during this period. Among adults, most physical contact is associated with informal greetings and gestures of departure between friends and colleagues, expressions of intimacy and sexual activities, and expressions of hostility and aggression.

Levels of contact and comfort with touching vary to some extent from one culture to another. In some Asian or African cultures, for example, male friends may walk down the street hand-in-hand as they talk. In Middle Eastern cultures, casual acquaintances stand so close together when talking that North Americans assume they are intimates. By comparison, ours is a low-contact culture. In general, North Americans go to great lengths to avoid touching whenever possible. In an elevator or crowded shopping mall, for instance, we generally touch strangers only when absolutely necessary and then often with discomfort.

Because tactile data are often associated with aggression or sexual intimacy, touch is a very impactful communication mode. Depending upon the circumstance, persons involved, and the culture, touch may lead us to react with considerably more intensity than we would to verbal or other nonverbal data.

Touching or grabbing another person without his or her consent is regarded in most societies as considerably more disturbing than verbal abuse, name calling, obscene gestures, or other verbal violations of an individual.

The Use of Space

To some extent the intensity of tactile messages occurs because we have well-defined expectations as to how much personal space we will have around us. When our *personal space*, the *portable territory* we carry with us from place to place, is invaded, we respond. Being bumped unnecessarily on an elevator, having a beach towel walked across or practically shared by a stranger, or being unnecessarily crowded while shopping generally cause us discomfort for this reason. Our response is to readjust our own position to regain the amount of space we think we need. Research suggests that in some instances the extreme violation of personal space over a time, such as occurs in

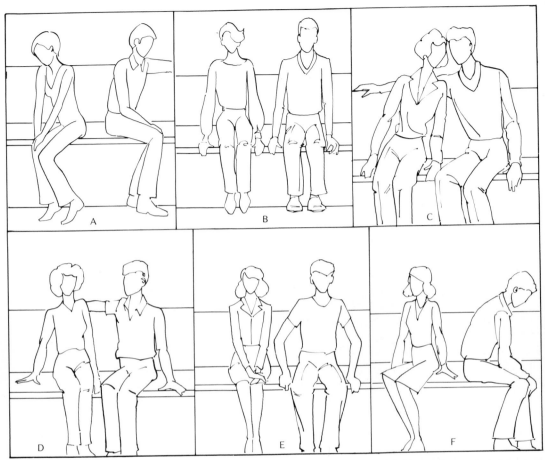

FIGURE 6.11 Body positioning and the way space is used often serve as significant factors in inferences as to the nature, duration, and intensity of a relationship between individuals.

hysterical crowds and very high density neighborhoods, can lead to extreme reactions, frustration, and even aggression.

Edward Hall has done much to broaden our understanding of the way space is used during face-to-face conversations.[37] Hall found that in public setting, the space between individuals ranges from twelve feet to the limits of visibility. Informal and business conversations take place with individuals between four and twelve feet apart, and one and a half to four feet separate persons engaged in casual-personal discussions. For intimate conversations and relations space between individuals varies between zero and eighteen inches. Fluctuations with each category depend upon a number of factors. The culture in which the conversation takes place, the ages of the individuals, topic being discussed, setting, nature of the relationship, attitudes and feelings of the individuals, and so on.[38]

The use of space and position is also important in seating. In a group situation, for instance, certain positions are more often associated with high levels of activity and leadership than others. Being in front of a group, for instance, separated more from the group as a whole than are any of the individual members from one another, affords the isolated individual a position of distance and authority. Examples are a teacher in front of a class, a judge in front of the court, the speaker and an audience, the religious leader at the front of the church, and so on.

Position within a large room—a classroom, for example—can also have an influence on verbal behavior. In typical classes over fifty per cent of the comments are initiated by class members located in the front and center positions within the room. For many individuals, position is the most influential factor explaining their participation.[39] In smaller groups, particularly where furniture is involved, the head of the table is traditionally a position of leadership, honor, respect, and power.

In a conference room, a similar association often attends to the individual sitting at the head. Some researchers have found, for instance, that in experimental jury deliberations, the person sitting at the head of the table was chosen much more often as leader than persons in other positions.[40] Our positions relative to others, whether in silence or active conversation,

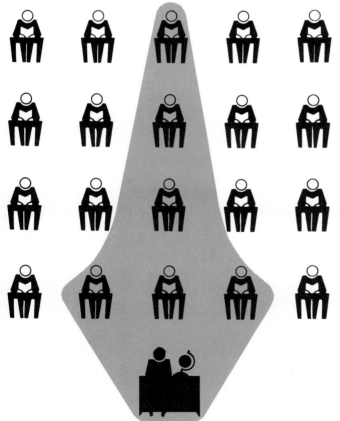

FIGURE 6.12 Studies suggest that classroom participation is highest in the front and center sections of a room. Researchers studying interaction in grades one, six, and eleven found that sixty-three percent of the contributions came from students located in only three positions, one behind another, down the center of the classroom.

SOURCE: Mark L. Knapp, *Essentials of Nonverbal Communication*. Adapted from R.S. Adams and B. Biddle, *Realities of Teaching: Explorations with Video Tape* (New York: Holt, Rinehart, Winston, 1970). Copyright © 1980, Holt, Rinehart, Winston. By permission.

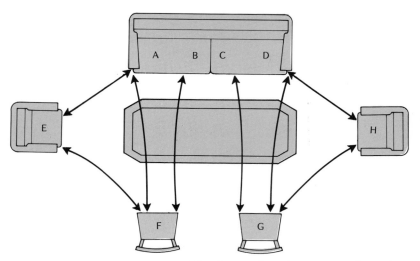

FIGURE 6.13 The arrangement of furniture and seating patterns play an important role in levels and direction of conversation. All other things being equal, the pairs marked by arrows would engage in the most frequent conversation. Those persons seated on the couch would be least likely to engage in interaction.

SOURCE: Albert Mehrabian, *Public Places and Private Spaces: The Psychology of Work, Play, and Living Environments* Copyright © 1976 by Basic Books, Inc. By permission.

standing or sitting, can be a significant factor in shaping communication and in contributing to others impressions of us and ours of them.

The Physical Environment

The use of space in our more permanent physical environment is also important to human communication. Though there are many aspects of the physical environment over which we have no direct control, other elements are directly shaped by human activity. Our buildings, furniture, decor, lighting, and color schemes are the result of human decision-making. In addition to providing shelter and housing, and facilitating our various human activities, the manmade elements of our physical environment also serve a number of informational functions—some intentionally, many by accident.

Whether one thinks of the arrangement of furniture and the selection of wall hangings in one's own apartment, the design and furnishing of an elegant restaurant, the layout of an outdoor mall or park, or the architecture of a massive airport complex, all have much in common in terms of communication.

Use Each environment with its furniture, decor, and color serves as a source of data that may have an impact on the people present. Some of the information is "designed-in" by the architect or designer to impact upon the way the environment or its parts are used. Sidewalks in a park, for example, direct our movement as we walk about. Similarly, chairs used by some for

Conversation	63%	17%	20%
Cooperation	83	7	10
Co-action	13	36	51
Competition	12	25	63

Conversation	42%	46%	11%	0%	1%	0%
Cooperation	19	25	51	0	5	0
Co-action	3	32	7	13	43	3
Competition	7	41	8	18	20	5

FIGURE 6.14 In studies of relationships and seating preference, Robert Sommer asked students to indicate how they would prefer to situate themselves for each of the following situations:

(1) *Conversation:* Casual discussions for a few moments before class.
(2) *Cooperation:* Sitting and studying together for a common exam.
(3) *Co-action:* Sitting and studying for different exams.
(4) *Competition:* Competing to see which person would be first to solve a series of puzzles.
Students were asked to indicate their preferences for round and rectangular tables, each with six possible seating positions. The results of the studies are shown under the diagrams.

SOURCE: Robert Sommer, "Further Studies of Small Group Ecology," *Sociometry,* **28,** 1965, pp. 337–348, and Mark Knapp, *Essentials of Nonverbal Communication* (New York: Holt, Rinehart, Winston, 1980), pp. 85–90.

fast food restaurants that are designed to be comfortable for only a short period of time and may well influence our decisions about how long to remain in the environment.

Symbolic Value Structures and their contents, by virtue of their size, shape, use of space, and decor, may also have symbolic significance for us. Religious buildings and their contents, for example, are often symbolic by their very nature. Large rooms with high ceilings, stained-glass windows, dimly-lit interiors, deep colors, and sacred books and objects, each have information value to those who use the environment.

The symbolic properties of houses of worship have their parallels in shopping malls, parks, restaurants, as well as in the structure and decor of homes and apartments. The differences, for instance, between dining in a candlelit room with elegantly upholstered armchairs and soft dinner music

FIGURE 6.15 The objects of our physical environment also serve as nonverbal information sources, providing clues as to how they are to be understood, related to, and whether and how they are to be used.

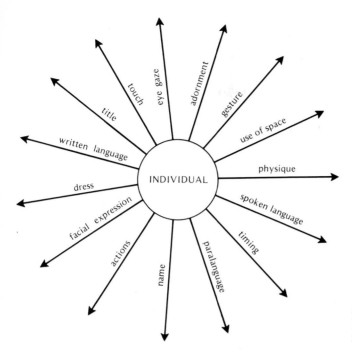

FIGURE 6.16 Every facet of our behavior is a potential source of information to those around us.

compared to the experience of having dinner at the counter of a truck stop are quite substantial.

Interaction Environments may also provide the basis for information which regulates—encourages or discourages—interaction. The study carrels of the library, for example, serve to separate and isolate their users, discouraging interaction, while a business office with no private offices or partitions encourages interchange. In a similar sense, a classroom with permanently attached chairs contributes to "one-way" message flow. Robert Sommer provides the following lucid description of the typical classroom and its impact.

The American classroom is dominated by what has been called the rule of two-thirds—two-thirds of the time someone is talking and two-thirds of the time it is the teacher, and two-thirds of the time that the teacher is talking, she is lecturing, giving directions or criticizing behavior. Movement in and out of classrooms and the school building itself is rigidly controlled. Everywhere one looks there are "lines"—generally straight lines that bend around corners before entering the auditorium, the cafeteria, or the shop.... The straight rows tell the student to look ahead and ignore everyone except the teacher, the students are jammed so tightly together that psychological escape, much less physical separation, is impossible. The teacher has 50 times more free space than the students with the mobility to move about. He writes important messages on the blackboard with his back to his students. The august figure can rise and walk among the lowly who lack the authority even to stand without explicit permission. Teacher and children may share the same classroom but they see it differently. From a student's eye level, the world is cluttered, disorganized, full of people's shoulders, heads, and body movements. His world at ground level is colder than the teacher's world. She looms over the scene like a helicopter swooping down to ridicule or punish any wrongdoer.[41]

The Use of Time

The use of *time* and *timing* is often another critical factor in communication. In fact, the reactions to our words and deeds generally depends far more on *when* we speak or act, than upon the content of the action.

Timing

It comes as no surprise to anyone who has ever asked for a raise or to borrow the family car that there are certain "times" which are better than others for presenting ideas or suggestions. The decisions people make—intentionally as well as accidentally—about when to speak and when to be silent, when they have said too much and when too little, when to "speak their piece" and when to "keep it to themselves" are among the most critical decisions people make relative to communication. The way time is shared within conversations can also be significant to communication. Too little talking can be read as disinterest, shyness, or boredom, while too much can be construed as aggressiveness, self-assuredness, presumptuousness, over-confidence, or rudeness.

Timeliness

Such adages as "time is money," "never put off until tomorrow what you can do today," "a stitch in time saves nine," and "the sooner the better" reflect the common North American view that time is a precious commodity. The sooner we can get something done, the less time we "waste."

Our "time-is-money" philosophy shows up in a great many of our activities. We like to drive as fast as we legally can, so we'll get where we're going quicker. When we have an appointment with someone, we like to get business transacted in as little time as possible, so we can get on to the next task. We want to leave work "on time" whenever possible to hurry home. En route every red light, wait at a pedestrian crossing, or slow-moving car is an annoyance as we rush home quickly, so that we can relax and enjoy our "leisure time." We find ourselves rushing to meet deadlines, keep appointments, avoid waste, and increase productivity.

Given the significance of *time* in our daily lives, it is not surprising that our use of it can have an important impact on behavior. Being "early" or "late" is data. The information provided by this data varies depending on a number of factors, including the amount of time one is early or late, the purpose of the appointment, who called the meeting, the length of the relationship between the persons involved, the relative status of the parties involved, and the orientation toward time of each of the individuals.

Being fifteen minutes late for a visit with a heart specialist may lead to the cancellation of the appointment, while being fifteen minutes late for a cocktail party may result in being embarrassingly "early." Being late for a business meeting carries different consequences than being late for a social engagement. Arriving two hours late—even with a good reason—for a first date will probably be reacted to differently than being as late for a meeting with one's spouse. In such circumstances, timeliness and the use of time— being on-time, late, or early—may be as significant a source of information to other persons as whatever one does or says after arriving.

Data and Information

In this and the previous chapter we have seen how verbal and nonverbal behaviors play a pervasive role in human communication. In considering precisely how they function in this process, however, it is important to cautiously avoid falling victim to the transmission-oriented, source-and-message centered thinking, characteristic of Source →Message →Receiver models of communication.

The Individual↔Data↔Environment paradigm views the creation and use of *data* as a means through which individuals adapt to their environment. In this perspective, verbal and nonverbal behaviors are seen as contributing to the vast pool of data that comprise the symbolic environment which surrounds us at any point in time.

Some of these data are created intentionally with a specific purpose, while others are not. In either case, the presence of particular verbal or nonverbal messages provides little assurance that they will be noted or interpreted in a predictable way by the individuals within that environment. *Messages sent (intentionally, or not) do not equal messages received.* Verbal and nonverbal data are *sources* of information, but they are not, in and of themselves, *information*. Nor are these *data* transformed into *information* automatically. Rather, they become information when attended to, given significance, and used through an active and complex process which we will examine in Chapter 7.

Summary

Nonverbal codes play an important role in human communication. Compared to language, there has been a lack of awareness and attention to nonverbal cues and their impact on behavior. While the processing of verbal codes is thought to occur primarily in the left hemisphere, the right hemisphere is essential for processing information related to nonverbal activity—music, art, face recognition, and spatial relations, for instance.

There are a number of similarities between the two code systems: 1) both make possible the production of unintended, as well as purposeful data; 2) rules and patterns are necessary to nonverbal, as well as verbal, communication; and 3) verbal and nonverbal cues may duplicate, contradict, or complement one another.

Appearance, action, touch, and the use of space and time are five primary sources of nonverbal data. Appearance plays an important role in interpersonal relations, particularly in initial impressions. The face is a central aspect of one's appearance, providing the primary source of information as to one's emotional state.

The eyes are perhaps the most important component of the facial system in terms of communication. Based upon direction and duration of eye gaze, or the absence thereof, cues are provided that serve as the basis of inferences as to interest, readiness to interact, and attraction. Pupil size, dress and adornment, and physique are other facets of appearance that provide data that serve as potential information sources.

Actions in general, and gestures, in particular, are also potential sources of information. Among the most common types of gestures are: baton signals and guide signs, yes-no signals, greetings and salutation displays, tie signs, and isolation gestures.

Touch is another source of potentially impactful nonverbal information, playing a central role in greetings, the expression of intimacy, and aggression. The intensity of tactile data is suggestive of the importance of the role of *space* in communication. When our *personal space* is invaded in other than intimate relationships, discomfort often results. The significance of spatial cues is also apparent in seating patterns. Certain seating positions are often associated with high levels of participation and leadership. The nature and placement of elements in the physical environment—furniture, decor, lighting and color schemes—also generate data that are potentially significant to behavior. They often provide cues which influence their use, symbolic value, and interaction patterns.

Time, *timing*, and *timeliness* can also be important in the communication process. The way time is shared in conversations, for instance, can be a source of information that is even more impactful than the content of those discussions. Definitions of *timeliness*—being "late" or "early"—vary a good deal from situation to situation and culture to culture. Being "late" or "early" can itself be a potential information source.

Our verbal and nonverbal behaviors—some intentionally enacted— create a pool of data that are part of the environment that surrounds us. It is important to keep in mind the implications of the I↔D↔E perspective. The presence of verbal and nonverbal data in the environment provides no assurance that they will be attended to or of significance to individuals within it. *Messages sent* (intentionally or not) *do not equal messages received; data* becomes *information* when attended to, given significance, and used.

Notes

1. Robert E. Ornstein, *The Psychology of Consciousness* (San Francisco: Freeman, 1977), pp. 20–21. See more detailed discussion in Springer, Sally P., and George Deutsch. *Left Brain, Right Brain* (San Francisco: Freeman, 1981), and Norman Geschwind, "Specializations of the Human Brain." *Scientific American* (September, 1979), pp. 180–182.
2. Ibid.

3. Sally P. Springer and George Deutsch. *Left Brain, Right Brain,* (San Francisco: Freeman, 1981), p. 15.

4. Cf. Paul Ekman, Wallace Friesen, and P. Ellsworth. *Emotion in the Human Face: Guidelines for Research and an Integration of the Findings* (New York: Pergamon Press, 1972); Paul Ekman, "Universal and Cultural Differences in Facial Expressions of Emotions," in J.K. Cole, ed., *Nebraska Symposium on Motivation, 1971.* (Lincoln: University of Nebraska Press, 1972), pp. 207–283; and discussion of these and other related works in Robert G. Harper, Arthur N. Wiens, and Joseph D. Matarazzo, eds., *Nonverbal Communication: The State of the Art* (New York: Wiley, 1978), especially pp. 92–109.

5. Paul Ekman, op. cit. (1972), p. 212.

6. Paul Ekman and Wallace V. Friesen, "The Repertoire of Nonverbal Behavior: Categories, Origins, Usage, and Coding," *Semiotica,* 1: (1969), p. 53.

7. Mark L. Knapp, *Essentials of Nonverbal Communication* (New York: Holt, 1980), p. 100.

8. Ibid., pp. 98–99.

9. Ibid., pp. 161–162.

10. Paul Ekman and Wallace Friesen, op. cit., 1972, p. 50.

11. Paul Ekman, op. cit. (1972), p. 216

12. Cf. discussion in Robert G. Harper, et. al., pp. 98–105, and Paul Ekman, op. cit., 1972.

13. Cf. Robert G. Harper, et. al., op. cit., p. 101.

14. P.C. Ellsworth, "Direct Gaze as a Social Stimulus: The Example of Aggression." In P. Pliner, L. Krames, and T. Alloway, eds., *Nonverbal Communication of Aggression.* (New York: Plenum, 1975), pp. 5–6.

15. Robert G. Harper, op. cit., 1972, p. 173. Based on earlier work by von Cranach, 1971.

16. G. Nielsen, *Studies in Self-Confrontation* (Copenhagen, Denmark: Munksgaard), 1962.

17. An excellent summary of research findings on the functions and perceived impact of eye gaze is provided in Robert G. Harper et. al., op. cit., pp. 181–215.

18. See discussion in Mark L. Knapp, pp. 190–194.

19. Mark L. Knapp, op. cit., pp. 198–199.

20. Ibid., p. 199.

21. A discussion of research on pupil dilation by E.H. Hess, *The Tell-Tale Eye.* (New York, Van Nostrand Reinhold, 1975); and E.H. Hess, A.L. Seltzer, and J.M. Shlien, "Pupil Response of Hetero- and Homosexual Males to Pictures of Men and Women: A Pilot Study," *Journal of Abnormal Psychology,* 70: 587–590 (1965), is provided in Mark L. Knapp, op. cit., pp. 169–172 and Desmond Morris, *Manwatching,* (New York: Abrams, 1977), pp. 169–172.

22. Edward T. Hall "Learning the Arabs' Silent Language," *Psychology Today* (August 1979), pp. 47–48.

23. Mark L. Knapp, op. cit., p. 116.

24. See discussion of L. Aiken, "Relationship of Dress to Selected Measures

of Personality in Undergraduate Women," *Journal of Social Psychology*, **59**: 119–128 (1963), in Mark L. Knapp, op. cit., p. 118.

25. Useful overviews of research on physique and communication are provided by Judee K. Burgoon and Thomas Saine, *The Unspoken Dialogue*, (Boston: Houghton Mifflin, 1978), pp. 160–161, and Mark L. Knapp, op. cit., pp. 102–107.

26. Mark L. Knapp, op. cit., p. 107.

27. A discussion of research and writings on the development of nonverbal capabilities in children is provided in Barbara S. Wood, *Children and Communication* (Englewood Cliffs, NJ: Prentice-Hall, 1976), pp. 194–200.

28. Desmond Morris, op. cit., pp. 17–23. The term *imitated actions* is used to refer to what Morris has labeled *absorbed actions*.

29. Ibid., p. 16–17.

30. Ibid., p. 52.

31. Ibid., pp. 68–69.

32. The discussion of baton signals, yes-no signs, guide signs, salutation displays, tie signs, and isolation gestures, is based upon the work of Desmond Morris, op. cit., pp. 56–100.

33. Ibid., p. 68.

34. Ibid., p. 79.

35. Cf. Desmond Morris discussion of "barrier signals" pp. 133–135, and "auto contact behaviour" pp. 102–105.

36. Cf. Mark L. Knapp, op. cit., pp. 136–137.

37. See discussion of personal space provided in *The Silent Language*, Edward T. Hall, (New York: Doubleday, 1959), especially Chapter 10.

38. A useful discussion of the work of Edward Hall and others in the area of personal space is provided in Mark L. Knapp, op. cit., pp. 81–87, and Judee K. Burgoon and Thomas Saine, op. cit., pp. 92–97.

39. A summary of research on position and participation is provided in Mark L. Knapp, op. cit. pp. 67–68 and 87–90.

40. F. Strodtbeck and L. Hook, "The Social Dimnensions of a Twelve Man Jury Table," *Sociometry*, **24**: 297–415 (1961). See, also, discussion of additional research on this topic in Mark L. Knapp, op. cit., p. 87.

41. Robert Sommer, *Personal Space* (Englewood Cliffs, NJ: Prentice-Hall, 1969), p. 99.

42. Cf. John M. Wiemann, "Explication and Test of Communication Competence," *Human Communication Research* **3**:195–213 (1977), and Brent D. Ruben and Daniel J. Kealey, "Behavioral Assessment of Communication Competency and the Prediction of Cross-Cultural Adaptation," *International Journal of Intercultural Relations*, **3**,1, pp. 15–48 (Spring 1979).

References and Suggested Reading

Adams, R.S. and B. Biddle, *Realities of Teaching*. New York: Holt, 1970.
Aiken, L. "Relationships of Dress to Selected Measures of Personality in

Undergraduate Women." *Journal of Social Psychology,* **59** (1963), 119–228.

Angeloglou, Maggie. *A History of Make-up.* New York: Macmillan, 1970.

Bass, Bernard M. and S. Klubeck, "Effects of Seating Arrangement on Leaderless Group Discussions." *Journal of Abnormal and Social Psychology,* **47** (1952), 724–726.

Berscheid, E. and E.H. Walster. *Interpersonal Attraction.* Reading, MA: Addison-Wesley, 1969.

———. "Physical Attractiveness." In *Advances in Experimental Social Psychology.* Ed. by L. Berkowitz. Volume 7, pp. 158–215. New York: Academic, 1974.

Bickman, L. "The Social Power of a Uniform." *Journal of Applied Social Psychology,* **4** (1974), 47–61.

———. "Social Roles and Uniforms: Clothes Make the Person," *Psychology Today,* **7** (1974), 48–51.

Budd, Richard W. and Brent D. Ruben. *Beyond Media.* Rochelle Park, NJ: Hayden, 1979.

Burgoon, Judee K. and Thomas Saine. *Unspoken Dialogue.* Boston: Houghton Mifflin, 1978.

Byrne, D., O. London, and K. Reeves. "The Effects of Physical Attractiveness, Sex, and Attitude Similarity on Interpersonal Attraction." *Journal of Personality,.* **36** (1968), 250–272.

Coombs, R.H. and W.F. Kenkel. "Sex Differences in Dating Aspirations and Satisfactions with Computer-Selected Partners." *Journal of Marriage and the Family,* **28** (1966), 62–66.

Cortes, J.B. and F.M. Gatti. "Physique and Propensity." *Psychology Today,* **4** (1970), 42–44, 32–34.

Ekman, Paul, "Universal and Cultural Differences in Facial Expressions of Emotions." In *Nebraska Symposium on Motivation, 1971.* Ed. by J.K. Cole. Lincoln: University of Nebraska Press, (1972), 207–283.

———, and Wallace V. Friesen. "The Repertoire of Nonverbal Behavior: Categories, Origins, Usage, and Coding." *Semiotica,* **1,** (1969), 49–98.

———, and Wallace V. Friesen, "Constants Across Cultures in the Face and Emotion." *Journal of Personality and Social Psychology,* **17,** (1971), 124–129.

———, Wallace Friesen, and P. Ellsworth. *Emotion in the Human Face: Guidelines for Research and an Integration of the Findings.* New York: Pergamon, 1972.

———, and Wallace V. Friesen. *Unmasking the Face.* Englewood Cliffs, NJ: Prentice-Hall, 1975.

Ellsworth, P.C. "Direct Gaze as a Social Stimulus: The Example of Aggression." Ed. by P. Pliner, L. Krames, and T. Alloway. *Nonverbal Communication of Aggression.* New York: Plenum, (1975), 53–76.

Geschwind, Norman. "Specializations of the Human Brain." *Scientific American,* September, 1979, 180–182.

Gibbins, K. "Communication Aspects of Women's Clothes and Their Relation to Fashionability." *British Journal of Social and Clinical Psychology,* **8** (1969), 301–312.

Gurel, L.M., J.C. Wilbur, and L. Gurel. "Personality Correlates of Adolescent Clothing Styles." *Journal of Home Economics*, **64** (1972), 42–47.

Hall, Edward T. *The Silent Language*. Garden City, NY: Doubleday, 1959.

———. *The Hidden Dimension*. Garden City, NY: Doubleday, 1969.

Hare A. and R. Bales. "Seating Position and Small Group Interaction." *Sociometry*, **26** (1963), 480–486.

Harper, Robert G., Arthur N. Wiens, and Joseph D. Matarazzo, Eds. *Nonverbal Communication: The State of the Art*. New York: Wiley, 1978.

Harrison, Randall P. *Beyond Words*. Englewood Cliffs, NJ: Prentice-Hall, 1974.

Henley, Nancy M. *Body Politics*. Englewood Cliffs, NJ: Prentice-Hall, 1977.

Hess, E.H. "The Role of Pupil Size in Communication." *Scientific American*, **233** (November 1975) 110–112, 116–119.

———. *The Tell-Tale Eye*. New York: Van Nostrand Reinhold, 1975.

——— and J.M. Polt. "Pupil Size as Related to Interest Value of Visual Stimuli." *Science*, **132** (1960), 349–350.

Hewes, Gordon W. "The Anthropology of Posture." *Scientific American*, 1957.

Howells L.T. and S.W. Becker. "Seating Arrangement and Leadership Emergence." *Journal of Abnormal and Social Psychology*, **64** (1962), 148–150.

Iliffe, A.M. "A Study of Preference in Feminine Beauty." *British Journal of Psychology*, **51** (1960), 267–273.

Ittelson, William H., ed. *Environment and Cognition*. New York: Seminar Press, 1973.

Jourard, S.M. "An Exploratory Study of Body-Accessibility." *British Journal of Social and Clinical Psychology*, **5** (1966), 221–231.

Kendon, A. Some Functions of Gaze-Direction in Social Interaction. *Acta Psychologica*, **26** (1967), 22–63.

Knapp, Mark L. *Essentials of Nonverbal Communication*. New York: Holt, 1980.

Koneya, W. "The Relationship Between Verbal Interaction and Seat Location of Members of Large Groups." Unpublished Ph.D. dissertation. Denver University, 1973.

Krout, Maurice H. "Symbolism." In *The Rhetoric of Nonverbal Communication*. Ed. by Haig A. Bosmajian. Glenview, IL: Scott, Foresman, 1971.

Leathers, Dale G. *Nonverbal Communication Systems*. Boston: Allyn & Bacon, 1976.

Lynch, Kevin. *The Image of the City*. Cambridge, MA: M.I.T. Press, 1960.

Mehrabian, Albert. *Public Places and Private Spaces*. New York: Basic Books, 1976.

Molloy, John T. *Dress for Success*. New York: Warner, 1975.

Morris, Desmond. *Intimate Behavior*. New York: Random House, 1971.

———. *Manwatching*. New York: Abrams, 1977.

Nielsen, G. *Studies in Self-Confrontation*. Copenhagen, Denmark: Munksgaard, 1962.

Norberg–Schulz, Christian. *Existence, Space and Architecture*. New York: Praeger, 1971.

Ornstein, Robert E. *The Psychology of Consciousness*. San Francisco: Freeman, 1977.

Parry, Albert. *Tattoo*. New York: Simon & Schuster, 1933.

Rosenfeld, L.B., S. Kartus, and C. Ray. "Body Accessibility Revisited." *Journal of Communication* **26** (1976), 27–30.

Ruben, Brent D. and Paolo Soleri. "Architecture: Medium and Message." In *Beyond Media*. Ed. by Richard W. Budd and Brent D. Ruben. 214–233. Rochelle Park, NJ: Hayden, 1979.

Scheflen, Albert L. "Quasi-Courtship Behavior in Psychotherapy," *Psychiatry*, **28** (1965), 245–257.

Sheldon, W.H., *Atlas of Man*. New York: Harper, 1954.

Sommer, Robert. *Personal Space*. Englewood Cliffs, NJ: Prentice-Hall, 1969.

Spiegel, John and Pavel Machotka. *Messages of the Body*. New York: Free Press, 1974.

Springer, Sally P., and George Deutsch. *Left Brain, Right Brain*. San Francisco: Freeman, 1981.

Strass, J.W. and F.N. Willis, Jr. "Eye Contact, Pupil Dilation, and Personal Preference." *Psychonomic Science*, **7** (1967), 375–376.

Strongman, K.T. and C.J. Hart. "Stereotyped Reactions to Body Build." *Psychological Reports*, **23** (1968), 1175–1178.

Strodtbeck F. and L. Hook. "The Social Dimensions of a Twelve Man Jury Table," *Sociometry*, **24** (1961), 297–415.

Walster, E., V. Aronson, D. Abrahams, and L. Rohmann. "Importance of Physical Attractiveness in Dating Behavior." *Journal of Personality and Social Psychology*, **4** (1966), 508–516.

Wiemann, John M. An Experimental Study of Visual Attention in Dyads: The Effect of Four Gaze Conditions on Evaluation of Applications in Employment Interviews. Paper presented at the Meeting of the Speech Communication Association, Chicago, 1974.

————."Explication and Test of Communication Competence." *Human Communication Research*, **3** (1977), 195–213.

Wood, Barbara S. *Children and Communication*. Englewood Cliffs, NJ: Prentice-Hall, 1976.

Information Reception

Chapter 7

Selection, Interpretation, and Retention

In the previous two chapters, we have examined the ways in which human language, paralanguage, appearance, gestures, touch, and the use of space and time create much of the data which comprises the symbolic environment with which we must adapt.

In this chapter, our attention is focused on *information reception*, and the processes involved in the sensing and making sense of our data-filled surroundings.

As is the case for other animals, human information reception involves the transformation of data into a form that can be used. Many animals inherit or very rapidly acquire the ability to determine what sorts of data are necessary to their life functioning, and how and when those data should be attended to. Our symbol and tool-using capabilities conspire to make our human environment more complex, and our ways of relating to it less predictable and less mechanical. For us, the identification of data and its conversion into a form for present and future use is an active process, one which involves three elements—*data selection, interpretation,* and *retention.* We will discuss each of these in detail in the pages ahead, beginning with an illustration.

Ed awoke this morning at 7:30 to a grey sky and light rain. He noticed the weather almost immediately, because it was a Saturday and he had looked forward all week to a chance to get outside. He chatted with his wife, Jane, about a variety of topics while he dressed and ate breakfast. He began to ponder his options as to how to spend the day, given that he was stuck inside. Ed left the breakfast table and walked down the hallway.

He glanced in the study and saw the piles of typed pages strewn about his desk. "I should work on the year-end report due next month," he thought to himself. "My future depends on how well that's received."

He continued into the family room where he noticed his children, Robert and Ann, sitting in front of the television set watching cartoons. He reflected to himself on how fast time goes by, and decided that he really ought to spend more time with the kids. "Maybe a game or some sort of craft project that we could work on together..." He exchanged a few brief words with his children, and it seemed that Woody Woodpecker was of more interest to the kids than he was, and he turned his attention to a stack of newspapers and magazines lying across the room on a table. As he looked at the pile of reading material, he thought about the fact that he had spent only a few minutes with the mail, newspapers, or magazines all week. "I really should go through them today," he noted to himself. "No...the report has got to come first!"

He made his way back to the study, turned on the radio, and tuned to a station that played the kind of music he liked as "background." He situated himself at the desk, and began to shuffle through the materials before him. He came across a book he had been using as a primary source in his report, picked it up, and began rereading sections of the text and leafing through the illustrations.

The radio station kept fading in and out, and the news was annoying him. He walked over to a nearby record rack, and picked several jazz instrumental albums, which he thought would be enjoyable, but not distracting.

As he walked back to the desk, Ed happened to glance out the window. Incredible! The grey skies had cleared; the rain had stopped and the sun was shining brightly. Ed heard the distant whine of a neighbor's lawn mower and glanced almost instinctively at his own lawn. "Damn, it really does need to be mowed...And the car is dirty," he thought to himself. "I could do both jobs tomorrow, if the weather holds."

He turned the radio on again and scanned for a local station and the weather report. "Clearing this afternoon, highs in the low 80's."

"I'll wash the car today, so it will be clean for the weekend, and put off mowing the lawn until tomorrow," he decided. "This grass is still a bit wet now, anyway...But what if the weather report is wrong? If it's wrong? It's always wrong. If I put off mowing until tomorrow, and it rains, I might not be able to mow until next weekend, and by then the grass will be so long it would take most of two days to mow."

"How ridiculous this is!" he concluded. "The lawn is ruling my life. It's amazing how one's priorities evolve by default. That settles it. Back to the report!"

The foregoing summary reveals a good deal about Ed's communication habits, values, orientations, and, at the same time, helps to illustrate how information processing works. To examine this process, let's briefly reconstruct the scenario, paying particular attention to the data Ed attended to, the meanings he attached to them, and the manner in which these meanings dictated his behavior.

There were, no doubt, an infinite number of things Ed might think about upon waking on a given day. Of these, he was primarily concerned with the day and the weather—*Saturday* and *rain*. That he chose to be concerned with these particular things and not others, had largely to do with the meanings each had for him. *Saturday* was a special day, one he had looked forward to all week. *Grey clouds* and *rain* meant it would be impossible for him to pursue some of the activities he had hoped and planned for. Together, *Saturday* and *rain* meant *plans ruined*, nothing more, nothing less.

Despite this reality, Ed moved through the information-processing sequence necessary to the activities he had come to think of as essential to the start of each day: taking a shower, shaving, selecting clothes, dressing, making his way to the kitchen, sitting down at the table, talking to his wife Jane, eating breakfast, and so forth.

As he chatted with Jane, new data were introduced into his purview. These data provided an opportunity for him to overcome the *plans ruined* aura, which to that point had been the dominant force in his message reception.

In talking to his wife (and himself), Ed determined that there was little to be gained by stewing over one set of plans ruined. There were, after all, a number of plans one might have which *Saturday-rain* would not ruin. As he began to attach new meaning to the situation, his attention was directed toward data and possible interpretations he was unaware of only minutes earlier.

Because Ed was ready to consider options as to how to spend the day, the stack of typed pages from his report was singled out from other potential data in the environment. At some level of awareness, those pages meant a variety of things to him at that point, including *job unfinished, frustration, guilt,* and *challenge*. None of these meanings were compelling enough to lead him to undertake work on the report at that instant.

In the family room, his children almost instantly became prominent message sources. They triggered a variety of meanings—*affection, enjoyment, responsibility, concern*. As with the significance of the year-end report, these meanings were central to his self-concept and sense of what he was about, and as a result they commanded his interest and receptivity.

In passing, he also attended momentarily to the television show they were watching. He recognized at some slightly-less-than-conscious level that the data generated by the cartoon were at that instant performing very different functions for Robert and Ann than for him. In some sense, Ed was competing with Woody Woodpecker for their attention.

The presence of the week's mail, magazines, and newspapers provided the basis for additional data which were significant to him. In the context of his own life they signified *knowledgeability, credibility, enjoyment,* and *obligation*. Ed was also aware of a need to be familiar with the "news" in order to appear intelligent, knowledgeable, and current to his friends and colleagues.

Though these meanings were also important to his definition of himself, they were not, at that instant, as critical as the meanings related to the report. Ed "decided"—again, in a less-than-wholly-aware manner—to reject these and other options in favor of returning to work on the report.

In the study, his message processing continued as he selected a particular information source—FM radio—and a particular frequency on the dial with a data set he had learned to associate with that station. His unstated objective in so doing was to control the background data in the immediate environment.

In looking through the materials on his desk, his eyes fell upon a book which had been significant earlier in his work. It became a primary object of attention for several minutes, as he recalled its contents and his reaction to them. "Noise" resulting from the fading of the radio station became another unavoidable message source, and he acted to replace the data from the radio with that from records which he assumed would better fulfill the intended function.

On glancing out the window, the clearing skies and sun were especially meaningful data. They signified *original plans O.K.; no need to pursue the present options, unless you want to*. As his attention shifted to the data in the environment outside his study, Ed noted the whine of a lawn mower, which triggered a variety of issues each of which required attention and resolution—the lawn, the car, and so on.

In examining the alternative meanings called up from memory, he inadvertently began a self-reflexive thought process. As he reflected on his own information processing, this time quite consciously, he decided to execute more control over himself and his surroundings and pursue what he had determined to be the most "logical" alternatives for use of his time.

In returning his attention to work on the report, in effect, Ed decided to attach less value to data related to the physical environment external to his study—the lawn, cars, etc. He chose instead to focus on information sources that were pertinent to his report. This decision was itself reflective of the relative importance he attached to the various information sources available to him at that point. At the same time, the act of selecting the option he did also had the effect of reaffirming his priorities.

Selection, Interpretation, Retention

Many interesting facets of message reception are illustrated in even a commonplace situation such as the one just described. As simple and automatic as such events may seem, they involve a complex of factors operating in a very active process of data selection, interpretation, and retention.

Selection

At any instant in time, we are surrounded in our environment by a number of persons, objects, and circumstances, which are the sources of the data that compete for our attention and interest. In the foregoing sequence, the radio, stereo, Ed's wife and children, the pages of his report, the outdoors, the lawnmower, and the weather were each potential information sources which confronted him and in a sense were competing for his attention.

Predictably in such circumstances we select certain data to attend to while disregarding others. The apparent simplicity of the activity often obscures its complexity. Even when one is faced with a basic decision like deciding what to do on a Saturday morning, we make a number of elaborate decisions—many of which we have little awareness of—as to which data we will focus on. In the foregoing illustration, Ed "decided" to give attention to the weather, the day of the week, his children and the year-end report rather than other sorts of data in his physical and symbolic environment—like the room that needed painting, the clothes that were to be taken to the cleaners, the unopened package on the table, the expressions on his children's faces when they exchanged words, and so on.

This same data selection process operates in other sorts of common situations such as when we pause in a hallway to chat with an acquaintance. First, the very act of noticing the other person involves the systematic selection of data. Triggered by the constellation of factors associated with the appearance of the other person, and perhaps some verbal data—"Hi"—we begin tuning ourselves to the other person and to the data necessary to the interchange which will follow. In so doing, we ignore other potential environmental data—the temperature, the color of the carpeting, the appearance of other persons who may pass by, the noise of a nearby copy machine, or the thunderstorm outside, through a complex process that has occupied the attention of many scholars over the years.[1]

In many situations the selective nature of information processing is apparent, as when we read a book or talk with friends in a room with a stereo

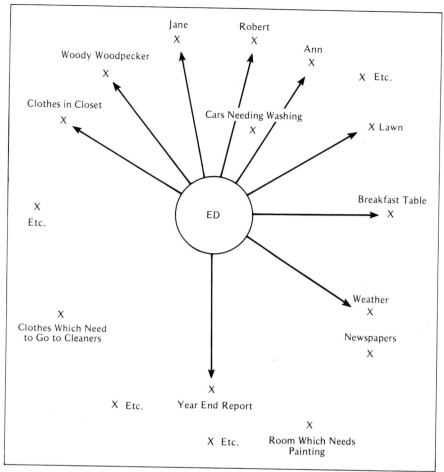

FIGURE 7.1 At any one point in time we are surrounded by a large number of persons, events, objects, and circumstances that are sources of the data competing for our attention.

or television set turned on or a lawn mower running outside. In such circumstances, we *selectively attend* to certain data while disregarding others, we define as background noise.

Another illustration of the selective nature of data reception is provided by cocktail parties and similar social gatherings. During such affairs one finds that it is not at all difficult to carry on a series of perfectly intelligible discussions with one or more individuals without being overly distracted by other conversations. It is even possible to tune into an exchange between several other persons a good distance away, without shifting one's position and while appearing to be deeply engrossed in conversation with a person close at hand.

In that same setting, we are able to tune out the entire external environment, periodically, in order to concentrate on our own feelings, decide what we ought to be doing, or think about how we are being perceived

A.

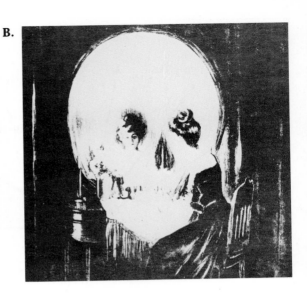

B.

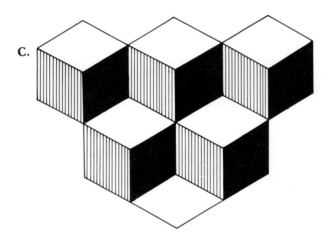

C.

D.

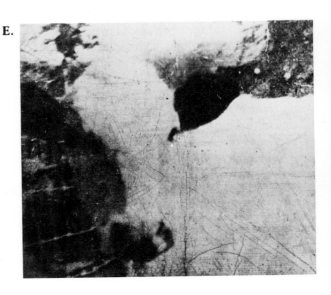

E.

by others. It is also possible to attend to the gathering as a whole, paying attention to the level, pitch, rhythm, number of interactions, and level of activity, as a basis for making some general assessments of the gathering as a whole—whether it is sedate or wild, winding up or down, and so on.[2]

Given these kinds of examples, it may seem as though information selection operates much like a filter, letting in some sounds, images, or smells, while screening out others.[3] Further examination reveals, however, that the process is often more complex than this way of thinking implies. For instance, we know that even when we have "tuned in" to a particular data source and "tuned out" others, the selected-out data may, nonetheless be taken note of. This is the case, for instance, when a honking horn interrupts our attention to a discussion with a colleague while crossing the street, or when the sound of one's own or a friend's name is heard "through" the otherwise unintelligible din of a party.[4] Additionally, there is some evidence to suggest that it is possible to take note of and attach meaning to data even when one is unaware of doing so.[5] And some studies suggest that under hypnosis we may be able to remember information that we were not fully aware of selecting for attention in the first place.[6]

The awareness of the complexity of the attention process has led to the adoption a "modified filter model" as a way of thinking about selection.[7] It is thought that the individual assigns priorities to competing data sources and allocates his or her attention among them, while monitoring other data and perhaps even attending to still other sources which are unknown even to the individual involved.

Interpretation

A second facet of information reception is the *interpretation* of data. When we interpret data, we determine what significance to attach to a word, sentence, circumstance, gesture, or event, and how to respond—whether to regard to it as fiction or nonfiction, serious or humorous, new or old, contradictory or

---

FIGURE 7.2 Depending upon the way we select and interpret data, very different consequences result. In the Illustration A below, for example, if we define the white area as the object to be looked at, then we see a vase. If on the other hand, we focus our attention on the black area, we see the silhouettes of two persons staring at one another.

In Illustration B, if we are drawn first to the large white portion, we see a skull. Attention to subtleties of the drawing in black, however, reveals a lady seated at a dressing table staring into a mirror. In Illustration C, we count either 3 or 5 cubes depending upon which cues we define as pertinent to interpreting the figure.

Again, depending upon data selection and interpretation, Illustration D—which was also reproduced on the beginning page of this chapter—either appears to be a stylish young lady with a feather in her hat or an older, haggard woman with a wart on her nose, staring downward in apparent depression. In each of these cases we see one or the other, depending upon which cues we attend to.

At first glance, Illustration E may appear to be a weather satellite photo, a highly magnified bacterial organism, or simply a random, nonsense image. Once our attention is directed to particular elements of the photo, it is no longer nonsense—we see a cow. Interestingly, once we see the cow, it becomes virtually impossible to see it any other way.

MAN DIES AFTER HEARING WIFE DIED

Linden, NJ (AP)-A Linden man collapsed and died after learning that his wife was killed in a plane crash earlier that day in Poland, police and hospital authorities said yesterday.

Police said that (the man) 61, had suffered an apparent heart attack Friday after learning that his wife. . .was one of 87 people who died in the Warsaw, Poland, plane crash.

FIGURE 7.3

SOURCE: Associated Press, March 17, 1980. By permission.

consistent, amusing or annoying. Even our reaction to a simple, "Hi, how are you?" will depend, among other things, on whether the person is male or female (and the significance we attach to each), whether we regard the individual as attractive or unattractive, whether the person is dressed in swimwear or formal dinner attire, whether we are situated on nearby blankets at the beach, or next to one another in a doctor's waiting room, whether we interpret the individual's motives as platonic or romantic, and a host of other factors.

The information-value particular objects, events, words, appearances, dress, gestures, will have for an individual depend upon the rules that have been acquired relative to processing data. As we know, for instance, the decoding of a spoken sentence requires an understanding of phonetic, syntactic, semantic, and pragmatic rules. Assigning meaning to particular dress or gestures involves a similar process.

Thus, our interpretations depend on a number of factors, including the data itself, rules we have learned for decoding the data, the source of the data, and most importantly, upon information values these data have for a given individual at a particular point in time. In the preceding narrative, for instance, the meaning Ed attached to the *year-end report* was influenced by the significance of *Saturday* and *rain*, as well as by the significance he had assigned to other elements of his environment, and to his long-term goals.

Retention—Memory

From the preceding discussion, it should be apparent that memory plays an indispensible role in the interpretative process. We are able to store and actively use an incredible amount of information—at least several billion times more than a large research computer—and yet we can locate and use it with an efficiency and ease of operation that is astounding.[8]

We have little difficulty accessing the information we need in order to go about our daily routine—to locate the bathroom, closet and kitchen; to select appropriate clothing and to dress; or start and operate an automobile, or find the way to the bus and train. And, with split-second timing and a high degree of accuracy, we can answer questions like "Who was the first President of the United States?" or "What is the name for the sound frequently heard following lightning?" While these seem like "simple" questions, the relatively longer time it would take to locate the answers in a book, library, or even many electronic databases using a table of contents, index, or other formal search techniques, underscores the sophistication of the human memory system.

As Morton Hunt notes:

> Although every act of thinking involves the use of images, sounds, symbols, meanings, and connections between things, all stored in memory, the organization of memory is so efficient that most of the time we are unaware of having to exert any effort to locate and use these materials. Consider the ranges of kinds of information you keep in, and can easily summon forth, from your own memory: the face of your closest friend...the words and melody of the national anthem...the spelling of almost every word you can think of...the exact place where you keep the pliers...the name of every object you can see from where you are sitting...the way your room looked when you were eight...the set of skills you need to drive a car in heavy traffic...and enough more to fill many shelves full of books....[9]

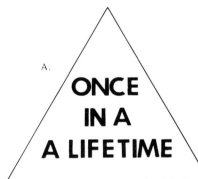

A.

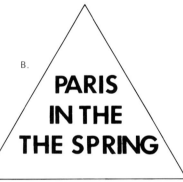

B.

C.

FIGURE 7.4 Memory plays an important role in the processing of information at any point in time. A quick glance at either of the two triangles below leads us to conclude that the sentences are "Once in a lifetime" and "Paris in the spring." Because these two phrases are familiar to most of us and because we expect such phrases to follow the normal rules for grammar we have learned, the repeated "a" and "the" are easy to miss. Looking at Illustration C, we have little trouble determining that the image is that of a "dog." Actually, very little detail is provided in the illustration. Were it not for substantial previous experience in selecting and interpreting messages relative to "dog," we would have great difficulty making sense of this image.

These are examples of *recall*—active, deliberate retrieval of information from memory, a capability that may well be unique to humans. In addition, we share with other animal systems the capacity to use data for *recognition*—to recognize objects, places, circumstances, and people when in their presence.[10]

Particularly in recent years, much effort has been directed to understanding the complex processes by which memory operates with promising results.[11]

Data enters the system through one or several communication modes. In selecting and attending particular sensory data we begin to attach meaning to those symbols following rules we have learned and frequently used.[12] A good deal of sensory information can be processed within the system at any one time. If, for example, you looked through the newspaper to determine what movie was playing a particular theater, not only that information, but additional sensory data relative to other items in the paper, such as other movies and other theaters, would also be processed at some level of awareness. The information other than that being sought, would be lost, *decay*, very rapidly—probably within a second or so.[13]

Information which is to be further used becomes a part of what is termed *short term memory*, and is available for a relatively short period of time—perhaps 15 seconds.[14] Our short-term memory capacity is limited under normal circumstances to a few pieces of information only—a phone number or a string of several letters or words. Most of us have had the experience of looking up a number, only to forget it by the time we walked across the room to the phone. This forgetting illustrates how rapidly information is lost from short-term memory. Through recitation or rehearsal, however, we can extend the time available to use information. Thus, if we repeat a phone number to ourselves several times as we walk across the room, the likelihood of remembering it for the needed time period greatly increases.

Some of the information is further processed and elaborated to become a part of our *long-term memory*. Generally, the longer time information is available to us in short-term memory the greater the chance it will become a part of our longer term memory. Therefore, a phone number looked up, rehearsed, and dialed several times over the period of an hour because of a busy signal, is far more likely to be remembered than a number successfully reached on the first try. Phone numbers that are often dialed become a part of an individual's long-term memory naturally, or actively—through memorization.

Much remains to be learned about the ways in which selected environmental data which are transformed into interpretable information and stored in a way that makes it quickly and easily accessible to us. It is thought by many scholars working in this area that much of the information is processed and stored in long term memory in a *semantic network*, whereby incoming messages are linked systematically to previously stored information based on common characteristics.

A canary, for instance, might become significant to an individual through a process of comparing its properties to those of previously observed

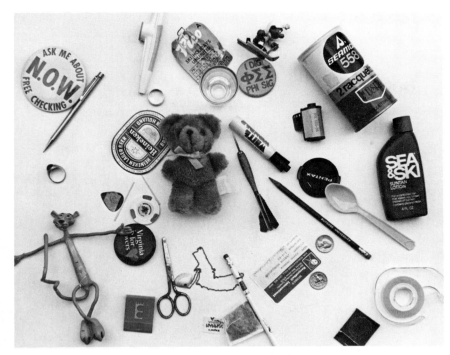

FIGURE 7.5 Glance at the items in the illustration above for 5 to 10 seconds, close the book, and list the items that your can remember on a sheet of paper. When one compares the resulting list with the picture, it is obvious that many items were forgotten and others were perhaps never noticed in the first place. Further study of those things noticed and remembered, and those not, can underscore aspects of the information reception process, the impact of memory on selection and retention of new data, and the complexity of information processing. Generally speaking, in any situation what one notices and remembers is greatly influenced by one's accumulated past experience. Objects, people, and circumstances that are a part of one's experience one can relate to are regarded as important; are noticed and remembered. Sometimes an item is taken note of precisely because one cannot relate to and identify it. In any case, those things noticed and remembered and those forgotten in any situation generally say as much or more about the individual involved—his or her past experiences, priorities, hobbies, and so on—as they do about the actual data and data sources present in the environment.

and classified objects. That it "has wings," "flies," and is "quite small" suggests it is similar to other animals one has learned to call *birds*—about which information has been previously processed and retained. That this *bird* "sings" and is "in a cage in a friend's house," suggests that while this canary has much in common with other birds, it also is different in some respects. A *canary* is a special kind of bird—a *pet bird*.

As Hunt explains:

> New material is added to this network by being plunked down in a hole in
> the middle of an appropriate region, and then gradually...tied in, by a host

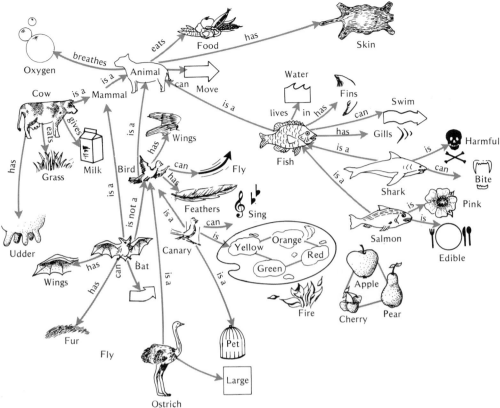

FIGURE 7.6 Humans interpret, store, and retrieve data according to the associations and meanings the objects, phenomena, and events of their experience have for them.

SOURCE: Adapted from *Cognitive Psychology and Information Processing,* R. Lachman, J.L. Lachman, and E.C. Butterfield. Copyright © 1979 by Lawrence Erlbaum Associates. By permission.

of meaningful connections, to the appropriate nodes in the surrounding network.

Thus, although remembered information is arranged by categories of subject matter, the arrangement is far less orderly and regular than in reference works or libraries. But also far more redundant: we have many ways of getting to something filed in long-term memory, many cues and routes to the item we are seeking. When no cue or route takes us directly to it, we can guide ourselves to the general area and then mentally run through the items in that area until we come across the one we're looking for.[15]

Factors That Influence Information Reception: The Individual

For each of us a complex set of elements work together to influence our decisions as to which sorts of data we will attend to and how we will interpret and retain the information that results. A great many of these factors have to do with the nature of the individual.

TABLE 7.1 Factors Affecting Information Reception.

1.   *THE INDIVIDUAL*
      — Needs
      — Attitudes, Beliefs, Values
      — Goals
      — Capabilities
      — Uses
      — Communication Style
      — Experience and Habit

2.   *THE DATA*
      — Type
      — Mode
      — Physical Character
      — Organization
      — Novelty

3.   *THE SOURCE*
      — Proximity
      — Attractiveness
      — Similarity
      — Credibility and Authoritativeness
      — Motivation and Intent
      — Delivery
      — Status, Power, and Authority

4.   *THE ENVIRONMENT*
      — Context and Setting
      — Repetition
      — Consistency
      — Competition

Needs

Among the most crucial factors which play a role in our message reception and decisions are what are commonly termed *needs*. Scholars generally agree that our most basic needs, like those of other animals, have to do with our physiological well-being—food, shelter, physical well-being, and sex.[16] These basic needs can be potent forces in directing our behavior in a number of respects. When fundamental needs are not met, our efforts to satisfy them are important guiding forces in information reception. To the individual who hasn't eaten for several days, for example, few data sources are as likely to be as noteworthy, or *salient*, as those relating to food. A knowledge that unsatisfied needs often increase the attention and importance attached to particular data has led popular authors to suggest that a good way to save money and diet is to shop for groceries after eating rather than before.

The same pattern occurs with regard to our health. A headache or upset stomach, which is readily dismissed by persons who believe themselves to be well, may become the focus of great attention and concern for an individual who has been diagnosed as or believes himself or herself to be ill. To the individual overcome with concern about his or her health, messages about the upcoming football game, a book manuscript, or grass that needs mowing, take on far less significance than they would under normal conditions. As these cases illustrate, the presence of unsatisifed basic needs in the areas of physical well-being, food, shelter, or sex increase the salience of information and potential information sources related to that need.

In addition to physiological needs, other needs or motives such as social contact, reality exploration and comprehension, socialization, and diversion, entertainment, and play have to do with our spiritual, psychological, social, and communicative well-being.[17] Perhaps the most basic of these types of needs has to do with maintaining and developing one's identity and self concept.[18]

Generally speaking, we want to be seen positively, as worthy, desirable, competent, or respectable. There are, of course, major differences between us as to the particular qualities for which we wish others to value us. For some of us, being valued for our creativity, intelligence, professional competence, and vocational success may be of primary concern, while for others, being seen as religious, honest, honorable, or empathetic, may be more important. Some of us would prefer to be admired for our leadership capacity, while others wish to be respected for our loyalty as followers, and so on.

Personal, social, and communicative needs play an important role in data selection, interpretation, and retention. The nature of that role has begun to be highlighted and clarified in recent years by scholars who have focused their attention on the "uses and gratifications" served by the mass media.[19] Their work helps substantiate the view that there is often a direct relationship between particular unsatisfied, or ungratified, needs and resulting patterns of exposure to mass media programs and other data sources.

There is also good reason to suppose that our specific personal needs and the information processing orientations that tend to accompany them are not rigid. Rather they may change over time as we move through various life stages and circumstances.[20] As children we adapt to a world in which we are highly dependent upon parents and other adults for the satisfaction of our needs, wants, and desires. That dependence carries with it a particular set of information-reception tendencies for most of us, in which our parents, relatives, and gradually peer relations are highly significant.

The thrust for independence which confronts many of us as a crisis, similarly signals a change in the sorts of data and data sources to which we are likely to respond. These changes generally are accompanied by new ways of interpreting information as well. *Dependence* on parents, for example, may give way to *counterdependence*, as a prior step to *independence*. Where we once "heard and agreed," we come to "hear and disagree," and later learn to "hear sometimes and agree sometimes." Every stage in our lives—adulthood, twenties, thirties, forties, fifties, sixties, and beyond—can present us with additional problems and challenges. Each of these stages and the many situations which compose them are accompanied by changes in our needs, and therefore in our selection, interpretation, and retention patterns, as we strive to adapt to the personal, social, and occupational circumstances which beset us.

Attitudes, Beliefs, and Values

The attitudes, preferences, and predispositions one has about particular topics, persons, or situations also play a critical role in information receiving activities and outcomes. Most people, for instance, will attend to and be favorably disposed toward new data, sources, and interpretations which support their views before they consider nonsupportive data, sources, or conclusions.[21] The person who supports candidate X for a particular elected office is likely to pay far more attention to articles and political ads and sources of new information about the candidate than he or she will to items about candidate Y or Z. And such a person may well prefer to spend time talking politics with others who share his or her view.

Values is a term used to refer to basic principles that we live by—our sense of what we ought and ought not do in our relations with the environment and the people in it. As with attitudes and beliefs, values also can substantially influence our selection, interpretation, and retention activities. Individuals who believe strongly that each able-bodied adult ought to be gainfully employed will likely take notice of and react strongly to persons who are complacent about receiving welfare checks and making only superficial attempts to find a job.

As implied in this example, there are instances where data which are likely to be interpreted as inconsistent and nonsupportive of our attitudes, beliefs, or values can lead to *more*, rather than *less*, attention and interest. We may devote considerable attention and effort to convert individuals who cling to beliefs or values which differ from our own. Similarly, we often spend more time reflecting upon people and events that trouble us than on those that reassure and comfort us, simply because we come to take the latter for granted.

Goals

Like the other factors discussed thus far, goals can play an important role in directing our information processing. Most of us are at best only partially aware of our needs, attitudes, beliefs, and values. By way of distinction, we consciously set our *goals*.

When an individual decides to pursue a particular plan, career, personal relationship, personal challenge, or the like, that goal serves to direct his or her attention toward certain sorts of messages and away from others.

If one has the goal of driving from Princeton, New Jersey, to JFK

Historian: "Yes, he's right few reporters have a solid grounding in history these days."

Journalism Educator: "It seems to me he's over-all generalizing. We have a number of good students graduating each year.

Economics: "Absolutely, few reporters are trained in economics, and that is essential today.

LET ME TAKE JUST A MINUTE OR TWO TO OUTLINE WHAT I SEE AS THE MAJOR PROBLEMS FACING THE MASS COMMUNICATION INDUSTRY TODAY AS IT RELATES TO COVERAGE OF FOREIGN NEWS. THERE IS A DANGEROUS SHORTAGE OF QUALIFIED PEOPLE WITH OVERSEAS EXPERIENCE. WE ARE ALWAYS LOOKING FOR SUCH INDIVIDUALS, BUT UNFORTUNATELY, THERE ARE FEW AND FAR BETWEEN. IT IS PARTICULARLY DIFFICULT TO FIND MINORITY PERSONNEL WITH PROPER BACKGROUNDS AND TRAINING.

Reporter: "I will go up and introduce myself after the speech. Sounds like a good job prospect.

Minority member: "Sounds like another racist hiding behind a facade."

A FURTHER PROBLEM IS THAT WHEN WE DO ACQUIRE MATERIALS ON FOREIGN EVENTS, OUR HUNCH IS THAT THE AUDIENCE FOR THIS KIND OF INFORMATION IS SMALL AND NOT WELL DIVERSIFIED.

Pollster: "If they would conduct a survey, they wouldn't have to talk about their "hunches."

Lay Member: "Why wouldn't they be satisfied with a small, elite audience for such information?"

I WISH I HAD TIME TO GO INTO MORE DETAIL ON THESE AND OTHER ISSUES, BUT I SEE MY TIME IS UP. THANK YOU ALL FOR YOUR ATTENTION. PERHAPS WE WILL HAVE TIME TO CARRY ON OUR DISCUSSION LATER.

Next Speaker: "I'll keep my comments brief, too, so they'll be plenty of time for questions and answers."

Master of Ceremonies: "OK., let's see, who's the next speaker. Jeff Johnson... from Detroit. . . .. fifteen years experience..." "THANK YOU ROY. I'M SURE THERE WILL BE A NUMBER OF QUESTIONS. I THINK IT WILL BE BEST IF WE HOLD THEM UNTIL ALL OF OUR GUESTS HAVE MADE THEIR OPENING COMMENTS. NOW, I'D LIKE TO INTRODUCE, JEFF JOHNSON..."

Lower case — thoughts and reflections
Upper case — spoken Comments

FIGURE 7.7 In a public communication situation, as in other circumstances, the data to which individuals attend and the way they interpret and retain information are largely reflective of their own backgrounds, attitudes, needs, orientations, goals, values, and interests, as the following scenario suggests. In the most literal sense, it is accurate to say that each of the individuals in the audience heard the speech on foreign news coverage. However, differences in the items on which particular persons focused and in their interpretations suggest that in a more basic sense each "heard" a different presentation.

Airport in New York to catch a specific flight, this objective plays a major role in guiding data selection, interpretation, and retention. On the way to the airport, he or she must process data concerning the location, direction, and rate of speed of his or her car and other vehicles in the vicinity. The driver must also attend to, interpret, and remember the road markings and signs which provide pertinent information, and those which indicate the path to the airport. The gauges, instruments, and other controls of the car must also be monitored. Additionally, the driver must take account of weather conditions, time remaining before arrival at the final destination, location of the long-term parking area, the proper terminal, the flight number, the assigned seat, and so on. Until the goal is achieved and the individual is comfortably seated aboard the airplane, a substantial amount of the person's information-receiving behavior is influenced by the commitment to the self-determined goal of catching a plane.

In a similar manner, a decision to pursue a particular career—to become a medical doctor, for instance—directs one's attention toward certain sorts of data and away from others. The aspiring doctor is directed by his or her goal toward a knowledge base in physiology, anatomy, chemistry and away from data pertinent to students of engineering, business administration, and journalism. Acquiring appropriate interpretations for these data is crucial, and a priority until the goal is met or changed. Interestingly enough, even a change of goals often involves information processing.

In a similar sense, when an individual sets the goal of achieving certain competence in an area—athletics, as an illustration—this objective shapes not only the data to which the individual attends, but also the interpretations of them that he or she makes. First, the goal increases the likelihood that the individual will expose himself or herself to data which pertain to athletics in general, and his or her sport, in particular. Secondly, the goal may well increase the individual's contact with other persons interested in a similar activity, and this will have an additional influence on information reception. The demands of physical fitness may also play an important role in determining how information having to do with food, drink, smoking, health, and drugs will be attended to, interpreted, and remembered.

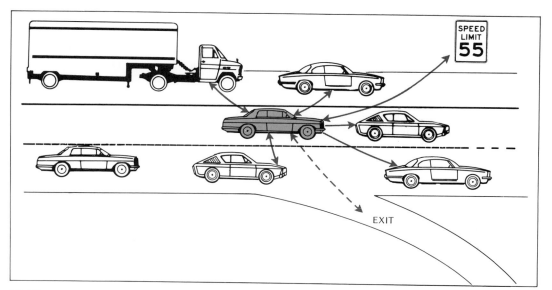

FIGURE 7.8 Even a relatively simple goal, like driving from point A to point B, makes incredible demands on one's data selection, interpretation, and retention skills. Data must be gathered and processed as to the location and rate of speed of other vehicles, and projections must be developed as to where nearby vehicles will be at future points in time. Road signs, gauges in one's own auto, and remembered information as to which exit to take, what lane to be in, and so forth, must also be utilized. In time, this complex information processing task becomes so natural that one can listen to the radio, plan a speech, or replay the days events while driving.

Capability

An additional factor involved in message-receiving activities is the capability of the individual. Our level of intelligence, previous experience with a particular topic area, and facility with language, have an obvious impact upon the kinds of data we attend to, and the manner in which we interpret and retain them. The probability of an English-speaking individual spending much time listening to Spanish-speaking radio, watching Spanish television programming, or reading Spanish publications is naturally very low, simply because he or she lacks the capability of processing these data meaningfully. By the same token, it is not likely an individual with no quantitative or research background will be drawn to reading articles in technical or scholarly journals. While the individual may possess the intellectual potential, his or her lack of familiarity with research and lack of facility in the technical language used in the publication would affect potential interest and comprehension, not to mention retention.

Use

One final factor related to the individual which affects message interpretation, and especially data selection and retention, is *use*. Generally speaking we will attend to and devote effort to understand and remember data that we think we will need or will be able to use. The learning of language offers an excellent example. It is a virtual certainty that individuals living in a social setting will learn to speak the language of those around them. For the most part, this learning occurs irrespective of whether there are efforts at formal schooling. We learn a language because attending to, learning how to interpret, and retaining messages about how to use spoken language is necessary to participate in most human activities.

In a school, one attends to and retains a large quantity of data on a variety of topics which may have no immediate personal relevance. Were it not for the opportunities and requirements to "rehearse" and "use" this retained knowledge to demonstrate course mastery on exams and quizzes, much less information would be remembered.

The same principle operates in many other domains. To the individual who is thinking about purchasing a new automobile, a number of statistics such as fuel capacity, estimated miles per gallon, wheel base, horsepower, 0 to 60 acceleration, price of accessories, and so on, are suddenly much more salient and far easier to remember than they were prior to the decision to shop for a new car.

Communication Style

Communication style can influence message-reception dynamics in two ways. First, depending upon our habits and preferences, we may be drawn to or actively avoid the chance to deal with other people. Persons who are shy or apprehensive about engaging in verbal communication in a group setting, for example, may well avoid such circumstances whenever possible.[22] Such an individual might well prefer to listen to a television show on health or consult a home medical guide for information on a particular illness rather than ask his or her doctor for information. Even when such persons push themselves to take part in interpersonal situations that make them uncomfortable, the discomfort may greatly affect the way they attend to, interpret, and retain data.

A somewhat less direct influence of style on information reception has to do with the manner in which we present ourselves communicationally to others. The way we "come across" to those with whom we deal can have a substantial impact on the way they react to us, and this in turn will influence both the quality and quantity of data they make available. Persons who are very talkative, for instance, often have less verbal data available to them than they otherwise might, simply because the persons with whom they are conversing are limited in their interest and in the time available to speak. Other aspects of the way we present ourselves such as our greetings, tone, word choice, level of openness, dress, and appearance also have an impact upon the sorts of data other persons make available to us, and this, in turn, has a direct bearing on our selection, interpretation, and retention.

Experience and Habit

As we have already noted earlier and will discuss in more detail in the next chapter, we develop a number of information reception habits or tendencies as a result of our experiences. These habits are no doubt the major guiding influence in how we select, interpret, or retain messages at any moment in time. Whether one thinks of reading a daily newspaper, viewing a particular television show, exchanging pleasantries with an acquaintance on the way to work, or arguing with a friend or family member, our previous experiences and the communication habits we have formed as a result of these experiences directly influence our message receiving decisions in very fundamental ways.

Factors That Influence Information Reception: The Data

In addition to *the individual*, the nature of the *data* also has a major impact on selection, interpretation, and reception. Five particularly important characteristics of data are type, mode, physical character, organization, and novelty.

Data Type

Some of the data we attend to have their origins in our physical environment. When we select an item on which to sit, identify a landmark to measure our movement, pick out an apartment in which to live, decide whether the temperature in our living room is too high, or develop a theory of why apples fall from trees, we do so using information based on the objects, events, relationships, or substances in the physical environment.

We also make frequent use of data we create ourselves. When we listen to and think about what we have said to someone else, try to recall our knowledge about a particular topic, or look at ourselves in a mirror before leaving for an important engagement, we are dealing with data of which we ourselves are the source.

We also use these data to assess our own internal feelings. Our sense of illness, fear, happiness, frustration, confusion, excitement, pain, and anxiety are associated with data that originate in our own physiological functioning.

Certainly the great majority of information of significance to us in our environment arises either directly or indirectly from the activities of other persons. Sometimes these data result from language use, other times from appearances, actions, gestures, the use of space, time, and so on. Often the messages which have importance to us originate out of direct, face-to-face encounters with others.

Other messages which are significant to us are a product of the activities of persons separated from us in either time or space or both. By means of various media, data created by persons in another time or place can play a highly significant role in our lives. A favorite television program, the evening news, a letter from a friend far away, a best-selling novel, the morning paper, a cherished painting, or the latest album by a favorite recording group often satisfy many of the same needs as face-to-face encounters, though the originator and receiver of the information are separated from one another physically.

In many circumstances we are limited as to which of these data sources we can use. If, for example, we wish to find out the temperature in Tokyo last night, we have little choice but to rely on messages provided by other persons through mass media. If we want to know how we feel about some situation facing us tomorrow, we are forced to rely on data we create ourselves. If we need to determine the exact temperature of our swimming pool, that data can be best derived by using data derived in a very different way—by placing a thermometer in water.

There are many instances in which we can choose among these sources. As an illustration, we can seek an answer to the question, "Is it hot in here?" using any of these types of data. We can make a determination based on our personal "feelings," we can ask the opinion of one or several other persons, or we can use a nearby thermometer. A similar situation occurs when we undertake a project such as assembling a swing set. We may choose to tackle the chore ourselves making use of the data provided by the manufacturer's instructions. We could seek the assistance of a neighbor. Or, we may "dig right in" without consulting the instructions, relying on our own resources and prior experience with similar projects. Or, as many of us do in such situations, we can use a combination of these data sources.

The availability or lack of availability of various sources of data has an obvious and direct impact upon the way in which we attend to, interpret, and retain information. Individuals may vary in terms of their preferences for particular types of sources, however, where there is a choice many people rely on self-created data first. That is, if we think we have the information necessary in a particular circumstance, we may go no further. When we feel we lack the internal resources to make sense of or handle a particular situation on our own that we turn to other types of data. We seek the advice of a doctor, consult a medical book, or undergo various diagnostic procedures, for instance, if a stomach pain persists or when we have determined that we lack the capability of adapting to the demands of the environment without assistance.

For a similar reason, when we enter a grocery store to shop for particular items, we will probably go directly to the shelves where we expect to find them. If, however, the store is an unfamiliar one, or the items are not where we expected, we are likely to glance at the signs hanging above the aisles or ask a clerk for assistance.

Mode

In a very basic sense the way data are processed may depend fundamentally on whether verbal or nonverbal channels are involved, as discussed earlier. In more obvious respects, information reception also varies depending upon whether visual, tactile, auditory, gustatory, or olfactory modes are involved. In any number of situations, for example, a touch or reassuring embrace will be taken note of and interpreted in quite a different way than spoken words of encouragement. In such an instance, "actions speak louder than words." In a similar sense, the smell of decaying garbage may be a much more poignant message than a newspaper story about the consequences of a garbage strike or a description of the odor from a friend who witnessed the accumulating trash. In certain other circumstances, however, words may be more salient than actions, such as in a brainstorming session, a term paper, a letter to a friend, a legal brief, or a debate.

Physical Character

Physical characteristics like size, color, brightness, and intensity can also be important to information processing. In general, symbols, actions, objects, or events that are large or prominent will attract more attention than those which are not. A bright light is more salient than a dim light; a loud noise more noticeable than a soft one. Similarly, a large headline is more noticeable than the small type used to designate the editorial staff of the newspaper or to list political notices. And, actions and circumstances that have major consequences for large numbers of people are more likely to be taken note of than less important events of less widespread impact. News items which appear on the front page of the newspaper or on the evening news—a fire, natural disaster, or international conflict—have an impact on large numbers of persons. The extent of their impact is a major factor in the information-reception processes of reporters and editors. For the same reason, readers and viewers are more likely to attend and be interested in these events than other news items that are given less prominence.

Other things being equal, message sources that have color, brightness, or intensity are more apt to be noticed and taken account of than those lacking these characteristics. A four-color advertisement, a brightly colored sport coat, a high intensity light are likely to be attended to before objects lacking these attributes. The *intensity* of potential visual or verbal messages can also be an important consideration in message reception. Visual nudity, explicit sexuality, and violence, for example, may well be responded to quite differently than images without these characteristics. People often attach quite a different meaning to "four-letter" words they regard as "obscene" than to other words that may have essentially the same meaning but lack intensity.

Organization

The way data are *organized* can also play a role in determining whether and how they will be attended and reacted to. A good deal of research in the area of persuasion has been directed toward determining the way in which the ordering of ideas or opinions affects listeners. More recent research on information processing has added to our knowledge in this area. This work, suggests, for instance, that when we are presented with a series of items, we devote greatest attention to the items listed first, and this information therefore has the greatest likelihood of becoming a part of our long-term memory.[23] When asked to recall items from a list after it has been completed, individuals do best with those things presented near the beginning and those near the end; the items at the beginning are thought to be recalled because they are still a part of one's short-term memory, while those at the beginning are remembered because the information can be retrieved from long-term memory.[24]

The significance of ordering of data in information reception is evident in a variety of settings. The arrangement of elements within a picture or paragraphs in a report can have a substantial impact on the overall impression created. The organization of material within a database is also an important factor in whether and how that material will be used.

Even the way in which various foods are arranged at a grocery store or in a cafeteria often has an impact on our data processing. How many times, for instance, do we pick up grocery items we hadn't intended to because we noticed them while on our way to the place in the store where bread or milk were shelved? In a wide range of circumstances, the arrangement and organization of things—objects, elements, or people—play a vital role in information reception.

Novelty

Often data which are novel, unfamiliar, or unusual stand out, "grabbing our attention" if only for the moment. While we may generally devote very little attention to the color of automobiles, a pink or purple car is likely to "catch the eye" of even the most preoccupied motorist.

FIGURE 7.9 Persons, objects, events, or patterns that are unique or novel often grab our attention far more than the usual, commonplace, or predictable. Barbara Cartland reports, for example, that during the two years after the Mona Lisa was stolen from the Louvre in Paris in 1911, more people came to stare at the place in the museum where the famous painting had hung than had come to see the actual painting during the 12 previous years.

Niagra Falls provides another interesting case in point. One of the first things that strikes most visitors to the falls is the pervasive sound created by the pounding of the falls to the river below. To residents of the area, however, the noise goes generally unnoticed. Ironically, it was the sudden absence of the thundering falls during a hard freeze in the winter of 1936 and a decade before in 1909 that reportedly awoke the residents.

SOURCE: Barbara Cartland, *Barbara Cartland's Book of Useless Information.*

The same principle applies in the areas of dress, language, appearance, greetings, and eye contact, where most of us devote little conscious attention unless the data dramatically violate what we have come to expect. An unfamiliar foreign language, unusual dress, or a normally tidy room in disarray often become very salient to us. And though we are typically only somewhat aware when we engage in a ritualistic handshake greeting, we certainly do take note when the other person squeezes our hand too firmly, too loosely, or continues to shake for seven or eight pumps. With eye contact, novel data often are met with the same reaction. We generally pay little attention to the length of another's eye contact unless the person stares at us "too long," or "not long enough."

FIGURE 7.10 Unusual objects, events, individuals, or actions often command attention and interest, at least initially.

Factors That Influence Information Reception: The Source

The most interesting and complex information reception decisions we make involve interpersonal data sources. Why do we listen to and believe some people more than others? Our decisions to attend to particular interpersonal sources and the manner in which we interpret and retain those messages depends upon a number of factors. Some of the most important of these are *proximity, attractiveness, similarity, authoritativeness, motivation, delivery, status, power, and authority.*

Proximity

One's distance from a source can have a major influence on the likelihood of our attending to particular data. Generally speaking, we are more likely to be exposed to sources which are close at hand than to those which are further away.[25] The closer we are, the less time, effort, and money that must be expended to avail ourselves of the data.

For example, if we are setting out to assemble a new lawn mower, we are much more likely to ask for the assistance of a neighbor if we reside in a housing development than if our home is two miles from the next residence. Or if we walk into a library and must pass by the reference librarian in order to get to the card catalogue, we may decide to ask his or her advice simply because of the person's proximity. For this same reason, it seems almost too obvious to note that we are far more likely to attend to the actions and reactions of a next door neighbor or colleague at work than to those of persons who live a block away or work in the next building.

The significance of distance as a factor in message reception is perhaps best illustrated by considering the function of communication technology. By means of television, radio, newspapers, magazines, books, and newer electronic technologies, data from thousands of miles away is available without leaving the comfort of one's home. It is, in fact, the ease of access to television and other media fare which have helped to make these technologies and the data they transport such a central part of our lives.

Physical and Social Attraction and Similarity

The way in which we process interpersonal messages often has a great deal to do with how attractive we believe a particular message source to be. Particularly when we are first meeting an individual, as we have discussed, we react largely to their dress, physique, manner, and general appearance. If, based on any of these messages, we are attracted to the person, it is likely that we will pay increased attention to, remember, and attach special significance to their words. In this way, attraction plays a significant, though often subtle, role in influencing the nature of selection, interpretation, and retention.

Though we tend to think of attractiveness primarily in physical terms, we often find persons appealing for other reasons, as well. An individual who appears to be friendly, warm, empathetic, concerned and who expresses interest in or respect for us may be quite attractive to us as a social companion. Like physical attractiveness, *social attractiveness* also can be an important influence in shaping our information-reception processes. When we determine that another individual is attractive to us, we are likely to pay more attention to them, expend more effort, and remember and attach particular significance to their actions and reactions to us and to other people, objects, and events in the environment.

Similarity is another factor of significance to message reception. The more like a source we are, or believe ourselves to be, the more likely we are to pay particular attention to that person and what they say.[26] Sometimes similarities that interest us in others are basic characteristics like gender, level of education, age, religion, background, race, hobbies, or language capacity. In other instances, we are particularly interested in persons because we believe they share our needs, attitudes, goals, or values.

The influence of similarity on reception is especially well-illustrated by the great impact of one's peer group, beginning in our early school years. Our cohorts have a role in shaping our reactions to clothing, movies, school, books,various occupations, and also to our parents, friends, and acquaintances. Preferences for persons with similar cultural, religious, racial, occupational, and educational background continue to play an important role in data selection, interpretation, and retention in a great many of our activities through the course of our lifetime.

Credibility and Authoritativeness

The credibility of a source is a key factor in information-reception decisions. We are especially likely to attend to and retain data from sources we believe to be experienced and/or knowledgeable.[27] Certain persons—or categories of persons—may be viewed as credible and authoritative, regardless of the topic. Data provided by medical doctors, clergymen, professors, or lawyers, for example, may be regarded as more noteworthy than messages from persons with other vocations even on topics which are outside the former's areas of expertise. Similarly, actors, television personalities, politicians, and other persons who are in the "public eye" may be given particular attention and significance. Thus, the actor speaking on politics or the medical doctor lecturing on religion may be afforded more than an average level of attention by receivers because of the credibility attached to the person by virtue of education or fame.

In many instances, the credibility accorded a particular person depends upon the topic in question. Most of us, for example, are more likely to attend to and retain information on international affairs presented by a network news commentator than to data on the same topic offered by our next door neighbor. When the topic is insurance, however, we may well attach more credibility to our neighbor who has twenty-five years experience working in that field than to reports provided by the newscaster. In any case, the relative credibility and authoritativeness attached to particular sources is generally a factor of prime importance in message reception dynamics.

Motivation, Intent, and Delivery

The manner in which we react to a particular interpersonal message source also depends upon the way we explain his or her actions to ourselves.[28] Depending upon what motives we attribute to an individual, our response may vary substantially. If we assume a person intends to inform us, we are likely to react to and interpret his or her messages in a different way than if we believe the intention is to persuade or deceive us. If we trust a person and believe he or she "has our best interests at heart," we are likely to be more receptive than if we believe he or she is just looking out for himself or herself, and so forth. The manner in which a source delivers a message is an additional factor which influences the way we select, interpret, and react to data.

Status, Power, and Authority

The presence or lack of status can also be important in determining how likely it is that a source or particular data will be selected and acted upon. The power of a source—the extent to which he or she is capable of dispensing rewards for selecting, remembering and interpreting data in a particular way—is also influential in information processing. Generally speaking, parents, teachers, employers, supervisors, or other persons who have status, power, or authority relative to us have a better than average chance of obtaining our attention to their messages. Our belief that such persons have power or status directs our attention to their words and actions in an effort to be aware of their opinions or to seek their favor. To the extent that we can be rewarded or punished through grades, money, praise, or other means for interpreting their messages in particular ways, we may be especially attentive to them.

Factors That Influence Information Reception: The Medium and Environment

Beyond the *individual*, the *data*, and the *source*, the *medium* and *environment* also have a substantial impact on selection, interpretation, and retention.

The Medium

Differences such as whether data are presented via print or illustration, gesture or dress, film or microfiche, radio broadcast or the spoken words of a friend, can have a direct, and in some cases obvious, influence on information reception in several respects. Simply in terms of availability, some media provide a greater likelihood of exposure to data than others. More consumers watch television, than read academic journals, and both of these numbers are greater, at present, than the number of individuals who subscribe to and use electronic consumer databases.

Beyond the rather obvious assets and liabilities of various mass media, there are less apparent distinctions in terms of information reception. Recent studies have shown, for instance, that newspapers have been declining as primary sources of national and international news among many individuals. Yet, it has also been suggested that newspapers are, in fact, a major data source for local news.[29] It has also been noted that depending upon the circumstances data provided by several media are often more influential than when available on a single medium alone.[30] Even the manner in which data are presented within a medium can have a bearing on information processing. In newspapers, for instance, factors such as sentence length, the number of different words used, punctuation, and language level can have an influence on comprehension, credibility, and interest associated with a publication.[31]

Of the various mass media, television has no doubt received the most attention among scholars in the past several decades. This interest is not surprising given the central role of television in the lives of most Americans. Even as early as 1951 families viewed television on the average of 4 hours and 35 minutes a day. That number jumped to 5 hours and 9 minutes in 1961, and to just over six hours in 1971. In 1981, the average family viewed 6 hours and 44 minutes of television per day.[32] In terms of exposure to data, alone, television is clearly a major force in our lives.

As noted in the recent summary of a National Institute of Mental Health report, *Television and Behavior,* "Television can no longer be considered as a casual part of daily life, as an electronic toy."[33]

> The simplest representations (on television) are literal visual and auditory pictures of something in the real world, for example, a car moving along a highway. To process this information, children probably depend on the same perceptual and cognitive skills they use in processing information in the real world. . . . At the next level are the forms and conventions that do not have real-world counterparts. Some of them are analogs of real-world experiences. . . . For example, a "zoom in," in which the object in front of the camera seems to get larger and more focused, is similar to moving closer to something in real life. But some effects, for example slow motion, do not appear in the real world, and children—and others who are unfamiliar with television—must learn what they mean.
>
> Once they are learned, these media conventions can be used by people in their own thinking. For example, children may learn to analyze a complex stimulus into its smaller parts by watching the camera zoom in and out. The forms can take on meaning, sometimes as a result of associations seen on television.[34]

The report also indicates that the rapid movement and visual and audio contrasts presented by television are particularly salient to very young viewers, who often become "passive consumers of audio-visual thrills."[35]

The Environment

Context and Setting The way we process data depends greatly on the environmental *context* or *setting.* Whether and how a particular person or event is reacted to depends, for instance, on whether we are at home or on vacation, at work or engaged in a leisure activity. It will often depend also on whether the messages are being processed in an office, a church, a bedroom, or an auditorium. It is not at all difficult to think of numerous examples of how the same data would be interpreted much differently depending upon the contexts in which the data were encountered.

An especially important factor, in this regard, is whether or not other people are present in a particular setting. And one may well react quite differently to data if the others present are friends than if they are strangers, members of the same as opposed to the opposite sex, few in number rather than a large group, and so on.

FIGURE 7.11 The context or setting in which potential information sources are encountered can be an important factor influencing whether and how data are selected, interpreted, and remembered.

The presence of others often has a very direct bearing on how we select as well as interpret and retain information.[36] How we want to be seen, how we think other persons see us, what we believe others expect from us, and what we think they think about the situation we are in are among the considerations that shape the way we react in social situations. If, for instance, we are in the company of a colleague or friend, we may pay particular attention to the people, events, and circumstances he or she attends to. And in our effort to decide how well we liked a particular movie, lecture, painting, or person, the reactions of other persons are often of major significance to our own judgments. Sometimes, we conform our own data processing to that of others for appearances only; in many other instances the influence is more subtle and far-reaching, as we shall discuss in Chapter 9.

Repetition Yet another factor that can make a difference in message reception is *repetition*. In general, as we have noted already, we are likely to take into account and remember data which are often repeated. Advertising slogans and jingles, the lyrics of popular songs, the multiplication table, an often-called phone number, and the birth dates of family members "stand out in our minds," largely because they have been repeated so often. In addition to its role in learning these sorts of data, repetition also contributes to our learning of our native language, our parents' and friends' opinions, the slang and jargon of our associates, and the accent of our geographic region.

Consistency and Competition The extent to which data on a particular topic are consistent has an impact on selection, interpretation, and retention. Where an individual has been exposed over a long period of time to one religious orientation, one political philosophy, or one set of values, there is a likelihood that the individual will come to select and accept data consistent with that position. *Brainwashing* is the extreme example of this sort of communication phenomenon. In such circumstances, an individual is bombarded with data which advocate a particular position, and data supporting alternative points of view are systematically eliminated from the environment. When coupled with the promise of reward (or absence of punishment), consistency and the lack of competitive data become powerful shaping forces influencing the probability of data selection and the manner of interpretation and retention.

In considerably less extreme forms, the educational process makes use of these same principles. Math, language, reading, and spelling are taught not only through repetition but also through consistency. And substantial effort—including the arrangement of classroom furniture, and the use of examinations, lectures, books, and homework assignments—is directed toward minimizing the influence of competing data.

Conclusion

Early S→M→R perspectives on communication often characterized the receiver as the passive recipient of messages. Our more recent knowledge of the information reception argues convincingly to the contrary, suggesting instead, that the individual plays an active and central role in the selection, interpretation, and retention of information. Morton Hunt makes this point eloquently in discussing the opening sentence of Gibbon's *Decline and Fall of the Roman Empire:*

> "In the second century of the Christian era, the Empire of Rome comprehended the fairest part of the earth, and the most civilised portion of mankind."

> A reader who finds this sentence perfectly intelligible does so not because Gibbon was a lucid stylist but because he or she knows when the Christian era began, understands the concept of "empire," is familiar enough with history to recognize the huge sociocultural phenomenon known as "Rome," has enough information about world geography so that the phrase "the fairest part of the earth" produces a number of images in the mind, and, finally, can muster a whole congeries of ideas about the kinds of civilization that then existed. What skill, to elicit that profusion of associations with those few well-chosen cues—but what a performance by the the reader! One hardly knows which to admire more....[37]

Without doing any injustice to Hunt's intent, we could extend the point to apply equally to the impressive accomplishments of a listener in a personal, group, public, or mediated setting, or to the observer of visual images in an art gallery, a baseball game, or of a television program.

Summary

In this chapter, our focus has been upon the nature of information reception, and the processes involved in sensing and making sense of the people, objects, and circumstances in our environment. Individuals play an active role in this process though we may have little awareness that it is taking place.

Data *selection, interpretation,* and *retention* are primary facets of information reception. The first, involves the *selective attention* to particular environmental data from all those to which an individual is exposed. The second consists of the transformation of those data into a form that has value and utility for the individual, a process which directly involves retention, and *short* and *long-term memory.* In actual operation selection, interpretation and retention are very much interrelated activities.

A number of factors influence selection, interpretation, and retention. Many of them have to do with the individual and his or her needs, attitudes, beliefs, values, goals, capabilities, uses, style, experience, and habits.

Other factors which influence information reception have to do with the *data* itself—type, mode, physical character, novelty, and organization. The sources also have an impact on message reception, including their proximity, credibility, authoritativeness, attractiveness, similarity, motivation, intention, style, status, power, and authority. Message reception may also be affected by factors related to the medium and environment in which data are created and or reacted to.

While early communication theory characterized humans as passive recipients of data, our knowledge of information processing underscores the active nature of the activity.

Notes

1. Cf. Stuart M. Albert, Lee Alan Becker, and Timothy C. Brock, "Familiarity, Utility, and Supportiveness as Determinants of Information Receptivity." *Journal of Personality and Social Psychology,* **14**: 292–301 (1970). D.E. Broadbent, "A Mechanical Model for Human Attention and Immediate Memory," *Psychological Review,* **64**: 205–215 (1957). Robert T. Craig, "Information Systems Theory and Research: An Overview of Individual Information Processing." In *Communication Yearbook 3,* Dan Nimmo, ed., (New Brunswick, NJ: Transaction, International Communication Association, 1979), 99–120. D. Deutsch, and J.A. Deutsch, "Attention: Some Theoretical Considerations," *Psychological Review,* **70**: 80–90 (1963). Lewis Donohew, and Philip Palmgreen, "An Investigation of 'Mechanisms' of Information Selection," *Journalism Quarterly,* **48**: 624–639 (1971). Lewis Donohew and Philip Palmgreen, "Reappraisal of Dissonance and the Selective Exposure Hypothesis," *Journalism Quarterly,* **48**: 412–420 (1971). Anne M Treisman, "Strategies and Models of Selective Attention," *Psychological Review,* **76**: 3, 282–299 (1969).
2. Samuel L. Becker, "Visual Stimuli and the Construction of Meaning," In *Visual Learning, Thinking and Communication.* Bikkar S. Randhawa, ed., (New York: Academic Press, 1978), pp. 39–60.
3. Cf. D.E. Broadbent, op. cit.
4. Robert T. Craig, op. cit., p. 102

5. See discussion of "Research on Behavior Without Awareness," In James V. McConnell, Richard L. Cutler, and Elton B. McNeil, "Subliminal Stimulation: An Overview." *American Psychologist*, **13**: (1958) pp. 230–232.

6. The issue of *what* is recalled under hypnosis and drugs is relatively controversial. While it was long believed that the information recalled was in its "original, unaltered" form, recent studies have suggested that often, what is remembered is a transformed, elaborated, and often distorted version, changed by time and circumstance. For a discussion of these issues, see Elizabeth Loftus, *Memory*, (Reading, MA: Addison-Wesley, 1980), pp. 54–62.

7. Cf. Robert T. Craig, op. cit., p. 103.

8. Morton Hunt, *The Universe Within*, (New York: Simon & Schuster, 1982), p. 85.

9. Ibid., p. 86.

10. Ibid.

11. For a more detailed description of information processing stages and dynamics see Geoffrey R. Loftus and Elizabeth F. Loftus, op. cit., and Peter H. Lindsay and Donald A. Norman, *Human Information Processing*, (New York: Academic, 1977).

12. Morton Hunt, op. cit., p. 104.

13. Geoffrey R. Loftus, and Elizabeth F. Loftus, op. cit., p. 8. The authors provide a useful overview and model of information processing and memory in their "Introduction." See also Morton Hunt, op. cit., especially Ch. 3, and Elizabeth Loftus, op. cit., especially Ch. 2.

14. Geoffrey Loftus and Elizabeth F. Loftus, op. cit., p. 8.

15. Morton Hunt, op. cit., pp. 107–108.

16. One of the most widely cited classifications in recent years was provided in the writings of Abraham Maslow, "A Theory of Human Motivation," *Psychological Review*, **50**: (1943) pp. 370–396. The framework differentiates between basic biological needs and "higher order" psychological and social needs.

17. Cf. Elihu Katz, Jay G. Blumler, and Michael Gurevitch, "Utilization of Mass Communication by the Individual," In *The Uses of Mass Communications*, Jay G. Blumler and Elihu Katz, eds., (Beverly Hills, CA: Sage, 1974) pp. 22–23.

18. Cf. William J. McGuire, "The Nature of Attitudes and Attitude Change," In *The Handbook of Social Psychology*, Vol. 3, Gardner Lindzey and Elliot Aronson, eds., (Reading, MA: Addison-Wesley, 1969). See especially the discussion of the needs for "preservation" and "growth."

19. Elihu Katz, Jay G. Blumler, and Michael Gurevitch, op. cit., pp. 20–21.

20. Cf. Elizabeth Loftus, op. cit., Ch. 6, and Daniel J. Levinson (with Charlotte N. Darrow, Edward B. Klein, Maria M. Levinson and Braxton McKee), *The Seasons of a Man's Life* (New York: Ballantine, 1978).

21. Lawrence R. Wheeless, "The Effects of Attitude, Credibility, and

Homophily on Selective Exposure to Information," *Speech Monographs,* **41:** (April 1974), pp. 329–338.

22. Cf. Phillip Zimbardo, *Shyness* (Reading, MA: Addison-Wesley); James C. McCroskey, "Oral Communication Apprehension: A Summary of Recent Theory and Research," *Human Communication Research,* **4:**(1977) pp. 78–96; Gerald M. Phillips and Nancy J. Metzger, "The Reticent Syndrome: Some Theoretical Considerations About Etiology and Treatment." *Speech Monographs,* **40:** (1973).

23. Elizabeth Loftus, op. cit., pp. 24–25.

24. Ibid.

25. Cf. Nan Lin, *The Study of Human Communication,* (New York: Bobbs-Merrill, 1973), pp 44–46.

26. Cf. Lawrence R. Wheeless, op. cit.

27. Carl I. Hovland and W. Weiss, "The Influence of Source Credibility on Communication Effectiveness," *Public Opinion Quarterly,* **15:** 635–650 (1951); for a discussion of the role of credibility in communication see James C. McCroskey, *An Introduction to Rhetorical Communication* (Englewood Cliffs, NJ: Prentice-Hall, 1978), especially Ch. 4.

28. The way we explain behavior to ourselves is the focus of work in an area called *attribution theory.* See, for instance, Edward E. Jones, David E. Kanouse, Harold H. Kelley, Richard E. Nisbett, Stuart Valins, and Bernad Weiner, eds., *Attribution: Perceiving the Causes of Behavior,* (Morristown, NJ: General Learning Press, 1971) for a overview of area.

29. R.C. Adams, "Newspapers and Television as News Information Media," *Journalism Quarterly,* **58:** 4 (Winter 1981), pp. 627–629.

30. Steve K. Toggerson, "Media coverage and Information-Seeking Behavior," *Journalism Quarterly,* **58:** 1 (Spring 1981), pp. 89–92.

31. Cf. Judee K. Burgoon, Michael Burgoon, and Miriam Wilkinson, "Writing Style as Predictor of Newspaper Readership, Satisfaction, and Image," *Journalism Quarterly,* **58:** 2 (Summer 1981), pp. 225–231.

32. "What is TV Doing to America?" *U.S. News and World Report* (August 2, 1982), p. 29.

33. *Television and Behavior: Ten Years of Scientific Progress and Implications for the Eighties, Vol. 1: Summary Report* (Rockville, MD: National Institute of Mental Health, 1982), p. 87.

34. Ibid., p. 24.

35. Ibid., p. 26.

36. An excellent overview of these dynamics is provided in Elliot Aronson, *The Social Animal,* (San Francisco: Freeman, 1972).

37. Morton Hunt, op. cit., p. 119–121.

References and Suggested Reading

Abelson, Herbert I., and Marvin Karlins. *Persuasion.* New York: Springer, 1970.

Albert, Stuart M., Lee Alan Becker and Timothy C. Brock. "Familiarity, Utility, and Supportiveness as Determinants of Information Receptivity." *Journal of Personal and Social Psychology, 14,* 4 (1970), 292–301.

Adams, R.C., "Newspapers and Television as News Information Media," *Journalism Quarterly, 58,* 4 (Winter 1981), 627–629.

Aronson, Elliot. *The Social Animal.* San Francisco: Freeman, 1972.

Baker, Stephen. *Visual Persuasion.* New York: McGraw-Hill, 1961.

Becker, Samuel L. "Visual Stimuli and the Construction of Meaning," in *Visual Learning, Thinking and Communication.* Bikkar S. Randhawa (Ed.), New York: Academic Press, 1978, pp. 39–60.

Bettinghaus, Erwin P. *Persuasive Communication.* New York: Holt, 1968.

Brembeck, Winston L., and William S. Howell. *Persuasion: A Means of Social Influence.* Englewood Cliffs, NJ: Prentice-Hall, 1976.

Broadbent, D.E. "A Mechanical Model for Human Attention and Immediate Memory." *Psychological Review, 64,* 3 (1957), 205–215.

Budd, Richard W. and Brent D. Ruben, *Beyond Media: New Approaches to Mass Communication.* Rochelle Park, NJ: Hayden, 1979.

Burgoon, Judee K., Michael Burgoon, and Miriam Wilkinson. "Writing Style as Predictor of Newspaper Readership, Satisfaction, and Image." *Journalism Quarterly, 58,* 2 (Summer 1981), 225–231.

Burgoon, Michael. *Approaching Speech Communication.* New York: Holt, 1974.

———, and Gerald R. Miller. *New Techniques of Persuasion.* New York: Harper, 1973.

Cathcart, Robert and Gary Gumpert, Eds. *Inter/Media.* New York: Oxford University Press, 1979.

Craig, Robert T. "Information Systems Theory and Research: An Overview of Individual Information Processing." In *Communication Yearbook 3,* Ed. by Dan Nimmo. New Brunswick, NJ: Transaction, International Communication Association, 1979, 99–120.

Craik, Fergus I.M. "A Process View of Short-Term Retention." In *Cognitive Theory, Volume 1.* Ed. by Richard M. Shiffrin, N. John Castellan, Harold R. Lindman, and David B. Pisoni. Hillsdale, NJ: Lawrence Erlbaum, 1975, pp 173–192.

Deutsch, D. and J.A. Deutsch. "Attention: Some Theoretical Considerations." *Psychological Review, 70,* 1 (1963) 80–90.

Donohew, Lewis and Philip Palmgreen. "An Investigation of 'Mechanisms' of Information Selection." *Journalism Quarterly 48* (1971), 624–639.

——— "Reappraisal of Dissonance and the Selective Exposure Hypothesis." *Journalism Quarterly 48* (1971), 412–420.

Douglas, Mary. *Rules and Meanings.* New York: Penguin, 1977.

Farnham-Diggory, Sylvia. *Information Processing in Children.* New York: Academic Press, 1972.

Freedman, Jonathan L. and David O. Sears. "Selective Exposure to Information: A Critical Review." *Public Opinion Quarterly, 31,* (1967).

Hovland, Carl I., and W. Weiss. "The Influence of Source Credibility on Communication Effectiveness." *Public Opinion Quarterly, 15,* (1951), 635–650.

Hunt, Morton. *The Universe Within.* New York: Simon and Schuster, 1982.

Jones, Edward E., David E. Kanouse, Harold H. Kelley, Richard E.

Nisbett, Stuart Valins, and Bernard Weiner, (Eds.) *Attribution: Perceiving the Causes of Behavior*. Morristown, NJ: General Learning Press, 1971.

Katz, Elihu, Jay G. Blumler, and Michael Gurevitch. "Utilization of Mass Communication by the Individual." In *The Uses of Mass Communications*. Ed. by Jay G. Blumler and Elihu Katz. Beverly Hills, CA: Sage, 1974, 19–32.

Kees, Weldon and Jurgen Ruesch. *Nonverbal Communication*. Los Angeles, CA: University of California Press, 1972.

Larson, Charles *Persuasion: Reception and Responsibility*. Belmont, CA: Wadsworth, 1979.

Levinson, Daniel J. (with Charlotte N. Darrow, Edward B. Klein, Maria H. Levinson and Braxton McKee). *The Seasons of a Man's Life*. New York: Ballantine, 1978.

Lin, Nan. *The Study of Human Communication*. New York: Bobbs-Merrill, 1973.

Lindsay, Peter H. and Donald A. Norman. *Human Information Processing*. New York: Academic, 1977.

Littlejohn, Stephen W. *Theories of Human Communication*. Columbus, OH: Merrill, 1978.

Loftus, Geoffrey R. and Elizabeth F. Loftus. *Human Memory: The Processing of Information*. Hillsdale, NJ: Lawrence Erlbaum, 1976.

Loftus, Elizabeth. *Memory*. Reading, MA: Addison-Wesley, 1980.

McConnell, James V., Richard L. Cutler, and Elton B. McNeil. "Subliminal Stimulation: An Overview." *American Psychologist*, 13 (1958), 229–242.

McCroskey, James C. and Lawrence R. Wheeless. *Introduction to Human Communication*. Boston: Allyn & Bacon, 1976.

———. "Oral Communication Apprehension: A Summary of Recent Theory and Research." *Human Communication Research*, 4 (1957), 78–96.

———. *An Introduction to Rhetorical Communication*. Englewood Cliffs, NJ: Prentice-Hall, 1978.

McGuire, William, J. "The Nature of Attitudes and Attitude Change." In *The Handbook of Social Psychology*, Vol. 3, Edited by Gardner Lindzey and Elliot Aronson. Reading, MA: Addison-Wesley, (1969), 136–314.

———. "Psychological Motives and Communication Gratification." In *The Uses of Mass Communications*. Ed. by Jay G. Blumler and Elihu Katz. Beverly Hills, CA: Sage, 1974, pp. 167–195.

McLeod, Jack M., Carl R. Bybee and Jean A. Durall. "Evaluating Media Performance by Gratifications Sought and Received. *Journalism Quarterly*, 59, 1 (Spring 1982), 3–12, 59.

Maslow, Abraham. "A Theory of Human Motivation." *Psychological Review*, 50 (1943), 370–396.

Maslow, Abraham H. *Motivation and Personality*, 2nd ed., New York: Harper, 1954.

Miller, Jonathan. *The Body in Question*. New York: Random House, 1978.

Norman, Donald A. *Memory and Attention*. New York: Wiley, 1969.

Paivio, Allan. "On Exploring Visual Knowledge." In *Visual Learning*,

Thinking, and Communication. Ed. by Bikkar A. Randhawa. New York: Academic Press, 1978, 113–131.

Paris, Scott G. "Integration and Inference in Children's Comprehension and Memory." In *Cognitive Theory, Vol. 1*. Ed. by Richard M. Shiffrin, N. John Castelan, Harold R. Lindman, and David B. Pisoni. Hillsdale, NJ: Lawrence Erlbaum, 1975, 223–246.

Phillips, Gerald M., and Nancy J. Metzger. "The Reticent Syndrome: Some Theoretical Considerations About Etiology and Treatment." *Speech Monographs, 4* (1973).

Potts, George R. "Bring Order to Cognitive Structures." In *Cognitive Theory, Vol. 1*. Hillsdale, NJ: Lawrence Erlbaum, Ed. by Richard M. Shiffrin, N. John Castellan, Harold R. Lindman, and David B. Pisoni. 1975, pp. 247–270.

Powers, William G. and Michael D. Scott. *Interpersonal Communication: A Question of Needs*. Hopewell, NJ: Houghton Mifflin, 1978.

Randhawa, Bikkar S. (Ed.). *Visual Learning, Thinking and Communication*. New York: Academic Press, 1978.

Restle, Frank, Richard M. Shiffrin, N. John Catellan, Harold R. Lindman, and David B. Pisoni, Eds. *Cognitive Theory, Volume 1*. Hillsdale, NJ: Lawrence Erlbaum, 1975.

Robinson, Edward J., and Ralph L. Rosnow, Eds. *Experiments in Persuasion*. New York: Academic, 1967.

Rokeach, Milton. *Beliefs, Attitudes and Values*. San Francisco: Josey-Bass, 1968.

Schroder, Harold M., Michael J. Driver, and Siegfried Streufert. *Human Information Processing*. New York: Holt, 1967.

Sheehy, Gail. *Passages*. New York: Dutton, 1976.

Shiffrin, Richard M. "Short-Term Store: the Basis For a Memory System." In *Cognitive Theory, Volume 1*. Ed. by Richard M. Shiffrin, N. John Castellan, Harold R. Lindman, and David B. Pisoni. Hillsdale, NJ: Lawrence Erlbaum, 1975, 193–217.

Sigel, Irving E. "The Development of Pictorial Comprehension." In *Visual Learning, Thinking and Communication*. Bikkar S. Randhawa, Ed. New York: Academic Press, 1978, 93–111.

Simons, Herbert W. *Persuasion: Understanding, Practice, and Analysis*. Reading, MA: Addison-Wesley, 1976.

Television and Behavior: Ten Years of Scientific Progress and Implications for the Eighties. Vol. 1: Summary Report. Rockville, MD: National Institute of Mental Health, 1982, p. 87.

Toggerson, Steve K. "Media Coverage and Information-Seeking Behavior." *Journalism Quarterly, 58*, 1 (Spring 1981), 89–92.

Treisman, Anne M. "Strategies and Models of Selective Attention." *Psychological Review, 76*, 3 (1969), 282–299.

Wheeless, Lawrence R. "The Effects of Attitude, Credibility, and Homophily on Selective Exposure to Information." (April 1973). *Speech Monographs, 41* (1974), 329–338.

Zimbardo, Phillip. *Shyness*. Reading, MA: Addison-Wesley, 1979.

Communication Technology

The Tool-Making Animal

Chapter

8

In addition to our ability to create and use symbolic languages, our capacity for tool-making also visibly distinguishes us from other animals. Although monkeys have been observed using sticks and coconuts as weapons, no other animal is able to create tools to assist in adapting to and altering the environment at anywhere near the level of sophistication of humans.[1] This capacity has given us better ways of growing food, creating shelter, and fashioning bodily coverings. It has also led to the creation of an impressive array of devices through which we extend our communication ability.

From Smoke Signals to Telecommunication

It was about 20,000 B.C. when early humans first carved symbols on the walls of caves and used drums and smoke to signal one another. With these very primitive communication devices, the foundations of our modern information processing technologies were put firmly into place. While smoke signals and cave drawings served their purpose well, the development of the first systems of writing dramatically increased the possibilities for making coded data both permanent and portable.

By about 1,000 B.C., early pictographic writing had given way to systems of writing that made use of an alphabet. Paper was invented around 100 A.D., and the oldest-known printed piece is a Sutra printed in Korea in 750 A.D. Although printing as it is known today began in Germany during the mid-15th century, Chinese, Japanese, and Koreans developed printing much earlier. By 1500 Johann Gutenberg had completed the printing of a Bible using movable type and printing process he had developed. In many ways the printing press helped to revolutionize the communication process, because it greatly increased the rate at which written and other visual documents could be produced.

Other communication technologies were also created during this period. The ancient Greeks, for example, built a series of high walls stretching across the countryside, from which messages were relayed using fire and smoke. The Persians and Romans had a postal system; official correspondence was carried by horseback between regular stations on a more or less regular basis.

The impact of printing began to be felt in the 1500s and 1600s, and it was during this period that newspapers appeared in their present-day form. In the 1600s, regular mail service was also established to link major cities in Europe, and by the 1700s postal services were operating in many countries. The 1800s brought the advent of telegraph and the Morse code, and with them the introduction of electronic technologies that greatly increased both *range* and *immediacy*.[2]

There were a number of other notable advances in the 1800s. In 1866, the Atlantic was crossed by cable, further extending the capability for rapid

Early humans use paintings and cave drawings to record events of the day.

Sumerians develop first system of writing using pictographs.

20,000 B.C.

3000 B.C.

1600 B.C.
1500–1000 B.C.

First hearing aid—called ear trumpet—developed.

Semites forerunner of present-day alphabet.

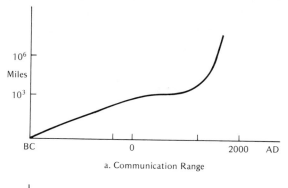

a. Communication Range

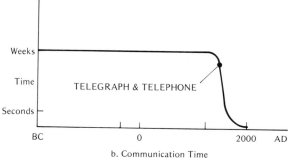

b. Communication Time

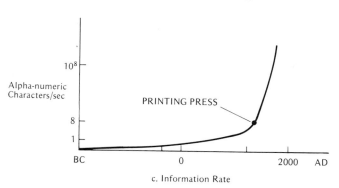

c. Information Rate

FIGURE 8.1 The evolution of communication technology in terms of *range, time,* and information *transmission rate.* The introduction of telegraph and telephone dramatically decreased the time involved in data transmission and the printing press marked the beginning of impressive increases in the range at which data can be dispersed.

SOURCE: Understanding Communications Systems, Don L. Cannon and Gerald Luecke, Copyright © 1980, Texas Instruments Learning Center, Dallas, Texas. By Permission.

data transmission, and it was during the same period when the typewriter and telephone were patented.

Prior to Marconi's development in 1895 of the wireless telegraph—or radio, as it is commonly termed today—the source and the destination had to be physically connected by wire. With a means for sending code and later voice through the air, many new options were available. These advances paved the way for the development of television in the 1930s.

The mid-1950s saw the widespread use of television, and the 1960s the

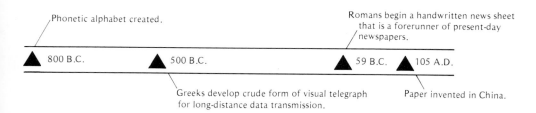

development of communication satellites which served much the same relay function as did the early and far less sophisticated "fire towers" of ancient Greece. In the years that followed, a number of new devices become widely available, including miniaturized transistor radios, stereophonic audio equipment, home movie systems, photocopying devices, and eight-track and cassette audio recorders.

More recent developments in the 1970s and early 1980s have included video games, cable television, video disc, home computers, video text, popular use of computerized databases, word processing, advanced telephone systems, and telecommunication technology.

Functions of Communication Technology

In the most obvious respects, it is difficult to see much similarity between such diverse technologies as smoke signals, telephones, typewriters, television, and computers. If we think of these in terms of basic concepts of communication and behavior, however, the relationship between tools such as these becomes more apparent. Each of these devices, along with many others, qualifies as communication technology if it *expands our visual, auditory, olfactory, gustatory, or tactile capacities*. We can define *communication technology*, then, as any *tool, special device, or medium which assists in the production, distribution, storage, reception, or display of data*.

Production, Transmission, and Display

Perhaps the most obvious contribution of communication technology has been the extension of our ability to create, transmit, and display auditory and visual data at great distances in time and space from their point of origin. Beginning with spoken language, early humans progressed in their utilization of auditory communication, to make use of drums, musical instruments, telegraph, telephone, and later commercial AM, FM, and citizen's band radio.

Our use of visual devices to extend our capacity for the production and dissemination of data began with cave drawings and early forms of the alphabet.[3] Later, the use of hand and arm signals, signs, billboards, flags, lanterns, printing, photographic, and copying equipment of all kinds further broadened our visual abilities. Television, film, projection systems, video disc, and video cassette have extended both the visual and auditory modalities simultaneously.

A number of other tools serve many of these same basic functions, though less obviously. For instance, pencils, pens, typewriters, and the materials of the artist further our human capability for creating, transmitting,

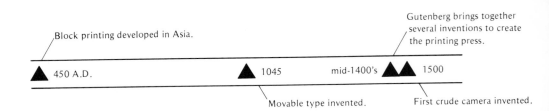

Block printing developed in Asia.

Gutenberg brings together several inventions to create the printing press.

▲ 450 A.D.   ▲ 1045   mid-1400's ▲▲ 1500

Movable type invented.   First crude camera invented.

and displaying visual messages. And computers, video games, and even many of the hand-held electronic games and calculators have equivalent uses. Without too much stretch of the imagination, even such devices as heating pads, saunas, and hot tubs would qualify as communication technologies, in that they extend our tactile capacities.

Multiplication, Duplication, and Amplification

Some of the data produced, transmitted, and displayed by means of communication technologies are sent by one individual to another person whose identity is known to the source. In situations such as this, technology essentially extends our capacity for *one-to-one*, or face-to-face, conversation. There are a number of times when we use communication technologies in this way, as when we call a friend on the phone, write a letter to a relative, or use an inter-office intercom. Communication technologies which assist in exchanges among two or several people in this way can be termed *interpersonal* (or *personal*) *media*, because they are being used in *interpersonal* communication.

In a great many other situations, messages are created and transmitted to a large number of individuals who are unknown to the originator. This sort of *one-to-many* situation is generally termed, *mass communication*, and, technologies used in this fashion are termed *mass media*. Whether one thinks of cave drawings, printing presses, video text, photocopying machines, or public address systems, the essential role of each in communication is quite similar. Tools such as these make it possible for what begins as a single message to be *multiplied, duplicated, amplified,* or *enlarged,* thereby making *mass* communication possible. In so doing, these technologies alter the proximity and availability of particular data and thereby heighten the probability of attention to them.

Reception, Storage, and Retrieval

In one sense, any technology which aids in the production, multiplication, display, or amplification of data plays a vital role in information reception. Other more specialized devices, however, play an even more basic role in message reception. Eyeglasses, mirrors, contact lenses, x-ray systems, microscopes, magnifying glasses, binoculars, radar, periscopes, and telescopes, for instance, are invaluable to us as devices for extending our capability for receiving visual information. And tools such as hearing aids, earphones, and stethoscopes give us capabilities for the reception of data unavailable to any other species.

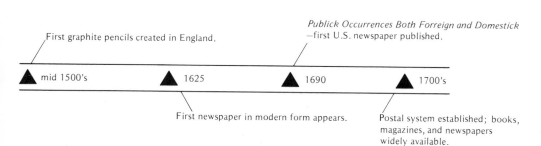

First graphite pencils created in England.

Publick Occurrences Both Forreign and Domestick —first U.S. newspaper published.

▲ mid 1500's   ▲ 1625   ▲ 1690   ▲ 1700's

First newspaper in modern form appears.

Postal system established; books, magazines, and newspapers widely available.

FIGURE 8.2

Our human tool-making capacity assists by extending our information retention abilities. Though we are not accustomed to thinking of diaries, wills, files, and appointment calendars as communication technologies, they fit the definition in that they further our capacity for storage and retrieval. Among the more familiar technologies that assist us in these ways are tape recorders, dictating and copying machines, phonograph records, microfiche and microfilm, video cassette and video disc. Certainly, the most noteworthy information-recording tool to be developed is the computer, through which data of all sorts can be stored, classified, reclassified, and retrieved at any point in time. Each of these tools—from the simple memo to the computer— greatly expands our data storage and retrieval capabilities.

The Evolution of Form

Over the course of human history the forms of communication technology have changed in dramatic, complex ways. Our first messages using communi-

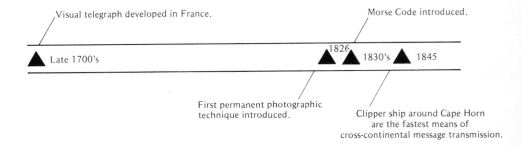

Visual telegraph developed in France.

Morse Code introduced.

▲ Late 1700's

1826
▲ ▲ 1830's ▲ 1845

First permanent photographic technique introduced.

Clipper ship around Cape Horn are the fastest means of cross-continental message transmission.

cation tools were fashioned from sticks, rocks, smoke, and fire. We have progressed today to the point where we are surrounded by a wide variety of machines and electronic devices which extend our information-processing modalities incredibly. While not too many years ago the advent of television made it possible for us to view as well as listen to local and national programming for the first time, we now have cable television, projection television, and even television sets that double as telephones. Where we once made our program selections from among a handful of stations, we are now able to choose among any number of offerings in most locales in the country. And with cassette, video disc, and home video game and computer systems, we are not limited in our selections to programs being broadcast to us. In effect, we are able to create our own programming with such luxuries as rewind, slow motion, stop-action, fast-forward, and stereo sound.

Further advances in computers, cable, and telecommunication technologies provide still other options. Using relatively inexpensive microcomputers and especially created software programs, one can send and receive acoustically coded alpha-numeric data through telephone lines. With this technology, the user has access to a number of large databases which contain current newspapers, magazines, stock market quotes, international weather reports, airline schedules, and a variety of games. Using this same equipment, it is possible to bank, shop, and make restaurant reservations from home, order "hard" printed copies of desired materials, and "converse" with other computers.

In a growing number of cities, "two-way" television has also become a reality. With cable systems like QUBE, subscribers not only select between standard and local programs but are also able to interact with the broadcast center.[4] Using a small keypad device similar to a hand-held calculator, users may participate in programmed instruction or an opinion poll without leaving home. A centrally located computer scans all sets connected to the cable system every few seconds, and in the case of opinion polls, tabulates viewer responses instanteously. The results of the polling can then be displayed on viewers' sets.

As impressive as these home technologies are, there is little doubt that they will seem elementary compared to the home-communication centers to which we will become accustomed in the years ahead. In all likelihood, these installations will combine the data storage and retrieval capacity of the computer and video disc, with video display, stereophonic audio reproduction, and print capability.

With these systems we will have at our disposal a wide variety of preprogrammed fare from which to choose—films, network shows, video concerts, news programs, documentaries, games, national and international

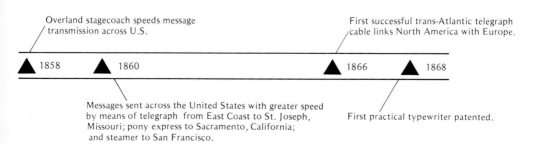

Overland stagecoach speeds message transmission across U.S.

First successful trans-Atlantic telegraph cable links North America with Europe.

▲ 1858   ▲ 1860   ▲ 1866   ▲ 1868

Messages sent across the United States with greater speed by means of telegraph from East Coast to St. Joseph, Missouri; pony express to Sacramento, California; and steamer to San Francisco.

First practical typewriter patented.

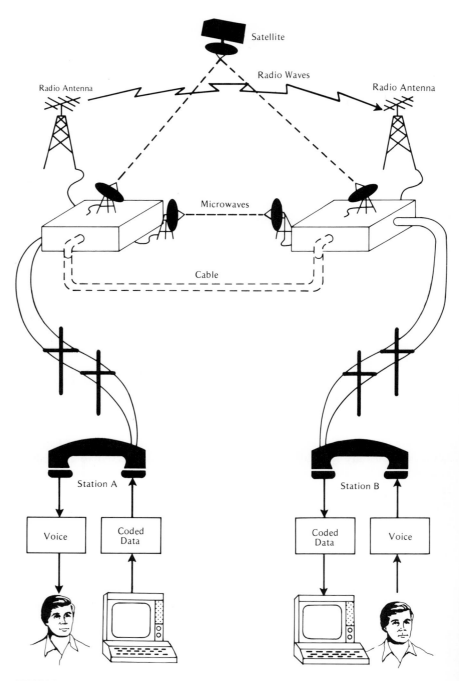

FIGURE 8.3 Voice and coded auditory or visual data are transmitted between home, office, or production studios via satellite, radio wave, microwave, or cable.

SOURCE: Understanding Communication Systems. Don L. Cannon and Gerald Luecke. Dallas: Texas Instruments Learning Center, 1980. By permission.

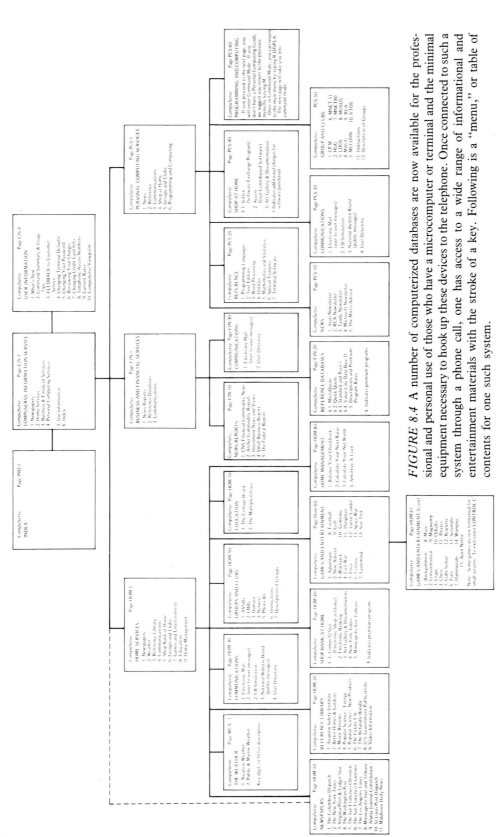

FIGURE 8.4 A number of computerized databases are now available for the professional and personal use of those who have a microcomputer or terminal and the minimal equipment necessary to hook up these devices to the telephone. Once connected to such a system through a phone call, one has access to a wide range of informational and entertainment materials with the stroke of a key. Following is a "menu," or table of contents for one such system.

SOURCE: Update, February, 1982, CompuServe Information Service, Columbus, Ohio. By Permission.

wire services, stock market quotation services, airline schedules, weather and travel data, a range of newspapers and magazines, and even off-track betting. Through these home centers, we will be able to electronically access and display back issues of newspapers, magazines, and other publications, or single out articles on particular topics of our choosing. With a press of a key, we will receive a printed, permanent copy of any of these documents.

Through the system, we will scan the pages of store catalogues and lists of sale items at supermarkets. With a touch of the keyboard, the order will be placed, the bank notified to forward payment, and our balance updated and displayed on the screen in front of us. If we need to know the phone number of a friend or whether a particular book is available in the local library, that information too will be available at the touch of a keyboard. A few additional keystrokes may well dial the necessary call or display the pages of the selected book on the screen.

Interconnected burglar and fire alarm systems will be linked to the center, and in the event that sensors detect a fire or break-in, information will be automatically conveyed to the fire or police department for immediate action. Our health records, favorite books, sets of encyclopedias, even family pictures, can all be stored on discs for immediate access and display, with "hard" copies available whenever desired. Writing a book, composing a song, creating visual art forms, and "personal publishing" of all sorts will be options for anyone who has access to the technology.

The new communication technologies have already begun to have a dramatic impact on our organizations and society, as well as upon us as individuals. Mechanical cash registers, typewriters, and checkwriting machines are rapidly becoming antiques, being replaced by electronic data processing systems. An entry in the electronic cash register not only records a sale, but also updates inventory records in the same transaction. Word processors tied to a central computer and printer are used in place of the single-function typewriter. The same technology that creates reports and memos, also prepares mailing labels, keeps personnel records, computes employee salaries, and writes out payroll checks. Increased capacities for data storage, production, transmission, and display make linking various divisions, offices, locations, or branches of any organization a trivial matter. At the same time, these devices provide instant access to a broad range of data that may be useful in management decision-making throughout an enterprise.

In hospitals, paper and pencil systems are being replaced by complex information-processing packages. Using these new tools, even the results of lab tests, x-rays, and other diagnostic procedures can be relayed to the appropriate destination electronically. And in the profession of law, the drafting of wills and many other documents requires no more than entering

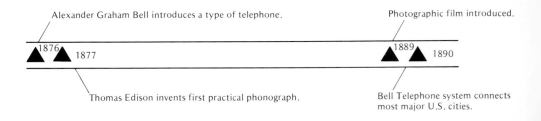

Alexander Graham Bell introduces a type of telephone.

Photographic film introduced.

1876 1877

1889 1890

Thomas Edison invents first practical phonograph.

Bell Telephone system connects most major U.S. cities.

the names, addresses, and special clauses and stipulations into a computer-printer facility capable of turning out such documents in a matter of seconds.

The Information Revolution

Throughout the history of human invention, our tools for communication have given our species capabilities wholly unmatched by other animals. Rapid advances in our technologies in the recent past and those projected for the immediate future promise even more dramatic impact upon our lives.

We are moving rapidly to the edge of what has been described as an "information revolution" which may well parallel the industrial revolution in its impact and far-reaching consequences. Given our current tools, we can already envision an "information society" in which communication technology will play a central role in virtually every facet of our personal, occupational, and social affairs.

There is little doubt that our rapidly changing technologies will have a number of implications for the way we live in the years ahead. Among the more obvious will be an ever-increasing volume of available data in our environment, merging of transportation and communication technologies, blurring of the distinction between home and office, blending of media uses, and a sharpening distinction between information "haves" and "have nots" based on economics. In the next section we will briefly discuss each of these and their implications for behavior.

Increase in the Volume of Data

With each new technological advance, particularly those with the capability of multiplication, amplification, or duplication, comes an increase in the amount of data available to us.

Today, collecting recordings of favorite singing groups, old television programs, classic movies, daily newspapers, magazines, books, articles, and monographs is a time, space, and money-consuming activity. In the near future, however, it will be possible for those who can afford certain basic technologies to have copies of nearly any visual or auditory material they desire available for instant access and use.

As this becomes possible, the real challenge facing humans will shift from "how to get it" to "what to do with it." The storage capacity of emerging technology literally boggles the mind. One side of a video disc can store 108,000 separate color television images together with stereo sound. At present, the quality of most video monitors is not adequate for reproducing a full printed page. As their quality is improved, the text of about 3,200 books

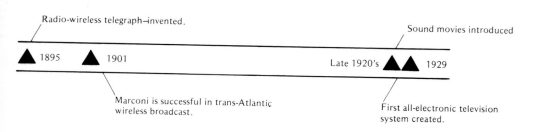

Radio-wireless telegraph–invented.

Sound movies introduced

▲ 1895   ▲ 1901   Late 1920's ▲▲ 1929

Marconi is successful in trans-Atlantic wireless broadcast.

First all-electronic television system created.

FIGURE 8.5 In terms of their functions transportation technology and communication have much in common.

could be stored on one two-sided disc and displayed for use as needed on a video screen, making "video publishing" a formidable new technology.[5]

As we move progressively toward a time when we will have ready access to virtually all current news and entertainment, as well as documents of all kinds, the problem of "information overload" may very well become even more critical than it is today. There seems little doubt that the increased volume of data will demand new information reception competencies for identifying those data which are relevant, organizing and categorizing them in an appropriate manner, and using them efficiently.

Merging of Transportation and Communication Technology

There has always been an interesting relationship between the functions of transportation technology and those of the tools of communication. Even with the earliest automated data-transmission devices this relationship was apparent. Instead of delivering a message in person, one sent it on horseback or ship. One need not go and look at something if information about it can be transported. One need not deliver a message personally if the message can be sent there on its own.

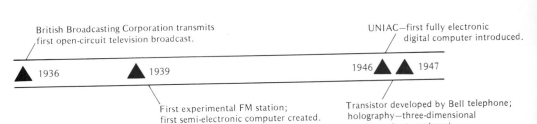

British Broadcasting Corporation transmits first open-circuit television broadcast.

UNIAC—first fully electronic digital computer introduced.

1936   1939   1946   1947

First experimental FM station; first semi-electronic computer created.

Transistor developed by Bell telephone; holography—three-dimensional photography introduced.

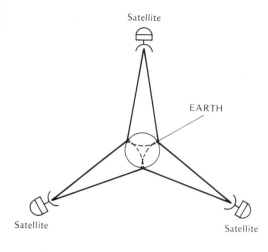

Satellite

EARTH

Satellite

Satellite

FIGURE 8.6 By means of telecommunication technology, data originated at one point on the earth's surface can be relayed via satellite to any number of remote destinations and back again.

Moving data can be an efficient, economical, and speedy alternative to moving things or people. More than ever before, our emerging communication technologies provide new options in this regard. Today, business conferences are held between individuals across the continent using telephones and video hook-ups. Using telephone lines, doctors at a hospital are now able to monitor the heart rate and other vital signs of a patient miles away. With similar systems, medical personnel also have access to current research findings in their efforts to diagnose and treat illness. And when connected to a nationwide network and computerized database, lawyers can instantly search through the equivalent of whole libraries to find key cases or legal opinions. The availability of newspapers, magazines, television, library documents, research reports, goods, services, health care, banking, and conferencing, without any travel whatsoever, promise to have a dramatic impact on our lives in the years ahead.

Evolving Concepts of Office and Home

It seems likely that the time will come when the concepts of *home* and *office* will be far less distinct than they are for most of us today. In the very near future, there will be little in the way of data sending and receiving that one cannot do from home. For most of us, *work* has been somewhere you traveled to—a place away from home. In the years ahead, it seems likely that *work* will be less a *place* and more an *activity*.

The idea of an *office* filled with individuals conversing face-to-face about social and business matters may gradually be replaced by an understanding of *office* which implies an individual alone, at home in front of a computer

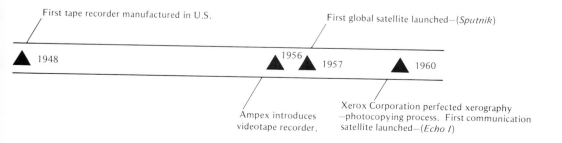

First tape recorder manufactured in U.S.

First global satellite launched—(*Sputnik*)

1948

1956

1957

1960

Ampex introduces videotape recorder.

Xerox Corporation perfected xerography —photocopying process. First communication satellite launched—(*Echo I*)

terminal, able to have access to the people and data he or she needs by a touch of the keys. At this point in time, one can do little more than speculate about the nature of these changes, and wonder about the kinds of lifestyles—personal, social, and occupational—that future communication technologies will inspire.

Changing Uses of Media

Traditionally, there has been a reasonably clear distinction between various communication technologies. Newspapers, for example, have historically provided their audience with a summary of current happenings of the day. Though they have increasingly broadened their scope to include features and other items, the primary focus has remained news.

Film has been essentially an entertainment medium. Radio and television, in terms of the majority of their content, have been primarily entertainment media, also. Telephones have been used socially and in business contexts, generally as a substitute for short, face-to-face conversations. Institutions like libraries and museums have served their users by providing documents which serve reference, archival, and to a somewhat lesser extent, entertainment functions.

Many of these traditional distinctions are rapidly becoming obsolete. Those who have cable television may now select channels that play recordings of rock groups much like those aired on radio, but these are accompanied by visual effects. Cable users also have a channel that functions as a local bulletin board much like what one is accustomed to finding in the newspaper or on the wall of a local supermarket. Other cable channels are available on a subscription fee basis, bringing films to television via satellite. Another cable channel displays stock market quotations, wire service copy, and the local weather.

With some fairly inexpensive equipment and a flip of the switch, television becomes a video arcade game. Connected to a microcomputer, television becomes a book—a self-instructional guide to French, finance, the stock market, or computer programming. With some additional hardware and software programming, the telephone also changes function to become a device for the transmission of acoustical data.

Together, the computer, telephone, and television can become a newspaper, magazine, game, reference tool, catalogue, index, and a variety of other things. When a printer is added, the telephone, television, and computer become a typewriter and paper, a card catalogue and the stacks of books at a reference library in medicine or law. When connected to a video disc or video cassette, television is a movie screen. When the tapes played are recorded on a portable video tape unit, television is a home movie—a family album.

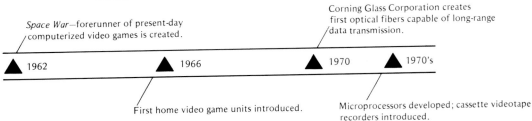

Space War—forerunner of present-day computerized video games is created.

Corning Glass Corporation creates first optical fibers capable of long-range data transmission.

▲ 1962   ▲ 1966   ▲ 1970   ▲ 1970's

First home video game units introduced.

Microprocessors developed; cassette videotape recorders introduced.

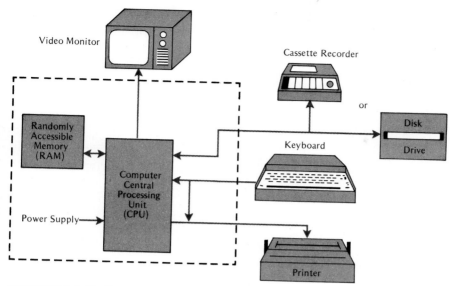

FIGURE 8.7 Until recently, typical desk equipment included a writing pad, pencils, a typewriter, and the necessary reference books. The computer "work station" links several pieces of electronic equipment that perform the tasks of creating information, storing it, retrieving it, and printing out copies or transmitting it to other work stations.

Coded data is loaded into the computer from cassettes or floppy disks. These data, which are stored in the memory section, provide the instructions necessary for the computer to carry out the desired activity—assist with instruction, play a game, or store and format the contents of a letter or report. Additional data can be input directly through the keyboard. The video monitor provides a means for displaying the data that are being processed by the computer, and a printer can be used to make permanent copies of programs or the results of the computer's operations, such as files, letters, charts, or graphics.

While these technologies are quite new, the trend toward converging uses of them is less so. Over ten years ago, Edwin Parker commented on the beginnings of this trend, which he saw as particularly significant because he believed it would lead to:

1. increased amounts of information available to the public, and increased efficiency...since everything need not be distributed to everyone in the audience

2. greater variety in the ways information packages can be constructed

3. individual receiver selection of information (both in content and timing)

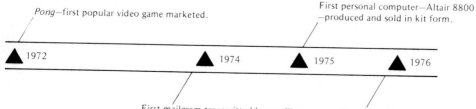

Pong—first popular video game marketed.

First personal computer—Altair 8800 —produced and sold in kit form.

1972   1974   1975   1976

First mailgram transmitted by satellite.

Steve Wozniak and Steve Jobs create forerunner of Apple computer in their garage.

Business	Games
Accounts receivable	Arcade-type games
Payroll	Mazes
Inventory control	Puzzles
Sales register	Logic games
Mailing label preparation	Word games
Electronic mail and bulletin board	Electronic pinball
Filing	Chess and checkers
Form letters	Casino games
Loan amortization	Sports--Football, bowling, etc.
Promotional signs	Adventure games
Calendars	
Check writing	**Other Entertainment**
Tab preparation	
Profit and loss statements	Astrology
Statistical analysis	Interactive counseling
	Rubik's cube solver
Text and Word Processing	**Education**
Text preparation	Spelling
Text editing	Language usage and comprehension
Print formating	Mathematics
Spelling verification	Foreign languages
Grammar and usage verification	Typing
Alphabetization	Computer programming
Graphics--graphs, charts, and tables	
	Aviation
Home	Flight simulations
Checkbook balance	Pilot flight planning
Household budget	Altitude determination
Installment payment projection	Navigation
Income tax preparation	
Automobile maintenance schedule	**Miscellaneous**
Gasoline usage comparisons	Stock market trends
Recipe categorization	Football scouting reports
Freezer inventory	Musical composition
Reminder calendar	Conversion to terminal for interfacing
Christmas card list	with other computers and data bases
Diary	via phone
Coin or stamp collection inventory	Bible study and key word index
Control of home appliances and lights	

Figure 8.8 A Sampling of Programs Available for Home Computers[6]

as opposed to source control of information selection, packaging and transmission

4. improved "feedback" capability (since the individual subscriber can "talk" to the system)....

5. greater convenience to the user....[7]

Carrying forth a trend begun a number of years ago, the old distinctions between communication technologies are not-so-gradually eroding.[8] The "consumer" is being provided with an increasingly active role, and media which were once primarily associated with mass communication are being

Radio Shack, Commodore, and Health introduce personal computers into the consumer market.

Several companies market videodisc systems and projection and large screen television equipment.

▲ 1977   ▲ 1978   ▲ Early 1980's

Computer game, *Space Invaders*, introduced in Japan, grosses estimated $600 million in one year.

increasingly used in interpersonal communication, and vice versa, perhaps an indication of even more fundamental shifts in the nature and use of these technologies in the years ahead.

The Economics of the New Communication Technologies

Overall sales of communication technologies, as well as the relative amount being spent on these technologies compared to other items, has been increasing dramatically in recent years. In 1980, for example, ten million color television sets were sold. Estimates place 1985 sales as high as fifteen million. During this same period unit sales in projection television, video disc, and video cassette recorders are expected to more than triple.[9] Figures also indicate that in 1981, $2.8 billion was taken in by the film industry, while some $5 billion was spent on electronic arcade entertainment, and another $1 billion on home video games.[10]

While the unit cost to play a video game, attend a movie, or even purchase a radio or television set is well within the range of most consumers, the newer technologies are much more expensive. The cost of home computers with the capability for transmitting and receiving data through phone lines range from about $300 to $6,000 with a printer. And while the prices of video cassette and disc recorders have dropped markedly, the base price is still nearly $500. The cost of satellite antennas, large screen and projection TV is even greater.

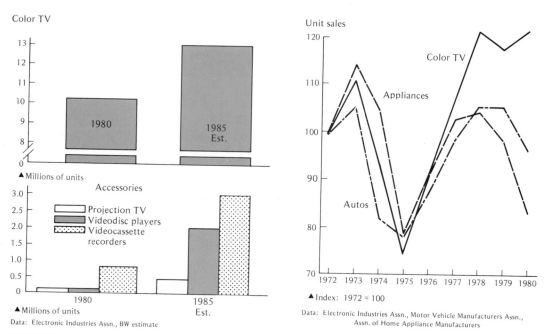

FIGURE 8.9 Given the broadening uses of television, the sales of sets and accessories have increased dramatically in relation to transportation and other household technology.

SOURCE: Reprinted from the February 23, 1981 issue of *Business Week* by special permission, © 1981 by McGraw-Hill, Inc., New York, N.Y. All rights reserved.

The relatively large expenditures now required to purchase some of the more advanced communication technologies may well have the potential to broaden the gap between the "haves" and "have nots" within our society, if not within the world. It seems quite likely that those who have financial resources will have much greater access to tools for creating and receiving information than those who do not.

Commenting on this issue, Alfred Smith said emphatically: "Today our primary resource is information. Today knowledge is the primary wealth of nations and the prime base of their power. Today the way we trade messages and allocate information is our communication economy."[11]

Discussing the same point, Parker noted:

> The development of a new technology for the storage, manipulation, and distribution of information raises significant social and political implications.... There is not a complete one-to-one correspondence between information and power. Nevertheless, information and information processing capacity does contribute a significant correlate of power such that, other things being equal, improved information services to different segments of the population are likely to increase their political power, if only by permitting them to find out where and how to best apply such political pressure as they can mobilize.[12]

To the extent that these technologies afford an individual or a society power over their own or other's lives, the economics of communication technology may well have important implications for human behavior in the decades ahead.[13]

Communication Technology and the Quality of Life

For all the obvious changes in the *forms* of our communication technologies over the years, it is important to question the extent to which their *functions* have also changed. There can be little doubt that data processing technology today is quicker, more flexible, and better displayed than ever before in our history. To what extent, however, have these changes been matched by improvement in the quality of life? In any given day, how much more do we know as a result of all the technology we have available? How much better entertained are we by all the new media? Are we better organized and better prepared by all the storage and retrieval technology? All in all, are our decisions better as a result of our improved technology? How much happier are we? Have the quality of communication and the nature of human life improved for all the advances?

In our excitement and enthusiasm for the new technologies, it is probably important to give at least passing consideration to these kinds of issues. Questions such as these remind us that communication technologies are, after all, no more than extensions of our own communication abilities and liabilities. They can do little more than display, transport, store, duplicate, or amplify the data *we* create. The nature and significance of those data and the uses to which they are put depend in the final analysis upon *us* and not our technologies.

Summary

The technologies of communication have a long and interesting heritage, beginning with the first drawings on cave walls and the earliest use of smoke signals. *Communication technology* is the appropriate label for any device, tool, or medium which assists in the production, distribution, multiplication, amplification, storage, display, or reception of data. These tools function by extending our message sending and receiving modalities, particularly visual and auditory modes.

The form of our technologies has changed greatly from early times, and we can predict even more dramatic change in the decades ahead. These changes can be expected to have a number of implications that may affect human behavior. Among these are the increased availability of data, increased storage and recording capacities, a blurring of lines between the technologies of communication and those of transportation, changing concepts of home and work, an erosion of the distinction between various communication technologies, and the uneven access to the new technologies due to economic factors. The impact of new technological forms on the quality of life ultimately depends upon the uses to which the data are put.

Notes

1. For a useful history of the development of communication technology upon which this summary is based, see George N. Gordon, "Communication," in *World Book Encyclopedia* (Chicago: World Book, 1981), Vol. 4, pp. 711–723, and Colin Cherry, *World Communication: Threat or Promise? A Socio-Technical Approach* (New York: Wiley, 1971), pp. 29–56. Summaries of major inventions and technological advances are provided by Wilbur Schramm, *Mass Communications* (Urbana, IL: University of Illinois Press, 1960), pp. 5–7; Edward J. Whetmore, *Mediamerica* (Belmont, CA: Wadsworth, 1979), pp. 36–37, 74–75, 96–97, 142–143, 197; and Michael G. Real, *Mass Mediated Culture*, Englewood Cliffs, NJ: Prentice-Hall, 1977.
2. Cf. Don L. Cannon and Gerald Luecke, *Understanding Communications Systems* (Dallas: Texas Instruments Learning Center, 1980), pp. 1.8–1.19.
3. Marshall McLuhan was perhaps the first to talk extensively of media as extensions of man. See especially, *Understanding Media* (New York: McGraw-Hill, 1964).
4. See J. Wicklein, "Wired City, U.S.A.: The Charms and Dangers of Two-Way TV" in *Mass Media Issues, Analysis and Debate*, George Rodman, ed (Chicago: Science Research Associates, 1981), pp. 242–251.

5. Lewis M. Branscomb, "The Electronic Library," *Journal of Communication*, **31**, 1, (1981), pp. 48–149.

6. The program categories are based upon an informal analysis of programs listed in *80 Micro: The Magazine for TRS-80 Users*, **32**, (September, 1982), and Charles D. Sternberg, *Using the TRS-80 in Your Home* (Rochelle Park, NJ: Hayden, 1980).

7. Edwin B. Parker, "Information Utilities and Mass Communication," in *The Information Utility and Social Choice*, ed by. H. Sackman and Norman Nie (Montvale, NJ: AFIPS Press, 1970), p. 53.

8. See discussion in Richard W. Budd and Brent D. Ruben, *Beyond Media* (Rochelle Park, NJ: Hayden, 1979), especially pp. 128–137.

9. "TV: A Growth Industry Again," *Business Week* (February 23, 1981), p. 89.

10. "Games That Play People," *Time* (January 18, 1982), pp. 50–58.

11. Alfred G. Smith, "The Cost of Communication," presidential address, International Communication Association, (1974). Abstracted as "The Primary Resource," in *Journal of Communication*, **25**, (1975), pp. 15–20.

12. Edwin B. Parker, *Op. Cit.*, p. 51.

13. For further discussion of the issues of communication technology and political and social control, often referred to as the "world information order," see the special section of the *Journal of Communication*, **29**, 1, (Winter, 1979), pp. 143–207. And *World Communication*. Colin Cherry, (New York: Wiley, 1971), especially Chapters 3–6.

References and Suggested Reading

Abel, V. "Electronic Playthings." *Apartment Life*, (Dec. 1980), 41–48.

Bagdikian, B.H. "Newspapers Face Troubles, But They'll Still Be a Good Deal." *Next*, 40–45.

Branscomb, L.M. "The Electronic Library." *Journal of Communication*, **31**, (Winter 1981), 143–150.

Budd, Richard W. and Brent D. Ruben. *Beyond Media*. Rochelle Park, NJ: Hayden, 1979.

Cannon, Don L. and Gerald Luecke, *Understanding Communications Systems*. Dallas: Texas Instruments Learning Center, 1980.

Cherry, Colin. *World Communication: Threat or Promise?* New York: Wiley, 1971.

Compaine, B.M. "Shifting Boundaries in the Information Marketplace." *Journal of Communication*, **31**, (Winter 1981), 132–142.

DeFleur, Melvin L. *Theories of Mass Communication*. New York: McKay, 1970.

deSola Pool, I. "Technology and Change in Modern Communication." *Technology Review*, (1980), 64–75.

Electronic Games. New York: Reese 1982.

"Games That Play People." *Time*, (January 18, 1982), 50–58.

Gordon, George. "Communication." In *World Book Encyclopedia*, Vol. 4, Chicago: World Book, 1981, 711–723.

Interface Age. Cerritos, CA: McPheters, Wolfe and Jones.

McLuhan, Marshall. *The Mechanical Bride*. New York: Vanguard Press, 1951.

———.*Understanding Media*. New York: McGraw-Hill, 1964.

Meyer, K.E. "Radio's Born-Again Serenity." *Next*, 52.

Navasky, V. "Books as We Know Them (1) May or (2) May Not Survive." *Next*, 59–61.

Parker, Edwin B., "Information Utilities and Mass Communication," in H. Sackman and Norman Nie, *The Information Utility and Social Choice*. Montvale, NJ: AFIPS Press, 1970.

Popular Computing. Peterborough, NH: McGraw-Hill Real, Michael R. *Mass Mediated Culture*, Englewood Cliffs, NJ: Prentice-Hall, 1977.

Sandman, Peter, David Rubin, and David Sachsman. *Media*. 3rd ed. Englewood Cliffs, NJ: Prentice-Hall, 1982.

Schramm, Wilbur. *Mass Communications*. Urbana, IL: University of Illinois Press, 1966.

Sigel, Efrem. *Videotext*. New York: Harmony, 1980.

Smith, Alfred G., "The Cost of Communication," Presidential Address, International Communication Association, 1974. Abstracted as "The Primary Resource," in *Journal of Communication*, 25, (1975), 15–20.

Smith, Anthony. *Goodbye Gutenberg*. Oxford, England: Oxford University Press, 1980.

"TV: A Growth Industry." *Business Week*, February 23, 1981, 88–102.

Whetmore, Edward J. *Mediamerica*. Belmont, CA: Wadsworth 1979.

Wicklein, J. "Wired City, U.S.A.: The Charms and Dangers of Two-Way TV." In George Rodman, *Mass Media Issues, Analysis and Debate*, Chicago: Science Research Associates, 1981, 242–251.

Williams, Raymond. *Television: Technology and Cultural Form*. NY: Schocken, 1975.

Willis, Jerry, *Peanut Butter and Jelly Guide to Computers*. Beaverton, OR: Dilithium, 1980.

Wright, C.R. *Mass Communication*. New York: Random House 1959.

Uses and Consequences of Information

The Individual

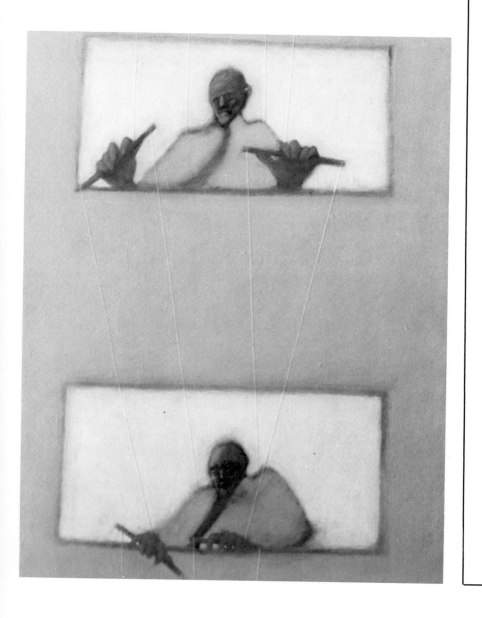

Introduction

In the previous section we discussed verbal and nonverbal information sources, the manner in which information is received and processed, and the role of communication technology in extending our capacities for each. In examining these facets of the communication process, our analysis was *microscopic* in nature. That is, we looked in detail at individual aspects of the communication such as language, paralanguage, appearance, gestures, selection, memory, individual needs, source credibility, data, organization, personal and mass media, focusing on the role each of these elements play in the overall process. Our examination of communication also tended to be relatively *static*, in that in order to analyze the individual elements it was necessary to "stop" the process.

In this section, our analyis will be more *macroscopic* and *dynamic*, extending the previous discussion to emphasize the broad nature and functions of communication as an ongoing process within and among individuals, groups, organizations, cultures, and societies. Our focus in this chapter will be on the individual and personal uses and consequences of information: *Acting and reacting*; *learning* and *mapping*; *developing an identity and self-concept*; *defining and reducing stress*; and *networking, socialization, and influence*.

Acting and Reacting

In the ongoing dynamics of human life, individuals must not only select, interpret, and retain data from their environment, but must also use the resulting information as the basis for their subsequent behavior. Carrying out these activities involves what we may think of as a *data-processing cycle* through which data is used as the basis for *description, classification, evaluation,* and *action*.

In nearly every circumstance, an initial use of data is to *describe*: to determine the nature, characteristics, appearance, size, composition, texture, color of an object, situation, or person. *Description* is necessary for the most basic communication functions like locomotion, food-finding, and courtship, as well as for creating or functioning in relationships, groups, organizations, or societies.

Based on our descriptions, *classification* is possible. When we *classify*, we compare our new observations with information stored from previous experience, to see where a person, object, or event "fits" in our "scheme of things"— in our semantic network.

Through *evaluation*, a third use of data, we identify the range of possible relationships between us and the objects, situations, or persons, and determine what, if any, actions or reactions are appropriate and/or necessary. A fourth step in the information-processing cycle—one which involves the *creation* of data—is to carry out particular verbal or nonverbal *actions* in the environment, based on our descriptions, classifications, and evaluations. Then, after acting, we often gather data as "feedback" to monitor and assess the impact of those actions. In so doing, we are once again involved in the description, classification, and (re)evaluation and action cycle.

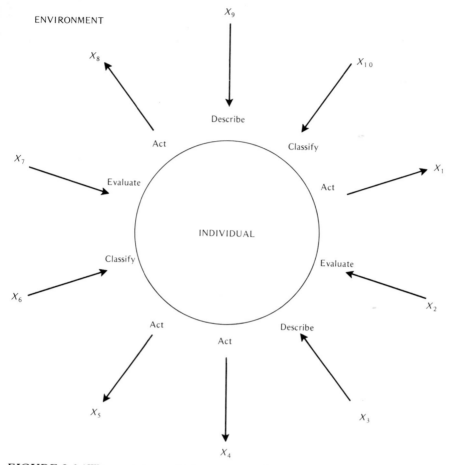

FIGURE 9.1)We use data to which we react to describe, classify, and evaluate the objects, people, and circumstances in our environment. When we *act* based upon our reactions, we create messages, completing the information processing cycle.

We can illustrate this cycle by considering a very simple activity. Imagine for a moment that you have just opened the door of your hotel room and stepped out into the corridor looking for a place to relax and kill ten minutes before your dinner reservation. As you begin to move through the hallway, you notice a chair ahead. Actually, of course, you don't notice a *chair*. Instead, you see a physical object from a particular point of view.

Based upon the visible characteristics of that object, you infer the existence of portions of it that you cannot see. You may only be able to make out two legs, for instance, connected by what appears to be a one-inch horizontal plane. Given the observation that the object is standing evenly on the floor, however, it seems safe to conclude that there are probably additional legs which are simply not visible because of your position relative to the object.

Determining that the object has four legs does not of course rule out the possibility that it is not a table, but a giraffe. Further efforts are necessary to determine its structure, composition, size, and decor.

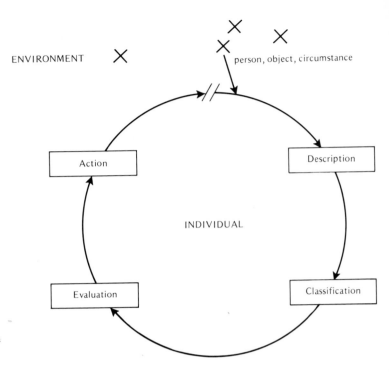

ENVIRONMENT ✕

✕
✕ ✕
person, object, circumstance

Action

Description

INDIVIDUAL

Evaluation

Classification

FIGURE 9.2 Information processing cycle.

As you continue to process data and derive information, you eventually *classify* the object as a *chair,* by which you mean "something to sit on." In the split second that this information-processing cycle requires, you observe it, walk over, and sit down, in full confidence that the object will support your weight.

With but a slight change in circumstance, the outcomes of information processing might be quite different. If, for example, the hallway were crowded with people and you were in a hurry, your attention might well be focused on *avoiding* rather than *using* the chair. In such a situation, the objective would be to negotiate past the object, perhaps without ever giving a thought to it as "something to sit on." The chair would be "a stationary object to be avoided," and you would act to move rapidly past it.

As this example suggests, in most respects, the way we process information

FIGURE 9.3 In observing an object such as a chair we infer—based on past experience—elements, properties, and characteristics that we often cannot actually see.

about people, circumstances, and objects is essentially the same. If you noticed someone walking toward you in the hotel hallway, their appearance, expressions, eye movements, actions, use of time and space would serve as the origins for data in the same way as did the properties of the chair. Their nonverbal (and perhaps, verbal) behaviors would serve as the basis for information as to their age, sex, race, attractiveness, and perhaps even their willingness to converse.

If, from your description, classification, and evaluation the person seemed friendly, interesting, and receptive, you might exchange glances, smile, or speak. If, however, you were in a hurry to check out and catch a plane, it is likely that you would relate to the individuals in the hallway precisely as you would to the chair in the previous example. They would be classified essentially as "objects to be avoided," with the major difference between people and objects being that the former were "mobile" while the latter were "stationary." Thus, whether the information sources which matter to us in a particular situation are people, objects, or circumstances, we go through a similar process of describing, classifying, evaluating, and then acting. Because of differing goals, needs, habits and other factors, however, the outcomes of this cycle may vary greatly from one situation to another.

Learning and Mapping

As O. J. Harvey notes so succinctly in the opening line of his book, "That the individual will come to structure or make sense of the personally relevant situation is one of psychology's most pervasive tenets."[1] During each instant we are involved in sensing, making sense of, acting and reacting to the objects, persons, and events in our environment, we are the same time engaged in a far more subtle activity with major long-term consequences for us. As we routinely create and respond to data necessary to the many circumstances we encounter, we are also developing and refining our internalized semantic networks, *maps*, and *images* of the world in which we live, and *rules* for behaving relative to it. Our maps, images, and rules develop over time in a very complex manner. The process begins very early in life:[2]

> The newborn baby is not capable of speech, symbolic, understanding, or directing skillful mobility. It has no ideas, words, or concepts, no tools for communication, no significant sensory experience, no culture. The newborn baby never smiles. He is unable to comprehend the loving phrases of his mother or to be aware of the environment.[3]

Facilitated and limited by the mental and physiological potentialities we inherit, we begin to learn about our environment and our relation to it.

> For some time. . .(the baby) see(s) just a mass of shifting shapes and colors, a single, ever-changing picture in front of (him). . . . The picture. . .is not made up, as it is for us, of many separate elements, each of which we can imagine and name, by itself, and all of which we can combine in our minds in other ways.
>
> When we see a chair in a room, we can easily imagine that chair in another part of the room, or in another room, or by itself. But for the baby the chair is an

integral part of the room he sees...This may be the reason, or one of the reasons, why when we hid something from a very young baby, it ceases to exist for him. And this in turn may be one of the reasons why peek-a-boo games are such fun for small babies to play, and may contribute much to their growing understanding of the world.[4]

The infant's awareness of mother, father, food and objects of potential sources of satisfaction, represents perhaps the first elements of the child's lifelong map-making enterprise. Gradually, the infant's world view expands to take account of the rapidly broadening environment of his or her experience. The fascination and attention to fingers, hands, and mouth, broadens to toys in and around the crib and, to the physical environment itself. The map continues to expand to define more and more detail of the child's room, other rooms in the dwelling, the neighborhood, the community, and eventually, the country and world. At the same time, the child is developing the communication rules necessary for making sense of and relating to his or her social environment— first family, then friends, relatives, acquaintances, teachers, peers, colleagues at work, and so on.

The manner in which our images, maps, and communication rules develop is very complicated. These images are not simply the result of an accumulation of data to which we have been exposed, though these data certainly play an important role.[5] Essentially, what we variously term our *maps, images, rules structures*, or *semantic networks, are the long-term informational consequence of our efforts to adapt to the data with which we have confronted over the course of our lifetimes.*[6]

Through this subtle self-programming process, as a consequence of communication, we acquire the rules, maps, and images, and associations

FIGURE 9.4 As we respond to the many circumstances, objects, and persons in our environment, we are developing our internalized semantic networks, *maps,* and images of the world.

FIGURE 9.5

which direct our behavior in any given situation. Whether we are aware of it or not, our maps and our rules tell us what to say, when to say it, how to act in this and that circumstance, how to tell one kind of circumstance from another, what to pay attention to and what to ignore, what to value and what to despise, what sort of people to seek out and which to avoid, what and who to believe, and so on.

Our images are our means for navigating about in our symbolic and physical environment and the basis for our functioning as human beings. They enable us to act and react, and to carry our knowledge of our environment forward in time. Without them, each experience would be totally new and bewildering.

The significance of these images is clearest when one considers an illustration such as the simple act of putting a key in a lock or opening a door. Our image of doors and our rules for door-opening tell us how to locate and use the handle, and whether to pull or push on the door in order to open it. Without this stored knowledge, each door-opening would be a wholly novel experience. Were it not for our maps, even the *identification* of a *door* would be a trial and error matter, since we would have no way other than by means of our images to identify and classify *doors* in the first place.

Maps are also invaluable in our dealing with interpersonal and intrapersonal facets of our environment. Standardized greetings such as a handshake and "Hi, how are You?" and "Fine, thanks, and you?" are easily accomplished. This is the case because our framework of communication rules permits us to categorize a particular situation as being like certain other situations in the past, for which we have learned a particular conversational pattern. Our rules also guide us in deciding when, "Hi! How are you?" is simply a request for a "routine" acknowledgement, and when the person wants more detailed information on our physical or mental health.

Characteristics of Maps, Images, and Rules

From the time we are infants, we begin to learn which data are important, what they mean to the people around us upon whom we depend, and how to interpret them ourselves. As we internalize the various symbols and the meanings that are necessary to adapt to the environment, meanings build upon meanings as we create our internal images of our world.

The maps and images are generalizations about the environment—*abstractions* of it based on our observations and inferences. Some of these are drawn from first hand experience. Many others are the result of second hand impressions from parents, peers, teachers, and the mass media.

We learn to read and write, add and subtract. We begin to understand how things work and where things are, what people should and should not do, what it means to be a male or female. We acquire an agenda of things to think and talk about, learn to be a consumer, and come to understand what people with varying jobs do, all with great ease and little, if any, awareness.[7]

As with many other human characteristics, our capacity for map-making is a mixed blessing. In emphasizing the obvious assets and values of our internal world-building capability, it is quite possible to overlook some of the shortcomings and dysfunctions of this capacity. Primary among these liabilities is the fact that once our maps become fairly well defined and internalized, they often take on an objective quality. Often, they seem so real to us that we forget their symbolic nature, and that they are in many senses our own personal creations.

We seldom give a second thought, for instance, to whether a paper dollar has buying power, or to the meaning of symbols like *dog* or *mother, Protestant* or *Catholic, Democrat* or *Republican, son* or *father.* We have so thoroughly internalized our images of *dollar bills, mother, father, Catholics,* and *dogs,* that we may behave as if our symbolic maps and images were in fact, identical to the persons, objects, situations, or ideas to which they refer.

This kind of problem comes about for several reasons: (1) *The environment is constantly changing while our images and rules may be relatively fixed*; (2) *any map or image is necessarily incomplete*; (3) *images are personal and subjective*; (4) *images and rules are social products*; and (5) *images and rules are resistant to change.*[8]

Change Like the map and the territory it characterizes, there can never be a point-for-point correspondence between our image and the environment. General semanticists, to whom we must be grateful for the map-and-territory analogy, point out several reasons why this match between our internal maps and external physical and symbolic reality is never complete. The first has to do with the *process-like* nature of the environment. The environment is ever-changing, and one "can never step in the same river twice."[9]

Our symbols and symbolic images are not always changing in the same *way* or at the same *rate* as the environment. Many everyday events illustrate this point well. For instance, long after we have moved a clock or wastebasket to a new location, we persist in looking for it where it used to be because of our well-learned maps.

The point to be mindful of is that the *usefulness of our rules, images, and maps is often time-bound*. Maps or rules appropriate at one point in time may be useless, even disadvantageous, at other times. The world and the behavior of it's inhabitants may change substantially from one point in time to another, and there is unfortunately no guarantee that our maps will be sensitive to these changes. If for no other reason, we should perhaps be grateful that our memories are imperfect, since forgetting contributes to the potential for change of our maps.[10]

Incompleteness As noted above, a second reason for mismatches between our maps and the environment is that a symbol or symbolic image is always *less complete* and *less comprehensive* than that which it symbolizes. Details are invariably left out. Much as a highway map highlights some features of the landscape and ignores others, our personal images are also selective. They are generalizations which categorize or stereotype aspects of the environment for our convenience. A symbol like *dog* illustrates this point. Each person has a different image of the environmental reality to which the term refers. When we think of *dog*, our images are based on our own personal experience, which may bear little similarity to standardized definitions.

Subjectivity A third characteristic of maps is that they are *personal and subjective*. As we know, our images develop in our efforts to adapt to the situations which confront us in our lives. We are not all confronted with the same situations, and the images and rules we develop as a result of our experiences vary greatly from person to person. Because our life experiences are to some extent unique, our maps are personal and unavoidably subjective.

An exchange between two characters in the well-known instructional film, *Eye of the Beholder*, makes this point well. The scene takes place on a sidewalk in an urban area. A landlord (Copplemeyer) and his artist tenant (Michael Garrard) gaze across the street at a passing woman:

Garrard:	"Do you see that woman over there? She isn't real."
Copplemeyer:	"That woman over there isn't real, huh? I made her up from my imagination?"
Garrard:	"Yes, exactly. One man looks and sees nothing, another looks and falls in love. Today I will put on a canvas what I see in a woman. To me the painting will be as real as that woman. To you it will only be a painting."
Copplemeyer:	"The painting will be as real as that woman?"
Garrard:	"Yes, Copplemeyer, yes! Do you understand?"
Copplemeyer:	"I understand you are a lunatic!
Garrard:	(laughing) "You see, Copplemeyer, you prove my point. The man you see in me does not exist."[11]

In a sense suggested so clearly by the dialogue, we do each create our own images and indeed their production is very much a creative effort.

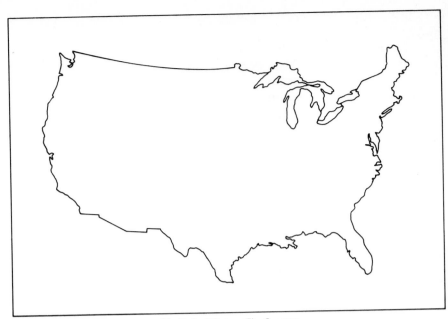

The United States: The Country

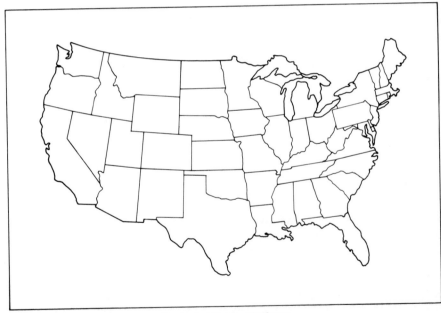

The United States: The States

FIGURE 9.6 Our symbolic maps, like physical maps of geographic territories, are necessarily selective. Maps highlight some characteristics of a territory and obscure others.

The United States: Interstate Routes and Major Cities

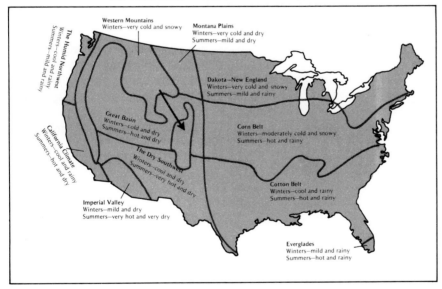

The United States: Climates

Social Nature A fourth facet of images is their *social nature*. Whether one considers a child striving to make sense of a toy jack-in-the-box, a physicist trying to integrate a new observation into his or her theory, or a salesperson trying to make a sale, the influence of other persons is unmistakable. From our earliest days, parents, family, and even previous generations, play a role in determining the data and experiences to which we will be exposed. Even the language we use is a product of our having developed the necessary knowledge and skills through social influence. We are not only influenced by these informal, developmental experiences, but also by our formal education and training. These social processes direct our attention in a highly selective fashion, highlighting certain phenomena and situations while obscuring others, shaping our images in a host of subtle and not-so-subtle ways through the course of our lifetime.

Stability A final characteristic of images is their *stability*. After our rule-structures are fairly well established, new data generally produce very little fundamental change. After we have developed a preference for one political party, for instance, it is unlikely that a single or even several advertisement or news articles will lead us to change our affiliation. Similarly, once we have decided we don't care for a particular job, television program, or individual, it is seldom that any single exposure to potentially-contradictory data will change our minds.

Our maps and force-of-habit tend to guide us toward data sources and data which are generally consistent with the framework or rules we have developed. In most instances, our tendency is to ignore or distort data which contradict or disconfirm our image, rather than revising our images in fundamental ways.

Like the scholar who has great difficulty discarding a particular theory or scientific paradigm, even in the face of seemingly disconfirming data, we part reluctantly with elements of our *personal paradigms*—our rules, maps, and images of the world. Nonetheless, in some instances, changes in our images and rule structures do occur. Sometimes the weight of accumulating evidence, the influence of persons who are important to us, and perhaps even accidents of history, lead us to change our ways of acting and reacting. Even a single incident can have a rather dramatic impact. For example, a car accident, illness, disappointment, or particular achievement sometimes seem to lead to fairly basic changes.

Identity and Self-Concept

Becoming is a term coined some twenty-five years ago by Gordon Allport to capture the dynamic process by which we as humans develop, modify, and refine our personal identity—our personality, our "self" and our concepts of our "self."[12] The role of communication in this becoming can be viewed as beginning with the very act of conception, at which instant the information necessary to the blueprint of growth for the offspring begins its work. The potentials we inherit are nourished and shaped by our life experiences in our physical and symbolic environment. Collectively, these experiences exert a subtle yet unmistakable influence upon us.

Our face-to-face dealings with parents, friends, acquaintances, and peers, along with our experiences with the various groups, organizations, technological and cultural facets of our lives provide much of the raw material for *becoming*. And, in reacting to and acting upon these influences, we provide fuel for the becoming process. Each encounter builds upon the last as we adjust to the demands and opportunities around us and fashion our identities for ourselves.

If a child lives with criticism
He learns to condemn
If a child lives with hostility
He learns to fight
If a child lives with ridicule
He learns to be shy
If a child lives with shame
He learns to feel guilty
If a child lives with tolerance
He learns to be patient
If a child lives with encouragement
He learns confidence
If a child lives with praise
He learns to appreciate
If a child lives with fairness
He learns justice
If a child lives with security
He learns to have faith
If a child lives with approval
He learns to like himself
If a child lives with acceptance and friendship
He learns to find love in the world.[13]

Though in a manner somewhat more complex and less predictable than suggested by the poem, we do in a very real sense become what we live. Whatever we are, have been, and will be—whether dominant or submissive, withdrawn or outgoing, self-confident or insecure, rigid or flexible, passive or aggressive—is very much influenced by the communication experiences we have had up to that point in time and the way we have adapted to them.

It is also through communication that we satisfy many of the needs that are so central to our personal development. Along with the need for making sense of the world, there is the need to grow emotionally—to affiliate with and compare ourselves to others, engage in fantasy, search for and find diversion and entertainment, discover our changing "selves," and so on.

In this becoming process we take much of our identities from those *significant others* around us as we grow and develop—parents, friends, colleagues—and in many respects we come to have much in common with these persons. But yet, as much as we grow like those significant to us, we also differentiate ourselves from them as well.

In addition to the role information processing plays in the *development* and *differentiation* of our personal identities, it plays an equally important role in the *expression* of our *self* to others, and in our capacity to react to others' expressions of their identities. It is through communication that we make known our anger, love, depression, affection, respect, and security, and it is also through this process that we are able to identify and comprehend these emotions in others.

Human communication is also important in the therapeutic process necessary to the preserving and nurturing our self-concept. Through communication we give and receive support and reassurance for our actions and reactions, and confirm the worth of our "self."

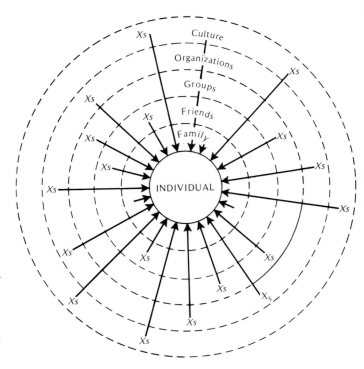

FIGURE 9.7 To a large extent our individual identities and self-concepts are a consequence of having adapted to the data created for us by our family and the relationships, groups, organizations, and culture of which we have been a part.

Sometimes this therapeutic process takes place in such an informal and indirect manner that we are unaware of it, as when we monitor others' expressions and reactions to our ideas as a part of causal conversation. Often this role is served by families, spouses, or intimate friends. In still other instances, therapeutic communication involves systematic efforts to develop relationships especially for that purpose, as is the case in counseling or therapy, and organized self-help groups like Weight Watchers or Alcoholics Anonymous. As should be apparent, the role of communication in the establishment, preservation, and nurturance of the individual "self" is complex, ongoing, and wholly essential to human life as we know it.

Defining Stress and Stress Reduction

In our efforts to act and react appropriately to the many demands and opportunities that we encounter in our environment, difficulties inevitably develop. When this kind of disharmony or *stress* occurs, we react instinctively to adjust to the challenge or threat.

From a biological point of view, the stress-adjustment cycle in humans directly parallels that of other living things.[14] However, in terms of the origins of the stress and the means available for dealing with it, humans are substantially unlike other animals. While most other animals detect and react to environmental threats in a direct, reflex-like manner, human stress is usually the consequence of a second-order communication event involving symbolic meaning. The threat of rejection by a loved one, a heated argument with a colleague, the prospect of a failure on an important exam, the tension of a long wait in line at a grocery store, or the pressure of an approaching deadline for an uncompleted project, are frequently potent stressors for humans. These *symbolic* threats are capable of triggering the same sorts of hormonal, muscular, and neural reactions that for other animals are associated only with *physical* threats to their safety and well-being.

For humans, the role of information processing in the stress-adjustment cycle has three facets: (1) like other animals, humans detect stressors in the environment through information processing; (2) unlike other animals, many of the stressors we face on a daily basis are the result of the communication activities of other humans. Stressors such as an argument between family members or the breakup of a long-term relationship are created through communication; (3) while other animals deal with stress only through physical means, humans often cope with stress through communication.

Unlike other animals, we do not simply fight or flee; we have learned through socialization that physical combat and running away are generally not regarded as "civilized" ways for dealing with problems. Because of this learning, we hold our bodies "in check" and usually react by "fight" or "flight" only in a symbolic sense. Ironically, our complex human environment not only increases the presence of stress factors in our lives, but has also decreased the opportunities for coping with that stress physically.

Though stress and adjustment are normal aspects of human life, evidence suggests that chronic and accumulated stress can have devastating physical as well as emotional consequences. Research indicates that stress lowers our resistence to illness and can play a contributory role in diseases of the kidney, heart, and blood vessels, as well as contributing to high blood pressure, migraine and tension headaches, and gastrointestinal problems such as ulcers, asthma, allergies, respiratory diseases, arthritis, and even cancer.[15]

Though there are a number of negative consequences of stress, it can also be a very positive force, bringing about personal and social growth and change.[16] The consequences of stress depend not only upon our biological means for coping, but also upon communication. The extent to which stress is productive or destructive ultimately depends not only on whether data which serve as stressors are present or absent in our environment, but perhaps more importantly, on the way in which we process this information.

Networks, Socialization, and Influence

As we know, much of the data we take notice of have their origins in the behavior of other people. When we react to these types of data, an ongoing sequence of action and reaction is set in motion. As the process unfolds, one consequence is we are *linked* to one another through the commonness of the emerging *communication network*.

At one extreme, these networks may take the simple form of an

Rank	Life Event	Mean Value
1	Death of Spouse	100
2	Divorce	73
3	Marital separation	65
4	Jail term	63
5	Death of close family member	63
6	Personal injury or illness	53
7	Marriage	50
8	Fired at work	47
9	Marital reconciliation	45
10	Retirement	45
11	Change in health of family member	44
12	Pregnancy	40
13	Sex difficulties	39
14	Gain of new family member	39
15	Business readjustment	39
16	Change in financial state	38
17	Death of close friend	37
18	Change to different line of work	36
19	Change in number of arguments with spouse	35
20	Mortgage over $10,000	31
21	Foreclosure of mortgage or loan	30
22	Change in responsibilities at work	29
23	Son or daughter leaving home	29
24	Trouble with in-laws	29
25	Outstanding personal achievement	28
26	Wife begin or stop work	26
27	Begin or end school	26
28	Change in living conditions	25
29	Revision of personal habits	24
30	Trouble with boss	23
31	Change in work hours or conditions	20
32	Change in residence	20
33	Change in schools	20
34	Change in recreation	19
35	Change in church activities	19
36	Change in social activities	18
37	Mortgage or loan less than $10,000	17
38	Change in sleeping habits	16
39	Change in number of family get-togethers	15
40	Change in eating habits	15
41	Vacation	13
42	Christmas	12
43	Minor violations of the law	11

exchange of smiles or a few words with a cab driver and his or her passengers. At the other extreme, they can involve all the complex legal, social, political, and religious data which bind us together as members of a society.

Often linking occurs through data produced and responded to in face-to-face settings. Where we are separated by one another geographically or in time, communication technology plays a vital role in the establishment and maintenance of networks.

Television, newspapers, magazines, radio, and other mass media provide the data and transmission devices that link members of groups, organizations, societies, and the world community in a common network. Even tools like telephones, intercoms, and duplicating machines serve this same function on a smaller scale. Human communication technologies also enable us to be linked with persons separated in time as well as space. Through books, archives, databases, photos, newspapers, art museums, and film we can be linked to those who lived one or many generations ago.

The linking which occurs through communication is no doubt one of the most taken for granted elements of our lives. It is so basic to our experience that it is difficult even to conceive of what life might be like were it not for the many communication networks in which we participate and upon which we so much depend. As Geoffrey Vickers put it: "Insofar as I can be regarded as human it is because I was claimed at birth by a communicative network, which programmed me for participation in itself.[17]

When we link ourselves to others, some mutual influence is inevitable. In a simple exchange like, "Hi, how are you?" "Fine, thank you, and you?" each individual exerts a controlling influence on the other. Even *exposure* to data can have a regulating consequence. In ongoing relationships, groups, organizations, and societies influence through communication is even more evident. Friends, husbands and wives, and members of a group or organization often come to share values, opinions, outlooks, use the same buzz words, jargon, dress, and even develop some of the same gestures.

The term *socialization* can be used to refer to this *primarily natural, regulatory consequence of communication which occurs as an individual adapts to*

FIGURE 9.8 The relationship between stress and illness has been dramatically demonstrated by Thomas Holmes and Richard Rahe, who have developed a scale (Social Readjustment Rating Scale) for classifying the severity of various stressful changes in life and relating these changes to the probability of becoming ill. Results of their research suggest that as stress increases, so does the likelihood of illness.

To complete the scale, check those events that have occurred within the past year and sum the point values. Holmes and Rahe found that with a score of 150 the chance of undergoing a major health change or contracting an illness was roughly 50%. With a score over 300 points within a single year the likelihood of illness or health change jumped to nearly 90 per cent.

SOURCE: Reprinted with permission from Thomas H. Holmes and Richard H. Rahe, "The Social Readjustment Rating Scale." *Journal of Psychosomatic Research*, **11** (2) (1967) Pergamon Press, Ltd.

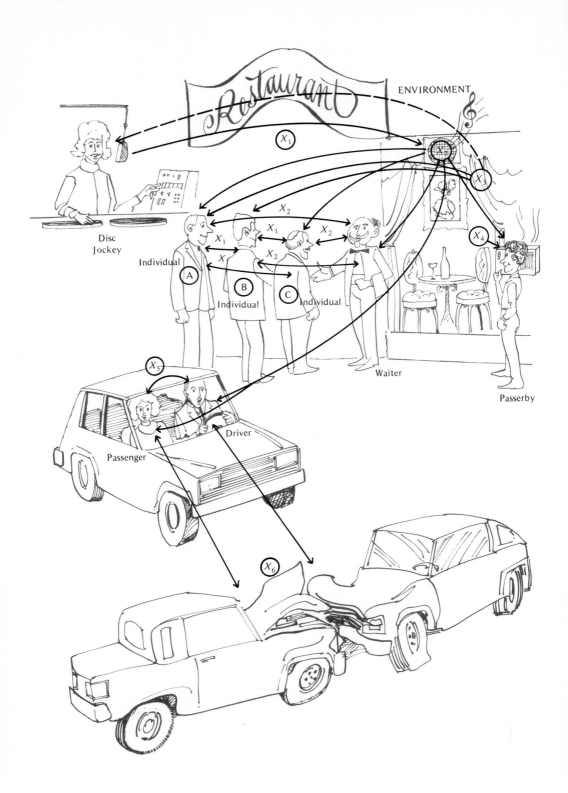

the demands of the various social units in which he or she becomes involved. In this process we learn language, dress standards, political preferences, values, and orientation to time, religion, greeting forms, and a whole host of symbols, patterns, rules, and meanings, quite apart from whether any of the persons with whom we dealt ever consciously tried to influence us.

Again, mass communication and communication technologies play an important role in this regard. Operating, not in a vacuum, but in the larger communication context, data transmitted via mass media—like messages in face-to-face situations—can and do serve to influence us, particularly in those areas in which our first hard knowledge is limited. As we have suggested earlier, the media play a role in setting the agenda of our knowledge and concerns, and in assisting us in making sense of and correlating parts of this agenda. They also provide a base of data that play a part in our socialization relative to such facets of life as masculinity and feminity, age, race, occupation, consumption, violence, criminality, eating and nutrition, and family and interpersonal relations.[18]

Not all of the influence which occurs through communication is unintended. As individuals, in relationships, groups, organizations, and societies, we expend a great deal of effort trying to persuade others—and vice versa—to agree, to buy, to accept, and so on.

How and when these attempts at influence are successful has perhaps been the most studied facet of human communication. A number of the factors involved in this process have been identified, many of which we discussed in Chapter 7 in our discussion of information reception. We know, for instance, that persuasion involves the selection, interpretation, and retention of information. We know, also, that attempts to influence begin when a source codes data, and selects media that are appropriate to his or her goals, the setting, and intended recipient(s). Next, the data must be available to the recipient, and the intended meaning generally compatible with the recipient's needs, goals, and map, at that point in time. When these conditions are present, there is some likelihood that influence will occur, though probably not if what is advocated represents a radical change from what is customary for the individual.

In sum, for all our knowledge of the factors and understanding of the process, the ability to combine these into a formula and make them work to persuade another individual in any particular situation is perhaps still more

---

FIGURE 9.9 When individuals react to data, the persons involved become linked together in a network by virtue of the commonness of their experience. The accident scene illustrates how such networks develop. Individuals A, B, and C are chatting with one another as they prepare to dine at a restaurant (X_1). The waiter approaches and exchanges words (X_2) with the individuals. The decor of the restaurant (X_3) is also of some significance to Individuals A and B. In the lower, left-hand corner of the network are two individuals driving along in a car chatting with one another (X_5). As they continue on their way they notice an accident as a busy intersection (X_6), while they listen to a favorite song on the radio (X_7). The sound system in the restaurant is tuned to the same station, and a passerby on the street listens to the same song on his transistor radio as he walks by and glances at the restaurant (X_4). The disc jockey dines at this particular restaurant often, finding the decor (X_3) one of the most memorable things about it.

TABLE 9.1 Summary of Uses and Consequences of Human Communication

1. *Acting and Reacting*
 	
  Description
  Classification
  Evaluation
  Action

2. *Learning and Mapping*
 	
  Environmental Maps
  Image Formation
  Rule Development
  Limitations
    Environmental Change
    Incompleteness
    Subjectivity
    Social Influence
    Resistance to Change

3. *Identity and Self-Concept*
 	
  Formation
  Differentiation
  Expression
  Maintenance

4. *Defining Stress and Stress Reduction*
 	
  Origins of Stress
  Defining Stress
  Stress Reduction

5. *Networks*
 	
  Network Formation
  Face-to-Face Linkages
  Technology-Mediated Linkages

6. *Standardization*
 	
  Creation of Symbols
  Standardization of Meaning
  Standardization of Rules and Rituals

7. *Influence*
 	
  Unintended—Socialization
  Intended—Persuasion

an art than a science. Regardless of which of these two perspectives one uses in thinking about persuasion, however, there is little doubt that some people are more skilled at it than others. It is also apparent that through an understanding of the communication process, and practice, one's skills for determining and providing data that are *appropriate* in a given situation for a given recipient or recipients, can be enhanced. As recipients of persuasion attempts, these same skills and understandings are equally valuable to us in reacting more consciously and with a greater sense of understanding of the process.

Summary

In this chapter we have examined a number of uses and consequences of information for the individual. Perhaps most basic among these is to *describe*, *classify*, *evaluate* and *act-toward* the circumstances, people, and objects in our environment.

Through information-processing we also learn and develop internalized *maps* and *images* of the environment, and a set of *rules* which guide us in selecting, interpreting, reacting, and acting toward the various situations in which we find ourselves over the course of our lifetimes.

Our maps, images, and rules may be limited in their usefulness because the environment changes with which we fail to keep pace. Additionally, the incompleteness, subjectivity, socially-influenced nature and stability of our images, maps and rules can be liabilities.

Communication also plays an important role in the formation and differentiation of our individual identities. At the same time, it is essential to expressions of our identity and self-concept to other persons, and in our interpretations of other's expressions of their identities. Information processing also enables us to seek, obtain, and provide necessary support and encouragement.

In the process of acting and reacting, we undergo *stress* in our efforts to adapt to the challenges and opportunities that present themselves. Many of the stressors to which we react are symbolic and themselves the product of communication. Through information processing we identify these stressors, and communication is also a primary means through which we react to and cope with such circumstances.

Still another use and consequence of human communication is *networking* and *linking*. When we act upon others' messages and they in turn act upon ours, linkages and networks form. Sometimes these occur throuugh face-to-face exchanges, while in other circumstances communication technology plays an important role. Through this process we develop the meanings, rules, and images that enable us to coordinate our activities with other persons.

As these interactions occur, *socialization* inevitably takes place. Much of the influence we exert over one another is a natural, unintended consequence of entering into linkages with one another. In other instances, influence results from systematic and purposeful attempts to influence or persuade one another.

In each of these respects, human comunication plays a critical role in enabling us to adapt and adapt to our complex and ever-changing physical and symbolic environment.

Notes

1. O.J. Harvey, *Motivation and Social Interaction*. New York: Ronald, 1963, p. 3
2. The term *map* is drawn from the writings of general semantics. Cf. Richard W. Budd, "General Semantics," In *Interdisciplinary Approaches to Human Communication*, Richard W. Budd and Brent D. Ruben, eds., (Rochelle Park, NJ: Hayden, 1979) for a discussion of the history of the term. *Image* was first used in the present context by Kenneth Boulding in *The Image* (Ann Arbor, MI: University of Michigan Press, 1956). The phrase *semantic network* comes from cognitive psychology. Cf. Morton Hunt, *The Universe Within*, (New York: Simon & Schuster, 1982) for a general discussion of the origin and uses of the term.
3. José M.R. Delgado, *Physical Control of the Mind* (New York: Harper, 1969), p. 45. See also "Neurophysiology" in *Interdisciplinary Approaches to Human Communication*. Richard W. Budd and Brent D. Ruben, eds. (Rochelle Park, NJ: Hayden), p. 126.
4. John Holt, *How Children Learn* (New York: Pitman, 1969), p. 61.
5. Cf. Kenneth Boulding, "General Systems Theory—The Skelton of Science," *General Systems*, 1: 1956, p. 15.
6. Cf. George Kelley, *A Theory of Personality* (New York: Norton, 1963). For a discussion of a similar notion which he refers to as *personal constructs;* see also the discussion of *schemata* in Edward E. Jones, David E. Kanouse, Harold H. Kelley, Richard E. Nisbett, Stuart Valins, and Bernard Weiner, *Attribution: Perceiving the Causes of Behavior* (Moorestown, NJ: General Learning Press, 1971).
7. Cf. discussion of the effects of mass communication in W. Phillips Davison, James Boylan, and Frederick T.C. Yu, *Mass Media: Systems and Effects* (New York: Praeger, 1976) especially Chapter 6, and *Television and Behavior: Ten Years of Scientific Progress and Implications for the Eighties Volume 1: Summary Report* (Rockville, MD: National Institute for Mental Health, 1982.
8. Cf. Richard W. budd, op. cit., 1979. See also Wendell Johnson, *People in Quandaries* (New York: Harper, 1946.)
9. Wendell Johnson, op. cit.
10. Cf. discussion of adaptive function of forgetting in Morton Hunt, op. cit., p. 111, and Elizabeth Loftus, *Memory* (Reading, MA: Addison, 1980), p. 19.
11. Dialogue based on *The Eye of the Beholder*, Stuart Reynolds Productions.
12. Gordon Allport, *Becoming* (New Haven, CT: Yale University Press, 1955)

13. Dorothy Law Nolte, "Children Learn What They Live," In *Looking Out/Looking In*, Ron Adler and Neil Towne, eds. (San Francisco: Holt, 1975), p. 43.

14. Cf. Hans Selye, *The Stress of Life*, rev. ed. (New York: McGraw-Hill, 1976)

15. A review of research and a rather detailed discussion of the relationship between stress and illness is provided by Kenneth R. Pelletier, in *Mind as Healer, Mind as Slayer*, (New York: Delacorte, 1977), pp. 117–188.

16. Cf. Brent D. Ruben, "Communication and Conflict: A System Theoretic Perspective," *Quarterly Journal of Speech*, **64**, 2, (1978) 202–210.

17. Geoffrey Vickers, "The Multi-valued Choice," In *Communication: Concepts and Perspectives*. Lee Thayer, ed. (New York: Spartan Books, 1967) p. 272.

18. Cf. W. Phillips Davison, James Boylan, and Frederick T.C. Yu, op. cit., and *Television and Behavior*, op. cit., for useful overviews of the role of the media in socialization.

References and Suggested Reading

Allport, Gordon W. *Becoming*. New Haven: Yale University Press, 1955.

Bateson, Gregory and Jurgen Ruesch. *Communication: The Social Matrix of Society*. New York: Norton, 1951

Berger, Peter. *The Sacred Canopy*. Garden City, NY: Doubleday, 1969.

———. "Sociology of Knowledge." In *Interdisciplinary Approaches to Human Communication*. Edited by Richard W. Budd and Brent D. Ruben. Rochelle Park, NJ: Hayden, 1979, 155–171.

———. and Thomas Luckmann. *The Social Construction of Reality*. Garden City, NY: Doubleday, 1967.

Blumer, Herbert. "Symbolic Interaction." In *Interdisciplinary Approaches to Human Communication*. Edited by Richard W. Budd and Brent D. Ruben. Rochelle Park, NJ: Hayden, 1979, 135–151.

Blumer, Jay G. and Elihu Katz, eds. *The Uses of Mass Communications*. Beverly Hills: Sage Publications, 1974.

Boulding, Kenneth. *The Image*. Ann Arbor, MI: University of Michigan Press, 1956.

———. "General System Theory: The Skeleton of Science." *General Systems*, 1: 1956, 11–17.

Bruner, J.S. *The Process of Education*. Cambridge, MA: Harvard Press, 1961.

Budd, Richard W. "General Semantics." In *Interdisciplinary Approaches to Human Communication*. Edited by Richard W. Budd and Brent D. Ruben. Rochelle Park, NJ: Hayden, 1979, 71–93.

Budd, Richard W. and Brent D. Ruben, Eds. *Beyond Media*. Rochelle Park, NJ: Hayden, 1979.

———. eds. *Interdisciplinary Approaches to Human Communication*. Rochelle Park, NJ: Hayden, 1979.

Church, Joseph. *Language and the Discovery of Reality*. New York: Vintage, 1961.

Dance, Frank E.X. and Carl E. Larson. *The Functions of Human Communication*, New York: Holt, 1976.

Davidson, Emily S., Robert M. Liebert and John M. Neale. *The Early Window: Effects of Television on Children and Youth*, New York: Pergamon, 1973.

Davison, W. Phillips, James Boylan, and Frederick T.C. Yu. *Mass Media: Systems and Effects*. New York: Praeger, 1976.

Delgado, José M.R. "Neurophysiology." In *Interdisciplinary Approaches to Human Communication*. Edited by Richard W. Budd and Brent D. Ruben. Rochelle Park, NJ: Hayden, 1979, 119–134.

————. *Physical Control of the Mind*. New York: Harper, 1969.

Dewey, John. *Experience and Education*. New York: Macmillan, 1938.

Douglas, Mary, ed. *Rules and Meanings*. New York: Penguin, 1973.

Duncan, Hugh Dalziel. *Communication and Social Order*. New York: Oxford University Press, 1962.

————. *Symbols and Social Theory*. New York: Oxford University Press, 1969.

Goffman, Erving. *Frame Analysis*. Cambridge, MA: Harvard University Press, 1974.

————. *The Presentation of Self in Everyday Life*. Garden City, NY: Doubleday, 1959.

Harvey, O.J., ed. *Motivation and Social Interaction*. New York: Ronald, 1963.

Holt, John. *How Children Learn*. New York: Pitman, 1967.

Holzner, Burkart. *Reality Construction in Society*. Cambridge, MA: Schenkman, 1968.

Hunt, Morton. *The Universe Within*. New York: Simon & Schuster, 1982.

Ittleson, William H. *Environment and Cognition*. New York: Seminar Press, 1973.

Johnson, Wendell. *People in Quandaries*. New York: Harper, 1946.

Johnson, Wendell and Dorothy Moeller. *Living With Change*. New York: Harper, 1972.

Jung, Carl G., ed. *Man and His Symbols*. New York: Dell, 1964.

Kelly, George A. *A Theory of Personality*. New York: Norton, 1963.

Kuhn, Thomas S. *The Structure of Scientific Revolutions*. Chicago: University of Chicago Press, 1970.

Levinson, Daniel J. (with Charlotte N. Darrow, Edward B. Klein, Maria H. Levinson and Braxton McKee). *The Seasons of A Man's Life*. New York: Ballantine Books, 1978.

Loftus, Elizabeth. *Memory*. Reading, MA: Addison-Wesley, 1980.

McHugh, Peter. *Defining the Situation*, New York: Bobbs-Merrill, 1968.

Mead, George H. *Mind, Self and Society*. Chicago: University of Chicago Press, 1967.

Nolte, Dorothy Law. "Children Learn What They Live," In *Looking Out/Looking In*. Ed. by Ron Adler and Neil Towne. San Francisco: Holt, 1975.

Pelletier, Kenneth R. *Mind as Healer, Mind as Slayer*. New York: Delacorte, 1977.

Postman, Neil and Charles Weingartner. *Teaching as a Subversive Activity*, New York: Delcorte, 1969.

Ruben, Brent D. "Communication and Conflict: A System Theoretic Perspective." *Quarterly Journal of Speech*, **64** 2 (1978) 202–210.

———. "General Systems Theory: An Approach to Human Communication." In *Interdisciplinary Approaches to Human Communication*. Edited by Richard W. Budd and Brent D. Ruben. Rochelle Park, NJ: Hayden, 1979, 95–118.

———. and John Y. Kim, Eds. *General Systems Theory and Human Communication*. Rochelle Park, NJ: Hayden, 1975.

———. "Intrapersonal, Interpersonal and Mass Communication Processes in Individual and Multi-Person Systems." In *General Systems Theory and Human Communication*. Edited by John Y. Kim and Brent D. Ruben. Rochelle Park, NJ: Hayden, 1975, 164–190.

Schroder, Harold M., Michael J. Driver and Siegfried Streufert. *Human Information Processing*. New York: Holt, 1967.

Schutz, Alfred. *On Phenomenology and Social Relations*. Chicago: University of Chicago Press, 1970.

Selye, Hans. *The Stress of Life*. rev. ed. New York: McGraw-Hill, 1976.

Shands, Harley C. *Thinking and Psychotherapy*. Cambridge, MA: Harvard University Press, 1960.

Sheehy, Gail. *Passages*. New York: Bantam Books, 1976.

Stark, Werner. *The Sociology of Knowledge*. London: Routledge & Kegan Paul, 1958.

Television and Behavior: Ten Years of Scientific Progress and Implications for the Eighties, Volume 1: Summary Report. Rockville, MD: National Institute for Mental Health, 1982.

Thayer, Lee. *Communication and Communication Systems*. Homewood, IL: Richard D. Irwin, 1968.

Vickers, Geoffrey. "The Multi-Valued Choice." In *Communication: Concepts and Perspectives*. Edited by Lee Thayer. Washington: Spartan, 1967, 259–278.

Watzlawick, Paul, Janet H. Beavin, Don D. Jackson. *Pragmatics of Human Communication*. New York: Norton, 1967.

Wilmot, William W. *Dyadic Communication*. Reading, MA: Addison-Wesley, 1979.

Whorf, Benjamin Lee. *Language, Thought and Reality*. Cambridge, MA: M.I.T., 1956.

Wood, Barbara S. *Children and Communication*. Englewood Cliffs, NJ: Prentice-Hall, 1976.

Wright, Charles R. *Mass Communication*. New York: Random, 1959.

Chapter 10

Relationships

We have explored some of the primary use and consequences of information processing from the perspective of the individual in the previous chapter. In the remaining pages of the book we will consider communication from the point of view of relationships, groups, organizations, cultures and societies.

The notion of *communication* and that of *relationship* are intertwined in several very basic ways. First, as we have seen, one of the most fundamental outcomes of human communication is the development of social networks, and no such networks are more fundamental to our lives than relationships. Second, our relationships—with parents, relatives, friends, and colleagues—are essential to the our learning, growth, and development. Third, it is in relationships of one sort or another that most of our purposeful message-sending activities take place. In the pages that follow, we will explore the connections between these two concepts in some detail.

Interpersonal Communication and Relationships

What is a *relationship?* Often, the term *relationship* is used as a way of talking about a friendship we regard as particularly significant. In recent years the term has also come to be used in a somewhat more specialized way, to refer to a particular type of friendship—a sexually intimate arrangement or agreement between two people. *Relationship* is also used to refer to other social units, such as those composed of a teacher-and-student, husband-and-wife, parent-and-child, employer-and-employee, or doctor-and-patient.

Whichever of these meanings one associates with the word, there is little question that relationships play an important role in our lives as humans. They are essential to our most basic biological and symbolic activities, and in fact to nearly every activity in which we take part.

While there is little reason to question whether friendships, sexually intimate arrangements, or the other social groupings mentioned qualify as relationships, few people would describe passengers riding on an elevator or strangers passing on a crowded street using the same term. From the point of view of communication, however, these can also be thought of as relationships.

In the most basic sense, a relationship is formed whenever *reciprocal data processing* occurs, that is, when *two or more individuals mutually take account of one another's verbal or nonverbal activities*. This reciprocal data processing, which we can term *interpersonal communication*, is the means through which relationships of all types are *initiated, develop, grow,* and *deteriorate*.

One of the simplest relationships is that created by people passing one another on a crowded sidewalk. In order for two individuals to negotiate past each other without bumping, they must process a good deal of data relative to the other's presence, location, direction, and rate of movement. They must use the resulting information to guide their actions in order to pass without colliding. In this situation all the essential elements of any relationship are in operation.

A somewhat more complex example is provided by people riding on an elevator. When alone in an elevator, most of us stand to the rear, often in the

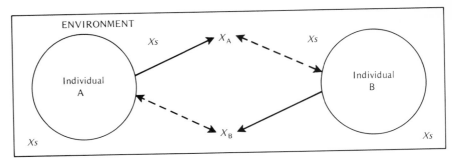

X_A — Words, actions, appearance, etc., created by A

X_B — Words, actions, appearance, etc., created by B

———▶ indicates data being created

◀ ‑ ‑▶ indicates data noted

FIGURE 10.1 Interpersonal communication. A relationship is formed when reciprocal data processing occurs—when two or more individuals take account of one another's verbal or nonverbal behavior.

center. Typically, as a second person boards, we move to one corner or another, leaving the remaining corner for the newly arriving passenger. In so doing, we initiate a simple relationship as we take note of and adjust our behavior—movements, gestures, and position—relative to one another. With little conscious awareness, mutual influence has taken place as we define and redefine the territory available for our use.

As a third person enters the elevator, further rejuggling is likely to occur as the social unit shifts from a two-person relationship to one composed of three individuals. Readjustments of this sort provide observable evidence that reciprocal data processing is taking place, and that a relationship has been formed.

Whether our point of reference is strangers passing on the street or an intimate, enduring friendship, the basic dynamics involved in the formation and evolution of relationships are quite similar. In each circumstance, the individuals enter the relationship behaving toward the other persons on the basis of the rules, maps, and images they have acquired as a result of their previous experiences. As relationships develop, mutual influence occurs as the individuals adopt or create *joint*, or *relational*, communication rules. These rules guide, shape, and in a sense govern the particular social unit from its initiation through the various stages of development to its eventual termination, in much the same ways as maps and images guide an individual's behavior.

In the case of strangers passing on the street, the information-processing rules the individuals use are relatively simple and the relationship itself is short-lived. By contrast, intimate relationships between persons who have lived or worked together for many years can be exceptionally complex.

We are unaware of many of relationships of which we are a part. Very often, we are taking account of messages and ourselves being taken account of, influencing and being influenced, without awareness or intention.

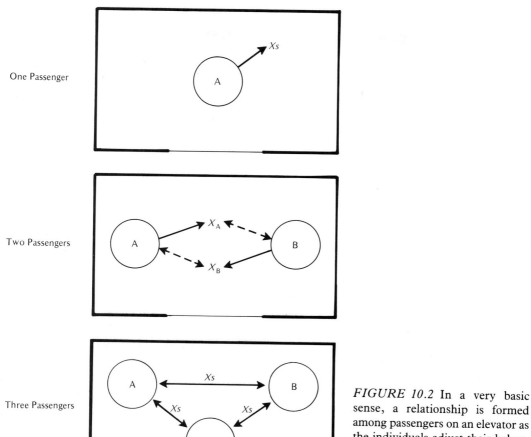

One Passenger

Two Passengers

Three Passengers

FIGURE 10.2 In a very basic sense, a relationship is formed among passengers on an elevator as the individuals adjust their behavior relative to the use of space, based on an awareness of one another's presence.

Perspectives on Relationships

In this chapter, the primary focus of our discussion will be upon those relationships which we are aware of and intentionally form and maintain. Relationships of this type can be classified based upon any number of factors. In our discussion we will consider the *number of persons* involved, the *purpose* of the relationship, its *duration*, and the *level of intimacy* attained.

Dyadic and Triadic Relationships

The vast majority of our relationships are *dyads*—two person units. As children, our first contacts with others are dyadic, and it is not until we reach the age of six to twelve years that we are able to engage in conversation with

FIGURE 10.3

several persons at the same time.[1] In our adult years each of us is a member of a large number of different dyads.

As William Wilmot notes in *Dyadic Communication*, each of the many dyads in which we participate is unique in a number of respects.[2] First, every dyadic relationship fulfills particular ends. The functions served by a teacher-student dyad, for instance, are generally quite different from those of a husband-wife relationship, and both are distinct from those served by doctor-patient or employee-employer relationships.

Second, each involves different facets of the individuals who participate in them. The demands placed on an individual as a student in a teacher-student relationship are different from those placed on that same person as a husband in a husband-wife relationship or as a supervisor in a work relationship. In this respect no two dyads in which we participate involve precisely the same demands or opportunities.

Third, in any dyad, unique language patterns, communication rules and patterns develop over time that differentiate each relationship from others. Slang and "in-phrases" among friends, terms of fondness between lovers, and ritualized greetings among colleagues at work are the result of these ongoing communication dynamics within relationships.

While the majority of the relationships in which we participate involve two persons, we also often find ourselves in social units composed of three or four persons.

Triads—three-person relationships—and *quadrads*—four-person relationships—differ from dyads in several respects, particularly in their complexity. In dyads, reciprocal data-processing takes place between two persons. With triads, there are six possible message-processing pairings: person 1 with person 2, person 1 with person 3, person 2 with person 3, persons 1 and 2 with person 3, persons 1 and 3 with person 2, and persons 2 and 3 with person 1. In quadrads, there are twenty-five such potential pairings.[3]

Beyond the increased complexity resulting from more possible data-processing pairs, triads and quadrads differ from dyads in several additional respects. One of these has to do with the likelihood of developing high levels of intimacy. While it is possible for members of triads or quadrads to develop very close relationships, there is certainly a far greater potential for intimacy when interaction is limited exclusively to two individuals.

Second, in relationships of more than two persons, differences of opinion can be resolved by "voting" to determine the "majority opinion." In dyads, negotiation is the only means available. A further distinction is that triads and quadrads have somewhat more stability than dyads. When only two persons are involved in a relationship, either party has the power to destroy the unit by withdrawing. In relationships involving three or four persons, the withdrawal of one party may well have a marked impact on the unit, but it would not necessarily lead to its termination.

Finally, it is rare that triads operate such that all parties are equally and evenly involved. Typically, at any point in time, two members of the relationship are closer to one another or in greater agreement than the other party or parties. The result is often the formation of coalitions, struggles for "leadership," and sometimes open conflict. Because of this, some authors have argued that there is actually no such thing as a triadic or quadratic relationship, but rather that such units are better thought of as a dyad plus one, or two dyads.[4]

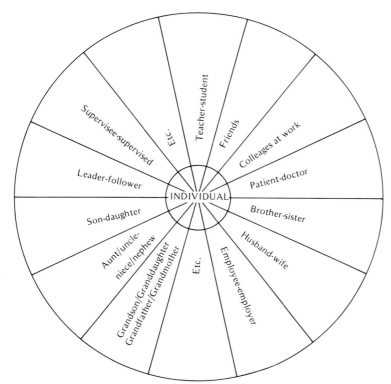

FIGURE 10.4 Relationships play a major role in the life activities and definition of the individual. Each relationship makes demands on the individual that are in some ways unique and at the same time contribute to the development of our identity and self concept.

FIGURE 10.5

Task and Social Relationships

In addition to thinking about relationships in terms of the *number of persons involved*, one can also look at the primary *purpose* for their formation. Many relationships are developed for the purpose of *coordinated action—completion of a task or project that one individual could not manage alone*. A simple example of this type of relationship is one person holding on to a board while another person saws off a piece.

The relationship created between a taxi driver and passenger, or that which develops between a newspaper carrier and a subscriber provide other illustrations of the simple relationships in which two individuals work together to accomplish a specific task.[5] Social units composed of colleagues at work, employer and employee, leader and follower, doctor and patient, teacher and student, therapist and patient are additional examples of task relationships which occupy a major role in our lives.

In some situations, accomplishing a task is of secondary importance, or perhaps of no significance whatsoever. In such circumstances, what can be termed, *personally* or *socially oriented goals*, take precedence. Making a new acquaintance, having a drink with an old friend, and spending time chatting periodically with a coworker during lunch, serve a number of important functions, even though they are not essential to completion of a task. Social relations can provide a means of diversion, recreation, intimacy, or companionship. They may also be a way of avoiding isolation or loneliness, confirming our own sense of worth, giving and receiving affection, or comparing our views and opinions to those held by others.[6]

Individuals may well be willing to devote more or less time, energy, and commitment to a relationship, depending upon whether they see it as essentially task or socially oriented. As a result, the communication patterns that develop will often vary substantially depending upon how the members regard their purpose for participating in a given relationship in the first place.

Short and Long-Term Relationships

Longevity is another factor which has a significant bearing on the nature of relationships. Most of us are engaged in at least several long-term relationships with members of our immediate families, relatives, lovers, and friends. By the same token, during any given day, we also participate in the formation and/or maintenance of any number of transitory relationships—an exchange of smiles and glances while walking down a corridor, a wave and hello to a familiar face in the apartment complex, or an exchange of pleasantries with the clerk at the shopping mall.

Between these two extremes are relationships of varying duration. In general, the older a relationship, the more the investment one has made in it, and the greater the investment he or she is willing to make in order to preserve it. Often too, a substantial investment in long-term relationships

FIGURE 10.6

PERSONALS

Single-White-Male—very successful genuine professional, interesting mid 50's, handsome, silver haired, distinguished, affectionate and understanding seeks mature. highly attractive, well groomed, sophisticated, intelligent, liberated, sexy, devoted, fun type S/W/F (under 35 yrs, 5' 6", 36" 24" 35", approx 120 lbs.) with no dependents for romantic, meaningful, permanent loving relationship. Private dinners, informal parties, social affairs, political functions, theatre, movies, recreational activities, sporting events, picnics, lost weekends, continental and foreign vacations and traveling. Kindly respond by sincere and descriptive letter enclosing recent color photo. Reply to Box #04211.

FIGURE 10.7

leads to a willingness to maintain them at costs greater than those we would pay in a newly formed relationship.

With short-term relationships there is little history, generally fewer personal consequences should the relationship not progress as intended, and relatively little personal involvement. In such circumstances, an individual is far less locked into a particular identity, and much less constrained by past actions and the images others may have of him or her. In many instances short-term relationships can be attractive and functional precisely because they are seen as requiring less investment, commitment, and follow-through.

Casual and Intimate Relationships

Relationships can also be characterized in terms of the level of intimacy, openness, honesty, trust, and receptivity that is present. On one extreme, we can think of relationships in which conversation consists primarily of a ritualized exchange of pleasantries:

Eric: "Hello. How are you?"
Pam: "Fine, thanks, and you?"
Eric: "Good."
Pam: "It's a beautiful day today, isn't it?"
Eric: "Sure is."
Pam: "How's the family?"
Eric: "Everyone is fine. How's yours?"
And so on.

In instances like this one, the specifics of the conversation are *highly predictable*. It is also an *impersonal* exchange in the sense that either person could—and probably would—share the same remarks with virtually anyone. There is little that suggests the uniqueness of the relationship to either person. Further, in such a conversation, there is a lack of *self, other, or topical disclosure*.[7] That is, neither person is disclosing much information as to his or her own opinions or beliefs at other than a surface level, and there is an obvious absence of personal feelings being expressed.

In more intimate relationships, individuals may share some of their private concerns about life, death, illness, their feelings about other persons and themselves. An exchange between persons who have attained greater intimacy would contrast markedly with the previous exchange:

Eric: "Hello. How are you?"
Pam: "Not that great, to be honest."
Eric: "What's the matter?"
Pam: "I went for my routine physical last week, and the doctor found a tumor."
Eric: "How serious is it?"
Pam: "They don't know yet. The test results aren't back, but I'm scared to death."
Eric: "I don't blame you. It scares the hell out of me even hearing about it. Is it something you want to talk about.?"
Pam: "I really think I need to, if it's O.K."
Eric: "Of course it's O.K...."
And so on.

Contrasted with the earlier example, this exchange is neither routine nor highly predictable. A high degree of topical information and self-disclosure is involved. Further, it seems likely that neither person would be participating in precisely the same kind of discussion with many other individuals, which suggests the uniqueness of this relationship for the persons involved. Generally speaking colleagues and casual friends fall somewhere near the center of the continuum between *acquaintances* and *intimates*.

Relationships of differing levels of intimacy have varying values for us. As Erving Goffman and other writers have noted, the ritualized exchanges which characterize casual acquaintances permit us to maintain contact with a large number of individuals with a minimum of effort and conscious attention. Such exchanges are a way of saying: "Hello, I see you. It seems to me it is worth acknowledging you. I want you to know that. I hope you feel the same way too." Ritualized conversation is also important because it is generally the first step in the development of closer relationships.

Intimate relationships, by contrast, require a substantial investment of time and effort. They can, however, provide opportunities for personal and social growth which may well be impossible to derive in any other way. They afford a context of trust in which the individual can express himself or herself candidly, be reacted to with a greater degree of continuity and honesty than is likely in other relationships, and openly explore and work to apply the insights gained over a period of time.

No doubt even more basic than the personal and social functions served by intimate relationships are the apparent medical aspects. In his book, *The Broken Heart: The Medical Consequences of Loneliness*, James Lynch discusses the importance of intimate relationships to our health. He cites research that suggests that the absence of intimate relationships can have negative medical consequences. Those studies have shown that a continual state of loneliness,

FIGURE 10.8

the absence or death of parents during the early years of childhood, or the loss of a loved one are significant factors contributing to the likelihood of premature death. This work vividly underscores the critical role of intimate relationships in our lives.[8]

The Evolution of Relationships

Whether a relationship is a *dyad* or *triad*, *task* or *socially oriented*, *short-* or *long-term*, *casual* or *intimate*, the dynamics by which they are initiated, develop, and eventually deteriorate and terminate are quite similar in terms of communication.

Stage One: Initiation

The initial stage in the formation of any relationship involves *social initiation* or *encounter*.[9] In this phase two or several individuals take note of and adjust to one another's behavior. Often the initial data to which the individuals adjust are nonverbal—a smile, glance, handshake, movement, or appear-

FIGURE 10.9

ance. Should the relationship continue, progressive reciprocity of message processing occurs. One person notices the other's actions, position, appearance, and gestures. The second person reacts, and those reactions are noted and reacted to by the first person, whose reactions are acted on by the second person, and so on. Except in the most fleeting relationships like passengers on an elevator, language comes to play an important role as the individuals move beyond first impressions.

During the early stages of a relationship, the individuals involved operate in terms of the communication patterns, rules, and habits they "bring with them" from previous experiences. As interpersonal communication progresses, each begins to acquire some knowledge of the other's maps and rules for sensing, making sense of, acting, and reacting. Gradually, through combination, recombination, blend, mutation, compromise, and unspoken negotiation, the *joint* rules by which their particular relationship will operate begin to emerge.

In *Pragmatics of Human Communication*, Watzlawick, Beavin, and Jackson point out that interpersonal communication in relationships serves both *content* and *relational* functions.[10] On the one hand, each person acquires information about the other from the *content* of his or her verbal and nonverbal behaviors—*what* is said or done. In the same process, the *way* things are said and done provides the cues that help define the nature of emerging relationships. Consider the following introductions:

Bill: "Hi, Mary. My name is Bill."
Bill: "Hello, Mary. My name is Dr. Remson."

While the *content* of each statement served essentially the same function—letting Mary know the other individual's name, the *relational implications* are quite different. In this brief exchange a tone and pattern is set in motion that is likely to impact upon the developing relationship.

Stage Two: Exploration

The second stage of relational development picks up just moments after the initial encounter, as the individuals begin exploring potentials of the other person and the possibility of further pursuing the relationship. In this phase the individuals gather information about the other person's communication rules, maps, images, motives, interests, and values. This knowledge serves as the basis for assessing the merits of continuing the relationship.

Stage Three: Intensification

If the relationship progresses, it moves into a third phase, which Mark Knapp has labeled the *intensifying* stage.[11] In reaching this level, the individuals have arrived at a decision—which they may or may not verbalize—that they wish the relationship to continue. As the relationship progresses, the individuals acquire a good deal of knowledge of the communication behavior of the others involved, and at the same time a number of joint rules, shared language, and relational rituals will have emerged. A relationship may stall at this stage, may deteriorate, or may continue to develop.

Stage Four: Formalization

Should the relationship progress further, some formal, symbolic, acknowledgement binding the individuals to one another is common. In the case of a love relationship, the formal bonding may take the form of engagement or wedding rings. With an individual being hired for a job, the employee and employer may sign a contract. Where two persons are entering a business partnership, the relationship may be formalized by ratifying legal agreements.

FIGURE 10.10

During and following the formalization stage, the individuals advance in their joint creation of relational rules, including the development of shared symbols, preferred and characteristic patterns of conversing, unintentional habits and customs, and standardized rituals. The meanings of these verbal and nonverbal behaviors become standardized. Sometimes the persons involved are aware the process is occurring; more often they are not. Over time, the relationship develops a distinctiveness that distinguishes it in subtle and not so subtle ways from the many other relationships in which the individuals have been involved.

Stage Five: Redefinition

With the passage of time, the individuals inevitably grow and develop. This change creates pressure for change on the other individual or individuals in the relationship, as well as upon the relationship itself. As a consequence, a need for redefining some of the joint rules of the relationship often arises. There are many classic illustrations of these sorts of situations: perhaps a woman who was once quite pleased to stay at home and take care of the children wishes to pursue a career. Or it may be that a teenager no longer wants to be so closely supervised by his or her parents, or an employee feels he or she deserves more latitude on the job than when first hired. In each such instance, changes in the individual place strains on their relationships and on the accepted and often difficult to change rules and patterns which have developed to date.

Sometimes the needed redefinition is a very gradual, natural, or easily manageable part of the evolution of a relationship. In other instances, when change is too rapid or extreme or resistance too great, a deterioration process begins.

FIGURE 10.11

Stage Six: Deterioration

Initially, the deterioration may go unnoticed, as parties in a relationship begin more and more to "go their own ways" physically and symbolically. Things that once were shared no longer are. Words or gestures that once mattered no longer do. Once glowing prospects for the future at a particular job become blurred and faded. Rules that grew naturally in a love relationship during its development now seem more like shackles and imposed statutes to be followed with resignation.

Once the deterioration process has reached this point, it is quite likely that the relationship is nearing dissolution, as the behaviors of each person come to make less and less difference to the actions and reactions of the other. Physical separation and the dissolution of any remaining legal or contractual obligations is the final step in the often painful process of terminating a relationship.

As we noted earlier, relationships do not necessarily move through these stages in an orderly way. They may stall in any one stage, back up and go forward again, or stop at one point for an extended period of time.

Relational Patterns

As we have noted, at various stages in relationships of all sorts, characteristic patterns develop. These relational patterns are the result of joint rules that have developed between the persons involved. In this section, we will briefly consider three of the most common of these patterns: (1) *dependencies and counterdependencies;* (2) *progressive and regressive spirals;* and (3) *self-fulfilling and self-defeating prophecies.*[12]

Dependencies and Counterdependencies

The dynamics of dependency and counterdependency are prevalent in many relationships at various points in time. What we can term a *dependency relationship* exists when one individual in a relationship who is highly dependent on another for support, money, a job, leadership, guidance, or whatever, generalizes this dependency to other facets of the relationship.

The classic example of this kind of relational dynamic is that which develops between the child and his or her parents, sometimes between therapists and their patients.[13] In both instances, one individual has particular needs or goals that are being met by the other individual or individuals in the relationship. The dependent pattern may become more generalized, so that one person comes to rely on the other in a broad range of circumstances that are unrelated to the original basis for dependency. When this occurs, a pattern is set in motion that can have far-reaching impact and consequences for the individuals as well as the relationship. Whether the people are discussing politics, sex, or religion, whether they are trying to decide where to eat or where to live, the dependent person will predictably take his or her cues from the other, on whom he or she has learned to rely, as the following conversation might suggest:

Robbi: "I think we should go to McDonald's for lunch. How does that sound?"
Jenny: "Fine."
Robbi: "Come to think about it, McDonald's is likely to be busy at this hour. How about the Corner Grill?"
Jenny: "Sure, that sounds great."

In other relationships, or in the same relationship at other points in time, the dependency is in the opposite direction. In these circumstances, one individual relates to the other not as a dependent, but instead as a *counter-dependent*. Where the dependent individual generally complies with the other individual in the relationship across a broad range of topics, the counter-dependent person characteristically disagrees, as the following scenario illustrates:

Robbi: "I think we should go to McDonald's for lunch. How does that sound?"
Jenny: "I'm tired of McDonald's."
Robbi: "How About the Corner Grill?"
Jenny: "That's no better. I was thinking of a place we could have a drink and relax."
Robbi: "What about The Attic?"
Jenny: "It's really not worth all this time deciding. Let's just go to McDonald's and be done with it."

In the first circumstance, we can assume that whatever Robbi suggested, Jenny would go along. In the second, it seems likely that whatever Robbi suggested Jenny would disagree.

As dependencies and counter-dependencies become a habitual way of relating, they guide, shape, and often overshadow the specific content of conversation. Eventually, at the extreme, the content of what the individuals say comes to have little impact on the dynamics. When person A says "yes," person B agrees. Or, When A says "no," B consistently disagrees.

Progressive and Regressive Spirals

When the actions and reactions of individuals in a relationship are consistent with their goals and needs, the relationship progresses on a positive tone with continual increases in the level of harmony and satisfaction. This circumstance can be termed a *progressive spiral*. In progressive spirals, the reciprocal message processing of the persons involved contributes positively and progressively to one another, leading to a sense of "positiveness" in their experiences. The satisfaction derived from others and from circumstance builds on itself and contributes at the same time to the satisfaction others derive. The result is a relationship that is a source of growing pleasure and value for the participants.

The opposite sort of pattern can also develop, in which each exchange between individuals contributes to a progressive decrease in satisfaction and harmony. In these sorts of circumstances—*regressive spirals*—the result is increasing discomfort, distance, frustration, and dissatisfaction for the parties involved. Perhaps the simplest example of this latter type of spiral is provided by an argument:

Ann: "Would you try to remember to take out the garbage tomorrow morning on your way to work?"
Mike: "You know I get really sick of your nagging all the damn time!"
Ann: "If you were a little more reliable and a little less defensive, we might not have to have these same discussions over and over again."
Mike: "You're hardly the one to lecture about memory or defensiveness. If you remembered half the things you committed to do, we would have a hell of a lot less arguments. And it's your defensiveness, not mine, that causes all of our problems...."

Relationships that begin on a "wrong note" may rapidly become regressive spirals as the individuals involved find they are unable to satisfy one another's needs. But, where the interpersonal communication serves the needs, goals, and aspirations of the persons involved, the relationship is likely to become a progressive spiral, at least at the outset. Over time, of course, the spirals that characterize any relationship alternate between progressive and regressive, as a reflection of the inevitable cycles of conflict and conflict resolution that characterize any social unit. In order for a relationship to maintain strength, momentum, and continuity, the progressive phases must outweigh and/or outlast the regressive periods.

Like dependencies, spirals often take on a "life of their own," fueled by the momentum they themselves create. What begins as a request to take out the garbage can easily become still another in a string of provocations, in a relationship where regressive spirals are common. And, by contrast, "Hi, how are you?" can initiate a very positive chain of events in a relationship characterized by frequent progressive spirals.

Self-Fulfilling and Self-Defeating Prophecies

Another pattern that often develops in relationships has to do with our own *expectations*. It is often the case that what we expect to happen will happen, or at the least what we expect to happen will influence what actually occurs. If a person expects, for example, that he or she will do poorly in an interview for a new job, that expectation alone is enough to set in motion a process that helps to fulfill his or her prophecy. Because the individual believes he or she will not get the job, the approach to the interview situation may well be negative. This negative outlook is reflected in what is said and done, with the result that the interviewer may well be convinced that the candidate is not appropriate for the position.

The reverse circumstance is also possible. When an individual is convinced that he or she is well-qualified for a particular job, this expectation can provide the energy and commitment needed to prepare for the interview and to respond competently during the interview, which greatly increases the chances of being selected for the position.

In a wide range of situations, the expectations we have play a major role in influencing the outcomes of our interactions with people and contribute to long-term patterns within relationships. In relationships, as in so many other facets of human activity, our own effort, commitment, and attitude play a major role in the outcomes that are realized.

Factors That Influence Patterns

We have looked at the role communication plays in the evolution of relationships and the patterns that develop within them. In this section, we will focus our attention on the factors which influence these patterns. A number of elements impact on the interpersonal communication dynamics which take place within relationships. Particularly important are: (1) *stage and context of interaction;* (2) *interpersonal needs and style;* and (3) *power and structure.*

Stage of Relationship and Context

It is almost too obvious to note that communication patterns in a relationship vary greatly from one stage to another. Naturally, individuals meeting each other for the first time interact in a different manner than they would had they lived together for several years. In a similar vein, the nature of the interpersonal patterns one observes varies depending upon the context in which conversation is taking place. People meeting in a grocery store are quite likely to act and react differently to one another than if they were interacting in a bar or at a business meeting. Together, these two factors account for much of the variation in the patterns of communication within relationships.

Interpersonal Orientation

Beyond the rather direct and obvious impact of *stage and context,* the *needs, goals, attitudes, habits,* and *values* of the individuals involved represent another source of influence on communication within relationships.

Often noted as especially important in this way are the *interpersonal needs* for *affection, inclusion,* and *control.* William Schutz has suggested that our desires relative to giving and receiving affection, being included in the activities of others and including them in ours, and controlling other people and being controlled by them are very basic to our orientations to social relations of all kinds.[14]

Presumably, we have each developed our own specific needs relative to control, affection, and inclusion, as we have in other areas. The particular profile of needs we ourselves have, and how these match with those of other persons, can be a major determinant of the sorts of relational patterns that result. For instance, we could expect that one person with high needs for control and another with similarly strong needs to be controlled would function well together. The former would fall comfortably into a dominant leadership role, while the latter would be very willing to follow. If, on the other hand, two persons who work or live together have similarly high (or low) needs for control, one might predict a good deal of conflict (or a lack of decisiveness) within the relationship. In any event, we would expect the match (or mismatch) between individuals' interpersonal needs for affection, inclusion, and control would often have a great impact on interpersonal dynamics.

Interpersonal *style* also plays a key role in shaping the communication patterns that emerge in relationships. As discussed earlier, some persons are more comfortable operating in an outgoing, highly verbal manner in their dealings with others, while other individuals characteristically adopt a more passive and restrained interpersonal style, due either to preference or apprehension about speaking in social situations.

Characteristically those who use a more outgoing style deal with their thoughts and feelings in a forthright, assertive manner.[15] If they want something, they ask for it. If they feel angry, they let others know. If they feel taken advantage of, they say so. If they don't want to comply with a request, they have little trouble saying "no!"

In contrast to what might be termed a *machine-gun style* of interpersonal communication, the more passive *marshmallow style* involves absorbing the verbal and nonverbal data of others, giving the outward appearance of acceptance, congeniality, and even encouragement, regardless of how one might feel or think about what is going on.[16] For any of several reasons, the individual who is prone to use the marshmallow style, often "holds onto" and "bottles up" his or her thoughts, opinions, and feelings.

If such a person is angry, it is seldom apparent from what they say. If they disagree, they seldom say so. If they feel taken advantage of, they may well allow the situation to continue rather than confront the other person openly with their feelings.

Though few people use either style exclusively, most of us probably favor one approach or the other in the majority of our dealings with people. And depending upon the style of the people with whom we are in relationship, this factor alone can become a primary influence in shaping our interactions and our relationships as is suggested in the following conversation:

Tom: "Georgia, you wouldn't mind taking me home tonight after work, would you? I know I impose on you a lot, but Mary needed the car again today, and I know you're the kind of person who doesn't mind helping out now and then."

Georgia: "Well, if you have no other way, I..."

Tom: "Hey thanks, Georgia. I was sure I could count on you. How are things anyway? Really busy, I'll bet. Well, listen, I'd better get back to work. I'll meet you by your car, at 5:00. Thanks again."

Tom's use of a *machine-gun style,* in combination with Georgia's *marshmallow style,* will no doubt be critical factors in defining most, if not all of the interactions that take place between them.

Structure and Power

Interpersonal communication within relationships is also shaped by the *structure* and the distribution of *power.* Where one individual, for instance, is employed by the other, the relationship is *asymmetrical,* or uneven, in terms of the actual power each has in the job situation.[17] The employer can exercise more control over that facet of their relationship—so long as the other person does not quit—simply as a consequence of their structural relationship.

There are many similar situations where asymmetries within the relationship affect the interpersonal communication. The relationship existing between a therapist and a patient, a teacher and a student, a parent and a child, or a supervisor and supervisee are among the most common examples of this situation. In each, one member of the relationship has control over certain facets of the other's life, a circumstance that generally has a substantial impact on the interpersonal communication patterns which develop.

In peer-peer, colleague-colleague, or other relationships of this type, there is the *potential* for symmetry. Where this possibility exists, interpersonal communication *creates* any dependencies which result, rather than *perpetuating* them as it does with asymmetrical relationships.

Summary

In this chapter, we have examined the role of communication in the development and evolution of relationships. We have also discussed a number of ways of thinking about and characterizing relationships, and explored common communication patterns which can occur. Communication plays a central role in the development and evolution of all human relationships. Relationships also provide perhaps the most important context in which we attempt to use our communication abilities to achieve particular goals and meet particular needs.

In the most general sense, a relationship exists whenever there is *reciprocal data processing*—when two or more individuals are reacting to one another's verbal and nonverbal messages. It is by means of reciprocal message processing—*interpersonal communication*—that relationships are initiated, develop, grow, or deteriorate.

Intentionally established relationships can be considered from several perspectives: whether they are *dyadic, triadic,* or *quadradic;* whether they are *task* or *social* in purpose; whether they are *short-* or *long*-term; whether they are *casual* or *intimate.*

Relationships progress through a series of relatively predictable stages, beginning from an initial social encounter, progressing to stages of increasing interaction and joint rule creation. Many relationships involve some formalized acknowledgement of their status, such as marriage or a legal business contract. A relationship may stall in one of these stages, back up and go foward again, or stop and remain in one stage for an extended period of time.

In the evolution of relationships, message processing serves both *content* and *relational* functions, providing the individuals with information about one another and about the topics of conversation, while at the same time shaping the nature of their relationship.

Over time, communication patterns develop in relationships. Often these dynamics take the form of *dependencies or counter-dependencies, progressive or regressive spirals,* or *self-fulfilling or self-defeating prophecies.* These dynamics can have a far more significant impact on the form and developmental patterns of relationships than does the content of interaction.

A number of factors such as *stage and context, interpersonal needs and style,* and *structure and power* play a role in facilitating the development of particular patterns.

Notes

1. The discussion of nature of dyads and triads draws upon the excellent summary of work on this topic provided by William Wilmot in *Dyadic Communication* (Reading, MA.: Addison-Wesley, 1979), pp. 14–30.
2. Ibid., pp. 14–15.
3. William M. Kephart, "A Quantitative Analysis of Intra-Group Relationships." *American Journal of Sociology*, **55**. 544–549 (1950).
4. William Wilmot, *op. cit.*, p. 21.
5. Cf. Fred Davis, "The Cabdriver and his Fare: Facets of a Fleeting Relationship," in Warren G. Bennis, David E. Berlew, Edgar H. Schein, and Fred I. Steele, eds., *Interpersonal Dynamics*, (Homewood, IL: Dorsey, 1973), pp. 417–426.
6. Cf. Michael D. Scott and William G. Powers, *Interpersonal Communication: A Question of Needs* (Boston, Houghton Mifflin, 1978), for a useful discussion of the role of needs in interpersonal communication and relational development.
7. Cf. Joseph Luft, *Of Human Interaction* (Palo Alto, CA: National Press Books, 1969); Sidney M. Jourard, *The Transparent Self* (Princeton, NJ: Van Nostrand, 1964); and Stella Ting-Toomey, "Gossip as a Communication Construct." Paper presented at the Annual Conference of the Western Speech Communication Association. Los Angeles, February, 1979.
8. James J. Lynch, *The Broken Heart: The Medical Consequences of Loneliness,* (New York: Basic Books, 1979).
9. The discussion of stages of development of relationships draws on the work of Mark L. Knapp in *Social Intercourse: From Greeting to Goodbye* (Boston: Allyn & Bacon, 1978), and Murray S. Davis, *Intimate Relations* (New York: Free Press, 1973).
10. Paul Watzlawick, Janet H. Beavin, and Don D. Jackson, *Pragmatics of Human Communication* (New York: Norton, 1967), pp. 51–54.

11. Mark L. Knapp, *op. cit.*, pp. 19–21.
12. Cf. discussion of spirals and prophecies in William Wilmot, op. cit., pp. 121–129, and in Paul Watzlawick, *et al., op. cit.*
13. Cf. Robert R. Carkhuff and Bernard G. Berenson, *Beyond Counseling and Therapy* (New York: Holt, 1967).
14. William Schutz, *The Interpersonal Underworld* (Palo Alto, CA: Science and Behavior Books, 1968).
15. Cf. Colleen Kelley, "Assertion Theory," in J. William Pfeiffer and John E. Jones, eds., *The 1976 Annual Handbook for Group Facilitators* (La Jolla, CA: University Associates, 1976); Sharon and Gordon Bowers, *Asserting Yourself* (Reading, MA: Addison-Wesley, 1976); and Colleen Kelley, *Assertion Training* (La Jolla, CA: University Associates, 1979).
16. Brent D. Ruben "The Machinegun and the Marshmallow: Some Thoughts on the Concept of Communication Effectiveness." Paper presented at the annual conference of the Western Speech Association (Honolulu: November, 1972), and Brent D. Ruben "Communication, Stress, and Assertiveness: An Interpersonal Problem-Solving Model." In J. William Pfeiffer and John E. Jones, eds., *The 1982 Annual Handbook for Group Facilitators,* (La Jolla, CA: University Associates, 1982).
17. Paul Watzlawick, et al., op cit., pp. 67–71.

References and Suggested Reading

Bales, Robert F. *Personality and Interpersonal Behavior.* New York: Holt, 1970.

Bennis, Warren G., David E. Berlew, Edgar H. Schein and Fred I. Steele, eds. *Interpersonal Dynamics.* 3rd ed. Homewood, IL: Dorsey, 1973.

Berger, Peter L. and Thomas Luckmann. *The Social Construction of Reality.* Garden City, NY: Doubleday, 1967.

Blumer, Herbert. *Symbolic Interactionism.* Englewood Cliffs, NJ: Prentice-Hall, 1969.

Davis, Murray S. *Intimate Relations.* New York: Free Press, 1973.

Eakins, Barbara W. and R. Gene Eakins. *Sex Differences in Human Communication.* Boston: Houghton Mifflin, 1978.

Gibb, Jack R. "Defensive Communication." *Journal of Communication,* **2** (1961), 141–148.

Goffman, Erving. *Interaction Ritual.* Garden City, NY: Doubleday, 1967.

———. *The Presentation of Self in Everyday Life.* Garden City, NY: Doubleday, 1959.

Jourard, Sidney M. *The Transparent Self.* Princeton, NJ: Van Nostrand, 1964.

Knapp, Mark L. *Social Intercourse.* Boston: Allyn & Bacon, 1978.

Levinson, Daniel J. *The Seasons of a Man's Life.* New York: Ballantine, 1978.

Luft, Joseph. *Of Human Interaction.* Palo Alto, CA: National Press Books, 1969.

Lynch, James J., *The Broken Heart: The Medical Consequences of Loneliness.* New York: Basic, 1977.

Manis, Jerome G. and Bernard N. Meltzer, eds. *Symbolic Interaction.* Boston: Allyn & Bacon, 1967.

Miller, Gerald R. and Mark Steinberg. *Between People.* Chicago: Science Research Associates, 1975.

Morris, Desmond. *Intimate Behaviour.* New York: Random, 1971.

Newcomb, Theodore M. *The Acquaintance Process.* New York: Holt, 1961.

Phillips, Gerald M. and Nancy J. Metzger. *Intimate Communication.* Boston: Allyn & Bacon, 1976.

Ruben, Brent D. "Machine-Guns and Marshmallows: Thoughts on The Concept of Communication Effectiveness." Paper presented at the Western Speech Communication Association, Honolulu, 1972.

Ruben, Brent D. "Communication, Stress, and Assertiveness: An Interpersonal Problem-Solving Model." In *The 1982 Handbook for Group Facilitators.* Edited by J. William Pfeiffer and John E. Jones. La Jolla, CA: University Associates, 1982.

Ruesch, Jurgen. *Disturbed Communication.* New York: Norton, 1957.

Ruesch, Jurgen and Gregory Bateson. *Communication—The Social Matrix of Psychiatry.* New York: Norton, 1951.

Schutz, William. *The Interpersonal Underworld.* Palo Alto, CA: Science and Behavior Books, 1968.

Scott, Michael D. and William G. Powers. *Interpersonal Communication: A Question of Needs.* Boston: Houghton Mifflin, 1978.

Sommer, Robert. "Further Studies of Small Group Ecology." *Sociometry,* **28** (1965), 337–348.

Stewart, John, ed. *Bridges Not Walls.* 2nd ed. Reading, MA: Addison-Wesley, 1977.

Ting-Toomey, Stella. "Gossip as a Communication Construct." Paper presented at the Annual Conference of the Western Speech Communication Association. Los Angeles, February, 1979.

Watzlawick, Paul, Janet H. Beavin and Don D. Jackson. *Pragmatics of Human Communication.* New York: Norton, 1967.

Wilmot, William W. *Dyadic Communication.* 2nd ed. Reading, MA: Addison-Wesley, 1979.

Groups and Organizations

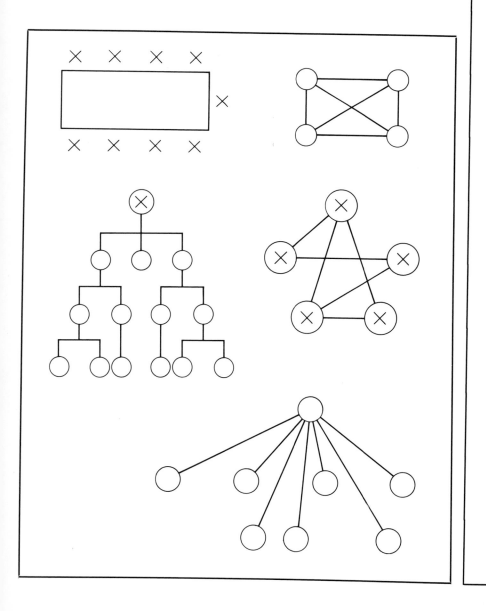

In this chapter we extend our discussions of the uses and consequences of communication to the groups and organizations which play such a vital role in human affairs. In discussing these social units, we will focus our attention on functions and goals, networks and networking, symbols, roles and responsibilities.

Functions and Goals

Each of us spends great quantities of our time in groups and organizations of various kinds—working at our jobs, participating in clubs and associations, attending church or civic functions, and taking part in any number of assorted social groups. We look to our social systems for fulfillment of many of our physiological, personal, and social needs and aspirations. Even the production of essentials of life such as food, shelter, and clothing requires the concerted effort of a good many persons working together in groups and organizations.

As with relationships, groups and organizations have their origins in individuals engaged in reciprocal data processing. Thus, in a very fundamental sense, the communication process makes groups and organizations possible. Once formed and operating, these social systems, in turn, serve a number of important communication functions for those who create and participate in them. Through participation in families, peer groups, clubs, religious orders, political parties, schools, and other groups and organizations we are selectively exposed to various facets of our environment. Beyond exposure, we receive additional guidance in learning how to transform environmental data into useful information. In this manner, groups and organizations have a substantial impact on the maps, images, and rules we acquire as individuals.

As a part of this mapping process, we also acquire the rules which are necessary to operate in the groups and organizations of which we are a part. In the same way that rules created among passengers on an elevator guide their actions, the rules of clubs, informal groups, business organizations, and other social units serve to direct the behavior of the persons who are members of them.

Groups and organizations also play an important role in the development and maintenance of our individual identities. As we grow from infancy to adulthood, the groups and organizations in which we participate provide a wide range of demands and opportunities for us, and in the process of adjusting to these we develop, change, and grow. Finally, groups and organizations are also essential to tool-making and to the creation of the communication technologies that enhance our capacity for the display, reception, storage, and retrieval of information.

Beyond these general functions, groups and organizations also serve more specific objects or goals. In many instances a group or organization is formed to complete a *task*—organize a party, build a house, put out a newspaper, or the like. Product and service business, labor unions,

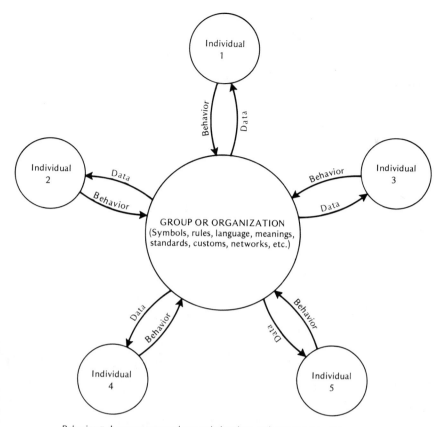

Behavior = Language use and nonverbal actions and appearances, etc.

Data = Used by the individual as information about the group or organization,
its symbols, rules, language, meanings, standards, customs, networks, etc.

FIGURE 11.1 Through their verbal and nonverbal behavior individuals collectively create the groups and organizations to which they belong and the symbols, rules, jargon, and other conventions characteristic of each. To become a member of an ongoing group or organization, the individual must accept the symbols, rules, and conventions that have developed. This process also occurs through communication.

professional organizations, and many civic groups exemplify this type of social unit.

There are also a good many other groups which serve primarily *personally* and *socially-oriented goals*, such as interpersonal support, encouragement, and diversion. Social fraternities and sororities, clubs, and rap groups, are examples.

To a greater or lesser extent, nearly all social systems serve a blend of these two kinds of functions. Even in what we might think of as a rigidly task-oriented organization, such as an industrial assembly line where productivity is the primary measure of success, personal and social goals are also regarded as important if only because of their impact on productivity. And, conversely, within social groups decision-making as to what movie to attend, where to go to eat, or what activities to pursue in spare time requires some degree of task orientation. A number of groups and organizations—such as families, service clubs, or religious organizations—require a fairly even balance among these kinds of goals for their continued existence.

Within relationships and small groups generally goals *emerge naturally* to meet our individual needs for such things as companionship, sexual intimacy, or the completion of a task. Often, in these circumstances, the goals are not clearly specified and the persons involved may not even be able to verbalize them.

By contrast, other groups and nearly all organizations are *contrived* rather than *emergent*—created, rather than naturally developed.[1] As such, these larger units typically have specific, stated goals or objectives—to serve the community, to share professional interests, to make a profit, or to advance a political candidate, for example.

Networks and Networking

In relationships and groups which are emergent, reciprocal data-processing networks develop naturally, often spontaneously. In newly formed units with minimal structure, such as discussion or growth groups, networks begin to form as individuals meet and get to know one another. Initially, the content of discussion may include such topics as the weather, composition of the group, the setting, circumstances that brought the individuals together, goals of the group, and so on. With the passage of time, the network becomes well developed as all members of the group participate in discussions on topics of central concern to them. Eventually the network includes all group members, at least minimally.[2] Some linkages in networks are utilized more and others

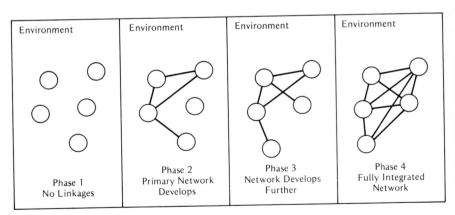

FIGURE 11.2 The development of linkages in a group or organization is marked by the emergence of networks that connect individuals to one another and define the unit. A given group or organization need not progress through all phases but may move from a stage of high integration to stages of lower integration and back again periodically.

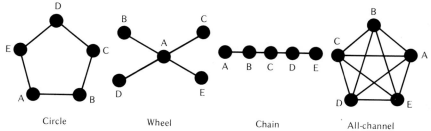

Circle   Wheel   Chain   All-channel

FIGURE 11.3 In studies of common group communication networks, such as those shown here, centralized networks (like the "wheel") contributed to rapid performance, but the error rate was high. Low centralization (such as provided in the "circle") was found to be associated with a high degree of individual satisfaction. Researchers also noted that being in a key position in a network, one requiring that information be channeled through an individual, led to information "overload."

SOURCE: Harold J. Leavitt, "Some Effects of Certain Communication Patterns on Group Performance," *Journal of Abnormal and Social Psychology,* **46**, 1951, pp 38–50; M.E. Shaw, "Some Effects of Unequal Distribution of Information Upon Group Performance in Various Communication Nets," Journal of Abnormal and Social Psychology, **49**, 1954, pp. 547–553.

less; some people become central to the network, others peripheral, still others may become isolated from others in the network.

It is thought that groups which are more clearly task-oriented go through quite a similar process involving an *orientation phase*, a *conflict phase*, an *emergence phase*, and a *reinforcement phase*.[3] The first stage consists of getting acquainted, the initial expression of points of view, and the formation of linkages relative to the task at hand. As the group proceeds, the expression of differing points of view lead to polarization. Gradually, accommodations are made among individuals and sub-groupings with differing view points. As the group's project nears completion, cooperation among individuals in the network increases as does support for the group's solution.[4]

Formalization

In relatively small informal groups, little may be done to formalize information networking. People can generally talk to whom they wish, whenever they wish, about what they wish. When the group gets together, whatever happens, happens.

Given the incredibly large number of potential two-person linkages in large groups and organizations, however, more formalization of communication is needed in order to avoid total chaos and random data sending and receiving.[5] To this end, *formal networks* are often established. The functions of formal networks include: (1) *coordinating what would otherwise be disparate activities of individuals and subunits;* (2) *maintaining lines of authority;* (3) *facilitating the exchange of data within the group or organization; and* (4) *ensuring the directed flow of data between the larger unit and the external environment in which it exists.*

Vertical and Horizontal Networks

Within some larger groups and organizations, the formalized *lines of data flow* correspond closely with the *lines of authority*. In such circumstances data flow "downward" from persons in leadership or management roles to others in the group or organization. Typically, such messages take the form of "assignments to be carried out," "requests for action," "information to be distributed," or "requests for input."

Upward flows refer to messages being channeled from individuals or subunits in a group or organization to persons occupying leadership roles. "Suggestions," "requests," and "advisory input" are common labels for data flowing "upward." What are often termed horizontal communication networks refer to linkages which connect individuals or subunits at the same level of authority.[6]

Informal and External Networks In addition to the formalized, intentionally designed linkages, other networks inevitably develop among individuals and subunits in any group or organization.[7] These *informal networks* serve to link individuals to one another in much the same way as formal networks. Unlike their formalized counterparts, however, informal linkages come into being primarily because of the personal and social needs of the members. Nonetheless, informal networks established during coffee breaks, at after-hours get-togethers, or on the tennis court or golf course, are also important channels within any group or organization. These networks have a substantial impact on both the content and shape of data flow in the more formalized networks.

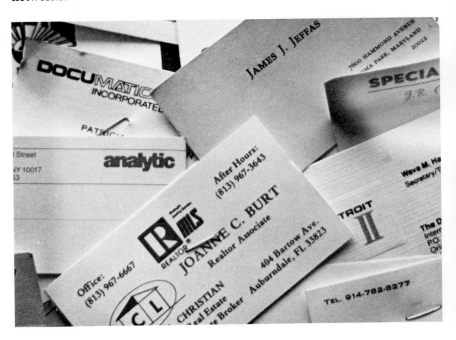

FIGURE 11.4

External Networks All groups and organizations depend on various constituencies in the larger environment for their survival. Voluntary groups rely on contributors, business organizations on consumers and the government, hospitals on patients and insurance companies, advertising agencies on their clients and the public, newspapers on their subscribers and advertisers, and so on. *External networks* connect the group or organization to these constituencies and to the larger environment.

These networks are used to provide the various external constituents with data which members of the group or organization think desirable, appropriate, or necessary. The terms *advertising, marketing,* and *public relations* are generally associated with group or organization activities which involve *the transmission data into the environment* with the aim of informing and systematically influencing constituents. These same networks, operating in reverse, enable the system to acquire the information necessary to identify and respond appropriately to environmental change, stressors, threat, opportunity, or challenge.

Symbols and Rules

As networks develop, symbols, rules, and codes of various types emerge and become standardized. Some develop naturally, as with slang phrases among members of a club or social group, or informal "dress codes" among employees of a company. In other instances, symbols, rules, and codes result from systematic efforts by members of a group or organization. In such cases,

FIGURE 11.5

symbols and rules are created to give the system an identity, to differentiate it from others, or to identify or differentiate individuals or sub-groups within the larger unit. The crests, handshakes, or "secret words" of fraternities or sororities serve these functions, as do the familiar trademarks and slogans of corporations.

Formalized dress codes may also serve a similar purpose. For example, the uniforms of police, doctors, nurses, military personnel, commercial pilots, and factory workers identify the tasks these individuals perform, provide members with a common identity, and distinguish the group from others.

In many organizations, rules are also developed for use in allocating space to employees, such that the location, size, and decor of an employee's office or work space reflect his or her position. Larger, more elaborately furnished and decorated offices, for example, go to individuals of a higher rank within the organization. Lesser officials may have smaller, less elegant offices; persons at still lower levels may have no private workspace at all, perhaps being separated from one another by portable partitions or bookcases and file cabinets. For reasons that may make little sense to an "outsider," carpeting in a vacated office might be ripped up and thrown away, as opposed to leaving it for a new occupant whose rank within the organization would not "call for" carpeted floors.

A number of other symbols and rules relative to operation of a unit emerge over time. In small groups, rules which guide the behavior of individuals toward one another are generally informal, as are "get-togethers" between members. In larger groups and organizations "get-togethers" are

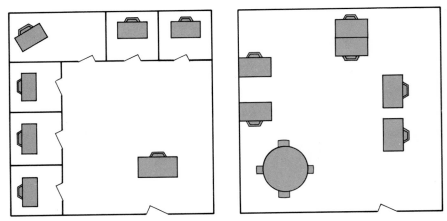

FIGURE 11.6 Architecture, interior design, and the arrangement of furniture can have major consequences for the communication dynamics within any social unit. In business and professional organizations, such factors are often intentionally manipulated to bring about particular outcomes. The placement of walls, desks, conference tables, and other structures directing the movement of individuals can have a substantial impact on the networks and working climate that develop within a particular environment.

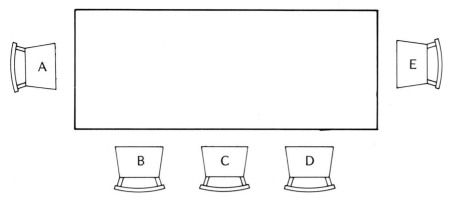

FIGURE 11.7 Studies of seating patterns in groups and communication behavior suggest that people who sit in positions A, C, and E are more vocal contributors to discussion than persons at positions B or D. Often, more dominant personalities tend to choose the high participation positions, while others who prefer to avoid high levels of participation, avoid them.

SOURCE: A. Hare and Robert Bales, "Seating Position and Small Group Interaction," *Sociometry*, **26**, 1963, pp. 480–486, and Mark L. Knapp, *Essentials of Nonverbal Communication* (New York: Holt Rinehart & Winston, 1980), p. 88.

generally convened, rather than naturally occurring. And, they are given a specific name—*meetings*—to suggest their relative formality. During *meetings*, the behaviors of individuals often follow a number of reasonably well-defined rules, some emerging naturally, others prescribed by *Roberts Rules of Order,* or the constitution or bylaws of the group. At such sessions, other symbols and rules operate. Certain locations and objects have symbolic value. The head of a table, for instance, is generally considered a symbol of power, as is a gavel.

Quite obviously, symbols, rules, and codes serve a central and pervasive role in the ongoing dynamics of groups and organizations of all kinds. They provide the individuals within these units with a sense of individual and collective identity, and contribute at the same time to the development of order, structure, and cohesiveness in overall operation of the system.

Roles and Responsibilities

In small informal groups, the roles individuals play and their responsibilities to others in the social unit generally develop as the unit evolves, along with the goals, networks, and symbols. They are primarily the result of informal, often unverbalized, negotiation.

In a now classic article on group roles, Benne and Sheat's outlined three broad kinds of roles assumed by members of a group over the course of time: (1) roles related to the completion of the task; (2) roles related to building and maintaining the group as a unit; and (3) individualistic roles.[7] Within each of these broad categories, a number of specific roles were identified.

TABLE 11.1 Group Task Roles.

Role	Description
(a) initiator-contributor	...suggests or proposes to the group new ideas or a changed way of regarding the group problem or goal.
(b) information seeker	...asks for clarification of suggestions made in terms of their factual adequacy, for authoritative information and facts pertinent to the problem being discussed.
(c) opinion seeker	...asks not primarily for the facts of the case but for a clarification of the values pertinent to what the group is undertaking or of values involved in a suggestion made or in alternative suggestions.
(d) information giver	...offers facts or generalizations which are "authoritative" or relates his own experience pertinently to the group problem.
(e) opinion giver	...states his belief or opinion pertinently to a suggestion made or to alternative suggestions.
(f) elaborator	...spells our suggestions in terms of examples or developed meanings, offers a rationale for suggestions previously made and tries to deduce how an idea or suggestion would work out if adopted by the group.
(g) coordinator	...shows or clarifies the relationships among various ideas and suggestions, tries to pull ideas and suggestions together or tries to coordinate the activities of various members of sub-groups.
(h) orienter	...defines the position of the group with respect to its goals by summarizing what has occurred, points to departures from agreed upon directions or goals, or raises questions about the direction which the group discussion is taking.
(j) evaluator-critic	...subjects the accomplishment of the group to some standard or set of standards of group functioning in the context of the group task.
(j) energizer	...prods the group to action or decision, attempts to stimulate or arouse the group to "greater" or "higher quality" activity.
(k) procedural technician	...expedites group movement by doing things for the group—performing routine tasks, e.g., distributing materials, or manipulating objects for the group, e.g., rearranging the seating or running the recording machine.
(l) recorder	...writes down suggestions, makes a record of group decisions, or writes down the product of discussion.

SOURCE: By permission of the *Journal of Social Issues.*

Within larger groups, and especially organizations, individual roles and responsibilities are often more explicit. In clubs, for instance, the responsibilities and duties of officers, committee persons, and other members' positions are generally detailed in written bylaws or a constitution. Particularly within larger organizations, roles are generally specified in great detail and described in written documents which outline the duties of each position. Thus, in comparison to most relationships and small, informal groups, larger social systems have structures, patterns and rules that are *formal rather than informal, created rather than natural,* and *explicit rather than implicit.*

TABLE 11.2 Group Building and Maintenance Roles.

Role	Description
(a) encourager	...praises, agrees with and accepts the contribution of others.
(b) harmonizer	...mediates the differences between other members, attempts to reconcile disagreements, relieves tension in conflict situations through jesting or pouring oil on the troubled waters, etc.
(c) compromiser	...operates from within a conflict in which his ideas or position is involved.
(d) gatekeeper/ expediter	...attempts to keep communication channels open by encouraging or facilitating the participations of others...or by proposing regulation of the flow of communication.
(e) standard setter	...expresses standards for the group to attempt to achieve in its functioning or applies standards in evaluating the quality of group processes.
(f) group- observer	...keeps records of various aspects of group process and feeds such data with proposed interpretations into the group's evaluation of its own procedures.
(g) follower	...goes along with the movement of the group, more or less passively accepting the ideas of others, serving as an audience in group discussion and decision-making.

SOURCE: By permission of the *Journal of Social Issues*.

Leadership and Management

No doubt the single role to receive the most attention in discussion of groups and organizations is the *leader* or *manager*. The basic function of *leadership*—or *management*, as it is often termed in the context of organizations—*is to coordinate the activities of individuals so that they contribute to the overall goals and general adaptability of the social system in its environment.*

In relationships of two, three, or four individuals, patterns of leadership and followership are almost totally the result of the needs, preferences, and communication styles of the individuals involved. Leadership may well be a subtle, even unnoticeable, aspect of the unit's operation. In organizations and larger groups, leadership is an essential, formalized, and highly visible element in the day-to-day and long-run functioning of the unit. In either case, the role involves the *design, implementation, and/or supervision of procedures, policies, or mechanisms necessary to bringing about the desired coordination of the individuals and activities of the unit.*

Leadership, most basically, has to do with the exercise of control over decision making. A great deal has been written concerning the various forms and styles this control may take.[8] In the extreme, there are two alternatives available. First, control over decision making can be wholly centralized. Secondly, this authority can be totally diffused among members of the group or organization. Where the former exists, the leadership style may be characterized as *autocratic*. Where the other pattern is present, leadership is generally described as *democratic* or *participatory*.

TABLE 11.3 Individual Roles.

Role	Description
(a) aggressor	...may work in many ways—deflating the status of others, expressing disapproval of the values, acts or feelings of others, attacking the group or the problem it is working on, joking aggressively, showing envy toward another's contribution by trying to take credit for it, etc.
(b) blocker	...tends to be negativistic and stubbornly resistant, disagreeing and opposing without or beyond reason and attempting to maintain or bring back an issue after the group has rejected it.
(c) recognition seeker	...works in various ways to call attention to himself, whether through boasting, reporting on personal achievements, acting in unusual ways, struggling to prevent his being placed in an "inferior" position, etc.
(d) self-confessor	...uses the audience opportunity which the group setting provides to express personal, nongroup-oriented "feeling," "insight," "ideology," etc.
(e) playboy	...makes a display of his lack of involvement in the group's processes.
(f) dominator	...tries to assert authority or superiority in manipulating the group or certain members of the group.
(g) help-seeker	...attempts to call forth "sympathy" response from other group members or from the whole group.
(h) special interest pleader	...speaks for the "small business man" "the grass roots" community, the "housewife," "labor," etc., usually cloaking his own prejudices or biases in the stereotype which best fits his individual need.[8]

SOURCE: By permission of the *Journal of Social Issues*.

The orientation one takes relative to these alternative approaches to leadership depends upon one's view of human nature. If one believes that humans are most productive and creative when they are self-directed, the approach to leadership is likely to be different than if one assumes that people are most productive when given well-defined direction, structure, and guidance.[9]

A good deal of thought and writing has been devoted to determining the factors one might use in deciding where along this continuum the ideal position is in a given circumstance. While it is conceivable that a group or organization might have leadership which operates at one of these extremes, most often the approaches used are at a point between the two. The issue continues to be a matter of considerable discussion among leaders, followers, managers, and subordinates, as well as writers and researchers.[10]

Follower and Membership Issues

For the individual, leadership is an important element which differentiates the involvement in a group or organization from participation in relation-

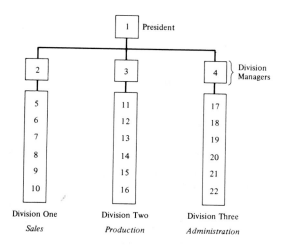

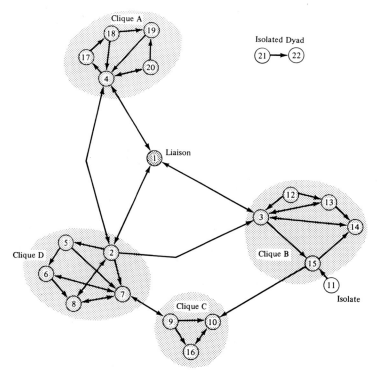

FIGURE 11.8 The chart at the top depicts the *formal organization* and *chain of command* within a typical company. The drawing underneath illustrates the *communication network* among members of the company. Within the company, there are four *cliques*—subsystems of individuals who interact with one another relatively more than with others. There is also an *isolate* (11), an *isolated dyad* (21 and 22), and a *liason* (1)— an individual interlinking various cliques.

SOURCE: *Communication in Organizations* by Everett M. Rogers and Rehka Agarwala-Rogers. Copyright © 1976 by The Free Press, a Division of Macmillan Publishing Co., Inc. By permission.

FIGURE 11.9 Offices.

SOURCE: "Presidentes Municipales," A Photo-essay of mayors of Mexican Cities and their offices by Richard Tichich, in *Studies in Visual Communication*, Vol. 6, 3, Fall 1980, pp. 76–83. By permission.

ships. In relationships, the individual can often have a direct hand in creating and controlling the enterprise. This is not often the case with most larger social systems, since we are generally *initiated into*—rather than *initiating*— groups and organizations. To the extent that we create relationships, we have a direct role in shaping the emerging patterns, rules, and structures. With most groups and organizations, the individual's role is often much more passive, at least initially.

Becoming a participant in any group, organization, or community involves an initiation into the symbols and communication patterns of the unit.[11] Our training for membership in these organizations begins during our earliest years. As a child in a family of three or four individuals, for instance, a good deal of compromise, accommodation, and fitting in is required. The child must learn the family's rules as to what to do, when to do it, what to say, and where to say it.

Later, as the child seeks to attain membership in various other groups, a similar process operates. Entry into certain clubs, fraternal orders, and religious groups makes this process of fitting in a very explicit part of the initiation of a new member into the unit. And even in those groups and organizations where there is no formal apprenticeship, internship, or adjustment, the individual must come to terms with the units' rules and realities in order to be accepted and function effectively as a member.

Thus, where the individual's role requires *adjusting* to—rather than *creating*—the initial function of communication is for *identifying* and *fitting oneself* to the ongoing rules and structures made by others over a long period of time. This generally makes *becoming* a member of a group or organization a less active, less creative, more accommodating—and for some a more frustrating—process than becoming part of a relationship.

TABLE 11.4 Three Main Schools of Organizational Behavior*

	Scientific Management School	Human Relations School	Systems School
Basic principles and assumptions about human behavior	A mechanistic view behavior: man is economically motivated, and will respond with maximum performance if material rewards are closely related to work efforts. Favors human engineering of worker effort and time in order to achieve maximum production, efficiency, and profit for the managers/owners.	A social view of man: informal groups affect production rates; attention to workers' needs and job satisfaction can motivate higher performance; worker participation in decision making; realization that the individual's goals may differ from the organization's goals; workers motivated by social needs and by their peer relationships.	The organization is an open system in continuous interaction with its environment; the system and its environment co-determine each other. The system must be analyzed as a whole in order to be understood properly. The organization is composed of subsystems, which are interdependent; individuals are the carriers of the organization.
Purpose of communication	To relay orders and information about work tasks, and to achieve obedience and coordination in carrying out such work.	To satisfy workers' needs, to provide for interaction among peers in work groups, and to facilitate the participation of members in organizational decision making.	To control and coordinate, and to provide information to decision makers; and to adjust the organization to changes in its environment.

*Theories of organization are reflective of more basic theories about the nature of humans. Three major orientations of thought as to the nature of human organizations are the Scientific Management Approach, the Human Relations Approach, and the Systems Approach. Each reflects a different set of basic principles and makes different assumptions about the nature of human behavior and the purpose of communication in an organizational setting.

SOURCE: *Communication in Organizations* by Everett M. Rogers and Rehka Agarwala-Rogers, Copyright © 1976 by The Free Press, A division of Macmillan Publishing Co., Inc. By permission.

Continuity and Change

Within an open system—individual, relationship, group, organization or society—there is an ongoing tension between influences that contribute to stability and continuity and those that contribute to *change*. As with *continuity*, *change* also occurs through communication. Whether one considers a family, a club, business organization, or other social unit, total compliance with the preexisting rules and symbols is neither necessary nor possible. Sometimes by design, other times by accident, individuals bring about very fundamental changes in the groups and organizations in which they become involved as a consequence of the way they cope with the rules, patterns, and structures of the unit.[12]

Communication, Groups, and Organizations

Communication, as we have seen, is essential to the emergence and evolution of groups and organizations, as it is for the development of individuals and relationships. Without information processing, even the simplest coordination between individuals would be impossible. In groups composed of several persons, as well as in organizations of several thousand persons, communication is critical to the creation and maintenance of the networks, symbols, rules, and roles that give life to the system.

The nature of these networks, symbols, rules, and roles, and the manner in which they develop, has a substantial impact, in turn, on the individuals involved and upon the functioning of the unit as a whole. The productivity and morale of members of groups and organizations, and the adaptability of the system in its environment, very much depend upon communication. Thus, communication processes are not only vital in the emergence and evolution of groups and organizations, but are also critical to every facet of day-to-day operations of these systems and the individuals who compose them.

Summary

Groups and organizations occupy an important place in our lives as humans. Communication is necessary for groups and organizations to develop. Once formed, these units have a number of important uses and consequences including: assisting us to meet basic needs, guiding our mapmaking, contributing to our personal development, and creating communication technologies.

Networks develop among individuals within groups and organizations. In small social units, these networks evolve naturally. In larger contrived units, they are specified and formalized. In larger groups and organizations, *formalized networks* are often established to regulate the flow of information. The functions of these networks are: (1) coordinating what would otherwise be disparate activities of individuals and subunits; (2) maintaining the lines of authority and leadership; (3) facilitating the exchange of information within the organization; and (4) facilitating the directed flow of data between the system and the external environment and constituencies.

Some of the formalized networks operate *within* the group or organization. Marketing, public relations, and advertising operate via external networks created to link the unit with its external environment.

Standardized symbols, rules, codes, and patterns of behavior develop in groups and organizations as they do in relationships. Roles and responsibilities also are central to the functioning of groups and organizations. In smaller groups roles and definitions of responsibility evolve gradually. Some roles are related to the task. Others have to do with group building and maintenance; still others are individualistic. In larger groups and organizations, roles and responsibilities are *formal* rather than *informal, created* rather than *natural, explicit* rather than *implicit*.

Leadership and management functions are often more formalized and specified with groups and organizations than with relationships. For the individual, the issue of leadership is an important element differentiating relationships from groups and organizations. Generally, a primary function of communication in relationships is the *creation* of structure and rules. In groups and organizations, a central function is the *identification of* and *fitting with* structures and rules already created by others.

Notes

1. Cf. Lee Thayer, *Communications and Communication Systems* (Homewood, IL: Irwin, 1968) p. 188, 190.

2. Cf. Richard W. Budd, "Encounter Groups: An Approach to Human Communication," in *Approaches to Human Communication*, Richard W. Budd and Brent D. Ruben, eds. (Rochelle Park, NJ: Hayden-Spartan, 1972), especially pp. 83–88; and Gerald Egan, *Encounter: Group Processes for Interpersonal Growth* (Belmont, CA: Brooks/Cole, 1970) pp. 69–71.

3. B. Aubrey Fisher, "Decision Emergence: Phases in Group Decision-Making," *Speech Monographs, 37:* 53–66 (1970) and *Small Group Decision Making* (New York: McGraw-Hill, 1974).

4. Cf. B. Aubrey Fisher, op. cit., and discussion in Stephen W. Littlejohn, *Theories of Human Communication* (Columbus: Merrill, 1978) pp. 276–280.

5. A formula for computing the number of such linkages has been provided by William M. Kephart "A Quantitative Analysis of Intra-Group Relationships," *American Journal of Sociology, 55:* (1950) 544–549:

$$PR = \frac{3^N - 2^{N+1} + 1}{2}$$

Note: *PR* is the number of potential relationships, and *N* is the number of persons involved.

6. For a discussion of directional flow in networks, see Gerald M. Goldhaber, *Organizational Communication* (Dubuque, IA: Brown, 1974), pp. 114–122.

7. Kenneth Benne and Paul Sheats, "Functional Roles of Group Members," *Journal of Social Issues, 4:* 41–49 (1948).

8. An excellent discussion of the functions and characteristics of leadership is provided by John E. Baird, Jr., and Sanford B. Weinberg in *Group Communication* Second Edition, (Dubuque, IA: Brown) Chapter 7, pp. 203–331.

9. Cf. Everett M. Rogers and Rekha Agarwala-Rogers, op. cit. for a discussion and comparison of three philosophical schools of thought regarding the nature of organizational behavior.

10. Cf. Robert Tannenbaum and Warren H. Schmidt "How to Choose a Leadership Pattern," *Harvard Business Review* (May-June 1973), pp. 162–164, 166–168.

11. Cf. Hugh D. Duncan, *Symbols in Society* (New York: Oxford University Press, 1968) especially Sections II and III; and Herbert Blumer, *Symbolic Interactionism* (Englewood Cliffs, NJ: Prentice-Hall, 1969), especially Chapter 1.

12. Cf. Georg Simmel, *Conflict and The Web of Group-Affiliations*, translated by Kurt H. Wolff and Reinhard Bendix (New York: Free Press, 1955) and Brent D. Ruben, "Communication and Conflict: A System-Theoretic Perspective," *Quarterly Journal of Speech, 64:* 202–210,

(1978), for a discussion and additional references on the dynamic tension within living systems.

References and Suggested Reading

Argyris, Chris. *Personality and Organization.* New York: Harper, 1957.
———*Understanding Organizational Behavior.* Homewood, IL: Dorsey, 1960.

Aronson, Elliot. *The Social Animal.* San Francisco: Freeman, 1972.

Baird, John E., Jr. *The Dynamics of Organizational Communication.* New York: Harper, 1977.

Baird, John E., Jr. and Sanford B. Weinberg. *Group Communication.* Dubuque, IA: Brown, 1981.

Bales, Robert F. *Personality and Interpersonal Behavior.* New York: Holt, 1970.

Barnard, Chester I. *The Functions of the Executive.* Cambridge, MA: Harvard University Press, 1938.

Benne, Kenneth and Paul Sheats. "Functional Roles of Group Members," *Journal of Social Issues,* 4 (1948), 41–49.

Berne, Eric. *The Structure and Dynamics of Organizations and Groups.* New York: Grove, 1963.

Berrien, Kenneth F. *General and Social Systems.* New Brunswick, NJ: Rutgers University Press, 1968.

Buckley, Walter. *Sociology and Modern Systems Theory.* Englewood Cliffs, NJ: Prentice-Hall, 1967.

Budd, Richard W. "Encounter Groups: An Approach to Human Communication." In *Approaches to Human Communication.* Edited by Richard W. Budd and Brent D. Ruben. Rochelle Park, NJ: Hayden, 1972, 75–96.

Campbell, James H. and John S. Mickelson. "Organic Communication Systems." In *General Systems Theory and Human Communication.* Edited by Brent D. Ruben and John Y. Kim. Rochelle Park, NJ: Hayden, 1975, 207–221.

Cathcart, Robert S. and Larry A. Samovar. *Small Group Communication.* Dubuque, IA: Brown, 1974.

Crane, Diana. *Invisible Colleges.* Chicago: University of Chicago Press, 1972.

Dobriner, William. *Social Structures and Systems.* Pacific Palisades, CA: Goodyear, 1969.

Downs, Cal W. and Tony Hain. "Productivity and Communication." In *Communication Yearbook 5.* Edited by Michael Burgoon. New Brunswick, NJ: Transaction-International Communication Association, 1982, 435–454.

Duncan, Hugh D. *Symbols in Society.* New York: Oxford University Press, 1968.

Eddy, William B., W. Warner Burke, Vladimir A. Dupre and Oron P. South, eds. *Behavioral Science and the Manager's Role.* La Jolla, CA: University Associates, 1969.

Egan, Gerald. *Encounter: Group Processes for Interpersonal Growth*. Belmont, CA: Books/Cole, 1970.

Eisenberg, Abné M. *Understanding Communication in Business and the Professions*. New York: Macmillan, 1978.

Fisher, B. Aubrey. "Decision Emergence: Phases in Group Decision-Making." *Speech Monographs*, 37, (1970).

——— *Small Group Decision Making*. New York: McGraw-Hill, 1974.

Goldhaber, Gerald M. *Organizational Communication*. Dubuque, IA: Brown, 1974, 276–280.

Homans, George C. *The Human Group*. New York: Harcourt, 1950.

——— *Social Behavior*. New York: Harcourt, 1961.

Jablin, Fred M. "Organizational Communication Theory and Research: An Overview of Communication Climate and Network Research." In *Communication Yearbook 4*. Edited by Dan Nimmo. New Brunswick, NJ: Transaction-International Communication Association, 1981, 327–348.

Koehler, Jerry, Karl W.F. Anatol and Ronald L. Applbaum. *Organizational Communication*. New York: Holt, 1976.

Leavitt, Harold J. "Some Effects of Certain Communication Patterns on Group Performance." *Journal of Abnormal and Social Psychology*, 46 (1951), 38–50.

Lewin, Kurt. "Group Decision and Social Change." In *Readings in Social Psychology*. Ed. by Theodore Newcomb and Eugene L. Hartley. New York: Holt, 1958.

Likert, Rensis. *The Human Organization*. New York: McGraw-Hill, 1967.

Lin, Nan. *The Study of Human Communication*. Indianapolis, IN: Bobbs-Merrill, 1973.

McGregor, Douglas. *The Human Side of Enterprise*. New York: McGraw-Hill, 1960.

Mayo, Elton. *The Human Problems of an Industrial Civilization*. New York: Macmillan, 1933.

Phillips, Gerald M. *Communication and the Small Group*. Indianapolis, IN: Bobbs-Merrill, 1973.

Ramsoy, Odd. *Social Groups as System and Subsystem*. New York: Free Press, 1963.

Richetto, Gary M. "Organizational Communication Theory and Research: An Overview." In *Communication Yearbook 1*. Edited by Brent D. Ruben. New Brunswick, NJ: Transaction-International Communication Association, 1977, 331–346.

Rogers, Everett M. and D. Lawrence Kincaid. *Communication Networks*. New York: Free Press, 1981.

———.and Rekha Agarwala-Rogers. *Communication in Organizations*. New York: Free Press, 1976.

Ruben, Brent D. and John Y. Kim, eds. *General Systems Theory and Human Communication*. Rochelle Park, NJ: Hayden, 1975.

Seiler, William J., E. Scott Baudhuin and L. David Schuelke. *Communication in Business and Professional Organizations*. Reading, MA: Addison-Wesley, 1982.

Simon, Herbert A. *Administrative Behavior*. New York: Macmillan, 1947.

Smith, Ronald L., Gary M. Richetto and Joseph P. Zima. "Organizational Behavior." In *Approaches to Human Communication*. Edited by Richard W. Budd and Brent D. Ruben. New York: Spartan, 1972, 269–289.

Tannenbaum, Robert and Warren H. Schmidt. "How to Choose a Leadership Pattern." *Harvard Business Review*, May-June, 1973.

Thayer, Lee. *Communication and Communication Systems*. Homewood, IL: Irwin, 1968.

——— "Communication and Organization Theory." In *Human Communication Theory*. Edited by Frank E.X. Dance. New York: Holt, 1967.

Chapter 12

Societies and Cultures

Characteristics, Dynamics, and Relations

In this chapter we extend our perspective on the role of communication in human affairs by exploring its significance for societies and cultures. Cultures and societies, like relationships, groups, and organizations, are created, defined, and maintained by the activities of their members. And, as with other social units, communication plays a central role.

National and International Networks

Even more obviously than with other social units, communication networks within a society are essential to coordinate the activities of the individuals and social units which compose them. These networks involve both interpersonal and mass communication.

In a democratic society, many of the critical linkages are provided through personal contact between a group or organization, the persons who are elected to *represent* and *speak on behalf of* them, and the various groups and organizations composed of these representatives. Individuals from a neighborhood, for instance, may meet to share local concerns and to select someone to *convey* their point of view to other groups within the community, region, or state. And, at a still higher level, representatives from communities, regions, states, and other groups and organizations join together to discuss still broader concerns, set priorities, and establish policies on a national level, creating the network Karl Deutsch termed the *nerves of government*.[1]

Information relative to the recommendations, policies, or laws that result are diffused among members of the society through interpersonal and mass communication processes. News and public affairs media programming, political campaigning, and government publications operate in combination with personal representation, elections, and referenda. Together, these networks link individuals and social units within a society to one another and to the whole which they collectively define.

In addition to these *internal* linkages, societies also depend on networks that interconnect them to other societies and the world community in their *external* environment. Interpersonal contact also plays a role in these international linkages through tourism, foreign service and embassy personnel, and representation in the United Nations and other international agencies. Other connections are created through international news and entertainment programming, governmental propaganda, and intelligence operations.

Collectively, these internal and external channels perform essentially the same functions for a society as they do for large organizations. They facilitate the coordination of the often diverse activities of the individuals, groups, and organizations that compose the society; permit the exchange of data among individuals and social units within a society; allow for the establishment and maintenance of a leadership or governance system; and ensure the directed flow of data between a society and the external environment in which it exists.

Culture

In addition to the development of networks and governance systems, long the objects of study in political science, the evolution of society involves the creation of common symbols, meanings, knowledge, rules, and behavior patterns. The role of communication in these facets of social life has been of central interest to scholars like George Herbert Mead, Alfred Schutz, Hugh Duncan, Peter Berger, and Herbert Blumer. In our discussions, we will use the term *culture* to refer to characteristic and defining symbols, meanings, knowledge, rules, and behaviors that bind individuals in social units together and give them a common identity.[2]

Culture, like *communication*, is a familiar term to most people. Perhaps partly because of this familiarity, there are a number of different ways the term is used. Probably the most common use of *culture* is as a synonym for *country* or *nation*. If, for example, one happens across several persons conversing in a language other than English, or notices a woman wearing a veil over her face and a ruby on her nose, they are likely to be described as being from another *culture*, by which is meant, another *place*.

At other times, the term is used to refer to *desired qualities or attributes*. For instance, someone who misuses his or her native language, is sloppy in his or her eating habits, or lacks a knowledge of the arts, may be described as *uncultured*, meaning—*unrefined, uneducated, or unsophisticated.*

To those who study human behavior, *culture* has a more precise usage. It is not regarded as something one *has* or *does not have*, nor is it something which is thought of as being *positive* or *negative*. In fact, culture is not some *thing* at all, in the sense that an object can be touched, physically examined, or located on a map. Rather, it is an idea or a concept, which E.B. Tylor in 1871 described as having to do with "that complex whole which includes knowledge, belief, art, morals, law, custom, and any other capabilities and habits acquird by man as a member of society."[3] From the point of view of communication, culture can be defined much as Tylor did, as *the complex combination of common symbols, knowledge, conventions, language, information processing patterns, rules, rituals, habits, life styles, and attitudes which link and give a common identity to a particular group of people at a particular point in time.*

Communication and Culture

To understand more fully the relationship between communication, culture, and society, it is helpful to briefly review the role of communication in the development of other less complex social units. As we know, in any ongoing relationships certain common symbols, understandings, rules, and characteristic verbal and nonverbal patterns develop as a natural consequence of reciprocal data processing.

As casual friendships between individuals evolve toward greater intimacy, each person adapts to the communication patterns, rules, and maps of the other. In a process of compromise and negotiation of which the individuals involved are only partially aware, the body of *joint* rules, habits,

FIGURE 12.1 A variety of verbal and nonverbal data sources provide the visible traces of culture that confront individuals within societies.

greeting forms, symbols, knowledge, and standardized meanings are forged in a developing relationship. This standardization and patterning occur in a very natural way, as the individuals involved adapt over time to one another and their environment. Collectively, these shared patterns represent what might be thought of as the *culture* of the relationship.[4]

The same process occurs in groups and organizations involving larger numbers of people. As networks are formed and evolve, shared patterns are created in families, clubs, prison communities, social groups, educational institutions, and business organizations. In each, particular words, phrases, gestures, conventions of dress, and greetings emerge over time as a result of communication and mutual adaptation of the members of the unit.

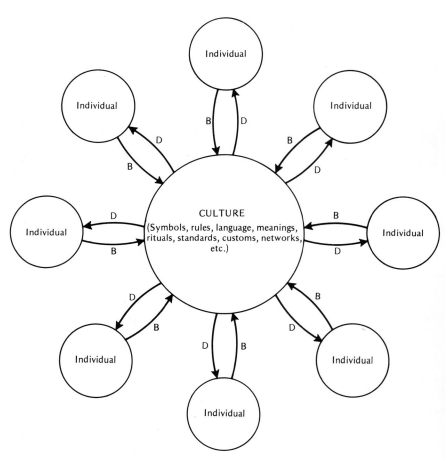

B= Behavior–Language use and nonverbal actions and appearances, etc.

D= Data–Used by the individual as information about the culture, its symbols, rules, language, meanings, rituals, standards, customs, networks, etc.

FIGURE 12.2 The relationship between individual and culture is mutually influencing and reciprocally defining. Culture is created and perpetuated through the communication activities of individuals. Collectively, their behaviors provide the realities—symbols, rules, language, standards, customs, etc.—with which each individual must adapt in order to be a part of the unit.

The intent of diplomatic language can become lost in the translation

By EARLEEN F. TATRO
Associated Press Writer

BEIRUT, Lebanon—What's in a word? When diplomats, revolutionaries and politicians are discussing the future of 52 American hostages in four languages on three continents, a wrong word here or misconstrued meaning there could prove fateful.

Take the word "ta'ahod." This every-day Persian noun threw the hostage crisis into still new confusion this week.

On Tuesday, Iranian Prime Minister Mohammad Ali Rajai emerged from a meeting with Ayatollah Ruhollah Khomeini in Tehran and told reporters the Iranian revolutionary leader had agreed to a proposal discussed with Algerian intermediaries to resolve the hostage crisis.

Rajai used the word "ta'ahod," which Persian-English dictionaries say can mean guarantee, commitment or undertaking.

Some reporters translated Rajai's comments as meaning the ayatollah had accepted unspecified "guarantees" by Algeria to help break the deadlock.

But other Iranian journalists translated Rajai's remarks as meaning that the ayatollah had accepted an Algerian "undertaking."

The difference—between Algeria be-coming an active party in an agreement ending the crisis, or simply continuing its role as a go-between—is significant.

Some Iranians residing in Beirut who are billingual in Persian and English say that when they hear "ta'ahod," the first English word that springs to mind is "guarantee."

But they agree it can also mean "com-mitment" or "undertaking," and they say that if they were to translate the English word "guarantee" into Persian, they would choose a more forceful word, "zemanat," over "ta'ahod."

The principals in the hostage talks are all working from different native tongues. The first lanaguages of the Algerian inter-mediaries tend to be Arabic and French. The Americans, of course, generally pre-fer English. Some of the Iranians are believed to speak French or English, but many of the top revolutionaries in power have little familiarity with the West and its languages.

Like many languages, Persian, or Farsi, is a tongue in which even the simplest words can have a variety of meanings. The Farsi word that is pronounced "sheer," for example, means either "milk" or "lion." Less tangible concepts can be more complicated to translate.

Some scholars say this because Farsi has remained basically unchanged for the past 1,000 years. But some Farsi speakers dispute this and claim their language is constantly growing. In general, they say, Farsi is a language where grammer has few rules, and this can lead to translation problems.

The translation often depends upon the context in which a word is used, and in the hostage crisis this is hindered by the absence of official English translations of many of the day-to-day statements by Iranian officials. Unofficial translators, such as Iranian reporters at news confer-ences, may be reluctant to use the most precise or strongest translations for fear of giving meanings to words that were not intended by those who uttered them.

The Translation problems generally do not occur in relatively straightforward statements, such as Iran's communiques on the war with Iraq, but they can crop up in more subjective matters.

For such reasons, negotiators on impor-tant international issues must often spend long hours working on translations after basic principles have been agreed upon.

When Egypt and Israel agreed to end a three-decade state of war, the peace treaty was written in Arabic, Hebrew and English, with the provision that in the event of any future dispute involving translations the English version would prevail.

FIGURE 12.3

SOURCE: Associated Press, Jan. 9, 1981. By permission.

Societies are larger, far more complex social systems, in which the same communication dynamics are at work. The *symbols* of a society are perhaps the most visible signs of the process. Of these, spoken and written *language* are the most pervasive. Coins and currency are other central symbol systems of any society, linking individuals to one another, providing a basis for a common identity, and creating a medium for interaction and negotiation among members. The terminology, graphics and values associated with the monetary system of any one society are of necessity fairly distinctive. Interestingly, however, in terms of physical characteristics such as their form, overall size, composition, weight, most are relatively similar.

There are also many other significant symbols—heroes and heroines, leaders, monuments, buildings, flags, songs, and places that have important symbolic value for the citizens. For us, George Washington, Martin Luther King, the Capitol Building, "Old Glory," "The Star Spangled Banner," the Statue of Liberty, and Gettysburg have important symbolic value. Shared communication patterns, orientations toward religion, politics, sex roles,

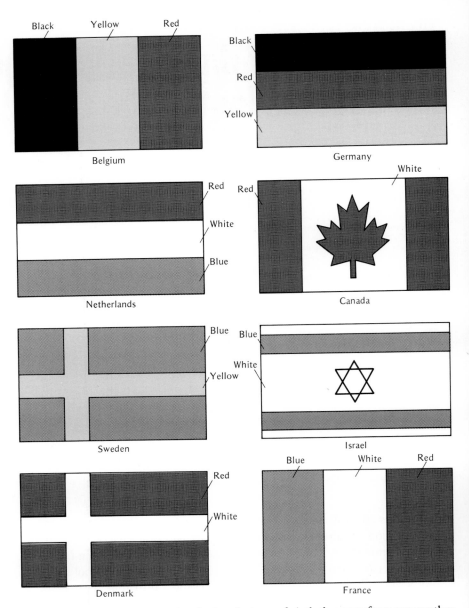

FIGURE 12.4 Composed only of colored pieces of cloth that vary from one another in little more than color, flags play important symbolic roles in human affairs. They mark territories, represent particular geographic locations, symbolize political or religious ideologies, and provide a symbol of commonality and unity for the residents of the territories they symbolize. For these reasons, burning or in any other way defiling the flag of a country is a blatant insult, punishable by law in some countries, and generally met with strong emotional reaction by residents. It is the importance of such symbols that also explains why fundamental changes in the governance of a territory are often accompanied by a change of flag or the name of that country.

SANDWICH DE BISTEC A LO McDONALD'S	1. 7 9
BIG MAC/HAMBURGER doble con queso	1. 4 5
QUARTER POUNDER, con queso	1. 5 0
QUARTER POUNDER/HAMBURGER 1/4lb.	1. 3 5
FILET-O-FISH/FILETE DE PESCADO	. 9 5
PAPAS FRITAS	5 5 / 7 5
HAMBURGER con queso	. 7 0
HAMBURGER	6 0

FIGURE 12.5

courtship, childrearing, race, and other facets of social life also become a part of the culture of any society.

Thus, in terms of the general dynamics underlying the creation of culture, relationships, groups, organizations, and societies have much in common.[5] In the same way that individuals in a small social unit come to share common symbols, knowledge, and rules—a *subculture*—members of a society are linked together and given a collective identity through the *culture* they jointly create and perpetuate through their activities.

As should be apparent, the relationship between *culture* and *communication* is an intimate one. Were it not for our human capacity for creating symbolic language, we could not develop the knowledge, meaning, symbols, values, rules, and rituals, that give definition and form to our ongoing relationships, organizations, and societies. And, without communication, it

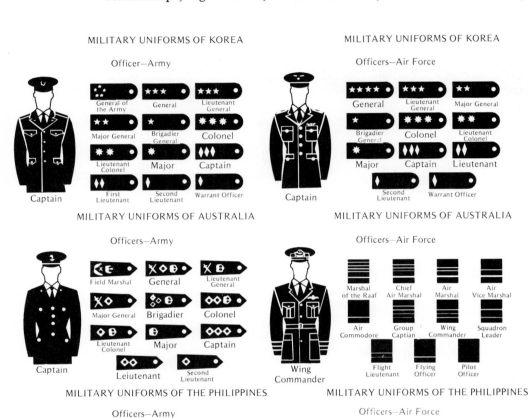

FIGURE 12.6 As with flags, military attire and the various emblems and insignias associated with them suggest both intercultural uniformity and distinctiveness. On the one hand, internationally accepted standards of formal military uniforms appear to have emerged, yet on the other hand, the attire of each country is distinctive in some ways as well.

SOURCE: Guidelines for United States Navy Overseas Diplomacy, (Washington, D.C.: Department of the Navy).

would be impossible to pass along the elements of our culture from one generation to the next and one place to another. Communication also provides the means through which we become aware of and adapt to the distinctive subcultures and cultures with which we are confronted.

As much as it is accurate to say that culture is defined, shaped, transmitted, and learned through communication, the reverse is equally correct.[6] Cultures and subcultures are the by-product of human activity in relationships, groups, organizations, and societies. The maps, images, rules, and behaviors we acquire as individuals are largely the result of our having adapted in particular ways to the demands and opportunities of these social systems. In effect, then, there is a reciprocally-influencing relationship between human communication and culture. Through communication we shape our cultures, and, in turn, our cultures shape our communication rules and patterns.[7]

Mass Communication and Culture

Communication technology plays a vital role in the development and evolution of culture in two ways. First, because they extend our creating, copying, and storing capabilities, our technology broadens the pool of data available in common to individuals within a society. This database consists of the news, information, and entertainment programming provided by traditional mass media, along with other mass communication institutions like libraries and museums.[8] Collectively, these institutions provide members of a society with a common menu and an agenda of concerns, issues, values, personalities, and themes which occupy a central role in the symbolic environment with which individuals must adapt.[9]

These data are a kind of societal mirror, providing potential information as to how society works and how the individual fits within it, as a child or adult, male or female, husband or wife, producer or consumer. As many popular and scholarly authors have noted, the mass media do provide society with a view of political, economic, social, aesthetic, and religious reality, and in this way communication technology also contributes to the "portability" of culture; the media play a fundamental role in the socialization process of the individual, and in so doing contribute at the same time to stability and social order within a society.[10]

It is also largely due to communciation technology that knowledge, symbols, and rules developed within one subculture or culture are available to individuals who were not involved in their creation. With the increased capability for transmitting, duplicating, and storing data, the knowledge of one generation need not die with its creators. Rather, it becomes a permanent part of the symbolic environment. And, these data can be transported through space. They are available not only to persons in the society where they were created, but to any individual or group with the appropriate technologies.

Characteristics of Culture

We can add clarity to our thinking about the idea of culture and its relationship to communication by discussing the following common characteristics of cultures (and subcultures): (1) Cultures are complex and multifaceted; (2) Cultures change over time; (3) Cultures are invisible.

Cultures are Complex and Multifaceted

Whether we examine the complex culture of a society, or the culture (what we have termed *subculture* for clarity) of a particular intimate relationship, prison community, ethnic group, or business or educational organization, a number of complex and interrelated facets come into play. Particularly, at the level of a society, so many elements are involved that it is exceedingly difficult to identify and categorize them. Some of the most basic dimensions of culture are language, social customs, family life, clothing, eating habits, class structure, political orientations, religion, customs, economic philosophies, beliefs and value systems.[11]

These elements do not exist in isolation from one another, but instead interact in a number of subtle ways. The values of a society influence its economics and vice versa, and both impact and are impacted upon by social customs, religion, and family life. In many cultures, for example, the tendency to have large families is explained not only by custom, but also by economics, religion, health, and the technological level within the society. In cultures where infant mortality is high due to disease and poor health conditions, a husband and wife may well need a large number of children in order to have enough healthy boys to farm and help with other duties necessary to the survival of the family unit. In contemporary North American culture, the decreasing size of families is also influenced by complex factors, such as economics, customs, available technology, social conditions, and evolving sex-role attitudes.

If we examine the verbal and nonverbal patterns in a given culture the same sort of complexity and interconnectedness are apparent. Greeting forms, gestures, conversational topics and formats, dress, language habits, courtship practices, eye contact preferences, use of space, orientation toward time, male-female roles, orientation toward elders, and attitudes toward work, all influence and are in turn influenced by a variety of cultural dimensions such as religion, economics, politics, and so on.

In Saudi Arabia, for example, women wear dark robes and veils in public, and it is customary for men not to introduce themselves or appear to take note of women in social situations. It is quite normal for a Saudi male to invite a married man to dinner at his home with the expectation that the guest will not bring his wife. Even in those situations in which a couple is invited, the wife may be met at the door by the women of the house and

---

FIGURE 12.7 Dimensions of Culture.

SOURCE: Language Research Center, Brigham Young University, 1976. By permission.

1. GREETINGS — appropriate or inappropriate gestures (such as handshake or touching), verbal greetings (what to say), how close together persons stand when greeting or conversing, conversation topics, etc.

   a. meeting a person the first time:
   b. everyday acquaintances:
   c. close friends:
   d. elderly people:
   e. women:
   f. youth:
   g. children:
   h. leaders in the culture:
   i. to show special respect:
   j. from a distance:
   k. use of family name or first name:
   l. use of titles (such as Mr. or Dr.):
   m. compliments with greetings: what to compliment, how to give and receive compliments, and when):

2. VISITING a family at home — what should and should not be done in the following situations.

   a. greeting:
   b. entering the house:
   c. gifts and flowers (what is appropriate; when and how to give, receive and open gifts):
   d. compliments on possessions, decor, or to family members:
   e. proper conduct (in the living room, parlor, or guest welcoming area):
   f. conversation (what topics are best and when people usually talk):
   g. table manners (seating arrangements, when a guest should begin to eat, excusing oneself from the table, etc.):
   h. utensils and how to use them:
   i. conversation at the dinner table:
   j. compliments on the food:
   k. saying farewell and leaving:
   l. parties and social events (What should be remembered by a guest to best interact with the host and other guests? What is expected of the guest?):
   m. words to avoid:

3. TALKS, SPEECHES AND PUBLIC ADDRESSES to groups of people.

   a. subjects or topics which these people are especially fond of or those which should not be referred to:
   b. gestures which help or hurt communication:
   c. the way the speaker stands or sits in front of the group:
   d. hints on using an interpreter.

4. MEETINGS — punctuality, best ways to begin and end the meeting, seating arrangement, eye contact, and using an interpreter.

   a. large formal meetings:
   b. small group sessions (about 3–15 people):
   c. private interview with an individual:

5. GESTURES — those which help to carry a message and those which should be avoided.

   a. with hands:
   b. head:
   c. eye and eye contact, eyebrows, face (Is it customary to look a person directly in the eyes when speaking to him? What would be the reaction to this by a person in this culture?):
   d. legs (such as crossing the legs when sitting down):
   e. feet (moving things with them, pointing them at

people, gesturing with them, putting them on one's desk, etc.):

f. posture (standing and sitting down, hands oh hips, etc.):

g. touching (another person, male and female, etc.):

h. shoulders:

i. arms (such as folding them or putting them around another's shoulders):

j. smiling and laughing customs (When is a smile appropriate or inappropriate? In what situations does a smile mean something other than happiness and good will?):

k. yawning:

l. calling someone to yourwith with your hands (palm facing up or down, etc.):

m. handing, passing, or giving things to another person:

6. PERSONAL APPEARANCE.

a. clothing:

b. eye glasses and sun glasses:

c. hats:

d. other:

7. GENERAL ATTITUDES of
(1) adults, a. male b. female; (2) teenagers, a. male b. female, about.

a. nature and man's role in it:

b. society, groups, and the individual, self:

c. wealth, clothes, possessions:

d. work, success, failure, and fate:

e. government, politics, taxes, police welfare assistance:

f. personality traits that are considered good or bad in a person:

g. role of men and women:

h. sexual promiscuity, abortion:

i. time, punctuality:

j. youth, teenagers:

k. elderly people:

l. physically or mentally handicapped:

m. business and economic progress:

n. war and the military:

o. crime and violence:

p. majority groups, races and minority groups (special likes, dislikes, or problems):

q. other nations and their people (Special likes, dislikes, or problems):

r. longevity, retirement and death:

s. political systems (socialism, communism, imperialism, democracy, etc.):

t. humor:

u. promises, agreements, and trust:

v. community participation

w. revenge, retributions, repayment of wrongs received:

x. animals, pets:

y. showing emotions:

z. gambling, drinking alcoholic beverages, drugs:

aa. giving and receiving criticism:

bb. making decisions in business, among peers:

cc. education:

dd. what possessions or achievements indicate status (for men and women, adult and youth):

8. LANGUAGE — dialects, use of English, etc.

9. RELIGION — general attitudes toward religion, predominant beliefs.

10. SPECIAL HOLIDAYS — specific dates and how these holidays are celebrated).

11. THE FAMILY.

a. average size of family:

b. attitudes about the family and its role in society:

c. teenagers' role in the family:

d. role of the elderly in the family:

e. authority, obedience,

roles of father, mother, and children (making decisions in the family):

f. system of family inheritance:

g. milestone experiences in life for a male:

h. milestone experiences in life for a female:

i. special activities which are used to show that a person has become an adult (or otherwise changed social status):

j. who in the family works (father, mother, children):

k. average daily schedule and activities for fathers, mothers, children:

12. DATING AND MARRIAGE CUSTOMS.

a. from what age does dating begin? How important is dating? Why?:

b. is dating in larger groups or individual couples?:

c. common dating activities:

d. chaperones:

e. acceptable and unacceptable dating behavior:

f. engagement customs:

g. attitude about marriage:

h. age at which most men marry:

i. age at which most women marry:

j. how much influence the family has in deciding about marriages:

k. prerequisites to marriage (such as completion of education or financial independence):

l. desirability of children (birth control):

m. attitude about divorce:

n. attitude toward displaying affection in public (such as between husband and wife or parents and children):

13. SOCIAL AND ECONOMIC LEVELS — including size of different general classes,

average income and what it provides for the family, general housing conditions and possessions (such as refrigerator, range, toaster, cars, radios, telephones, televisions, etc.).

14. DISTRIBUTION OF GROUP — rural or urban, what cities or areas, group population for areas concerned and what ratio group population is to total population in these areas.

15. WORK.

a. the economy of the group (What are the main occupations of the people, industries, and important products?):

b. individual work schedules (hours per day, days per week):

c. age at which people begin working:

d. choosing a job:

16. DIET.

a. average diet, size of meals, when they are eaten:

b. special foods which are usually given to guests:

c. Is mealtime important for some other reason than just nutrition?

17. RECREATION, SPORTS, ARTS, MUSIC, LEISURE TIME.

a. family cultural and physical recreation and sports activities (including vacations):

b. individual recreation, games, sports of children, youth, adults, and elderly:

c. distinctive arts of the culture which a visitor should known about):

18. HISTORY AND GOVERNMENT.

a. history of the group, including facts and events

considered most important
by the people and why:

b. heroes, leaders of the group
and why they are esteemed:

c. group government systems,
differences from regular
local government:

19. EDUCATION.

a. education in the group:

b. any private education
systems within the group:

20. TRANSPORTATION AND
COMMUNICATION SYS-
TEMS — their use and
significance to the group.

a. bicycles:

b. individual cars and road
system:

c. buses:

d. taxis:

e. other:

f. mass communication
(such as TV, radio,
newspapers, magazines):

g. individual interpersonal
communication (such as
telephones, postal service):

h. any special or unusual meth
methods of trade, exchange

change, communication
or transportation:

21. HEALTH, SANITATION,
MEDICAL FACILITIES —
including general attitude
about disease.

22. LAND AND CLIMATE —
including geographical effects
on the history of the group,
problems posed today by the
geography or climate where
these people are located.

23. "UNIVERSAL" SIGNALS
OR NON-VERBAL CUES
a newcomer should know
that indicate approval or
disapproval, acceptance or
rejection in this society.

This list is a partial summary
of some aspects of culture which
can unite people who share the
same basic attitudes, backgrounds,
and lifestyles. Since these characteristics can vary widely between cultures they can be a
source of misunderstanding and
miscommunication.

entertained in a separate area of the home, leaving the men to dine alone. And
many restaurants have separate entrances and special areas where women and
children are expected to dine.

These Saudi customs, objectionable as they may at first seem to a North
American, must be understood in relation to the entire Arab culture. They
are the "tip" of what can be thought of as the "cultural iceberg."[12] In the case
of the Arab culture, for example, the Islamic religion and tradition prescribe
a very different role for women than men. Saudi women are treated the way
they are because of a long-standing concern for protecting the female from
the harsh realities of life. For this same historical reason, the traditional dress
of the Saudi women is designed to conceal and protect her from visual
intrusions that are presumed to be undesirable. Similarly, the practice of
polygamy, which is permitted by Saudi law and religion, has as its origin a
concern for ensuring that no woman would have to live alone or fend for
herself.

Yet another example of the way in which facets of culture and
communication impact one another comes to light in business situations in

Saudi Arabia. In general, Saudis place great value on family, and friends, and relationships. As a result, in Saudi business dealings, a substantial amount of time is spent discussing family, friends, and "how things are going." In fact, two businessmen meeting one another for the first time might spend their first one or two initial sessions together discussing only these topics, engaged totally in what we think of as "small talk." Only after the Saudi feels he knows and trust the other, does he feel disposed to talk business—what *he* is more apt to regard as "small talk." From the perspective of North American culture, where a great premium is placed upon time, efficiency, and problem solving in business affairs, the Saudi communication behavior may well be frustrating and difficult to comprehend.[13]

Cultures are Invisible

Most of what characterizes a culture or subculture—regardless of whether it is a relationship, group, organization, or society is as invisible to the individuals it envelops as is the air which surrounds them. The presence of culture is so subtle and pervasive that it simply goes unnoticed. It's there now, it's been there as long as anyone can remember, and few of us have reason to think much about it.

As adults living in the United States, most of us simply take the English language for granted as we do the characteristic two-or three-pump handshake greeting, the intermittent eye glances, and two and a half to four feet separating us from others in casual conversation. In a similar way we have come to accept our subcultures without much thought about them: The romantic glances and expressive touch between intimates and the conventions of dress and jargon in our various groups and organizations, are completely natural to the persons involved.

When we happen to become aware of the existence and nature of our cultures and subcultures, it generally happens in one or two ways. The first is when someone within our subculture or culture violates the taken-for-granted standards. Consider the customary handshake greeting as an illustration. Few of us think much about handshakes unless our expectations about them are violated. If, when meeting an individual for the first time, for instance, he or she takes hold of our hand with a very limp or exceptionally overpowering grip, we are likely to take note. Even more dramatic is our response when an individual continues to pump our hand four, five, six, or seven times, and only then reluctantly lets go. We have a similar reaction when a new acquaintance stares incessantly or stands only one or two feet from us in during casual conversation.

The same process occurs in the subculture of relationships. Perhaps the most striking example is when one individual in an intimate relationship "senses that something is wrong," because the other person doesn't look at him or her "in the way he or she is used to," or no longer seems to "joke around" or "touch" his or her partner in the accustomed way. When our expectations are violated, we come to recognize at some level of awareness that we have developed a number of taken-for-granted patterns, customs, habits, and meanings of which we are generally unaware.

The second way in which we can be alerted to the presence and impact of our culture is when we happen across someone from another culture or subculture, and observe major differences between their behavior and our own. To the Arab, men kissing one another on the cheek as a greeting goes unnoticed, while this same behavior startles and often upsets the European. And the Japanese habit of closing the eyes when concentrating on a question, may be quite traumatic to the Canadian businessman who has no idea how to interpret the action. Similarly, the "street language" of the urban black youth may be shocking to the suburban, white middle-class youth, whose verbal and nonverbal behavior, in turn, may also seem equally strange to the blacks.

Without our necessarily being aware of it, these circumstances afford us some of our only opportunities to observe the subtle and pervasive influence our own cultures and subcultures have upon us. In either of these two sorts of circumstances, we know intuitively that "something is wrong" and that we feel somewhat uncomfortable, though we may not know exactly what is troubling us.

Because we have grown up with and take out cultures so much for granted, we are largely unaware of their subjective nature. We may easily come to assume that things are the way they should be—one wife for every husband, intermittent glances during casual conversation, kissing only among intimates of the opposite sex, and so on. A more realistic view, of course, is that our culture and subcultures are the way they are because we and our ancestors created them in a particular way, and we have come to accept their rightness in the same way that other persons have come to accept the rightness of their cultures and subcultures—through communication.

Cultures Change Over Time

Whether one considers the subculture of an intimate relationship, ethnic group, organization, or the culture of a society, changes inevitably occur over time. Cultures and subcultures do not exist in a vacuum. Each of us participates in any number of relationships, groups, or organizations. We carry the subcultures of each with us in our dealings in all the others. And as we change as individuals we bring about changes in cultures and subcultures of which we are a part. In this sense we are each agents of cultural change.

In addition to natural, evolutionary cultural change which inevitably occurs, other cultural and subcultural change occurs in a more intentional revolutionary way. In recent years, for example, concerned Blacks, Hispanics, women, and handicapped individuals have dramatically called attention to the discriminatory conventions and practices which have become a part of our society's culture. Efforts by members of these groups have not only accelerated and directed cultural change within the society as a whole, but

FIGURE 12.8 A characterization of the culture of the United States.

SOURCE: Language and Intercultural Research Center, Brigham Young University, Provo, Utah, 1979. By permission.

Customs and Courtesies

Greetings: Americans* are an informal people. A handshake, smile, and "Hello, I'm pleased to meet (or see) you," are their most common forms of greeting. They usually do not embrace in public, except with members of their own family. People are not too concerned about rank or social position. They often call each other by their first name, even when first meeting. In business and political situations, things are often more formal.

Visiting: Although Americans think of themselves as informal, they appreciate it when their guests arrive on time. If you are invited to "drop by sometime" it might be a good idea to phone ahead to see if it is convenient for your host, or even to set a specific date and activity yourself. They will usually greet you at the door with a "Hi, make yourself at home." By this they mean relax and do not worry about being very formal. You are not normally expected to bring a gift when visiting. However, if you are staying overnight it is acceptable to bring some small token, such as candy or an inexpensive gift from your country.*

You might be asked what you may consider to be many personal questions. Your hosts are not trying to be rude; this is how people get acquainted or "keep in touch" in America. They are usually trying to find out what interests or viewpoints they have in common with you.

Eating: While eating, Americans usually hold the knife in the right hand and the fork in the left, when cutting food. Then the knife is placed on the plate and the fork is switched back to the right hand before eating. However, a visitor may feel free to use almost any style of eating providing he uses his utensils. With some foods, however, even utensils are not required, such as with fried chicken, fruit, or hamburgers and other sandwiches.

Elbows on the table are generally considered bad manners. It would be better to put the hand you are not using for eating in your lap. When you have finished your meal, place your utensils on your plate. The evening meal is usually early (sometime between 5–7 p.m.) and the most leisurely. Dress varies with the host. It would be perfectly acceptable to ask your host beforehand whether a dinner is to be formal or casual, then dress accordingly.

Meals are usually served family style or buffet style. Family style means everyone serves themselves from common platters, which may be passed around the table. Buffet style is when the serving dishes are lined up on a separate table and guests serve themselves then return with their plate to the eating table. Children usually eat with their parents and visitors unless the occasion is a very formal one.

*If invited to stay as a houseguest, remember that most American homes do not have domestic servants. You might expect to make your own bed or to volunteer to help with other family responsibilities. Ask your host what you can do to help.

Gestures and Nonverbal Communication: Many people move quite frequently while conversing. Hands on hips or in pockets while talking is a common posture. So is motioning with the index finger or with hands when trying to emphasize an idea. In informal situations, people basically sit however they please—slouched, legs together or crossed, or even with their feet up, as on their desk. To Americans, motioning with the palm turned upwards means "come here." Waving the palm down means "good-by". People generally like to keep about an arm's length between themselves and the person they are conversing with or standing near. People of the same sex rarely walk hand in hand. A gesture to be avoided is extending the middle finger upward, since it may be considered vulgar.

Talks and Topics: In their conversations, Americans often try to be relatively frank. They like to talk fairly openly about their families, jobs, and feelings. This is their way to express friendliness and sincerity. They like to use phrases such as "Tell it like it is", "Don't beat around the bush", and "Get right to the point." They are trying to say that they do not want to hear only what may be polite or pleasant, but rather they want to know the way things really are or seem to be, as well as a person's real feelings on many matters.

Sports are often a topic of interest, as are jobs or domestic concerns. There are a few subjects that Americans sometimes do not like to discuss. Asking an adult his or her age is one of those things. Asking how much a possession costs or how much someone earns for a living are also questions not usually considered polite. Many people do not like to be asked how much they weigh or details about their marital arrangements, especially in mixed company. If people start raising their eyebrows at you, this may mean your questions or conversation are unexpected or may not be in good taste.

Personal Appearance: In the United States you can dress just about any way you please and still be acceptable. Slacks are now an accepted fashion for women, even formally. Jeans and sandals are particularly popular among the young, but may be worn by anyone. Dress is generally more casual in the West than in the East. Short shorts and brief tops are seen just about anywhere the weather permits. A good rule is if you are ever in doubt about what to wear, just ask someone you know well or notice what others are wearing.

Lifestyle

The Family: The nuclear family (parents and their children) is the most common type in the United States. This family, which averages 3–4 members, is considered one of the most mobile units in the world. It has been estimated that the average American family moves about every five years. Social mobility is also very common, meaning families are continually moving to other jobs and neighborhoods.

Many claim that reverence for the aged is sadly lacking and that the young are much idolized. Grandparents, however, usually prefer to maintain their independence and live separately from their children. Those incapable of caring for themselves often live in nursing homes. Divorce is quite common, but families are still very important. Though there are many who are poor or rich, the typical family is middle class. Ideally, families strive for some kind of equality between the husband, wife, and children, although this is not always achieved.

Dating and Marriage: Couples rarely live with their parents, and many choose to have no children at all. These couples may prefer their "freedom" and greater economic advantages of not having children. Others are concerned about population growth. Though not universally acceptable, premarital sex is common, and birth control devices are readily available. There is now widespread legalization and availability of abortion, but the abortion issue is still an emotional one in the United States.

Dating may begin as young as 13–14 years old but becomes common around 16–18. Teenagers date many people and are not chaperoned. Hand holding and light kissing in public are common. Anything more than light kissing

can also be seen at times and is tolerated, but not generally approved of in public.

Attitudes: It would be impossible to label all Americans with a set of identical additudes. You will find almost every attitude imaginable in the United States. However, there are characteristics a majority of Americans seem to display that make them different from other cultural groups.

Although Americans take pride in their nation's achievements, they are also very good at criticizing its shortcomings. But Americans often do not appreciate it when a foreigner initiates or joins in with complaints.

In general, they are very strong believers in the principle that all people are created equal—that is, to have equal opportunities. But some discrimination still exists. Americans enjoy stories of the "self-made man" who, by hard work and initiative, rose from poverty to riches. They believe that every person is in control of his or her own destiny, and, with determination and work, each one can achieve whatever he or she really wants to do. You should treat a person who works in a service job as an equal.

Individual freedom is very important to Americans. The younger generation has coined a few phrases which are now popular and express a general current feeling on the matter. They are "Do your own thing" and "If it feels good, do it." Religious tolerance is expected. Not all holidays are holy days. Even holy days such as Christmas and Easter are highly commercialized.

You may notice what you might consider an obsession with time and efficiency. Americans are often looking for a faster and more efficient way of doing things. The more that is accomplished each day, the better. This is a common sentiment.

Housing: Most families live in individual homes and either rent or buy them. In large urban areas, however, apartments are more common. Buying a home is becoming more and more difficult, since inflation has made housing costs very high. Taxes have risen considerably in the last few years. Condominiums are becoming popular. They are groups of small houses with common walls and

common yards and often have swimming pools. They allow residents more freedom from yard care, since the grounds are cared for by a hired person.

Transportation and Communication: Most families own at least one automobile and often two or three. Public transportation varies from city to city and ranges from excellent to nonexistent. Automobile, bus, and air travel are the most common forms of transportation. Trains are used mainly as freight carriers except in the East and urban Mid-west where they still carry passengers. Taxicabs can be very expensive.

There is a huge newspaper and magazine publishing industry. Most homes have at least one radio and one television. While radio and television are chiefly private businesses, they are licensed and regulated by the federal government.

Education: American education encourages a high degree of individual participation and independent study programs. School is mandatory until age 16. About two-thirds of the people graduate in 12 years from high school. Ninety-seven percent finish at least eighth grade, and only one out of every 100 citizens cannot read or write. Many people continue their education after high school in technical and business training, or in one or more of the roughly 3,000 state and private universities.

Income and Possessions: Household appliances such as washing machines, dishwashers, and refrigerators are as common as television, telephones, and automobiles. The per capita income is one of the highest among large nations of the world.

Work Schedules: The average business day is from 8 a.m. to 5 p.m., Monday through Friday. Retail stores, however, often do not open until 10 a.m. and close anywhere from 6 to 10 p.m. Grocery stores open as early as 8 a.m. and remain open as late as midnight or even all night. Stores do not close during lunch but are often closed on Sundays. Small "never close" stores are available in larger communities.

Typically, the husband and wife both work unless there are several children at home. Even then, many mothers work, probably due to a combination of economic reasons and the changing social climate. Working women represent almost half (42.2 percent) of the total U.S. work force.

Diet: A hearty American breakfast usually consists of cereal or pancakes, bacon, eggs, toast, coffee or tea, milk or juice. A light lunch of sandwiches, salads, or soups is common. The main and largest meal is eaten between 5–7 p.m. and consists of a main dish (some sort of meat or the economical casserole), salad, vegetable, bread, drink, and dessert. Quick-food restaurants are very popular and plentiful. Food in great variety is available in supermarkets. Ethnic foods (pizza, tacos, etc.) as well as salads and salad bars (make your own salad) are very popular now. So are low calorie meals in restaurants, diet soda pop, and other weight-loss foods. Health foods are growing in popularity.

Recreation and Sports: In their free time, Americans love to go to movies, dance (discos are now quite popular), watch TV, and read. Almost all workers receive at least a two-week paid vacation each year, plus several one-day holidays. They often spend these vacations camping and traveling around the country. Football, baseball, basketball, golf, and bowling are the major spectator sports and can often be seen on television. Popular participant sports include tennis, jogging, cycling, skiing, racquetball, and many others. Rugby and soccer are becoming popular. Children play just about anything from marbles to hopscotch to jacks. Little League teams flourish in baseball, football, basketball, and soccer.

The Nation

Geography and Climate: The United States covers the central portion of the North American continent and is geographically the fourth largest nation in the world. The climate is typical for inland areas, temperate at the coasts, and subtropical in areas of the south. Extensive deserts are found in the Southcentral and Southwest areas, and mountain ranges run north to south—inland of the East and West Coasts. Rainfall varies widely with season and area.

Language: American English is the highly flexible, predominant language throughout the country— with dialectical variations in spoken form, especially in rural areas. Many other languages are spoken extensively at home or in groups by members of minority groups, but most of these people also speak English.

Religion: There is nearly complete freedom of worship in the U.S. Almost two-thirds of the population belong to some organized religious group. Of these, more than 90 percent are members of various Christian denominations, and about 5 percent are Jewish. There are also places of worship for Moslems, Buddhists, and other religions throughout the country.

Population: The population is beyond 220,000,000 and is expected to reach 250 million by 2,000 A.D. About three-fourths of the people live in towns and large cities.

Ethnic Groups: The population is largely of white, anglo-saxon descent with significant minorities of non-anglo-saxon whites, blacks, Asians, Spanish-speaking, and American Indians.

Holidays: Christmas (December 25) and Easter (March or April) are the only national religious holidays—though nonreligious customs often predominate. Other prominent holidays include: New Year's Day (January 1), Valentine's Day (February 14), President's Day (third Monday in February), St. Patrick's Day (March 17), April Fools Day (April 1), Mother's Day (second Sunday in May), Memorial Day (last Monday in May), Father's Day (third Sunday in June), Independence Day (July 4), Labor Day (first Monday in September), Columbus Day (October 8), Halloween (October 31), Veteran's Day (November 11), and Thanksgiving (third Thursday in November). Much commercial emphasis is placed on these holidays.

History: The country was occupied by American Indians until it was explored and settled by Europeans, starting in about the sixteenth century. Much of the territory was under Spanish, French, and English colonial rule until the mid-eighteenth century. A revolution in the late eighteenth and early nineteenth centuries

brought independence. Westward expansion extended territorial control to the Pacific Ocean. There is a significant Spanish influence in the Southwest and East. Since the early part of the 1900s, the U.S. has been one of the world's major political and economic powers.

Government: The United States of America is a federal republic of 50 states. The Constitution of 1787 established the basic political framework which still exists. The legislature consists of the Senate with two representatives from each state and a House of Representatives with representation based upon population. Presidential elections occur every four years. Each state has its own constitution and government and exercises considerable autonomy in internal self-government. The political system is stable, with two primary political parties. The Communist Party is not legally recognized. County and city governments vary in format but allow democracy. The respective powers invested in the legislative, executive, and judicial branches of the government maintain the "checks and balances" in American democratic law.

Economy: The economic system is a modified free enterprise system with considerable government regulation. American currency is the U.S. dollar. The United States is slowly converting to the metric system, but most Americans are more familiar with the system of measurements and weights which uses miles, pounds, yards, feet, inches, pints, quarts, and gallons. America is one of the world's leading agricultural nations. Its technological systems are pervasive.

Tipping: Courtesy suggests that tips are generally in the 15–20 percent range, but there are no absolute rules. DO tip helpful waiters, taxi drivers, porters, doormen, and for extra care in personal service such as barbers may perform. DO NOT tip government employees or customs officials, bus drivers, gas station attendants, theater ushers, or hotel room clerks. "Bribes" are punishable by law. Courtesy is expected of all public servants.

have also undoubtedly have had an impact on the subcultures of these groups, as well.

While most of us would probably regard cultural change—whether of the inevitable or intentional sort—as desirable, not all people share this view. To some groups, for example, the intrusion of messages from other cultures and subcultures is negatively valued. Communication across subcultural or cultural boundaries can contribute to a "melting pot" effect, whereby the distinctions between the groups or societies tend to become increasingly blurred. To those who see this melting down of differences as threatening the identity and distinctiveness of a particular relationship, group, organization, or society, intercultural communication and change may be actively resisted.

Cultural Adaptation

Adjusting to a culture or subculture is a learning, mapping, rule-internalizing process through which we adapt to the symbolic and social realities created by the relationships, groups, organizations, and society of which we are a member. Most of the learning is natural and inevitable. We would learn to speak our native language, for example, whether we were ever *taught it* or not. But cultural adaptation also involves persuasion, as with the education provided by family, church, and school aimed at providing the knowledge, values, and rules which others deem necessary.

ENGLISH:

red	orange	yellow	green	blue	purple

SHONA:

cipsuka	cicena	citema	cipsuka

BASSA:

ziza	hui

FIGURE 12.9 The taken-for-granted language people use to describe color and the ways they categorize and perceive color around them may vary considerably from one culture to another. In Western cultures and language communities, we divide the color spectrum into six more or less distinct categories—red, orange, yellow, green, blue, and purple. These divisions are arbitrary, as are the labels. They are the result of the historical influence of European culture in the Western World. People in certain other language communities divide the color spectrum differently. The Shona of Rhodesia and the Bassa of Liberia, for instance, have few categories. The Shona divide the spectrum into three parts, which are pronounced *cipsuka, cicena,* and *citema. Cipsuka* appears two times, because it refers to colors at both the red and purple ends of the spectrum. The Bassa use two major categories—*ziza* and *hui.*

SOURCE: *Word Play: What Happens When People Talk,* Peter Farb. Copyright © 1979 by Alfred A. Knopf, Inc. By permission.

For the most part we absorb cultures—become Americans, Swiss, Tanzanians—with virtually no effort on our part or awareness that it is happening. Even less obviously, we adapt to and absorb the subcultures of relationships, groups, and organizations in which we become involved. We become "a corporate person," "a salesman," "a Protestant," or "a female," with very little effort on our part, as we "take on" the subcultural conventions of our gender, friends, family, ethnic group, profession, and society.

Because we so thoroughly adapt to our own cultures and subcultures, it is often a difficult and stressful matter to readjust to others. Newly retired, divorced, or widowed partners, for instance, often find the adjustment to thier new situation extremely difficult. Adjusting to the subculture of a prison often presents the same problems, and once this adjustment has taken place, readjustment to the culture of the "outside world" upon release can be even more difficult.

These kinds of adjustments represent what has been called *culture shock*—a term whose popularity is attributed to the writings of Kalvero Oberg.[14] Initially, culture shock was thought to be a disease contracted by persons who were suddenly transplanted from one geographic locale to another. Symptoms associated with the illness were noted to include: frustration, anger, anxiety, feelings of helplessness, overwhelming loneliness, and excessive fears of being robbed, cheated, or eating dangerous items.[15] As the following story indicates, the turbulence that goes with the experience of physical relocation can apparently be as traumatic for some animals as for humans:

> In the spring of 1972, the United States and China exchanged gifts of animals as a gesture of goodwill between countries. The Chinese pandas, Hsing-Hsing and Ling-Ling, quickly adjusted to the National Zoo in Washington, D.C. After a few days, they were in excellent health, standing on their heads and wiggling their rumps. Milton and Matilda, the two musk oxen sent to Peking, did not make a healthy adjustment to the Peking Zoo— they suffered from post-nasal drip and a skin condition that caused them to shed their hair....[16]

The explanation provided by Dr. Theodore Reed, director of the National Zoo, who accompanied the oxen to Peking, was that their runny noses and other symptoms were the result of culture shock and the rigors of travel—"hearing Chinese spoken instead of English, seeing new faces, new uniforms, new surroundings, and eating Chinese hay and grain."[17] Within several months, Milton and Matilda recovered, as a result of antibiotics and what Reed termed "tender loving care."

As one might predict even from this brief story, the medical view of cultural adjustment has broadened in recent years to include an emphasis on psychology, sociology, and especially, communication. In fact, in his classic book, *Silent Language*, Edward Hall described culture shock as "simply the removal or distortion of the familiar cues one encounters at home and the substitution of them for other cues which are strange."[18]

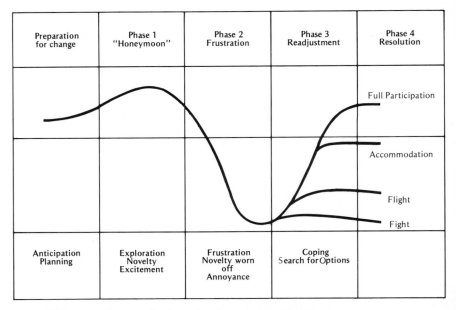

Preparation for change	Phase 1 "Honeymoon"	Phase 2 Frustration	Phase 3 Readjustment	Phase 4 Resolution
				Full Participation
				Accommodation
				Flight
				Fight
Anticipation Planning	Exploration Novelty Excitement	Frustration Novelty worn off Annoyance	Coping Search for Options	

FIGURE 12.10 Stages of adaptation in a new environment.

SOURCE: Based on review of literature on stages of adaptation presented in "Adaptation to a New Environment," by Daniel J. Kealey (Ottawa, Canada: Canadian International Agency, Briefing Centre, 1978).

Stages of Adaptation

There have been numerous attempts to describe and delineate the stages of cultural adaptation.[19] These writings suggest that there are generally four phases:

(1) Phase 1 is a "honeymoon" period during which individuals adjusting to a new culture are excited by the novelty of the people and new surroundings or situations.

(2) Phase 2 is a period where fascination and novelty often turn into frustration, anxiety, and even hostility, as the realities of life in an unfamiliar environment or circumstance become more apparent.

(3) Phase 3 marks the beginning of the readjustment process, as individuals begin to develop ways of coping with their frustrations and the challenge of the new situation.

(4) In phase 4, the readjustment continues. During this period, several outcomes are possible. Many individuals regain their balance and comfort level, developing meaningful relations and an appreciation of the new culture. Other individuals are unable to fully accept the new culture, but find a way to cope with it adequately for their purposes. A third response is simply to find a way to "survive," though with substantial personal

discomfort and strain. Some are unable to reach even this level of adjustment, and find their only alternative is to retreat from the situation.

When an individual is adjusting to the culture of a new society thousands of miles from home, where the geography, climate, rituals, customs, life styles and languages are unfamiliar, with no companions and no prospect of returning to one's home country for several years, cultural adaptation may well be a very intense and stressful experience.

The same dynamics of adaptation occur in situations which are more common and familiar. Any time one ends one intimate relationship, starts a new job, moves in with new roomates, joins a sorority or fraternity, or moves from one community to another, he or she is likely to go through stages of cultural or subcultural adaptation on some level, as the adjustment to new people, new expectations, new symbols, and often new rules takes place.

Often, the initial enthusiasm in a new job, relationship, organization, or community gives way to frustration, disappointment, and even some degree of depression, as it becomes apparent that the new situation is not all we had hoped it would be. Gradually, we begin to adapt, as we revise our expectations downward, develop new understanding, and apply the skills necessary to cope with the new relationship, group, organization, or circumstance. In some instances, we adjust fully. In others, we give the appearance of fitting in, but never really become comfortable. Sometimes we may be unable to continue and decide to withdraw.

TEA RITUAL STARTED BLAZE

Pilgrim lit jet fire

JEDDAH, Saudi Arabia (UPI) – A Moslem pilgrim who lit a gas stove to make tea started the fire that turned a Saudi Arabian jetliner into a flying inferno, killing 301 people in history's second-worst single-plane disaster, officials said yesterday.

In the panic that ensued as flames swept down the aisle, passengers blocked the emergency exits and jammed the doors, turning the Lockheed L-1011 Tristar into a flaming tomb for all aboard, the officials said.

As investigators searched the wreakage to answer the two most important questions—how the fire started and why the emergency doors jammed — the death toll from Tuesday's disaster rose to 301.

King Khaled ordered $15,000 to be paid to the families of each of the victims to show his "deep condolences" and "to ease their grief," the Saudi news agency said. The total payment comes to $4,515,000.

The pilot's account of what happened as recorded on the black box said a Moslem pilgrim sitting in the rear economy section ignited a gas stove to make a cup of tea. A fire started and it quickly spread from back to front, sweeping from the economy section through first-class while the plane was still in the air.

A statement by the Saudi Civil Aviation Directorate said searchers found the gas stove that started the blaze in the rear of the plane, along with a fire extinguisher used in a vain attempt to douse the flames.

The directorate said it found passengers jammed against the exit doors, apparently preventing them from opening.

Travellers in the Middle East, particularly those bound for the hardship of piligrimage to the Moslem shrine at Mecca, often carry gas stoves to make tea in flight and on several occasions they have touched off fires on airplanes.

FIGURE 12.11 This tragic story provides a vivid example of what can occur when cultures or subcultures clash. In this case, the clash is between the time-honored traditions of heating tea to serve one's friends and the demands of modern technology.

SOURCE: Excepted from a story by United Press International, August 21, 1980.

Intercultural and International Relations

Face-To-Face Contact

In a very basic sense, we are engaged in an intercultural (or intersubcultural) adaptation process any time we come into contact with individuals, data or an environment that is unfamiliar. From the first moments of contact between two individuals, for example, they begin a process of mutual exploration and accommodation. At the instant we take notice of a person, we don't know whether we have similar knowledge levels, backgrounds, orientations toward time, political philosophies, gestural patterns, greeting forms, religious orientations, or even a common language capability. We may not be certain whether we share a common flag, race, or nationality. And, we don't know whether or not we have in common, experiences in similar sorts of relationships, groups, or organizations.

We use communication to reduce our uncertainty about the situation and the person or persons involved. We study their appearance, dress, adornments, posture, and walk. We listen to them speak and talk to them. Gradually, we begin to acquire information that helps us to determine what we have in common and where we differ. If the process continues, the pool of common data available to us grows steadily, and with it the possibilities for adjusting to and shaping the culture or subculture of which we are becoming a part.

Mediated Contact

Not all of the contact between different societies, cultures, and subcultures takes place through interpersonal contact. Often, the linkages between individuals from various cultures involves communication technology. Through telecommunications, cable, video cassette recording, and more traditional media like newspapers, magazines, radio, and film, citizens of the world are coming to share an increasingly common symbolic environment. In many parts of the globe one can hear the same popular records, read the same newspapers and magazines, watch the same television programs, and even play the same video games.

Will these new technologies and the increasingly common international database they provide increase world understanding and the prospects of peace? Not necessarily. The capability of communication and the sharing of a common symbolic environment does not automatically lead to shared or converging maps, rules, images, values orientations, or information processing patterns for the individuals involved. In all fundamental respects, an argument, a divorce, or a war are as much a product of communication as are a reconciliation, a marriage, or peaceful coexistence. Occasionally, "negative' outcomes develop because of a lack of a common base of data or reciprocal message processing. More often, however, these results occur because of the *presence* rather than *absence* of communication. Even when two individuals are confronted by the same data, their ways of selecting, attaching meaning and significance, and retaining the information which results may inhibit— or even preclude—the chances for mutual understanding, agreement, or convergence.

The problem of people starving in many countries of the world, for instance, does not seem to be the result of a "breakdown" in reciprocal data processing. Vitually all of us have access to data relative to the problems of world hunger and some "awareness" of the problem. But *access to* and *awareness of* data are not necessarily good predictors of whether and how the data will be transformed into information, nor of subsequent behavior. How many of us who are aware of the problems of hunger and starvation have taken steps to alter the situation?

In the short run, at least, the presence of communication and commonly available data is probably not much more likely to produce convergence than divergence, love than hate, understanding than misunderstanding, peace than war. In the longer run, we can speculate that the ever-increasing pool of shared environmental data—along with new common needs and goals—will lead to a more predictable world culture than the one guiding relations between countries of the world today.

Summary

Communication networks within a society are essential and even more visible than in other social systems. These networks involve both interpersonal and mass communication, and serve to coordinate the activities of individuals within a society as well as linking the system to the larger environment in which it exists.

Culture is a familiar term with a variety of meanings. For our purposes, culture is defined as the complex combination of common symbols, knowledge, meanings, conventions, rules, rituals, customs, practices, habits, life styles, values and attitudes which characterize and distinguished a particular group of people at a specific point in time.

These common patterns emerge in any ongoing relationship, group, or organization, and are particularly complex in societies. Cultures have a number of characteristics: They are *complex* and *multifaceted, change* over time, and are largely *invisible*.

Adjusting to one's culture and subculture is a matter of adapting to the relationships, groups, organizations, and societies of which one is a member. Once we have thoroughly adapted to a subculture or culture, it is often a difficult matter to readapt to others. *Culture shock* is a term used to refer to the process of adjusting to a new culture.

Moving from one familiar society to another perhaps many miles away, where language, customs, and habits are totally alien is perhaps the most difficult sort of cultural adaptation. The same basic dynamics are at work each time we leave a long-term relationship and begin a new one, leave one group and join another, or move from one job to another. In each case, we use communication to reduce uncertainty in the new situation, to discover commonalities and differences, and to adapt to and shape the subculture or culture of which we are becoming a part.

Intercultural adaptation occurs when an individual from one culture or subculture comes into contact with individuals or data from other relationships, groups, organizations, or societies. Intercultural and international relations occur through both face-to-face and mediated contact. The availability of common data among members of different societies does not assure common understanding, acceptance, or peace.

Notes

1. Karl Deutsch, *The Nerves of Government* (New York: Free Press, 1966).
2. Cf. Robert A. LeVine, *Culture, Behavior, and Personality* (Chicago, Aldine, 1973) especially Chapter 1.
3. E.B. Tylor, quoted in Marvin E. Wolfgang and Franco Ferracuti, *The Subculture of Violence* (New York: Tavistock, 1967), p. 95.
4. Cf. Lee Thayer, *Communication and Communication Systems* (Homewood, IL: Irwin, 1968), p. 47.
5. Ibid.
6. Cf. Edward Hall, *The Silent Language* (New York: Doubleday, 1959) pp. 50–52.
7. An acknowledgement for this phraseology is due to Marshall McLuhan and the well-known adage of his time: "We shape our tools and thereafter our tools shape us."
8. A broadly-based view of communication and mass communication institutions is provided by Richard W. Budd and Brent D. Ruben, *Beyond Media* (Rochelle Park, NJ: Hayden) 1979.
9. What is often referred to as the "agenda-setting function" is detailed by Maxwell E. McCombs and Donald L. Shaw in "The Agenda-Setting Function of Mass Media." *Public Opinion Quarterly, 36,* 1, (1972) pp. 176–187.
10. Cf. "Socialization and Concepts of Social Reality," in *Television and Behavior: Ten Years of Scientific Progress and Implications for the Eighties. Vol 1: Summary Report,* (Rockville MD: National Institute of Mental Health, 1982), pp. 54–66, and Hugh D. Duncan, *Communication and Social Order* (London: Oxford University Press, 1962) and Hugh D. Duncan, *Symbols in Society* (New York: Oxford University Press, 1968), especially Parts II and III.
11. Cf. "How to Map a People" (Brigham Young University, Language Research Center, 1976) and Brent D. Ruben, *Human Communication Handbook: Simulations and Games, Volume 2,* (Rochelle Park, NJ: Hayden, 1978), pp. 116–120.
12. For the phrase "cultural iceberg" I am indebted to the writings of Donald Timkulu, "The Cultural Iceberg," (Ottawa, Canada: Canadian International Development Agency, Briefing Center).
13. Cf. Alison Lanier, *Saudi Arabia* (New York: Overseas Briefing Associates, 1978), especially Sections II and V.

14. Kalvero Oberg, "Culture Shock and the Problem of Adjustment to New Cultural Environments." Unpublished paper, Washington, DC: Department of State, Foreign Service Institute, 1958.
15. *Guidelines for United States Navy Overseas Diplomacy,* (Washington, DC: Department of Navy,) p. 33.
16. Ibid.
17. Ibid.
18. Edward Hall, op. cit., p. 199.
19. Excellent summaries of writing and research in the area of cultural adaptation are provided by Marjorie H. Klein, "Adaptation to New Cultural Environments," in *Overview of Intercultural Education, Training and Research. Volume I: Theory.* David S. Hoopes, Paul B. Pedersen, and George W. Renwick, eds. (Washington, DC: Society for Intercultural Education, Training and Research, 1977) pp. 50–56; David Reed Barker, in "Culture Shock and Anthropological Fieldwork," Paper presented at the Conference of the Society for Intercultural Education, Training and Research, Mount Pocono, PA., 1980; and by Daniel J. Kealey in "Adaptation to a New Environment," (Ottawa, Canada: Canadian International Development Agency, Briefing Centre, 1978).

References and Suggested Readings

Berger, Peter L. "Sociology of Knowledge." in *Interdisciplinary Approaches to Human Communication.* Edited by Richard W. Budd and Brent D. Ruben. Rochelle Park, NJ: Hayden, 1979.

———. and Thomas Luckmann. *The Social Construction of Reality.* Garden City, NY: Doubleday, 1966.

Berrien, F. Kenneth. *General and Social Systems.* New Brunswick, NJ: Rutgers University Press, 1968.

Blumer, Herbert. "Symbolic Interaction." In *Interdisciplinary Approaches to Human Communication.* Edited by Richard W. Budd and Brent D. Ruben. Rochelle Park, NJ: Hayden, 1979.

———. *Symbolic Interactionism.* Englewood Cliffs, NJ: Prentice-Hall, 1969.

Bostain, James. "How to Read a Foreigner Like a Book." Parts I and II. Videotape. Produced by the Canadian International Development Agency, Briefing Centre, Hull, Quebec, 1977.

Brislin, Richard W. *Cross-Cultural Encounters.* New York: Pergamon, 1981.

Budd, Richard W. and Brent D. Ruben, *Beyond Media.* Rochelle Park, NJ: Hayden, 1979.

Buckley, Walter. *Sociology and Modern Systems Theory.* Englewood Cliffs, NJ: Prentice-Hall, 1967.

Cherry, Colin. *World Communication.* New York: Wiley, 1971.

Duetsch, Karl W. *The Nerves of Government.* New York: Free Press, 1966.

Douglas, Mary, ed. *Rules and Meanings.* New York: Penguin, 1972.

Duncan, Hugh D. *Communication and Social Order.* London: Oxford University Press, 1962.

———. *Symbols in Society.* New York: Oxford University Press, 1968.

Ellingsworth, Huber W. "Conceptualizing Intercultural Communication." In *Communication Yearbook 1*. Edited by Brent D. Ruben. New Brunswick, NJ: Transaction-International Communication Association, 1977, 99–106.

Farb, Peter. *Word Play: What Happens When People Talk*. New York: Knopf, 1979.

Fersh, Seymour, ed. *Learning About Peoples and Cultures*. Evanston, IL: McDougal, Littell, 1974.

Fischer, Heinz-Dietrich and John C. Merrill, eds. *International Communication*. New York: Hastings House, 1974.

Frank, Lawrence. "Cultural Organization." In *General Systems Theory and Human Communication*. Edited by Brent D. Ruben and John Y. Kim. Rochelle Park, NJ: Hayden, 1975, 128–135.

Gerard, R.W. "A Biologist's View of Society." *General Systems*, **1** (1956).

Gudykunst, William and Young Kim. *Communicating With Strangers*, Reading, MA: Addison-Wesley, 1984.

Hall, Edward T. *Beyond Culture*. Garden City, NY: Doubleday, 1979.

———. *The Silent Language*. Garden City, NY: Doubleday, 1959.

Holzner, Burkart. *Reality Construction in Society*. Cambridge, MA: Schenkman, 1968.

Hoopes, David S., Paul B. Pedersen and George W. Renwick, eds. *Overview of Intercultural Education, Training and Research. Volume I: Theory*. Washington, DC: Society for Intercultural Education, Training and Research, 1977.

Laszlo, Ervin. *The Systems View of the World*. New York: Braziller, 1972.

———, ed. *The World System*. New York: Braziller, 1973.

LeVine, Robert A. *Culture, Behavior, and Personality*. Chicago: Aldine, 1973.

Lippman, Walter. *Public Opinion*. New York: Free Press, 1922.

Lynch, James J. *The Broken Heart: The Medical Consequences of Loneliness*. New York: Basic Books, 1977.

McClelland, Charles A. "Systems and History in International Relations." *General Systems*, **3** (1958).

Maruyama, Magorah. "Metaorganization of Information." *Cybernetica*, **4** (1965).

Mead, George Herbert. *Mind, Self and Society*. Chicago: University of Chicago, 1934.

Merritt, Richard L. "Transmission of Values Across National Boundaries." In *Communication in International Politics*. Edited by Richard L. Merritt. Urbana, IL: University of Illinois Press, 1972.

Monane, Joseph H. *A Sociology of Human Systems*. New York: Appleton-Century-Crofts, 1967.

Morris, Desmond. *Manwatching*. New York: Abrams, 1977.

Rivers, William L. *The Adversaries*. Boston: Beacon Press, 1970.

Ruben, Brent D. and Daniel J. Kealey. "Behavioral Assessment of Communication Competency and the Prediction of Cross Cultural Adaptation," *International Journal of Intercultural Relations*. **3**, 1 (Spring 1979), 15–48.

Ruben, Brent D. and John Y. Kim, eds. *General Systems Theory and Human Communication*. Rochelle Park, NJ: Hayden, 1975.

Samovar, Larry, A. and Richard E. Porter, eds. *Intercultural Communication*. 2nd ed. Belmont, CA: Wadsworth, 1976.

———, Richard E. Porter, and Nemi C. Jain. *Understanding Intercultural Communication*. Belmont, CA: Wadsworth, 1981.

Sarbaugh, L.E. *Intercultural Communication*. Rochelle Park, NJ: Hayden, 1979.

Schiller, Herbert I. *Mass Communications and American Empire*. New York: Kelley, 1969.

Siebert, Fredrick, S., Theodore Peterson and Wilbur Schramm. *Four Theories of the Press*. Urbana, IL: University of Illinois Press, 1956.

Simmel, Georg. *Conflict and the Web of Group-Affiliations*. Translated by Kurt H. Wolff and Reinhard Bendix. New York: Free Press, 1955.

Smith, Alfred G., ed. *Communication and Culture*. New York: Holt, 1966.

Stark, Warner, ed. *The Sociology of Knowledge*. London: Routledge and Kegan Paul, 1958.

Thayer, Lee. "On Human Communication and Social Development." A paper presented at the First World Conference on Communication for Development, Mexico City, March, 1970.

Wiener, Norbert. *The Human Use of Human Beings*. New York: Avon, 1954.

Wilson, Joan and Margaret Omar. "A Self-Taught Guide to Cultural Learning." Revised in *Human Communication Handbook Simulations and Games Volume II*, Rochelle Park, NJ: Hayden, 1978. 116–121.

Vickers, Geoffrey. *Value Systems and Social Process*. New York: Basic, 1968.

Author Index

Subject Index

C

Caesar, Julius, 43
Carter, Jimmy, 139
Cell(s), 23
Chemical data, 19
Chromatin, 23
Chromosomes, 23, 80
Cicero, 42
Circle sign, 143
Closed systems, 14
Code(s), 76–78, 201, 241
    systems, 128
Coded language, 77–78
Coded messages, 83
Cognitive factors, in language usage, 103–104
Communication
    and adaptation, 26–35
    animal, 15–35, 51–52, 163
    apprehension, 180, 266
    books and publications, 52–53
    breakdown, 317
    characteristics of, 4–9, 81–93
    and communications, 9
    content functions, 259
    and courtship, 21–22, 24–25, 31
    and culture, 294–301
    definition of, 11, 15
    and economics, 215–216
    factors which affect, 174–192
    and feeding, 23–24
    and food identification, 26
    functions of, 20–35, 272–273, 285–286
    habits, 164
    and images, 227–234
    journals, 52
    and learning, 227–234
    and locomotion, 26–29
    and mapping, 227–234
    and maps, 227–234
    and mating, 21–22
    modes, 16–20, 49
    popularity of, 9
    programs, 53
    relational functions, 259
    and reproduction, 21, 23
    and survival of a species, 20–26, 30
    and uncertainty, 316
Communication technology, 64, 82, 89, 107, 182, 187, 200–217, 224, 239, 241, 272, 301
    definition, 202
    evolution of, 201, 204–209
    forms of, 204–209, 216
    functions, 202–204, 216
    primitive, 200

and the quality of life, 216–217
and transportation technology, 210–211
Communications, 9
Computers, 53, 82, 212–215
Connotative meaning, 107
Consistency theory, 54
Corax, 41
Correction channel, 46, 59
Counter-dependencies, 262–263
Courtship, 21–22, 24–25, 31
Cultural iceberg, 306
Culture, 89–90, 131, 236, 294–317
    adaptation, 312–315
    and change, 308, 312
    characteristics of, 302–312
    and color, 312
    and communication, 294–301
    complexity of, 302–307
    invisibility of, 307–308
    culture shock, 313–315
Cultures
    African, 147
    Arab, 302, 308
    Asian, 147
    Canadian, 308
    English, 143, 312
    European, 308
    French, 143
    Japanese, 143, 308
    Liberian, 312
    North American, 143, 147, 154, 302, 306–311
    Rhodesian, 312
    Saudi Arabian, 302, 306–307

D

Dance's model of communication, 55–56, 60
Data, 16–35, 59, 99–100, 104, 119, 200
    access to, 317
    amplification of, 203
    auditory, 21, 23, 102, 206
    awareness of, 317
    coded, 104, 200, 213
    complementary, 129
    contradictory, 129
    definition of, 15
    display of, 202–203
    duplication of, 203
    duplicative, 129
    exposure to, 239
    factors that affect, 181–185
    and information, 15–35, 101–102, 155
    interpretation of, 163, 169–170, 171, 241

Left hemisphere of the brain, 127–128
Life stages, 176
Living systems, 14–35, 76
Locomotion, 26–29
Long-term memory, 172, 174, 184

M

Mammals, use of visual data, 17
Management, 276, 281–282
Mapping process, 272
Maps, 227–234, 250, 272, 301, 316
　characteristics, 230–234
　definition, 228
Marketing, 276
Mass communication, 43–44, 49–50, 89, 203
　and culture, 301
Mass media, 43–44, 49, 109, 176, 182, 189–190, 203, 212–215, 239, 241, 293, 316
　agenda-setting function, 241
　and the creation of reality, 91
　uses, 212–215
Mating, 21–22, 24, 80, 88
Meaning, 54, 57, 60–61, 78, 86–91, 108
　standardization of, 88
　subjectivity of, 109
Media content, 89
Membership, in groups and organizations, 282–286
Memory, 165, 170–174
　capacity, 172
　decay, 172
　long-term, 172, 174, 184
　recall, 184
　short-term, 172, 184
Message(s), 60, 77, 83, 155
　processing, 316
　reception, 77, 187
　sending, 77
　sources, 165, 184
　tactile, 147
　verbal, 184
　visual, 184
Metacommunication, 115
Microcomputer, 212–215
　programs, 214
Middle Ages, 108
Models of communication, 41–42, 44–50, 53–62
　Aristotle, 41–42
　Berlo, David, 53–54
　circular, 60
　convergence, 57
　Dance, Frank, 55–56, 60

I↔D↔E, 155
　information-transmission, 54
　interpretation-oriented, 54–55
　Katz, Elihu, and Paul Lazarsfeld, 48–49, 60
　Lasswell, Harold, 44–45
　meaning-centered, 60
　Newcomb, Theodore, 54–55, 60
　one-way, 60
　Rogers, Everett, and D. Lawrence Kincaid, 57–58, 60
　S→M→R, 155, 192
　Schramm, Wilbur, 47–48, 59–60
　Shannon, Claude, and Warren Weaver, 45–46, 48, 59
　straight line, 55
　transmission-oriented, 54–55
　unidirectional, 60
　Watzlawick, Paul, Janet Beavin, and Don Jackson, 56–57
　Westley, Bruce, and Malcolm MacLean, Jr., 49–50, 59
Modes of communication, 16–20, 183
Modified filter model, 169
Monetary symbols, 80
Monetary system, 78
Morse Code, 76–77

N

National Association of Elocutionists, 43
National Association of Teachers of Public Speaking, 43
National Society for the Study of Communication, 44
Needs
　interpersonal, 265–269
　communicative, 176
　personal, 176, 276
　physiological, 175–177
　social, 176, 276
Networking, 274–277, 283
Networks, 237, 240–241, 274–277, 283
　circle, 275
　downward, 276
　external, 277
　formal, 275
　formalization of, 275
　informal, 275–277
　international, 293
　national, 293
　phases in development, 274–275
　upward, 276
　vertical, 276
　wheel, 275

Newcomb's model of communication, 54–55, 60
Noise, 46
Nonverbal behavior, 126–155, 227
    cold behavior, 131
    deception, 131
    engagement, 133
    information, 128
    information sources, 129–155
    masking, 131
    message sources, 129–155
    stages of development, 140
    warm behavior, 131
Nonverbal codes, 126–155
    cultural differences, 143, 147, 154
    phonetics, 128
    pragmatics, 128
    semantics, 128
    syntax, 128
    and verbal codes, 126–128
Nonverbal cues, 126, 129
Nonverbal data, 101–102, 129–155, 181, 183
    actions, 139–147
    adornment, 129, 137–139
    appearance, 129–139
    display of, 128
    dress, 129, 137–139
    eyes, 132–136
    face, 129–131
    physical environment, 150–154
    physique, 139
    production of, 128
    pupil dilation, 136
    space, 147–154
    time, 154–155
    touch, 144–147

O

Old Testament, 41
Olfactory information, 19
Opinion leaders, 49, 60
Organization(s)
    chain of command, 283
    change in, 286
    continuity in, 286
    formal organization in, 283
    functions, 272–274
    goals, 272–274
    management, 281–282
    networking, 274–277
    networks, 274–277
    roles, 279–286
    rules, 277–279
    symbols, 277–279, 284–285

P

Paradigm(s), 58–61
    I↔D↔E, 60, 62, 155
    personal, 234
    S→M→R, 59–60, 155, 192
Paralanguage, 102, 115–120, 129
Parent-offspring relations, 23–26
Patterns of communication
    asymmetrical, 267
    symmetrical, 267
Personal paradigms, 234
Personal space, 33–35, 147–148
Persuasion, 42, 58, 241, 243
    and mating, 21–22
Pheromones, 19, 21
Phonetic skills, 105
Phonology, 102
Photosynthesis, 14–15
Physical contact, 18
Physical environment, 150–154, 166
    and interaction, 153–154
    and symbolic environment, 83–86
    use of, 150–151
Physiological factors in language usage, 102–103
Physique, 129
Pictographic writing, 200
Pitch, 102–103, 115
Position and communication, 17
    and seating, 148–149
Pragmatics, 102
    skills, 105
Preening behavior, 144
Prenatal contact, 144
Progressive spirals, 263–264
Propaganda, 51
Public relations, 277
Publick Occurrences Both Forreign and Domestick, 43
Pupil dilation, 136

Q

Quadratic relationships, 252–253
Quarterly Journal of Public Speaking, 43
Quarterly Journal of Speech, 43
QUBE, 205
Quintilian, 42

R

Reciprocal message processing, 249–250, 259
Reflexes, 86
Regressive spirals, 263–264

Relational patterns
  counter-dependencies, 262–264
  dependencies, 262–264
  progressive spirals, 263–264
  regressive spirals, 263–264
  self-defeating prophecies, 264–265
  self-fulfilling prophecies, 264–265
Relationships, 120, 248–268
  casual, 256–258
  conflict in, 253, 264
  context and, 265
  counter-dependent, 262–263
  decision-making in, 253
  dependent, 262–263
  deterioration of, 262
  disclosure in, 256–257
  dyadic, 251–253
  encounter in, 258–259
  evolution of, 258–262
  exploration in, 260
  formalization in, 260–261
  initial impressions in, 258–259
  initiation of, 258–259
  intensification of, 260
  interpersonal communication and, 249–250
  interpersonal orientation and, 265–267
  intimate, 256–258
  long-term, 255–256
  medical consequences of, 257–258
  "one-down" position in, 120
  patterns, 262–267
  perspectives on, 251–258
  progressive spirals, 263–264
  quadrads, 252–253
  redefinition of, 261
  regressive spirals, 263–264
  relational patterns, 262–265
  rules, 252
  self-defeating prophecies, 264–265
  self-fulfilling prophecies, 264–265
  short-term, 255–256
  social, 254–255
  stage and, 265
  stages of, 258–262
  task, 254–255
Rhetoric, history of, 41–43
Right hemisphere, 127–128
Rogers and Kincaid's model of communication, 57–58, 60
Roles, 279–286
Rules, 127, 131–133, 227–234, 250, 262, 273, 276–279, 301, 316,
  and change, 230–231
  characteristics of, 230–234
  definition of, 228
  and incompleteness, 231

  joint, 250, 259–261, 294
  phonetic, 170
  pragmatic, 170
  relational, 250, 261
  semantic, 170
  stability, 234
  subjectivity, 231, 234
  syntactic, 170

S

S→M→R model, 155, 192
S→M→R paradigm, 59–60, 155, 192
Sammonicus, Quintus Serenus, 108
Schramm's model of communication, 47–48, 60
Second-order communication event, 86–87, 236–237
Self-concept, 234–236
Self-defense, 18, 29–31
Self-disclosure, 256–257
Self-reflexivity, 91, 165
Semantic network(s), 172, 227–228
Semantic skills, 105
Semantics, 108
Severus, 108
Shannon and Weaver's model of communication, 45–46, 48, 59
Short-term memory, 172, 184
Significant others, 235
Social initiation, 258
Socialization, 23–26, 81, 176, 237, 239, 241
  definition of, 239, 241
Song
  birds, 21–22
  pattern, 31
Space, 30–32, 130
  allocation of, 278
  arrangement of furniture, 150
  in conversations, 148–149
  and leadership, 149
  personal, 33–35, 147–148
  portable, 147–148
  seating and, 149–150
  and territory, 31–35
  use of, 147–150, 250–251, 302
Spatial relationships, 127
Speech, history of, 41–43
Speech Association of America, 43
Speech patterns, 105
Stages of nonverbal development, 140
Stages of relationships, 258–262
Stress, 30–31, 88, 236–237
  and communication, 236–237
  defining, 236–237
  fight-and-flight response, 30–31, 88
  reduction, 236–237